S0-CJE-290

Instructor's Manual
to Accompany

THE WESTERN HUMANITIES

Roy T. Matthews
F. DeWitt Platt
Michigan State University

Mayfield Publishing Company
Mountain View, California
London • Toronto

Copyright © 1992 by Mayfield Publishing Company

All rights reserved. No portion of this book may be reproduced in any form or by any means without written permission of the publisher.

International Standard Book Number: 1-55934-165-3

Manufactured in the United States of America

10 9 8 7 6 5 4 3 2

Mayfield Publishing Company
1240 Villa Street
Mountain View, California 94041

CONTENTS

PREFACE

This Instructor's Manual for *The Western Humanities* is written to serve several purposes. First, it provides teachers with advice on how to approach the subject of the humanities and how to make the classroom a more lively environment for students. Second, it also supplies a list of resources to enhance the classroom presentation. Third, this manual makes the instructor's work easier by offering various types of test questions. It also supplies a list of resources to enhance the classroom presentation.

The organization of the Instructor's Manual reflects the same emphases that characterize *The Western Humanities;* that is, one-third of each chapter's content focuses on political, social, and economic trends—material history—and the remaining two-thirds on the artistic, literary, musical, and intellectual developments—cultural history. We have followed these ratios, especially in preparing the examination questions.

The manual provides both teaching strategies and suggestions, which are explained in greater detail at the beginning of Part One. In addition to hints on improving teaching, the manual also offers a detailed lecture outline of each chapter of *The Western Humanities.* The instructor may adopt the lecture outline as given, reduce it in scope, or supplement it with new material, as the need arises. A unique feature of the manual is that we list significant developments in other cultures that parallel the events described in each chapter of our textbook. Instructors, particularly those interested in improving the multicultural awareness of students, can draw on these notations about non-Western happenings in order to relate Western events to a global setting.

The manual offers the instructor three different types of sample tests: identifications, discussion/essays, and multiple-choice questions. The identifications—the Key Cultural Terms found in each chapter—are included as a quick reference for the teacher and as a reminder that each term is important to the central themes in the text. The discussion/essay questions can help students improve their analytical and writing skills while reviewing the material in each chapter. The fifty multiple-choice questions per chapter are designed to test the students' knowledge of the text and also to challenge them to relate ideas and to draw interpretations from their reading.

Each chapter of the manual also provides a judicious list of film and music selections that are intended to supplement the classroom lectures. The recommended films have been produced in the past twenty years and have proven their usefulness as teaching devices. Because ancient music has virtually disappeared, the music selections begin only with Chapter 9, The High Middle Ages; these selections are meant to augment the music listed in the textbook. The Books for Further Reading section is for intellectually curious teachers who want sources for their lectures; those books listed in *The Western Humanities* are primarily for students.

Accompanying the Instructor's Manual and the textbook are auxiliary teaching aids—100 slides of art and architecture; 23 color slides of maps; a computerized test bank; tape cassette and compact disc recordings of music; and a video package. If used on a regular basis in the classroom, these teaching aids will certainly enhance the quality of instruction. Those instructors who are fortunate to live near museums and art galleries can schedule field trips for their students. Instructors can also make use of on-campus plays, poetry readings, films, concerts, and other performing arts presentations for both extracurricular activities and classroom credit.

TEACHING STRATEGIES FOR THE WESTERN HUMANITIES

A key feature of this Instructor's Manual is the section in each chapter called Teaching Strategies and Suggestions. We are motivated to offer these teaching suggestions by two interrelated classroom ideals: First, we believe that university and college students should have a working knowledge of the basic vocabulary, major milestones, and general history of the Western arts and humanities; and, second, we believe that students should use that information to help them think critically—the goal of education at every level. These educational principles reinforce the message of our textbook, *The Western Humanities*, since it is based on these same ideals.

Presented with the challenge of offering advice to instructors who adopt our textbook and ruminating on the knowledge we have gained through years of university teaching, we have concluded that there are five general teaching strategies and seven specific lecture suggestions that we can recommend. Although not an exhaustive list, these strategies and suggestions represent basic approaches to teaching and are flexible enough to be adaptable to many different settings. For this reason we have organized the *Teaching Strategies and Suggestions* sections around these basic approaches, suggesting their use in various combinations depending on each chapter's demands. Instructors, of course, may develop their own teaching strategies and suggestions, since not all pedagogical methods will work in the same way for each person. Following are the five basic teaching strategies and the seven specific lecture suggestions we use in the Instructor's Manual.

FIVE BASIC TEACHING STRATEGIES

1. *Standard Lecture.* The Standard Lecture teaching strategy is the oldest and most frequently used teaching tool in the world. It involves a single instructor, with or without teaching aids, who gives a lecture that conveys a large quantity of information to note-taking students. When well done, the Standard Lecture method can be extremely effective; when done poorly, it is a deadening experience. We believe that the Standard Lecture strategy is best when done with the following teaching aids: a well-thought-out outline made available to students before the lecture (projected on a screen, written on a blackboard, or distributed in a handout); adequate time for students to ask questions or request clarification about the lecture; a summary at the lecture's end to drive home the vital points; and the instructor's vigor in varying voice level, using appropriate gestures, writing on the blackboard or using an overhead projector, and moving about the classroom.

   We envision that the Standard Lecture strategy will be the one used most frequently by instructors who adopt *The Western Humanities*. It is ideal for topics that lend themselves to a direct approach—specifically historical issues like the rise of Rome or the causes of the Crusades, for instance. The Standard Lecture approach is also flexible enough to add new instructional ingredients and our suggestions for the next two strategies are variations of this basic method.

2. *Slide Lecture.* A variation on the Standard Lecture approach, the Slide Lecture strategy is centered on the presentation of slides of art and architecture with running commentary by the instructor. This particular model is the preferred method for introducing the visual arts of a specific historical era, such as the Hellenic style of ancient Greece. Instructors will want eventually to amass their own art slide collections. In the meantime the slides in the auxiliary

materials accompanying *The Western Humanities* provide the beginning of a collection, since five slides of key artistic works are included for each chapter. With these five slides instructors can illustrate the leading characteristics of each artistic style, and when juxtaposed with slides from another period, can demonstrate differences between styles. For maximum educational benefit, instructors should provide students with slide lists, giving the name of each artist or architect and the full title and the date of each work of art or building under review. The slide lists serve both as reminders of the art viewed and as writing areas for students to record lecture notes.

3. *Music Lecture.* Another variation on the Standard Lecture approach, the Music Lecture strategy is excellent for illustrating musical styles as well as significant monuments of Western music. A set of key musical recordings, with helpful notes, is provided to instructors in the auxiliary materials accompanying *The Western Humanities*. With these materials instructors can play recordings in class and provide students with handouts that set forth the composer and title of each selection along with general instructions for listening.

4. *Discussion.* The Discussion strategy is just what its name implies, a class conducted by the discussion method. This strategy works best when the class size is limited to twenty-five or fewer students so that there can be maximum interaction between the discussion leader and the students. If the class is too large, the discussion fails to engage most of the students and they end up being bored or hostile. In those instances when the classroom size is favorable, we recommend that discussion questions be based on the *Teaching Objectives* section of the Instructor's Manual. Even in larger classes, ten or fifteen minutes of discussion can provide variety and be illuminating to students. Particularly helpful in such settings is the use of open-ended questions that cause students to think for themselves. For example, when teaching Greek civilization, the instructor might ask, "Which is the more beautiful style of art: the Hellenic or the Hellenistic?" Because there is no "correct" answer, this question allows many students to express their opinions. While encouraging a democracy of opinions, a good discussion leader will ask students to back up their points of view with sound reasoning based on specific works of art.

5. *Film.* The Film strategy is a teaching technique in which the instructor presents a film on a certain topic. For the Film strategy to work best, films must be used as teaching aids and not simply be treated as ends in themselves. At a minimum this means that the instructor should "frame" each film by giving it an introduction that explains what it is about and a conclusion that places its message into the context of the course being taught. The Film strategy is especially good for dealing with the arts and architecture and for presenting sweeping surveys of a historical period. Only high-quality and well-made films should be shown, however; otherwise this technique is counterproductive of sound educational goals, since it leads students to ridicule what they view and to judge a poorly made film to be a waste of learning time.

SEVEN SPECIFIC LECTURE SUGGESTIONS

1. *The Diffusion Model.* If the classroom topic involves the interaction of two societies or cultures, then the Diffusion model is probably the best way to organize that part of the lecture. Such an organization involves an identification of the cultural ideas, values, and techniques that pass from one society to another and an elaboration of the ways in which the things borrowed are assimilated into the receiving culture. This is a highly valuable lecture-organizing technique for instructors to master, since nearly every chapter of *The Western Humanities* touches on cultural interaction in some way, particularly regarding the enduring influence of Greece and Rome on later phases of Western culture.

2. *The Pattern of Change.* The Pattern of Change organizing device is a convenient way to deal with the many different types of change that recur in Western culture, such as moving from relatively simple to more complex ideas, from an original to an imitative artistic style, from a pure to an eclectic artistic style, or from unadorned to richly ornamented architectural works. A good lecture topic that would lend itself to the Pattern of Change model is the shift in the Middle Ages from the Romanesque to the Gothic style, a shift that retained many ingredients of the plain

Romanesque style while laying the foundation for a soaring Gothic style that went through several complex and elaborate phases.

3. *The Spirit of the Age.* "The Spirit of the Age" is a phrase borrowed from the thought of the German thinker G.F.W. Hegel, who believed that every historic period had a distinct spirit—*Zeitgeist*—that was expressed unconsciously in its achievements, both cultural and material. Although controversial, Hegel's theory is a useful way to help students understand the traits that distinguish one age from another. Instructors interested in adopting this approach to their lectures may consult the introductory paragraphs and each chapter legacy of *The Western Humanities,* for these sections are often compatible with Hegel's point of view.

4. *Case Study.* The Case Study method is an excellent tool for drawing lessons from history. In this approach, the instructor focuses on a well-defined historic incident or set of events that permit comparisons with later developments. For example, a lecture on the collapse of the Roman republic or the Roman Empire would provide the instructor with a Case Study that touches on contemporary issues; students could be asked to assess parallels between Rome and the United States in the areas of involvement in world affairs, the rise of popular spectacles, and the upsurge in urban violence.

5. *Comparison/Contrast.* The Comparison/Contrast model is a teaching tool that is a part of many lecture models, such as the Diffusion or the Patterns of Change models, but it also can stand on its own. Highly flexible, the Comparison/Contrast method can be used in those situations where there are strong similarities and differences, as in art (Impressionism and Post-Impressionism), in culture (fifth-century B.C. Athens and fifteenth-century Florence), and in politics (seventeenth-century England and France.

6. *Historical Overview.* The Historical Overview is a method of surveying a vast sweep of history, usually illustrated with a time line that can be projected on a screen. Instructors who adopt *The Western Humanities* have been provided with twenty-six time lines that list decisive dates of historical events along with significant cultural achievements. Though limited in its use, the Historical Overview can be quite effective at the beginning of a course or at any major point in the course when a new phase of history is introduced, such as in a survey course when the instructor moves from the Middle Ages to the Renaissance.

7. *Reflections/Connections.* The Reflections/Connections approach is based on the notion that a civilization's creative works are closely linked to its political, social, and economic institutions. This means that the arts and humanities are not produced in a vacuum, but rather mirror the dominant values of a society. This Reflections/Connections model can be used throughout the book. For example, this model can be used to treat the Late Middle Ages, when the rise of capitalism and its secular spirit was reflected in the Chaucer's descriptions of the middle-class pilgrims in *The Canterbury Tales.*

PREHISTORY AND NEAR EASTERN CIVILIZATIONS

I. TEACHING STRATEGIES AND SUGGESTIONS

The instructor can approach the topic of prehistory and early culture through the Historical Overview model and use the Comparison/Contrast model to explain the differences between culture and civilization. An important point to emphasize is that human creativity is a basic human activity that predates the rise of civilization.

Using the Historical Overview, the instructor can easily survey Mesopotamian and Egyptian civilizations in separate lectures. Having explained the major phases of these earliest Western civilizations, the instructor can then shift to the Comparison/Contrast model and lay out their similarities and differences. The instructor can also use the Patterns of Change model to explain the evolution of each of these civilizations from its earliest beginning to its height of power. Another model the instructor can use is the Reflections/Connections model. For example, a lecture on the Sumerian civilization and the *Epic of Gilgamesh* would show how the two are connected and also demonstrate that the themes of the epic are common to most human concerns.

II. LECTURE OUTLINE

Non-Western Events

A. Prehistory and Early Cultures
  1. Definitions of culture and civilization
  2. The time frame
    a. Origins of human life and culture
      (1) Old Stone Age and New Stone Age
        (a) Artistic developments
        (b) Other achievements
      (2) The Neolithic period
        (a) Artistic developments
        (b) Other achievements
    b. Rise of civilizations

4000–3000 B.C.
First year of Jewish calendar (3760 B.C.)
First date in Mayan calendar (3372 B.C.)
Multicolored ceramic ware made in Russia reaches China

B. The Civilizations of the Tigris and Euphrates River Valley: Mesopotamia
  1. The Sumerian, Akkadian, and Babylonian kingdoms
    a. Historical overview of the three kingdoms
    b. Economic, social, and political developments

3000–2000 B.C.
First of the "Sage Kings" in China
Lake dwellings in middle Europe
In China, the Yao, Shun, & Hsia dynasties; tithe system with annual distribution of fields
Rock carvings in southern

2. The Cradle of Civilization
   a. Writing
   b. Religion
   c. Literature
      (1) Epics, tales, and legends
      (2) The *Epic of Gilgamesh*
   d. Law
      (1) The Code of Hammurabi
      (2) Judicial system
   e. Art and architecture
      (1) Carvings
      (2) The ziggurat

C. The Civilization of the Nile River Valley: Egypt
1. Prehistory to 3000 B.C.
   a. Characteristics
   b. Upper and Lower Egypt
   c. Neolithic developments
2. Continuity and change over three thousand years, 3100–525 B.C.
   a. Survey of Egypt's dynasties
   b. Common threads in politics, economics, and society
3. A quest for eternal cultural values
   a. Religion
      (1) The theocratic state
      (2) The pharaoh's defining role
      (3) The abortive Amarna revolution
      (4) The promise of immortality
   b. Writing and literature
      (1) Hieroglyphics
      (2) Literary genres of the Old Kingdom, the First Intermediate Period, and the Middle Kingdom
      (3) The rich heritage of the New Kingdom
         (a) *Hymn to Aten*
         (b) Love lyrics, model letters, wisdom literature, and fairy tales
   c. Architecture
      (1) The pyramid
         (a) The earliest version
         (b) The true pyramid
      (2) The funerary temple
   d. Sculpture, painting, and minor arts
      (1) Colossal sculpture: the Sphinx
      (2) Sculptures in the round
      (3) Portrait sculptures
      (4) The break in tradition: Amarna
      (5) The artistic canon
      (6) Minor arts

Norway depict skiing
Weaving loom in Europe
Start of regular astronomical observations in China and India; equinoxes and solstices determined in China
Cultivation of cotton in Peru
In China, first bamboo musical pipe; five-tone musical scale; painted and black pottery
Indus civilization in India (to 1500 B.C.)

2000–1500 B.C.
In China, Shang dynasty
First of seven periods of Chinese literature
Jomon people settle in Japan
Teutonic settlements in southern Norway
Beginning of the building of Stonehenge, England
Four basic elements known in India: earth, air, fire, and water

1500–1000 B.C.
Earliest settlement in Mexico
First Chinese dictionary
"Upanishad" tradition in India (hymns of the Rig Veda)
The Phoenicians import tin from England
Ethiopia becomes independent power
Silk fabrics in China
Founding of Corinth
Moses receives the Ten Commandments
Dorians conquer the Peloponnesus
Mexican Sun Pyramid in Teotihuacán
In China, elaborate bronze sculptures
Ganges civilization in India (to 400 B.C.)
The Lion Gate, Mycenae

D. Heirs to the Mesopotamian and Egyptian
   Empires, after 1000 B.C.
   1. The Hittites
   2. The Assyrians
   3. The Medes and the Persians
      a. Persian art
      b. The religion of Zoroaster

E. The Legacy of Near Eastern Civilizations

Chou dynasty in China
Blooming of Cretan-
   Mycenaean culture
The Trojan War

III. LEARNING OBJECTIVES

To learn:

1. The difference between *culture* and *civilization*

2. The great age of the earth and the relatively recent nature of human development

3. The distinction between prehistory and history

4. The stages of early human development

5. The earliest forms of artistic expression

6. How agriculture brought about the Neolithic period and the significance of this cultural period

7. How the discovery of metalworking led to the Bronze Age, which in turn produced the first civilizations in the West

8. The leading characteristics and major historical periods of the three civilizations that arose in Mesopotamia and the Egyptian civilization that began in the Nile river valley

9. The interaction between geography and cultural development in Mesopotamia and the Nile river valley

10. How Mesopotamia's and Egypt's cultural developments were each an outgrowth of specific political, economic, and social settings

11. Contrasts between Mesopotamian and Egyptian civilizations

12. The defining role played by religion in Mesopotamia's and Egypt's civilizations

13. Historic "firsts" achieved in Mesopotamia or Egypt or both that became legacies for later Western developments: writing, music, musical instruments, musical forms (such as hymns), astronomy, medicine, sound engineering principles rooted in mathematics, a law code, religious ideas, mathematical and geometrical knowledge, the 365-day, 12-month calendar, town life, town planning, standard weights and measures, literary genres, the column with capitals, the pyramid, post-and-lintel construction, sculpture in the round, portrait sculptures, relief sculptures, sculptural and painting techniques, and an aesthetic canon for artists

IV. SUGGESTIONS FOR FILMS

Ancient Egypt: Digging Up Her Rich Past. Time-Life, 51 min., color.

Ancient Mesopotamia. Coronet, 10 min., color.

Dr. Leakey and the Dawn of Man. Films, Inc., 27 min., color.

Egypt—The Gift of the Nile. Centron Educational Films, 29 min., color.

The Mysteries of the Great Pyramid. Wolper Productions, 50 min., color.

Persia: The Sudden Empire. Time-Life, 30 min., color.

Prehistoric Man in Europe. International Film Bureau, 23 min., color.

Yesterday's World: The Missing City Gates. NET, 29 min., color. [On ancient Assyria]

V. SUGGESTIONS FOR FURTHER READING

Mesopotamia

Frankfort, H. *Before Philosophy.* New York: Penguin, 1949.

Hallo, W., and Simpson, W. K. *The Ancient Near East.* New York: Harcourt, Brace, 1971.

Lloyd, S. *The Archaeology of Mesopotamia: From the Old Stone Age to the Persian Conquest.* London: Thames and Hudson, 1978.

Moortgat, A. *The Art of Mesopotamia.* Translated by J. Filson. New York: Phaidon, 1969.

Egypt

Aldred, C. *Egyptian Art: In the Days of the Pharaohs, 3100–320 B.C.* London: Thames and Hudson, 1980.

Davis, W. *The Canonical Tradition in Ancient Egyptian Art.* Cambridge: Cambridge University Press, 1989.

Schafer, H. *Principles of Egyptian Art.* Edited with an epilogue by E. Brunner-Traut; translated and edited with an introduction by J. Baines; foreword by E. H. Gombrich. Oxford: Humanities Press, 1986.

Smith, W. S. *The Art and Architecture of Ancient Egypt.* Rev. ed. New York: Penguin, 1981.

Trigger, B.B.G., and others. *Ancient Egypt: A Social History.* Cambridge: Cambridge University Press, 1983.

VI. IDENTIFICATIONS

culture   polytheism
civilization   anthropomorphism
Paleolithic   pantheism
Neolithic   stele
pictogram   post-and-lintel construction
ideogram   ziggurat
phonogram   hieroglyphs
cuneiform   canon

VII. DISCUSSION/ESSAY QUESTIONS

1. Define the Neolithic revolution. What was its importance in the development of material institutions and the arts of early civilizations?
2. Discuss the common characteristics of the religions practiced by the Sumerians, Akkadians, and Babylonians.
3. Discuss the themes and characters in the *Epic of Gilgamesh.*
4. What were the general characteristics of Mesopotamian art? How did the ziggurat manifest these characteristics?
5. Discuss the impact that geography had on Egyptian civilization.
6. Describe the Egyptian religious system. How did Egypt's religion affect developments in art, architecture, and literature.
7. Why is the pyramid the supreme symbol of Egyptian civilization?
8. Define the Amarna revolution. What was the significance of the Amarna revolution for Egypt, in both art and history?
9. What were the legacies of Mesopotamian and Egyptian civilization to the West?
10. How did Persian civilization differ from that of the Assyrians whom they conquered? What was the most enduring achievement of Persian civilization?

VIII. MULTIPLE-CHOICE QUESTIONS

1. The term *culture* usually refers to:
   a. the sum of all human endeavors
   b. the political, social, and economic institutions of a people
   c. a people's values and beliefs
 * d. all of the above (p. 1)

2. One of the primary traits of civilization is:
 * a. writing (p. 1)
   b. farming
   c. worshiping deities
   d. hunting

3. The earliest primate ancestors of present-day humans probably originated in:
   a. eastern Europe
   b. eastern India
 * c. eastern Africa (p. 2)
   d. western China

4. The term *Paleolithic* is another name for the:
   a. New Stone Age
   b. Bronze Age
 * c. Old Stone Age (p. 2)
   d. Iron Age

5. *Homo sapiens* or human beings evolved into their present form in about:
   a. 500,000 B.C.
 * b. 200,000 B.C. (p. 3)
   c. 10,000 B.C.
   d. 3,000 B.C.

6. Surviving evidence from the Upper Paleolithic period shows paintings of:
   a. human forms on canvas
 * b. animals on the walls of caves (p. 3)
   c. scenes of everyday life on walls of houses
   d. abstract designs on rocks

7. The Neolithic or New Stone Age arrived by about:
   a. 3,000 B.C.
   b. 80,000 B.C.
 * c. 8,000 B.C. (p. 4)
   d. 15,000 B.C.

8. Human beings in the early Neolithic Age began to:
   a. domesticate wild animals
   b. gather and sow wild grains
   c. establish an agrarian way of life
 * d. all of the above (p. 4)

9. As a consequence of the coming of the Neolithic Age:
   a. The domestication of wild animals declined.
   b. Villages lost population.
 * c. Communities grew and became more complex. (p. 4)
   d. Human beings stopped worshiping their deities.

10. The two geographical areas where civilizations first arose in the Near East were located:
    a. on the islands of the eastern Mediterranean and in Egypt
 * b. in the Tigris-Euphrates river valley and in the Nile river valley (p. 4)
    c. in southern Greece and in Egypt
    d. in the Tigris-Euphrates river valley and in southern Africa

11. The arc of land that swings through some of the most productive land in the Near East is called:
    a. the Womb of Civilization
    b. the Breadbasket of the World
 * c. the Fertile Crescent (p. 5)
    d. the Bountiful Valley

12. The three successive civilizations that flourished in the Tigris-Euphrates area, in chronological order, were:
    a. Akkadian, Babylonian, Sumerian
    b. Sumerian, Babylonian, Akkadian
 * c. Sumerian, Akkadian, Babylonian (p. 6)
    d. Babylonian, Sumerian, Akkadian

13. The first and greatest leader of the Akkadians was:
    a. Gilgamesh
    b. Moses
    c. Hammurabi
    * d. Sargon (p. 6)

14. The lawgiver for the Babylonians was:
    a. Moses
    * b. Hammurabi (p. 6)
    c. Enlil
    d. Gilgamesh

15. The Babylonian law code (Question 14) can be described as:
    a. claiming to be originated by a deity or god of justice
    b. setting forth a legal tradition that must be obeyed by future rulers
    c. establishing a type of justice based on retaliation
    * d. all of the above (p. 9–10)

16. The civilization that is credited with the invention of writing is:
    a. Egyptian
    * b. Sumerian (p. 7)
    c. Akkadian
    d. Babylonian

17. One of the earliest surviving written epics is the:
    a. Epic of Sargon
    * b. Epic of Gilgamesh (p. 8)
    c. Epic of Moses
    d. Epic of Achilles

18. This epic (Question 17) touches on which of the following themes?
    * a. the power of the gods over mortals (p. 8)
    b. the issue of free will
    c. the role of slaves in society
    d. the rights of free citizens

19. The hero in the epic (Question 17) can be described as:
    a. a man full of self-confidence all of his life
    * b. a person who learns that humans are mortal (p. 9)
    c. an individual who outwits the gods
    d. all of the above

20. Within the epic (Question 17) is another tale that:
    a. recounts the deeds of a noble warrior
    b. explains the origins of the deities
    * c. tells about a great flood (p. 9)
    d. praises the power of human beings

21. As is often the case in epics, the main character:
    * a. takes on characteristics of a superhuman being (p. 8)
    b. is transformed into another person
    c. finds peace and happiness in this life
    d. discovers that one can do whatever one desires in life

22. The central architectural feature of a Mesopotamian city usually was:
* a. a temple (p. 10)
  b. the city hall
  c. the palace of the king
  d. the market place

23. The proper name of the architectural work in Question 22 is:
  a. basilica
  b. cathedral
  c. mosque
* d. ziggurat (p. 11)

24. The basic type of construction for buildings in Mesopotamia was:
  a. vaulted ceiling and columns
  b. arches and columns
* c. post-and-lintel (p. 10)
  d. flying buttresses and arches

25. In Mesopotamian religion:
  a. The priests in each city had much power.
  b. The land and the periodic flooding helped to define the faith.
  c. Worshipers believed that the gods could come down to earth.
* d. all of the above (p. 8)

26. Geography influenced Egyptian culture in all these ways EXCEPT:
* a. Heavy rainfall made Upper Egypt the breadbasket of the country. (pp. 12–13)
  b. Isolated by deserts on either side, Egypt was little influenced by neighboring cultures.
  c. The Nile's periodic flooding made civilized life possible in Egypt.
  d. Proximity to the Mediterranean made Lower Egypt more cosmopolitan than Upper Egypt.

27. The first king of Egypt was:
  a. Hatshepsut
  b. Djoser
* c. Menes (p. 13)
  d. Kheops

28. A permanent feature of Egyptian civilization was:
  a. rulers who claimed to be divinities
  b. the construction of elaborate royal tombs
  c. the control of the foreign trade by the rulers
* d. all of the above (pp. 13-15)

29. Egypt fully entered the Bronze Age after being conquered by:
  a. the Persians
* b. the Hyksos (pp. 13 and 15)
  c. the Greeks
  d. the Sea Peoples

30. The New Kingdom in Egyptian history was significant because:
  a. Egypt became a great power, dividing the Near East with the Assyrians and the Hittites.
  b. Egypt, for the first time in its history, experimented with religious innovation.
  c. Egyptian art, for the only time in its history, underwent a short-lived revolution.
* d. all of the above (pp. 13 and 20)

31. Egyptian religion was characterized by all of the following EXCEPT:
    a. the belief in immortality
    b. the worship of the ruler
  * c. a single national deity for the state (p. 16)
    d. polytheism

32. Which pharaoh brought about the Amarna revolution?
  * a. Akhenaten (p. 16)
    b. Menes
    c. Hatshepsut
    d. Amenemhat

33. Which was an aspect of the Amarna revolution in Egypt?
    a. Aten, the god of the sun's disk, was elevated to supremacy over the other deities.
    b. Egyptian art became more fluid and natural than it had previously been.
    c. Later rulers tried to erase the name and memory of the pharaoh who instigated the revolution.
  * d. all of the above (pp. 16 and 20)

34. The most famous work of Egyptian literature is:
    a. the *Epic of Gilgamesh*
    b. *An Argument between a Man Contemplating Suicide and His Soul*
  * c. the *Story of Sinuhe* (p. 17)
    d. the *Hymn to Aten*

35. Egyptian writing is called:
  * a. hieroglyphs (p. 17)
    b. cuneiform
    c. minuscule
    d. all of the above

36. The model for the Step Pyramid of King Djoser was:
    a. an original Egyptian design
  * b. borrowed from the Mesopotamian ziggurat (caption for Fig. 1.12)
    c. a variation of the earlier pure pyramid design
    d. adopted from a Chinese design

37. In Egypt, the building of pyramids occurred:
    a. throughout Egyptian history
  * b. only in the Old Kingdom (p. 19)
    c. during the Amarna revolution
    d. only in the Middle Kingdom

38. What was the cultural significance of the Egyptian pyramid?
    a. It was the product of sound engineering principles rooted in mathematics.
    b. It was the resting place of a ruler preparatory to the afterlife.
    c. Its shape seemed to embody a constant and eternal order.
  * d. all of the above (pp. 17 and 18)

39. All of the following are aspects of Hatshepsut's temple EXCEPT:
  * a. Its central shrine is in the pure pyramid shape. (p. 19)
    b. It is built with post-and-lintel style of construction.
    c. It uses columns with decorated capitals.
    d. Its colonnaded courtyards lead to a hidden sanctuary in a cliff.

40. Which does NOT apply to the Great Sphinx?
    a. It represents a mythical creature, part-human and part-animal.
*   b. It is carved from Libyan stone that was transported to the Giza site. (p. 19)
    c. Its original purpose was to guard the nearby pyramid group.
    d. Its face depicts Khephren, the ruler who commissioned it.

41. The classical Egyptian style of sculpture did NOT include this trait:
    a. left leg forward
    b. fists clenched
*   c. completely nude (p. 19)
    d. unemotional countenance

42. This female pharaoh built a temple at Deir el Bahri, near Luxor:
*   a. Hatshepsut (p. 19)
    b. Neferit-iti
    c. Mykerinus
    d. Akhenaten

43. Egypt's outstanding contribution in relief sculpture was:
    a. the ability to depict figures facing straight ahead
    b. the development of the principles of perspective
*   c. the invention of a canon of proportions for depicting the human figure (p. 21)
    d. the creation of a vast repertory of poses for portraying human actions

44. The most famous discovery in Egyptian antiquities, made by archaeologists in the twentieth century, is the tomb of:
    a. Hatshepsut
    b. Djoser
    c. Akhenaten
*   d. Tutankhamen (p. 21)

45. Which was a successor kingdom to the Mesopotamian and Egyptian empires in the period after 1000 B.C.?
    a. the Hittite
    b. the Assyrian
    c. the Persian
*   d. all of the above (p. 22)

46. What new subject was introduced into sculpture during the Amarna revolution?
*   a. intimate scenes of court life (p. 20 and caption for Fig. 1.17)
    b. royal portraits
    c. banqueting scenes
    d. all of the above

47. Persian art was characterized by:
    a. violent and savage images
    b. abstract and nonfigurative shapes
*   c. contemplative themes with less action (p. 23)
    d. all of the above

48. Which was NOT an aspect of the Zoroastrian religion?
    a. It taught that the universe was engaged in a cosmic struggle between good and evil.
*   b. It originated in Assyrian culture. (p. 23)
    c. It advocated puritanical behavior as a way to gain favor in the afterlife.
    d. It prophesied a Last Judgment.

49. Egypt's legacy to the West did NOT include:
    a. a solar calendar of 360 days, divided into twelve 30-day months, plus 5 holidays
    * b. the novel (p. 24)
    c. the decorated column
    d. medical learning and knowledge of drugs

50. Mesopotamia's legacy to the West did NOT include:
    * a. the dome (p. 24)
    b. a mathematical system based on 60
    c. standard weights and measures
    d. writing

2

AEGEAN CIVILIZATION
The Minoans, the Mycenaeans,
and the Greeks of the Archaic Age

I. TEACHING STRATEGIES AND SUGGESTIONS

A good approach to Aegean civilization is for the instructor to begin with a lecture that combines elements of the Historical Overview with the Diffusion model. In this opening presentation the teacher should provide a clear survey of early events in the Aegean area from about 2000 to 479 B.C.; clarify the influences operating on Archaic Greece from the Near East, Crete, and Mycenae; and set forth the basic differences between Archaic Greece and earlier civilizations. The instructor should then focus on Archaic Greece, identifying its leading characteristics and stressing the primary role played by religion in shaping culture. To give a well-rounded view of this earliest stage of Greek civilization, the instructor can use four different strategies: the Slide Lecture model to set forth the artistic achievements; the Reflections/Connections model to establish the linkages between cultural and material history; the Comparison/Contrast method to deal with the dominant literary forms of epic and lyric poetry; and the Spirit of the Age approach to show the unity amid the artistic and literary diversity. The instructor can also employ the Case Study method to deal with the rise of philosophy/science, one of the most enduring legacies of this remarkable age. And above all else, the instructor should show how the Archaic Greeks laid the foundation for the humanities, since the evolution of the humanistic tradition is a leading theme for the rest of *The Western Humanities*.

II. LECTURE OUTLINE

Non-Western Events

A. Introduction and Overview
  1. Brief contrast of Greek civilization
     with that of Mesopotamia and Egypt
     a. Human-centered *versus*
        god-centered
     b. Protagoras: "Man is the measure of
        all things"
  2. The Greek foundation of Western
     civilization
  3. Greek borrowings from the Near East

B. Prelude: Minoan Civilization, 3000–1300 B.C.
  1. The source of the term *Minoan*
  2. Characteristics of Minoan civilization
  3. Its outstanding architectural creation:
     the palace at Knossos

[See Chapter 1 for
developments in other
parts of the world.]

            a. Layout
            b. Decorative plan
        4. Cretan script, Linear A and B
        5. Religion
            a. Worship of a mother goddess
            b. The bull cult
        6. Commerce
        7. Mythology and its later impact on
           Greece

    C. Beginnings: Mycenaean Civilization,
       1900–1100 B.C.
        1. A source of legends for Greece
        2. Power center: Mycenae and the
           Peloponnesus
        3. Political, social, and economic
           structure
        4. The chief symbol of this militaristic
           civilization: the fortress-palace
            a. Ashlar construction
            b. The Lion Gate, Mycenae
        5. Religion
            a. Worship of divinities
            b. Burial practices
            c. Contribution to later Greek
               practice of worship of heroes
        6. The Trojan War
            a. The realities of the war
            b. The inspiration for Homer's *Iliad* and
               Odyssey
        7. Mycenae and the Homeric tradition

    D. Interlude: The Dark Ages, 1100–800 B.C.
        1. The collapse of one form of civilized
           order
        2. The emergence of a new civilized order

1000–800 B.C.
In India, the religions
    of Brahmanism and
    Atmanism begin
In China, sun's height
    measured in relation to
    incline of polar axis
Peking founded
Beginning of mass
    migration of Germanic
    peoples
Beginning of Hebrew
    literature
Brush and ink painting
    in China
Pinto Indians build huts
    in California

    E. The Archaic Age, 800–479 B.C.
        1. Historical overview: Age of innovation and
           experimentation
        2. The origin of *Hellas* and *Hellene*

800–700 B.C.

Founding of Rome
Celts move into England

3. Political, economic, and social
   structures
   a. The rise of the polis
      (1) The acropolis
      (2) The agora
      (3) The goal of the polis
   b. The shift from monarchy to oligarchy
      (1) Exemplary leadership, civil
          idealism, and cultural and
          artistic patronage
      (2) New military tactics
      (3) Overseas expansion and colonization
          (a) The coasts of Spain and North
              Africa, and the Black Sea
              area
          (b) Southern Italy and Sicily:
              Magna Graecia
          (c) Social developments
          (d) The rise of tyrants
   c. The shift from oligarchy to democracy
      (1) The rights of male citizens
      (2) Few rights for women
      (3) The hard lot of foreigners and
          slaves
4. Case studies of the Greek polis:
   Sparta and Athens
   a. Sparta, the symbol of Dorian
      civilization
      (1) Origins of oligarchic rule
      (2) Limited cultural achievements
   b. Athens, the symbol of Ionian
      civilization
      (1) Origins of democratic rule
          (a) Mounting social problems
          (b) Solon's reforms
          (c) Cleisthenes' democratic
              constitution
      (2) Inauguration of the Golden Age
5. The Persian Wars
   a. The threat from Persia
      (1) The war against Darius
      (2) The war against Xerxes
   b. The consequences of a Greek victory
      for the West
6. The emergence of Greek genius: the
   mastery of form
   a. The role of the muses in artistic
      creativity
   b. Religion
      (1) Olympian and chthonian deities
      (2) The concept of *hubris*
   c. Epic poetry
      (1) The *Iliad*

Babylonian and Chinese
   astronomers understand
   planetary movements
In India, medicine is
   freed from priestly
   control

700–600 B.C.
Beginning of second
   period of Chinese
   literature (to 200 B.C.)
Lao-tse, Chinese
   philosopher
Indian Vedas completed

600–500 B.C.
Mayan civilization in
   Mexico
Babylonian Captivity of
   the Jews
Siddhartha (550–480
   B.C.), the founder of
   Buddhism
Mahavira Jina (Vardhamana)
   founds Jainism
   in India; first known
   rebel against caste
   system
Shwe Dagon Pagoda built
   in Burma
Kung Fu-Tse (Confucius),
   Chinese philosopher
   (551–479 B.C.)
First recorded sea voyage
   around Africa, by
   Phoenicians
Decline of China
   under Chou
   dynasty
Rome declared a
   republic
La Tene culture in Europe
First Roman stone bridge
High point of Etruscan
   influence in Italy
"Ramayana," Hindu poem
   (about 500 B.C.)
In Persia, first coin
   with picture of ruler

500–479 B.C.
Greek civilization begins
   to be adopted in Rome
Indian surgeon Susrata
   performs cataract
   operations
Plebeians in Rome begin
   to agitate for more
   rights
Hanno the Carthaginian
   travels down the west
   coast of Africa

III. LEARNING OBJECTIVES

To learn:

1. How Greek civilization borrowed from Near Eastern civilizations

2. How the Greeks laid the foundation of Western civilization

3. The cultural contributions of the Minoans, the makers of the first high civilization in what became the Greek area

4. The cultural contributions of the Mycenaeans, the makers of the first high civilization on the Greek peninsula

5. The origin of the Dorians and the Ionians and the significance of these cultural terms for Greek civilization

6. The significance of the Dark Ages

7. The characteristics and major forms of cultural expression of Archaic Greece

8. The meaning of "polis" and the central role it played in Greek civilization

9. The evolution of the polis, from monarchy to oligarchy to democracy

10. The significance of Sparta and Athens, symbols respectively of Dorian and Ionian civilization

11. How Athens's victory over Persia laid the groundwork for the Athenian dominance of Greece

12. How religion helped to shape Greek culture, especially the muses, the Olympian gods and goddesses, and the chthonic deities

13. The epic tradition as established by Homer in the *Iliad* and the *Odyssey*

14. The lyric poetic tradition as expressed in the verses of Sappho

15. The early history of natural philosophy and the contributions of Thales, Pythagoras, and Heraclitus

16. To recognize visually the Doric style of temple building and to identify its components, decorative details, and aesthetic principles

17. To recognize visually the Archaic style in sculpture and to identify its distinguishing characteristics, with special reference to kouros and kòre statuary

18. To recognize visually the changes taking place in Archaic-style sculpture that were leading to Hellenic-style sculpture and to identify significant changes in this transition period

19. Historic "firsts" achieved in Archaic Greece that became legacies for later Western developments: the polis, epic poetry, lyric poetry, the post-beam-triangle temple, the kore and kouros sculptures, natural philosophy, and the humanities

IV. SUGGESTIONS FOR FILMS

The Aegean Age. Coronet, 14 min., color.

The Glory That Was Greece: The Age of Civil War. Time-Life, 36 min., black and white. [On the Persian Wars]

The Glory That Was Greece: The Age of Minos. Time-Life, 36 min., black and white.

The Greek Myths. Encyclopedia Britannica, 54 min., color.

The Greek Temple. Universal Education and Visual Arts, 54 min., color.

The Search for Ulysses. Carousel Films, 53 min.

V. SUGGESTIONS FOR FURTHER READING

Austin, M. M. *Greece and Egypt in the Archaic Age.* Cambridge: Cambridge Philological Society, 1970.

Boardman, J. *Pre-classical: From Crete to Archaic Greece.* New York: Penguin, 1967.

Charbonneaux, J., Martin, R., and Villard, F. *Archaic Greek Art, 620–480 B.C.* Translated by J. Emmons and R. Allen and maps by J. Person. London: Thames and Hudson, 1971.

Higgins, R. A. *Minoan and Mycenaean Art.* Rev. ed. London: Thames and Hudson, 1981.

Homann-Wedeking, E. *The Art of Archaic Greece.* Translated by J. R. Foster. New York: Crown, 1968.

Hussey, E. *The Presocratics.* New York: Scribner, 1973.

Jaeger, W. W. *Paideia: The Ideals of Greek Culture.* Translated by G. Highet. 2nd ed. New York: Oxford University Press, 1945.

Jeffery, L. H. *Archaic Greece: The City-states, c. 700–500 B.C.* London: Ernest Benn, 1976.

Matz, F. *The Art of Crete and Early Greece: The Prelude to Greek Art.* Translated by A. E. Keep. New York: Crown, 1965.

Snodgrass, A. M. *Archaic Greece: The Age of Experiment.* London: Dent, 1980.

Wilbur, J. B., and Allen, H. J. *The Worlds of the Early Greek Philosophers.* Buffalo, N.Y.: Prometheus Press, 1979.

VI. IDENTIFICATIONS

frieze	pediment
fresco	entablature
ashlar	cornice
shaft graves	stylobate
muse	cella
Olympian deities	capital
chthonian deities	triglyph
hubris	metope
epic poetry	relief
bard	entasis
Homeric epithet	fluting
lyric poetry	kouros
post-beam-triangle	kore
construction	Archaic
architrave	humanities

VII. DISCUSSION/ESSAY QUESTIONS

1. Explain the relationship of Archaic sculpture to Egyptian art. How did Archaic sculpture differ from Egyptian art?
2. What were the achievements of Minoan civilization? Discuss the impact of Minoan civilization on Archaic Greece.
3. What were the achievements of Mycenaean civilization? Discuss the impact of Mycenaean civilization on Archaic Greece.
4. Summarize the leading aspects of Greek religion and show how religion helped to shape cultural developments.
5. Select a work of Archaic sculpture and show how it expresses the Archaic style of art.

6. In what way did Archaic Greece lay the foundations for Western civilization?
7. Define "polis." Why was the development of the polis one of the most important contributions of Greek civilization?
8. What was the significance of Homer for Greek civilization?
9. Compare and contrast epic poetry with lyric poetry. What different audiences would be attracted to each of these poetic genres?
10. Show how Protagoras's statement that "Man is the measure of all things" was realized in Archaic Greek civilization.
11. Explain briefly the philosophies of Thales, Pythagoras, and Heraclitus. Why were their accomplishments so momentous?
12. Describe a typical Doric temple, and name and identify its chief features.
13. Explain the differences between Athens and Sparta. What cultural features did they have in common?
14. Define "the humanities." What role did the humanities play in the life of Archaic Greece?
15. What were the legacies of Archaic Greece to later Western civilization?

VIII. MULTIPLE-CHOICE QUESTIONS

1. Minoan civilization was centered on:
* a. the island of Crete (p. 27)
   b. the Greek mainland
   c. the coast of Asia Minor
   d. all of the above

2. Which is NOT an aspect of Minoan civilization?
   a. It was named for the legendary king Minos.
   b. Its major center was Knossos.
* c. Its cities were ringed with massive walls (p. 29)
   d. Its leading nobles lived in palaces.

3. Minoan art reveals this religious practice:
   a. the worship of a mother goddess
   b. bull leaping
   c. snake handling
* d. all of the above (pp. 29 and 30)

4. Which of the Greek deities was also worshiped by the Minoans?
   a. Athena
* b. Zeus (p. 31)
   c. Apollo
   d. Dionysus

5. Minoan civilization eventually fell to the:
   a. Egyptians
   b. Etruscans
* c. Mycenaeans (p. 31)
   d. Dorians

6. Mycenaean civilization was centered:
* a. on the Peloponnesus (p. 31)
   b. in northern Greece
   c. on the Greek islands
   d. on Crete

7. Which was NOT an achievement of Mycenaean civilization?
    a. gold funeral masks
*   b. imaginative literature (pp. 33 and 34)
    c. strong bureaucracies
    d. shaft graves

8. Mycenaean civilization transmitted which legacy to Archaic Greece?
    a. fortress-palaces
    b. ashlar-style construction
*   c. legends and myths of gods and heroes (pp. 33 and 34)
    d. imaginative literature

9. Mycenaean civilization had what political system?
*   a. rule by kings (monarchical) (p. 31)
    b. rule by the people (democratic)
    c. rule by god-kings (theocratic)
    d. rule by chieftains (tribal)

10. Homer's writings drew on legends of:
    a. Egyptian civilization
    b. Minoan civilization
*   c. Mycenaean civilization (p. 33)
    d. Etruscan civilization

11. Which occurred in the Greek Dark Ages?
    a. the adoption of iron age technology
    b. the migration of Greek-speaking peoples to the coast of Asia Minor
    c. the fragmentation of the Greek world
*   d. all of the above (p. 34)

12. Who is the originator of the epic literary tradition?
*   a. Homer (p. 40)
    b. Hesiod
    c. Sappho
    d. Archilocus

13. Greeks of the Achaic Age were NOT bound together by:
    a. a common language
*   b. a unified state (p. 34)
    c. a shared tradition of heroic stories and folk tales
    d. a standard set of myths and religious practices

14. Which was NOT one of the three major Greek tribes?
    a. the Ionians
    b. the Dorians
    c. the Aeolians
*   d. the Corinthians (p. 34)

15. The Archaic Greeks called their land:
*   a. Hellas (p. 34)
    b. Peloponnesus
    c. Morea
    d. Greece

16. A typical polis included:
    a. a citadel where the rulers resided
    b. a sanctuary for temples and shrines
    c. a central gathering area for business and socializing
  * d. all of the above (p. 34)

17. An "acropolis" is:
    a. a wealthy city-state
    b. a king
  * c. a fortified hilltop (p. 34)
    d. a tyrant

18. An "agora" is a(n):
    a. theater
  * b. open area that serves as a marketplace and city center (p. 34)
    c. military organization
    d. devotee of the god Dionysus

19. Which is the correct sequence to describe governmental shifts in a typical polis during the
    Archaic Age?
  * a. oligarchy to tyranny to democracy (pp. 34–35)
    b. democracy to tyranny to oligarchy
    c. oligarchy to democracy to tyranny
    d. tyranny to democracy to oligarchy

20. All of these had happened by the end of the Archaic Age EXCEPT:
    a. Greek colonies dotted the coasts of Spain, North Africa, the Black Sea and southern Russia,
       and Sicily and southern Italy.
    b. Foot soldiers had replaced warriors in horse-drawn chariots.
    c. Most adult male property owners enjoyed citizenship rights.
  * d. Women joined their husbands in carrying out public duties. (p. 35)

21. Which is NOT an aspect of ancient Sparta? The Spartans:
  * a. welcomed foreigners into their midst (p. 36)
    b. prided themselves on their hierarchical social system
    c. restricted the accumulation of wealth by citizens
    d. treated their slaves ruthlessly

22. The rest of Greece admired Sparta for its:
    a. artistic creativity
    b. contributions to philosophy
  * c. military might (p. 36)
    d. all of the above

23. Who introduced true democracy into Athens in about 500 B.C.?
    a. Solon
  * b. Cleisthenes (p. 36)
    c. Pericles
    d. Themistocles

24. What was the significance of the Persian Wars?
    a. The victory created a euphoric mood in Athens that set the stage for the ensuing Golden Age.
    b. The victory meant that the Persians would have little impact on the course of Western
       civilization.

c. The victory ensured the continuation of Greek democratic institutions and humanistic values that were just then being established.
* d. all of the above (p. 37)

25. A major victory of the Persians during the Persian Wars was at the battle of:
* a. Thermopylae (p. 37)
  b. Marathon
  c. Salamis
  d. Plataea

26. Which is NOT a correct pairing of a Muse with her area of creativity?
* a. Niobe   painting (p. 38)
  b. Calliope   epic poetry
  c. Clio   history
  d. Terpsichore   dance and song

27. The Olympian deities had all of these aspects EXCEPT:
  a. They lived in the sky or on mountain tops.
  b. They were associated with the Homeric heroes.
* c. They originated among the peasants and lower social orders. (p. 38)
  d. The Greeks endowed them with bodies and individual personalities.

28. Greek religion taught the faithful to avoid the sin of *hubris* or:
  a. greed
* b. pride (p. 38)
  c. sexual immorality
  d. murder

29. Which is NOT a correct pairing of an Olympian deity and his/her duty?
  a. Zeus   king of the gods and goddesses
* b. Athena   goddess of love (p. 39)
  c. Artemis   virgin goddess who aided women
  d. Hermes   god of merchants and thieves

30. Chthonian religious cults had all of these aspects EXCEPT:
  a. They were called mystery cults.
  b. They originally were intended to invoke the powers of the earth to ensure a successful planting and a rich harvest.
  c. They later claimed to promise immortality to worshipers.
* d. They began among the aristocratic population. (p. 39)

31. What cultural institution grew out of the worship of Dionysus?
* a. the theater (p. 39)
  b. the library
  c. the school
  d. all of the above

32. The hero of the *Iliad* is:
  a. Odysseus
  b. Menelaus
* c. Achilles (p. 41)
  d. Hector

33. Which applies to the *Odyssey?*
    a. It recounts events after the Greeks defeat the Trojans.
    b. It focuses on Odysseus's efforts to return to his home in Ithaca.
    c. It portrays the faithful Penelope awaiting the return of her husband.
  * d. all of the above (p. 41)

34. Homer influenced Greek civilization by:
    a. giving texture to the Greek language
    b. acting as a theologian of the Greek religion
    c. serving as a moral guide
  * d. all of the above (p. 41)

35. Which was NOT an aspect of lyric poetry?
  * a. Its richest period occurred before the time of Homer. (p. 41)
    b. It expressed an author's personal, private thoughts.
    c. It reflected the rising democratic spirit of the Archaic Age.
    d. Its inspiration was credited to the muse Euterpe.

36. Sappho's lyric poetry was mainly on the subject of:
    a. victorious athletes
  * b. passionate love in all of its aspects (p. 41)
    c. political and social problems
    d. nature

37. Who was the first philosopher/scientist?
  * a. Thales (p. 42)
    b. Pythagoras
    c. Heraclitus
    d. Democritus

38. Pythagoras was author of which scientific theory?
    a. the notion that the basic stuff of nature is water
    b. the concept of Atomism
    c. the view of the four elements, earth, air, fire, and water
  * d. the belief that everything is based on numbers (p. 42)

39. What was the significance of the philosopher/scientists of Archaic Greece?
    a. They believed that there is regularity in the universe.
    b. They thought that human reason could understand the natural order.
    c. They called into question divine explanations of human events.
  * d. all of the above (p. 42)

40. Typical Greek temple architecture did NOT have this feature:
    a. post-beam-triangle construction
    b. a cornice
  * c. arches (p. 43)
    d. a cella

41. All of these features are unique to the Doric temple style EXCEPT:
    a. columns with undecorated capitals
  * b. a pediment with sculptures (p. 43)
    c. triglyphs
    d. metopes

42. The beauty of the Temple of Aphaia, Aegina, is the result of:
    a. fluting on the columns
    b. mathematical proportions
    c. refined details
 * d. all of the above (p. 45 and caption for Fig. 2.13)

43. An Egyptian influence on Archaic Greek sculpture was:
    a. left foot forward
    b. clenched fists
    c. frontality
 * d. all of the above (p. 46)

44. Unlike the Egyptian style, the Archaic style was characterized by:
    a. archaic smile
    b. nude male figures
    c. musculature based on careful study of the human body
 * d. all of the above (pp. 46 and 48)

45. A frequent subject in Archaic Greek sculpture was:
    a. portrait busts
 * b. youths and maidens (pp. 45–46)
    c. scenes of everyday life
    d. all of the above

46. The Ptoon Kouros is a statue of a:
    a. standing maiden
    b. creature with an animal's body and a man's face
 * c. standing youth (p. 46)
    d. kneeling archer

47. In the Archaic style, how did a statue of a Kore differ from a statue of a Kouros?
    a. A Kore was given an archaic smile.
 * b. A Kore was portrayed clothed. (p. 48)
    c. A Kore was portrayed with stylized hair.
    d. all of the above

48. What change occurred in Archaic sculpture at the end of the period?
    a. Faces became more emotional.
 * b. Realistic tension was now depicted in the body. (p. 48)
    c. Frontality was introduced.
    d. all of the above

49. The humanities are:
    a. the things that human beings do in any culture
    b. the beliefs that arise out of religious worship
 * c. the original artistic and literary forms of the Greeks (p. 50)
    d. the attitudes and practices that make human beings more sympathetic to others

50. In what way did the Archaic Greeks lay the foundation for Western civilization?
    a. They originated the spirit of scientific inquiry.
    b. They developed a human-centered consciousness.
    c. They launched a literary, artistic, and philosophic tradition.
 * d. all of the above (p. 27, 50)

3

CLASSICAL GREEK CIVILIZATION
The Hellenic Age

I. TEACHING STRATEGIES AND SUGGESTIONS

The instructor can introduce this chapter with the Comparison/Contrast model, noting similarities and differences between the Archaic and Hellenic Greek civilizations with emphasis on the political, economic, and social institutions. The instructor can use the Historic Overview approach to set forth the principal historic divisions and then give a more detailed analysis of the causes of the Peloponnesian War. Thucydides' account of the war could be effectively used along with an explanation of the changing "climate of opinion" in late fifth-century Athens. The instructor could connect these events with Greek philosophy just before the time of Socrates.

The teacher should utilize the Reflections/Connections model to discuss Greek theater and its relationship to the arts and civic institutions. Having the students read one or two tragedies will introduce them to Greek values and ideals. Two or more hours of Standard Lecture on Greek philosophy are essential to lay the foundation of the major schools of Western thought whose influences come down to the present day. Arguably, this will be the most important set of lectures of the entire term. The instructor can adopt the Comparison/Contrast model for treating Platonism and Aristotelianism; the discussion of these systems of thought must be in simple enough terms so that students will be able to recognize them when they resurface in later philosophy.

A variety of approaches may be used in dealing with Greek architecture and sculpture. The Reflections/Connections model will enable students to relate Greek values to the visual arts. The Diffusion method can illustrate the changes that occurred in Hellenic art as compared with Archaic art. This method can also illustrate the influence of the Greek Classical style on later revivals of this style, in particular as found in the United States in the late eighteenth century. The Case Study approach will permit the instructor to note how America's leaders looked to Greece (and to Republican Rome) for inspiration regarding political systems and architecture.

A summary lecture, using the Spirit of the Age model, should identify the most significant legacies of Hellenic Greece and the common artistic and moral values that were expressed in those achievements.

II. LECTURE OUTLINE

Non-Western Events

A. Geography and Historical Overview

B. General Characteristics of Hellenic Civilization
1. Competitiveness
2. Religious
3. High regard for moderation

a. Dionysus
b. Apollo

C. Domestic and Foreign Affairs:
War, Peace, and the Triumph of Macedonia
1. Economic changes
2. The Delian League
   a. A mutual defense organization
   b. The central role of Athens
3. Wars in Greece and with Persia and the
Thirty Years' Peace
   a. Instability in Greece
   b. The Golden Age of Athens
   c. The connection of Athenian imperialism
   and cultural exuberance
   d. The Age of Pericles
      (1) Cultural zenith
      (2) Fear of Athens among other city-states
4. The Peloponnesian War
   a. Its origins
   b. The death of Pericles
   c. The Sicilian expedition
   d. The defeat of Athens by Sparta
5. Spartan and Theban hegemony and the
triumph of Macedonia
   a. Shifting fortunes in Greece
   b. Conquest of Greece by Philip of
   Macedonia
   c. The reign of Alexander the Great
      (1) Alexander's dream
      (2) Alexander's sudden death

D. The Perfection of the Tradition:
The Glory of Hellenic Greece
1. Brief overview of Athens in the Hellenic
Age
   a. Definition of Classic
   b. Definition of Classicism
2. Theater: Tragedy
   a. Its origins
   b. Features of the Tragic Theater
      (1) The actors and chorus
      (2) The physical theater
      (3) The staging of the plays
      (4) The structure of the Great Dionysia
   c. Tragic Drama
      (1) Essence of Greek tragedy
         (a) The moral nature of tragedy
         (b) The source of the plots
         (c) The issues treated in
         the plays
         (d) Aristotle's theory of tragedy
      (2) Aeschylus and the *Oresteia*
      (3) Sophocles

479–323 B.C.
Developments in
technology and
agriculture in
feudal China

          (a) *Antigone*
          (b) *Oedipus the King*
          (c) *Oedipus at Colonus*
     (4) Euripides
          (a) *The Trojan Women*
          (b) *The Bacchae*
3. Theater: Comedy
   a. Nature of Greek comedy
     (1) Characteristics
     (2) Comedy and democratic values
   b. Aristophanes
     (1) Old Comedy
     (2) *Lysistrata*
4. Music
   a. Role in Greek society
     (1) Music as one of the humanities
     (2) A partially reconstructed legacy
          (a) The diatonic system of
              Pythagoras
          (b) The series of scales, called
              modes
   b. Music's dependent status
5. History
   a. Herodotus, the founder of secular
      history
     (1) The *Histories*
     (2) The methodology
   b. Thucydides, the founder of scientific
      history
     (1) *History of the Peloponnesian War*
     (2) The methodology
6. Natural Philosophy
   a. Historic overview
   b. The pre-Socratics
     (1) The School of Elea
          (a) Parmenides
          (b) Empedocles
     (2) Atomism
     (3) Anaxagoras
   c. The Sophists
     (1) Source of the name
     (2) Their teachings
     (3) Their influence
   d. The Socratic revolution
     (1) Comparison with Sophists
     (2) The life and teachings of
        Socrates
          (a) The Socratic method
          (b) The teaching that "Virtue
              is Knowledge"
          (c) The revolutionary nature
              of his thinking
          (d) The death of Socrates

Indian vina: the ancestor
of hollow string
musical instruments

e. Plato
   (1) The influence of Socrates
   (2) The author of Western idealism
   (3) Platonism
      (a) The doctrine of the Forms,
           or Ideas
      (b) Platonic dualism
      (c) The Form (Idea) of the Good
   (4) The originator of political
        philosophy—the *Republic*
f. Aristotle
   (1) The influence of Plato
   (2) Emphasis on empiricism
   (3) Aristotelianism
      (a) The indivisibility of Form
           and Matter
      (b) Focus on purpose
      (c) The First Cause
      (d) The ethical ideal of
           moderation: a sound mind
           in a sound body
      (e) Political theory based on
           research
   (4) His enduring influence
7. Architecture
   a. Sanctuaries
      (1) Apollo's shrine at Delphi
      (2) The effect of the rise of the polis
   b. The temple: The perfection of the form
      (1) The style of western Greece
         (a) Characteristics
         (b) The Second Temple of Hera
              at Poseidonia
      (2) The style of eastern Greece
         (a) Characteristics
         (b) The Parthenon
      (3) The Ionic temple
         (a) Characteristics
         (b) The Erechtheum
8. Sculpture
   a. The Severe style
      (1) Characteristics
      (2) *Kritios Boy*
      (3) *Mourning Athena*
   b. The High Classical style
      (1) Characteristics
      (2) *Poseidon,* or *Zeus*
      (3) The *Doryphoros*
      (4) The Parthenon sculptures
         (a) *Centaur versus Lapith*
         (b) *Apollo, Poseidon, and
              Artemis*

c. Fourth Century style
      (1) Characteristics
      (2) *Hermes with the Infant Dionysus*

E. The Legacy of Hellenic Civilization

III. LEARNING OBJECTIVES

To Learn:

1. The general characteristics of Hellenic civilization

2. The Greek examples and images of balance and harmony

3. The causes, phases, and results of the Peloponnesian War

4. The reasons for and results of the coming of the Macedonians

5. The definitions of Classic, Classical, and Classicism

6. The origins and characteristics of Greek drama, the names of the major playwrights, and their contributions

7. The origins and characteristics of Greek comedy, the name of the chief comic playwright, and his contributions

8. The origins and moral purpose of Greek music

9. The writing techniques and contributions of the first Greek historians

10. The leading thinkers, their contributions, and the phases of philosophy in Hellenic Greece

11. The characteristics of the Ionic order of Greek architecture and its similarities and differences from the Doric order

12. The characteristics of Greek Hellenic sculpture, its various phases, and examples of sculptural works from each phase

13. The historic "firsts" of Hellenic civilization that became part of the Western tradition: humanism; a school curriculum based on humanistic studies; Classicism; the literary genres of tragedy, comedy, and dialogue; written secular history; the Ionic temple; the open-air theater; the Hellenic art style; the idea of democracy; the skeptical spirit rooted in scientific knowledge; and Platonism, Aristotelianism, and Atomism

14. The role of Hellenic civilization in transmitting the heritage of Archaic Greece: redirecting philosophy away from the study of nature and into humanistic inquiry, redefining sculpture along more realistic lines, and elaborating the basic temple form

IV. SUGGESTIONS FOR FILMS

The Acropolis of Athens. Media Guide, 26 min., color.

Athens: The Golden Age. Encyclopedia Britannica, 30 min., color.

The Greek Temple. Universal Education and Visual Arts, 54 min., color.

Plato's Apology—The Life and Teachings of Socrates. Encyclopedia Britannica, 30 min., color.

V. SUGGESTIONS FOR FURTHER READING

Andrewes, A. *The Greeks.* London: Hutchinson and Co., 1967.

Biers, W. R. *The Archaeology of Greece.* Ithaca, N.Y.: Cornell University Press, 1980.

Goldhill, S. *Reading Greek Tragedy.* New York: Cambridge University Press, 1986.

Robertson, M. *A History of Greek Art.* Cambridge: Cambridge University Press, 1975.

Shorey, P. *What Plato Said.* Chicago: University of Chicago Press, 1965.

Taylor, A. E. *Aristotle.* New York: Dover, 1955.

————. *Plato.* Ann Arbor: University of Michigan Press, 1962.

————. *Socrates: The Man and His Thought.* Garden City, N.Y.: Doubleday, 1953.

VI. IDENTIFICATIONS

Hellenic	idealism
maenad	Platonism
Classic (Classical)	Doric
Classicism	Ionic
tragedy	Severe style
chorus	High Classical style
orchestra	Fourth Century style
skene	contrapposto
satyr-play	Praxitelean curve
Old Comedy	humanism
modes	

VII. DISCUSSION/ESSAY QUESTIONS

1. Discuss the general characteristics of Hellenic civilization.

2. What were causes of the Peloponnesian War and what were its results?

3. Discuss the features of Greek tragedy and explain how they were manifested in Sophocles' *Antigone.*

4. Compare and contrast the works and techniques of Herodotus and Thucydides.

5. Who were the pre-Socratics? Note the contributions to philosophy of *two* of the schools of pre-Socratic thinkers.

6. Compare and contrast Plato's and Aristotle's approaches to truth, and note their basic contributions to Western philosophy.

7. What is meant by the High Classical style? Discuss at least two examples of this style as found in Greek sculpture.

8. How did the Greeks define humanism? How was this concept manifested in Greek tragedy and in Aristotle's writings on ethics?

VIII.   MULTIPLE-CHOICE QUESTIONS

1. One of the ideals the Greeks strived for was:
   a. a high standard of living for all citizens
   b. a uniform religion with one major deity
   * c. a balance or moderation in life (p. 53)
   d. a recognition in life that all human beings are equal

2. The organization that the Greeks founded to protect themselves after the Persian War was:
   a. the League of Samos
   * b. the Delian League (p. 56)
   c. the Anti-Persian Alliance
   d. the Peloponnesian League

3. At the height of its power Athens was dominated by:
   a. Quales
   b. Leonidas
   c.. Philip
   * d. Pericles (p. 57)

4. The Age of Pericles was characterized by:
   a. a retreat from Athens's policy of imperial control
   b. a lessening of political democracy in Athens
   * c. an outburst in the arts and literature in Athens (p. 57)
   d. the establishment of a communal economy in Athens

5. The primary cause of the Peloponnesian War was:
   a. the rise of Sparta
   * b. Athens's growing domination over the other city-states (pp. 56–57)
   c. the emergence of Thebes
   d. the threat from Philip of Macedonia

6. What event provoked the outbreak of the Peloponnesian War?
   a. Athens attacked her long time enemy Sparta.
   b. Corinth was conquered by the Thebans.
   * c. Athens sent troops to aid the Corcyrians. (p. 57)
   d. Sparta called for help against the Athenians.

7. The Peloponnesian War was noteworthy for:
    a. its disruptive influence on Spartan political affairs
    b. its quick and decisive outcome
    c. the triumph of Athens over the other city-states
*   d. the weakening of Greece that made it an easy prey for outsiders (p. 57)

8. This fourth-century Macedonian leader conquered the Greeks:
    a. Themistocles
    b. Pericles
*   c. Philip (p. 58)
    d. Leonidas

9. Which fourth-century leader had a dream that he would conquer the known world?
*   a. Alexander the Great (p. 58)
    b. Charles of Macedonia
    c. Attila the Hun
    d. Pericles the Conqueror

10. The dream of Alexander the Great was:
*   a. to create a united world based on Greek and Persian culture (p. 58)
    b. to set up an international league of city-states
    c. to destroy all cultures except the Greek culture
    d. to fuse African and Macedonian civilizations

11. The Greek god associated with Greek drama was:
*   a. Dionysus (p. 59)
    b. Zeus
    c. Hera
    d. Aphrodite

12. According to tradition, the first playwright to introduce an actor with whom a chorus could interact was:
    a. Aeschylus
    b. Aristophanes
*   c. Thespis (p. 60)
    d. Sophocles

13. Greek drama had this feature:
    a. The plays were full of on-stage action.
*   b. The themes often dealt with serious moral issues. (p. 61)
    c. Most of the dramas were based on current political events.
    d. The plays had many characters and elaborate scenery.

14. This Greek philosopher wrote a book on tragedy:
    a. Plato
    b. Socrates
*   c. Aristotle (p. 61)
    d. Pythagoras

15. The most prolific Greek tragedian was:
*   a. Sophocles (p. 62)
    b. Aristophanes
    c. Thespis
    d. Euripides

16. The *Oresteia* trilogy involved:
    a. a conflict of strong personalities
    b. many moral issues
    c. three plays organized around a central theme
  * d. all of the above (pp. 61–62)

17. Euripides wrote plays that can be described as:
    a. concerned with human behavior
    b. basically humorous satires of Greek manners
    c. skeptical about religion
  * d. a and c are correct (p. 63)

18. Greek Old Comedy can be described as:
    a. relatively unpopular with Greek audiences
    b. developed before tragedy
  * c. showing political criticism (p. 63)
    d. expressed through clever and subtle dialogue

19. The most famous and most successful comic playwright was:
    a. Aristotle
    b. Agisthenes
  * c. Aristophanes (p. 63)
    d. Aeschylus

20. The most important legacy of Greek comedy was:
  * a. Old Comedy (p. 63)
    b. New Comedy
    c. burlesque style
    d. New Satire

21. This Greek philosopher contributed to the development of music theory:
    a. Protagoras
  * b. Pythagoras (p. 64)
    c. Pericles
    d. Anaxagoras

22. Empedocles, a Greek philosopher, claimed that:
    a. everything is made up of atoms
  * b. the four elements are the basis for all things (p. 65)
    c. the world is static and never changes
    d. water is the basic ingredient of all things

23. The Greek thinker who developed the Atomic theory was:
  * a. Democritus (p. 66)
    b. Empedocles
    c. Parmenides
    d. Pythagoras

24. The Sophists could be described as:
    a. teachers who claimed that they could make their students successful
    b. critics of all types of philosophical speculation
    c. experts in rhetoric and advocates of the use of language
  * d. all of the above (p. 66)

25. The Greek philosopher who is reputed to have said that "Man is the measure of all things" was:
    a. Pythagoras
  * b. Protagoras (p. 66)
    c. Plato
    d. Socrates

26. Socrates criticized the Sophists for their:
    a. inability to present a reasoned argument
    b. beliefs in the Olympian deities
  * c. rejection of an enduring moral order in the universe (p. 66)
    d. all of the above

27. What Socrates meant by "Virtue is Knowledge" was that:
    a. Everyone who does good will be rewarded in heaven.
  * b. If one knows what is good, that person will not commit evil acts. (p. 67)
    c. Everyone will reach understanding if they have faith.
    d. Being virtuous is all one needs to exist.

28. Socrates was condemned to death because:
    a. he aided Athens's enemies during the Peloponnesian War
  * b. he corrupted the youth of Athens (p. 67)
    c. he would not swear loyalty to the Athenian government
    d. he could not pay his debts

29. The Socratic method of teaching can be described as:
    a. a step-by-step memorization process to learn terms
  * b. a step-by-step system of asking and answering questions (p. 67)
    c. a progression of theories based on numbers
    d. a line of argument that refutes all basic values

30. Socrates' most famous pupil was:
    a. Aristotle
    b. Alcibiades
    c. Zeno
  * d. Plato (p. 67)

31. Plato's most important contribution to Western philosophy was:
    a. his theory of numbers
  * b. his founding of the school of idealism (p. 67)
    c. his establishment of the Academy
    d. his legacy of a new set of deities

32. In the *Republic*, Plato created:
    a. an ideal society under a government run by soldiers
  * b. an ideal society run by philosopher-kings (p. 68)
    c. a capitalist economic system
    d. a utopian land of peace and plenty

33. To many persons in the modern world, Plato's *Republic:*
    a. is an ideal to strive toward
  * b. is more like a totalitarian state than a democracy (p. 68)
    c. can be achieved only in a world of peace
    d. is possible if the economy becomes socialistic

34. Unlike Plato, Aristotle:
    a. was more practical in creating a social system
    b. felt that ethics reflected everyday experiences
    c. argued that knowledge is derived from studying the material world
    * d. all of the above (p. 68)

35. Aristotle has had an incalculable influence on Western thought because:
    a. his reputation led later thinkers to believe that Aristotle knew all there was to know
    b. his writings formed the core of much of Classical learning
    c. his ideas were later accepted as authoritative by the Catholic Church
    * d. all of the above (p. 68)

36. Greek Classical art concerned itself with:
    a. a set of ideal proportions
    b. a striving to create a balance and harmony
    c. an emphasis on the bigness of the object
    * d. a and b, but not c (p. 69)

37. In general terms Hellenic Greek architecture:
    a. achieved balanced proportions through mathematical rules
    b. expressed the ideals of Greek art
    c. was characterized by restrained decorative schemes
    * d. all of the above (pp. 68–69)

38. Athens's major religious shrines were located:
    a. in the agora
    b. outside the city's walls
    * c. on the Acropolis (p. 71)
    d. around the city's burial grounds

39. The two architects responsible for the building of Athens's temples in the mid-fifth century were:
    * a. Ictinus and Callicrates (p. 71)
    b. Pericles and Alcibiades
    c. Aeschylus and Euripides
    d. Myron and Praxiteles

40. The central temple on the Acropolis was the:
    a. Erechtheum
    * b. Parthenon (p. 71)
    c. Pantheon
    d. Athena Nike

41. The Parthenon has become one of the most important architectural landmarks in Western art because:
    a. it embodied most of the ideals of Greek architecture
    b. despite being nearly destroyed, it has survived and serves as a reminder of Greece's accomplishments in architecture
    c. it has been used by later builders as a model for proportions and harmony
    * d. all of the above (p. 71 and caption for Fig. 3.15)

42. The two most popular orders of columns used by the Hellenic Greeks were the:
    a. Corinthian and Ionic
    * b. Doric and Ionic (p. 71)
    c. Doric and Corinthian
    d. Ionic and Tuscan

43. A comparison of the Doric and Ionic orders of columns reveals that:
    a. the Ionic is more decorated than the Doric
    b. most of the early temples were built with Doric columns
    c. the Ionic column has a capital that looks like a double scroll or the horns of a ram
  * d. all of the above (p. 71)

44. Next to the Parthenon, the second most important temple on the Acropolis was the:
    a. Athena Nike
    b. Propylaea
  * c. Erechtheum (p. 71)
    d. Pantheon

45. The architect of the Erechtheum was:
    a. Ictinus
  * b. Mnesicles (p. 71)
    c. Praxiteles
    d. Myron

46. The three phases of sculpture, in chronological order, as they evolved during the Hellenic Age were:
  * a. Severe, High Classical, and Fourth Century (p. 72)
    b. Severe, Fourth Century, and High Classical
    c. High Classical, Severe, and Fourth Century
    d. Severe, High Classical, and Baroque

47. Greek sculptors carved the human form in a graceful pose known as the:
    a. three-point stance
  * b. *contrapposto* (p. 72)
    c. *sfumato*
    d. flat-footed pose

48. Statues carved during the Hellenic Age often:
    a. exhibit a sense of the correct bodily proportions
    b. tend to idealize the facial features
    c. were commissioned to stand in the inner sanctums of temples
  * d. all of the above (pp. 72–75)

49. The sculptor who supervised the carvings that decorated the Parthenon was:
    a. Praxiteles
    b. Ictinus
  * c. Phidias (p. 75)
    d. Mnesicles

50. The frieze that decorated the Parthenon:
    a. depicted a procession of Athenians
    b. included humans, animals, and Olympian deities
    c. was carved in low relief
  * d. all of the above (pp. 75–77)

4

CLASSICAL GREEK CIVILIZATION
The Hellenistic Age

I. TEACHING STRATEGIES

The instructor should begin the study of Hellenistic civilization with a Historic Overview that sets forth the imperial dream of Alexander the Great, the general trajectory of history after his death, and the general characteristics of the culture and society that now developed. The best introductory approach to cultural achievements in this volatile age is with the Reflections/Connections model, showing how art, literature, and philosophy reflected changes in material history. Special attention should be paid to the rise of enormous cities that caused a change in consciousness, which, in turn, had an impact on art, philosophy, religion, and propaganda. A related development was the rise of Hellenistic Classicism, rooted in Hellenic forms but emotional, violence-loving, and playful. The instructor can use a combination of five strategies when treating the rich diversity of Hellenistic civilization: the Diffusion model can show the impact of Persian, Egyptian, and Babylonian cultures on the Greek tradition; the Patterns of Change approach can illustrate the shift from the pure Hellenic to the eclectic Hellenistic style; the Comparison/Contrast method is excellent for analyzing the premier Hellenistic philosophies; the Spirit of the Age technique can demonstrate the harmony amid the cultural confusion; and the Case Study approach will enable the instructor to apply lessons from Hellenistic civilization to today's similarly multicultural and multiracial world.

II. LECTURE OUTLINE

Non-Western Events

A. The Hellenistic World
1. Meaning of "Hellenistic"
2. The legacy of Alexander the Great
3. Brief summary of key Hellenistic concepts
4. Overview of Hellenistic politics, society, and economics

B. The Stages of Hellenistic History
1. The end of the empire and the rise of the states
   a. The shattering of Alexander's dream, 323–307 B.C.
   b. The era of the successor states, 307–215 B.C.
      (1) Freedom of movement of Greeks and barbarians
      (2) Common *koine* language

            (3)   The Macedonian kingdom
            (4)   The Seleucid kingdom
                  (a)   Parthia and Bactria
                  (b)   Pergamum
            (5)   The Ptolemaic kingdom
                  (a)   Alexandria as the capital
                  (b)   Its agricultural and
                        commercial riches
      c.   The arrival and triumph of Rome
            (1)   The fall of Macedonia, 146 B.C.
            (2)   The fall of the Seleucid
                  kingdom, 65 B.C.
            (3)   The gift of Pergamum
            (4)   The fall of the Ptolemaic
                  kingdom, 31 B.C.

C. The Cities of Hellenistic Civilization
    1.   Alexander's vision of the city
    2.   Pergamum
          a.   The capital of the Pergamum kingdom
          b.   Artistic and intellectual center
    3.   Alexandria in Egypt
          a.   The capital of the Ptolemaic kingdom
          b.   The largest city of the Hellenistic
                world
          c.   An unmatched cultural center
                (1)   The world's first museum
                (2)   The largest library of the
                      ancient world

D. The Elaboration of the Greek Tradition:
    the Spread of Classicism to the
    Hellenistic World
    1.   Hellenistic cultural style
          and Classicism
    2.   Drama and literature
          a.   New Comedy
                (1)   Definition
                (2)   Menander, the leading exponent
                      (a)   The comedy of manners
                      (b)   *The Girl from Samos*
                      (c)   His later influence
          b.   Alexandrianism—the Hellenistic
                literary style
                (1)   Important genres
                (2)   Characteristics
          c.   Theocritus
                (1)   The pastoral
                (2)   The idylls
    3.   Philosophy and religion
          a.   Nature of Hellenistic society
                (1)   Everyday life in the Hellenistic
                      cities

323–146 B.C.
The Indian heroic epic
    "Mahabharata" being
    written (perhaps to
    A.D. 350)
The first important
    Chinese poet, Ch'u Yuan
    (343–277 B.C.)
Chandragupta Maurya
    reconquers northern
    India from Alexander
    the Great's general
    and founds the Mauryan
    dynasty (319 B.C.)
Beginning of Mauryan
    culture in India
Appian Way being built
    in Rome, 312 B.C.
Rain is measured in
    India
Iron is used as a working
    material in China

(2) The rise of contradictory points
of view
b. The four chief Hellenistic
philosophies
(1) Cynicism
(a) Definition
(b) Least impact on
Hellenistic civilization
(c) The goal of *autarky*
(d) Diogenes
(2) Skepticism
(a) Definition
(b) Later influence
(c) The goal of *autarky*
(d) Carneades
(3) Epicureanism
(a) Definition
(b) Epicurus and his school
(c) Appeal to women
and slaves
(d) Based on Democritus's
Atomism
(e) The goals of happiness
and *ataraxia*
(4) Stoicism
(a) Definition
(b) Key concepts
(c) The goal of *autarky*
(d) Similarity of Stoic
ideals and Alexander
the Great's dream
c. Hellenistic religious alternatives
and fatalistic beliefs
(1) Fate, a Babylonian belief
(a) Astrology
(b) Magic
(2) The mystery cults
(a) Greek chthonic
religions
(b) Egyptian cults of Serapis
and Isis
(c) Babylonian cult of Cybele,
the Great Mother goddess
(d) Persian Mithraism
(e) Contributions to the
atmosphere in which
Christianity was born
4. Architecture
a. The defining role of religion
(1) The altar
(2) The temple
b. The Corinthian temple
(1) Characteristics of the Corinthian
column and temple

Mexican sun temple
Atetello at
Teotihuacán, 300 B.C.
Jewish scholars in
Alexandria develop
"Septuagint," a Greek
version of the Old
Testament (*ca.* 255 B.C.)
End of First Punic War,
241 B.C.
Invasion of Britain by
La Tene, Iron Age
people, about 250 B.C..
Asoka, the Indian
emperor, erects 40-
foot-high columns
inscribed with his
laws, about 250 B.C.
Death of Sun-tsi
(233 B.C.) marks end
of Chinese classical
philosophy
Standardization of all
Chinese measures and
weights, 221 B.C.
Great Wall of China
built to keep out
invaders, 215 B.C.
Rome conquers northern
Italy, 222 B.C.
Ch'in dynasty in China,
221–206 B.C.
End of Second Punic War,
201 B.C.
Third period of Chinese
literature
Shunga dynasty replaces
Mauryan dynasty in
India, 185–30 B.C.
"The Book of Daniel"
written, *ca.* 165 B.C.
First known paved
streets in Rome,
ca. 170 B.C.
End of Third Punic War,
146 B.C.; Rome now
master of the
western Mediterranean
Hu Shin produces Chinese
dictionary of 10,000
characters, 149 B.C.

        (2)   The Corinthian column as a symbol of Hellenistic influence

        (3)   The Olympieum in Athens
            (a)   History
            (b)   Description

   c. The altar
        (1)   General changes to altars in the Hellenistic period
        (2)   The altar of Zeus at Pergamum
            (a)   Description
            (b)   Its role in the beautification of Pergamum
            (c)   The idea of a "new" Athens

5. Sculpture
   a. Comparison with Hellenic style
   b. *Gaul and Wife*
        (1)   Why it was created
        (2)   Description
        (3)   Characteristics
   c. *Old Market Woman*
        (1)   Description
        (2)   A genre subject
   d. Pergamum altar frieze
        (1)   Subject and description
        (2)   Characteristics
        (3)   Moral purpose of the art
   e. *Aphrodite of Melos*
        (1)   Subject and description
        (2)   Characteristics
   f. *Horse and Jockey*
        (1)   Subject and description
        (2)   Characteristics
        (3)   Contrast with the Hellenic style

6. Rhodes: Late Hellenistic style
   a. The persistence of Rhodes as a center of Hellenistic culture, until the early Christian era
   b. The Rhodian style
        (1)   *Crouching Aphrodite*
            (a)   Subject and description
            (b)   Characteristics
         (2)   *Aphrodite of Cyrene*
            (a)   Subject and description
            (b)   Characteristics
         (3)   *The Laocoön Group*
            (a)   Subject and description
            (b)   Characteristics
            (c)   Later influence of this sculptural group

E. The Legacy of the Hellenistic World

III. LEARNING OBJECTIVES

To learn:

1. That Hellenistic society was one of the first world-states to be organized on multiracial lines

2. The role of Alexander in giving a vision to Hellenistic civilization

3. A brief summary of Hellenistic economics and society

4. The two historic stages of Hellenistic civilization

5. The major Hellenistic successor states to Alexander the Great's unified empire, their leading cultural characteristics, and how each state eventually fell to Rome

6. The two largest Hellenistic cities, Pergamum and Alexandria, and their chief contributions to the civilization of this age

7. How Hellenistic artists and writers adopted the Hellenic style and modified it into Hellenistic Classicism

8. How Menander developed New Comedy and the ways it differed from the Old Comedy of the Hellenic period

9. The characteristics of Alexandrianism, the unique literary style of the Hellenistic Age

10. The contributions and enduring influence of Theocritus, the chief writer of the Hellenistic period

11. The principles of the main Hellenistic philosophies (Cynicism, Skepticism, Epicureanism, and Stoicism), their leading spokespersons, and how they differed from one another

12. The teachings of the Hellenistic mystery cults and the belief in Fate

13. How Hellenistic religions and philosophies reflected the then-prevailing climate of opinion, especially in the cities

14. The characteristics of the Corinthian temple, as seen in the Olympeium, Athens

15. How today the Corinthian style is a symbol of Hellenistic influence

16. To describe and recognize the altar of Zeus at Pergamum

17. How Hellenistic rulers wanted to identify with Greek culture and to create cities that were "new" versions of Athens

18. The identifying characteristics of Hellenistic sculpture

19. To recognize visually key examples of Hellenistic sculpture

20. How Hellenistic sculpture differs from Hellenic sculpture

21. Historic "firsts" of Hellenistic civilization that became part of the Western tradition: the union of Greek culture and politics for propaganda purposes; the concept of a capital city as a "new Athens"; the Corinthian temple; the literary forms of the pastoral and the idyll; the Alexandrian literary style; the earliest museum; a mutiracial and multiethnic empire; the Hellenistic art style; and the philosophies of Cynicism, Skepticism, Epicureanism, and Stoicism

22. The role of Hellenistic civilization in transmitting the heritage of earlier civilizations: redefining Classicism to meet new needs, adopting the humanities as the curriculum in the schools, preserving the chief texts of Greek literature in Alexandria, expanding Greek science, making libraries into primary institutions in the large cities, and adopting the Near Eastern idea of a ruler-god

IV. SUGGESTIONS FOR FILMS

Alexander the Great and the Hellenistic Age. Coronet, 14 min., color.

Aristotle's Ethics—The Theory of Happiness. Encyclopedia Britannica, 30 min., color.

The Search for Alexander the Great: The Young Lion; The Young Conqueror; Lord of Asia; The Last March. Time-Life, each segment 60 min., color.

You Are There: The Triumph of Alexander the Great. McGraw-Hill, 26 min., black and white.

V. SUGGESTIONS FOR FURTHER READING

Fowler, B. H. *The Hellenistic Aesthetic.* Madison: University of Wisconsin Press, 1989.

Havelock, C. M. *Hellenistic Art: The Art of the Classical World from the Death of Alexander the Great to the Battle of Actium.* 2nd ed. New York: Norton, 1981.

Lewis, N. *Greeks in Ptolemaic Egypt: Case Studies in the Social History of the Hellenistic World.* New York: Oxford University Press, 1986.

Long, A. A., and Sedley, D. N. *The Hellenistic Philosophers.* New York: Cambridge University Press, 1987.

Rosenmeyer, T. G. *The Green Cabinet: Theocritus and the European Pastoral Lyric.* Berkeley: University of California Press, 1973.

Strozier, R. M. *Epicurus and Hellenistic Philosophy.* Lanham, Md.: University Press of America, 1985.

Welles, C. B. *Alexander and the Hellenistic World.* Toronto: A. M. Hakkert, 1970

VI. IDENTIFICATIONS

Hellenistic	*autarky*
koine	Skepticism
New Comedy	Epicureanism
comedy of manners	*ataraxia*
Alexandrianism	Stoicism
pastoral	*logos*

idyll   Corinthian
Cynicism   genre subject

VII. DISCUSSION/ESSAY QUESTIONS

1. What was Alexander the Great's vision for the world-state that he founded? To what extent did the Hellenistic era's successor states embody Alexander's dream? Include both material and cultural aspects in your essay.

2. Identify the Hellenistic states that arose as a result of the partition of Alexander the Great's far-flung empire. What forces unified these states during the Hellenistic period? Explain the circumstances under which these states eventually fell to the rising Roman empire.

3. Compare and contrast the two largest cities of the Hellenistic Age: Pergamum and Alexandria. Be specific as to the cultural contributions of each city.

4. Discuss the changes made to Classicism by Hellenistic writers and artists. What was retained from Greek Classicism and what became the hallmark of Hellenistic Classicism?

5. Define New Comedy. Which playwright dominated this literary genre? What impact did this playwright's works have on the Western theatrical tradition?

6. Define Alexandrianism. Discuss this literary style in relation to the greatest writer of the Hellenistic period, Theocritus. What were the contributions of Theocritus to Western literature?

7. Why was the Hellenistic age so rich in new philosophies and religions? What contradictory points of view emerged and why?

8. Identify the four philosophies that dominated the Hellenistic period, and compare and contrast their differing principles and goals. Indicate the relative long-term importance of each of these philosophies to the Western tradition.

9. Discuss Hellenistic religions with special focus on the belief in Fate and the mystery cults. Why were these religions so popular with the masses?

10. Describe a Corinthian-style temple, using the Olympieum in Athens as the model. Explain how the Olympieum mirrored the propaganda goals of the rulers who commissioned it.

11. What changes occurred in the design of altars during the Hellenistic Age? Describe the altar of Zeus at Pergamum. Why was this altar made into such a spectacular work of art?

12. Which work of Hellenistic sculpture epitomizes the Hellenistic style? Explain.

13. *The Laocoön Group* is the most famous sculpture from the Hellenistic period. What makes this such a well-known work of art? Which sculptural school produced the *Laocoön*? Describe the artistic style of this famous sculptural group.

14. What was the legacy of the Hellenistic Age to the West? Discuss both material developments and cultural contributions. What was original and what was simply a transmission of ideas, beliefs, and genres from earlier civilizations?

VIII. MULTIPLE-CHOICE QUESTIONS

1. What role did Greece play in the Hellenistic world?
    a. furnished its diplomatic and commercial language
    b. provided the dominant literary and artistic forms
    c. staffed its bureaucracies
    * d. all of the above (p. 81)

2. What contributions did Near Eastern civilizations give to the Hellenistic world?
    a. They gave the concept of a ruler-god.
    b. They provided the aesthetic ideal that identifies earthly majesty with grandiosity.
    c. They introduced new religious cults that promised immortality.
    * d. all of the above (p. 81)

3. Which was NOT a characteristic of Hellenistic material civilization?
    * a. united into a single political state (p. 82)
    b. governed by men who declared themselves deities
    c. composed of multiracial and multiethnic populations
    d. dominated by huge metropolitan centers

4. What was Alexander's political dream?
    a. a world divided into rival, but friendly states, each pursuing its own direction
    * b. a world united into a single empire under a single ruler, dominated by its Greek and Persian peoples (p. 82)
    c. a world fragmented into small poleis [pl. of polis] that were guided by their citizens
    d. a world composed of a single ethnic group and governed as a constitutional monarchy

5. What was the name of the colloquial Greek language that was spoken throughout the Hellenistic world, from Gaul to Syria?
    a. kouros
    b. kore
    * c. *koine* (p. 83)
    d. hubris

6. In the partition of Alexander's empire, successor states were established in all EXCEPT:
    a. Macedonia
    b. Asia Minor
    * c. Libya (p. 83)
    d. Egypt

7. The Seleucid kingdom lost lands to a state that became:
    a. Parthia
    b. Bactria
    c. Pergamum
    * d. all of the above (p. 84)

8. Which was the last Hellenistic state to fall to Rome?
    * a. Egypt (p. 84)
    b. Pergamum
    c. Macedonia
    d. the Seleucid kingdom

9. The last ruler of Egypt prior to its fall to Rome was:
*   a. Cleopatra (p. 84)
    b. Ptolemy Soter
    c. Seleucus
    d. Antigonus

10. What was Alexander's enduring legacy to the Hellenistic world?
    a. his dream of a unified, single world-state
*   b. his new image of the city (p. 84)
    c. his ideal of a Greco-Oriental civilization
    d. his goal to found a peaceful world community

11. Which was NOT an aspect of the brilliant city of Pergamum?
    a. It was founded by the Attalid dynasty.
    b. Its library was second only in the number of volumes to the one in Alexandria.
*   c. It was the capital of the Seleucid kingdom. (pp. 85, 91)
    d. Its most famous structure was the altar of Zeus, one of the seven wonders of the ancient world.

12. The largest city of the Hellenistic world was:
    a. Pergamum
*   b. Alexandria (p. 85)
    c. Antioch
    d. Athens

13. Which was NOT an aspect of the city of Alexandria?
*   a. Its population was relatively homogeneous. (p. 85)
    b. Its rulers built the first museum in the world.
    c. Its library was the largest of antiquity.
    d. Its scholars collected the classic texts of Greek civilization.

14. Hellenistic Classicism was characterized by:
    a. emotionalism
    b. theatricality
    c. interest in everyday themes
*   d. all of the above (p. 86)

15. Hellenistic Classicism shared with Hellenic Classicism the ideal that:
*   a. Art must serve moral purposes. (p. 86)
    b. Art should be expressed in simple terms.
    c. Art should be characterized by restraint.
    d. all of the above

16. Which was NOT a characteristic of Hellenistic civilization?
    a. New philosophies and religions abounded.
    b. Grandiose architecture was the norm.
*   c. Tragedies were preferred to comedies. (p. 86)
    d. Exotic scholarship replaced imaginative literature.

17. How did productions of comic dramas change in the Hellenistic Age?
    a. Actors began to wear realistic costumes.
    b. Masks became more representative of the character portrayed.
    c. The chorus now took second place to the actors.
*   d. all of the above (p. 86)

18. New Comedy, the style of comic drama during the Hellenistic period, was characterized by:
*   a.   gently satirical scenes from aristocratic life (p. 86)
    b.   casual obscenity
    c.   political criticism
    d.   all of the above

19. The favorite subject of New Comedy was:
    a.   political satire
*   b.   comic romances (p. 86)
    c.   slapstick comedies
    d.   burlesques of Greek tragedies

20. A defining characteristic of New Comedy was:
    a.   the support of the traditional social order
    b.   the reliance on stock characters
    c.   the inevitable happy ending
*   d.   all of the above (p. 86)

21. The originator of New Comedy was:
    a.   Aristophanes
*   b.   Menander (p. 86)
    c.   Plautus
    d.   Theocritus

22. Which aspect of Menander's *The Girl from Samos* is typical of New Comedy plays?
    a.   It is filled with absurd misunderstandings.
    b.   It concludes with a marriage ceremony.
    c.   It features stock characters, including two comic servants.
*   d.   all of the above (p. 86)

23. New Comedy influenced:
    a.   Roman Comedy
    b.   Shakespeare's comedies
    c.   Molière's comedies
*   d.   all of the above (p. 86)

24. Alexandrianism is:
*   a.   the literary style of the writers in the city of Alexandria (p. 86)
    b.   the political style of Alexander the Great
    c.   the cultural style of the era of Alexander the Great
    d.   all of the above

25. A characteristic of Alexandrianism is:
    a.   simplicity
*   b.   arid scholarship (p. 87)
    c.   clarity
    d.   all of the above

26. The dominant poet of the Hellenistic period was:
    a.   Menander
    b.   Euclid
    c.   Aristarchus
*   d.   Theocritus (p. 87)

27. Theocritus developed the new literary genre called:
    a. the epic
 * b. the pastoral (p. 87)
    c. the sonnet
    d. all of the above

28. What was the subject of the "idylls" of Theocritus?
 * a. vignettes of Hellenistic life (p. 87)
    b. the lives of shepherds described in an artificial way
    c. comedies of manners
    d. all of the above

29. Which Hellenistic philosophy encouraged a type of self-sufficiency called *autarky?*
    a. Cynicism
    b. Skepticism
    c. Stoicism
 * d. all of the above (pp. 87–90)

30. This philosophy denounced all religions and governments; shunned physical comfort; and taught that if one wanted nothing, then one could not lack anything:
 * a. Cynicism (p. 87)
    b. Skepticism
    c. Epicureanism
    d. Stoicism

31. This philosophy encouraged a philosophy of doubting, arguing that nothing could be known for certain:
    a. Cynicism
 * b. Skepticism (p. 88)
    c. Epicureanism
    d. Stoicism

32. This philosophy taught that the best life is lived withdrawn from the world, cultivating simple pleasures and avoiding fame, power, and wealth:
    a. Cynicism
    b. Skepticism
 * c. Epicureanism (pp. 88–99)
    d. Stoicism

33. This philosophy taught that the order of things cannot be changed and hence wisdom lies in doing one's duty, without complaining, and in a spirit of dedication:
    a. Cynicism
    b. Skepticism
    c. Epicureanism
 * d. Stoicism (pp. 89–90)

34. A key principle of Stoicism was:
    a. the identification of God with Nature, Reason, Law, and the *logos*
    b. the brotherhood of humankind
    c. the kinship of mortals with God
 * d. all of the above (pp. 89–90)

35. Epicureanism was partially based on:
    a. Thales' belief that all things are made of water
  * b. Democritus's Atomism (p. 89)
    c. Pythagoras's belief that all things are made of numbers
    d. Heraclitus's dialectical reasoning

36. The Hellenistic world adopted the concept of Fate from:
  * a. the Babylonians (p. 90)
    b. the Egyptians
    c. the Chinese
    d. the Persians

37. A mystery cult deity worshiped in the Hellenistic Age was:
    a. Dionysus of Greece
    b. Isis and Osiris of Egypt
    c. Cybele of Babylonia
  * d. all of the above (pp. 90–91)

38. All of these were facets of Mithraism EXCEPT:
    a. It was an offshoot of Zoroastrianism.
  * b. It was especially attractive to women. (p. 91)
    c. It had an emphasis on duty and loyalty.
    d. It originated in Persia.

39. Hellenistic temples were characterized by:
    a. massive size
    b. elaborate decoration
    c. slender, delicate columns crowned with capitals decorated with carved acanthus leaves
  * d. all of the above (p. 91)

40. During the Hellenistic period, temples were altered so that:
    a. Space was made inside to seat the congregation of worshipers.
  * b. Their grandeur enhanced the earthly majesty of the ruler who built them. (p. 91)
    c. No statues of gods or goddesses would be placed inside.
    d. all of the above

41. The first temple to use Corinthian columns was:
    a. the Parthenon in Athens
    b. the Serapeion in Alexandria
  * c. the Olympieum in Athens (p. 91)
    d. the Pantheon in Rome

42. Which was NOT an aspect of the altar of Zeus at Pergamum?
  * a. It was the largest altar in Hellenistic times. (p. 91 and caption for Fig. 4.9)
    b. The actual altar was enclosed in an Ionic colonnaded courtyard, raised on a podium.
    c. It was constructed by the Attalid dynasty to glorify their capital.
    d. It was decorated with a sculpted frieze depicting the deities at war.

43. This Hellenistic sculpture depicts a genre subject:
    a. *Crouching Aprodite*
    b. *Gaul and Wife*
  * c. *Old Market Woman* (p. 93)
    d. all of the above

44. Hellenistic sculpture usually depicted:
    a. realism
    b. eroticism
    c. violence
 * d. all of the above (p. 93)

45. Aphrodite in the Hellenistic-style sculpture *Aphrodite of Melos* and Hermes in the Hellenic-style sculpture *Hermes with the Infant Dionysus* share the characteristic of:
    a. exaggerated contrapposto
    b. sensuous, even erotic modeling of the body
    c. a serene countenance with an unmistakable gaze
 * d. all of the above (p. 95)

46. This sculpture was produced by the sculptural school of Rhodes:
    a. *Gaul with Wife*
    b. *Aphrodite of Melos*
 * c. *The Laocoön Group* (p. 96)
    d. all of the above

47. All of these are aspects of *The Laocoön Group* EXCEPT:
 * a. It was based on a story in Homer's *Odyssey*.
    b. When rediscovered by Michelangelo it helped to launch the Baroque style. (pp. 96–97)
    c. It depicts the violent struggles of three athletic males.
    d. The face of Laocoön is contorted in deep anguish.

48. All are legacies of Hellenistic civilization EXCEPT:
 * a. the practice of democracy (p. 99)
    b. the idea of a "new Athens"
    c. a multiracial society
    d. state support of the arts

49. A typical Hellenistic city included:
    a. a library
    b. a school of philosophy
    c. marble buildings
 * d. all of the above (p. 99)

50. The eventual conqueror of the Hellenistic kingdoms was:
    a. the Carthaginians
    b. the Etruscans
 * c. the Romans (p. 99)
    d. the Germans

5

ROMAN CIVILIZATION
The Pre-Christian Centuries

I. TEACHING STRATEGIES AND SUGGESTIONS

The instructor can use every one of the teaching strategies with this chapter. An introductory lecture, combining the Historical Overview model with the Diffusion approach, can present a brief survey of the 1,200 years of Roman history and show the evolutionary development of Rome from a small city-state to master of the world to an empire in shambles. The Diffusion model can also be employed to discuss how Rome conquered Greece but became, in the end, conquered by Greek ideals and art. The instructor can drive this point home with a Slide Lecture, showing Roman art and architecture's dependence on Greek styles and models.

An especially useful method for presenting Roman culture is the Reflections/Connections approach, relating political, economic, and social changes to shifting Roman values as manifested in sculpture, architecture, and history. The Patterns of Change technique blended with a Slide Lecture can then show the evolution of Roman styles of architecture. With the aid of the Spirit of the Age strategy, the instructor can provide a brief summary of Roman cultural achievements that stresses the unity underneath this complex civilization.

A good conclusion to the Roman unit can be achieved by presenting Roman civilization as a Case Study of a society that self-destructs, not once but twice in its history, although with different outcomes each time. First, at the end of the Late Republic, Augustus saves Rome from collapse by transforming the republic into an empire; and, second, during the Late Empire, none of the emperors, despite heroic and innovative efforts, can halt Rome's long and slow slide into oblivion. A Discussion approach is also appropriate when considering the causes of Rome's decline and fall.

II. LECTURE OUTLINE

Non-Western Events

A. Historical Overview

B. The Colossus of the Mediterranean World
1. General characteristics of Roman civilization
   a. Contrast with Greeks
   b. The Roman character
      (1) The agrarian tradition
      (2) The sanctity of the family
      (3) Religious values
2. The Etruscan and Greek connections
   a. The Etruscans
      (1) A people with a high culture
      (2) Their legacy to Rome

b. The Greeks of the Hellenistic Age
   (1) A people with a high culture
   (2) Their legacy to Rome

3. Rome in the Age of Kings, 753–509 B.C.
  a. Impact on Roman institutions
  b. The first appearance of class
     struggle in Rome

4. The Roman Republic, 509–31 B.C.
  a. The Early Republic, 509–264 B.C.
    (1) The domestic crisis
      (a) Struggle between patricians
          and plebeians
      (b) The emergence of the Senate to
          leadership
    (2) The foreign crisis
      (a) The threat of nearby peoples
      (b) Conquest of the Italian
          peninsula
      (c) Rome's genius at dealing with
          conquered people
  b. The Middle Republic, 264–133 B.C.
    (1) The assimilation of Italy into
       the Roman orbit
    (2) The challenge of Carthage
      (a) The issues making for war
      (b) The three Punic Wars
      (c) Ultimate Roman victory
    (3) The conquest of the Hellenistic
       world
  c. The Late Republic, 133–31 B.C.
    (1) Oligarchy
    (2) The problem of the equestrian
       order
    (3) The changing nature of the masses
      (a) Landless citizens, slaves, and
          foreigners
      (b) "Bread and circuses"
    (4) Julius Caesar's lofty vision and
       failed reforms
    (5) Civil war

5. Growing autocracy: Imperial
Rome, 31 B.C.–A.D. 284
  a. Historical overview
  b. *Pax Romana*, 31 B.C.–A.D. 193
    (1) Keeping the peace
    (2) The key role of Egypt
    (3) The spread of Roman civilization
    (4) The burgeoning economy
  c. Civil wars, A.D. 193–284
    (1) The problem with choosing new
       emperors
    (2) The Barrack Emperors
    (3) Other imperial problems

753 B.C.–A.D. 500

Han Dynasty in China
  206 B.C.–A.D. 220
Japanese state begins

C. The Style of Pre-Christian Rome:
From Greek Imitation to Roman Grandeur
   1. Foundation in Hellenistic Culture
   2. Roman religion
      a. Native cults and beliefs
      b. Its syncretistic nature
         (1) The gods and goddesses of Greece
         (2) Innovative cults in the post–Punic
             War period
         (3) Emperor worship
   3. Language, literature, and drama
      a. The Latin language
      b. The first literary period, 250–31 B.C.
         (1) Characteristics
         (2) The birth of Roman theater:
             Roman comedy
             (a) Plautus
             (b) Terence
         (3) Roman poetry
             (a) Lucretius's *On the Nature
                 of Things*
             (b) Catullus's "small" epics,
                 epigrams, and love poems
         (4) Cicero, the greatest writer of
             the age
             (a) Philosophy
             (b) Oratory
             (c) Letters
      c. The second literary period:
         The Golden Age, 31 B.C.–A.D. 14
         (1) Characteristics
         (2) Vergil
             (a) Pastorals: *Eclogues* and
                 Georgics
             (b) Epic: the *Aeneid*
         (3) Horace
             (a) Odes
             (b) Letters in verse
         (4) Ovid and the *Metamorphoses*
      d. The third literary period:
         The Silver Age, A.D. 145–200
         (1) Characteristics
         (2) Seneca and Roman tragedy
         (3) Juvenal and satire
         (4) Tacitus's *Annals* and *Histories*
             (a) Heir to the Greek tradition
             (b) History with a moral purpose
   4. Philosophy
      a. Characteristics of Roman thought
      b. Stoicism
         (1) Seneca
             (a) The *Letters on Morality*
             (b) His influence
         (2) Epictetus

End of Chinese classical
   philosophy period
Chinese dictionary

Sanskrit inscriptions
   in India, 150 A.D.

    (a) Background
    (b) *Discourses* and *Handbook*
   (3) Marcus Aurelius
    (a) Background
    (b) *Meditations*
  c. Neo-Platonism
   (1) Origins in Platonism
   (2) Plotinus
 5. Law
  a. Rome's most original contribution
  b. The idea of natural law
  c. The evolution of Roman law
   (1) The Twelve Tables
   (2) The role of the praetors
   (3) The *jurisconsults*
   (4) The legal codifications of the second and third centuries A.D.
 6. The visual arts
  a. Uses and influences
   (1) Roman practicality
   (2) Etruscan and Greek influences
  b. Architecture
   (1) Materials and style
    (a) Changing types of building materials
    (b) The temple, the chief Roman architectural form
    (c) Innovations: rounded arch, barrel vault, groined vault, and dome
   (2) The prototype of the Roman temple: the Maison Carrée
    (a) Features and characteristics
    (b) Influence
   (3) The round temple: the Pantheon
    (a) Features and characteristics
    (b) Influence
   (4) Urban planning: the Forum
   (5) The triumphal arch
    (a) A symbol of empire
    (b) Characteristics
   (6) Amphitheaters
    (a) The Colosseum
    (b) Its relation to the realities of Roman life
   (7) Provincial town centers
   (8) Bridges and aqueducts
  c. Sculpture
   (1) Tastes of artists and patrons
   (2) First phase, third to first centuries B.C.
    (a) *Head of Brutus*

Mayan Monuments, A.D. 164

        (b) Characteristics
    (3) Second phase, the Late Republic
        of the first century B.C.
        (a) *Anonymous Youth*
        (b) Characteristics
    (4) Third phase, 31 B.C.–A.D. 284
        (a) Characteristics
        (b) Prima Porta portrait of
            Augustus
        (c) The Ara Pacis altar
        (d) *March of the Legions,* a
            relief from the Arch of
            Titus
        (e) The frieze from Trajan's
            Victory Column
        (f) *Marcus Aurelius*
  d. Paintings and Mosaics
    (1) Techniques and subjects
    (2) The murals from the Villa of the
        Mysteries, Pompeii
    (3) Mosaics in the provinces
7. Music
  a. The dominant role of the Greek
     tradition
  b. The imperial period
    (1) Spectacles and pantomimes
        for the masses
    (2) Private orchestras and choruses
    (3) Lyric poetry
    (4) Musical instruments

Chinese octave
  subdivided

D. The Legacy of Pre-Christian Rome

[See Chapters 3 and 4 for
  more information on
  non-Western events.]

III. LEARNING OBJECTIVES

To learn:

1. The different phases of history in pre-Christian Rome and the major features of each phase

2. The geographic territories that made up the Roman Empire

3. The general characteristics of Roman civilization

4. The role played by religion in Roman life and culture

5. How women's role in Roman life differed from that of women in Greece

6. The influence of the Etruscans on Roman civilization

7. The influence of the Greeks on Roman civilization

8. The enduring features of Roman political life

9. The significance of the Punic Wars for Roman society and civilization

10. Rome's enlightened treatment of conquered peoples and the impact this had on Roman civilization

11. Rome as the heir of Hellenistic Greece

12. The cultural significance of Julius Caesar

13. The meaning of the *Pax Romana*

14. How Augustus saved the Roman state

15. Rome's three literary periods, including dates, characteristics, leading figures, literary genres, titles and descriptions of works

16. The characteristics of Roman Comedy

17. The principles of Roman Stoicism and Epicureanism, their leading advocates, and how they differed from both one another and the Greek originals

18. The beliefs of Neo-Platonism and its leading exponent

19. How Roman philosophy reflected Roman values and circumstances

20. The ideals of Roman law, the most original contribution of Rome

21. The innovations made by Roman architects

22. The identifying characteristics of the Roman temple, as seen in the Maison Carrée, Nîmes

23. The interrelationship between the arts and architecture and Rome's rulers

24. To recognize achievements in Roman architecture and the arts

25. The phases of Roman sculpture along with characteristic examples

26. The contributions of Roman music

27. Historic "firsts" of Roman civilization that became part of the Western tradition: the Latin language and its offspring, the Romance languages; Roman law; the educational ideal of the arts and sciences; the architectural innovations based on the rounded arch, including barrel vaults, groined vaults, and domes; providing "bread and circuses" for citizens; and the Idea of Rome

28. The role of Roman civilization in transmitting the heritage of earlier civilizations: adding to Greek architecture to make the Greco-Roman style; redefining the Greek educational curriculum into the *trivium* and *quadrivium*; perpetuating Greek ideals and models in the arts, literature, and music; adopting the Hellenistic Age's political legacy of ruler-gods; preserving and expanding Hellenistic Greek science; continuing to make libraries primary institutions in major cities as had been done in Hellenistic Greece; and making the Hellenistic goal of a just and well-regulated society of multiethnic, multiracial citizens the guiding ideal of imperial Rome

IV. SUGGESTIONS FOR FILMS

Buried Cities (Pompeii and Herculaneum). International Film Bureau, 14 min., color.

Julius Caesar—Rise of the Roman Empire. Encyclopedia Britannica, 22 min., color.

The Legacy of Rome. McGraw-Hill, 55 min., color.

Life in Ancient Rome. Encyclopedia Britannica, 14 min., color.

The Spirit of Rome. Encyclopedia Britannica, 29 min., color.

V. SUGGESTIONS FOR FURTHER READING

Bourne, F. C. *A History of the Romans.* Boston: D. C. Heath, 1966.

Ferguson, J. *The Religions of the Roman Empire.* Ithaca: Cornell University Press, 1970.

Henig, M., ed. *A Handbook of Roman Art: A Survey of the Visual Arts of the Roman World.* Oxford: Phaidon, 1983.

Rose, H. J. *A Handbook of Latin Literature.* London: Methuen, 1954.

Starr, C. *The Ancient Romans.* New York: Oxford University Press, 1972.

Strong, D. *Roman Art.* Baltimore: Pelican, 1980.

VI. IDENTIFICATIONS

syncretism	groined vault (cross vault)
Neo-Platonism	oculus
natural law	forum
voussoirs	mural
keystone	mosaic
vault	pantomime
barrel vault	

VII. DISCUSSION/ESSAY QUESTIONS

1. In what ways did Rome's values account for its successful civilization?
2. How did the Etruscans and the Greeks affect the rise of Roman civilization?
3. Which factions of Roman society were involved in the Struggle of the Orders, and what were the results of this conflict?
4. Discuss the expansion of Rome from about 250 to 31 B.C., and show how this expansion affected Roman society and values.
5. What were the major problems confronting Augustus as emperor, and how did he solve these problems?
6. In what ways was Vergil the voice of the Golden Age of Roman literature?

7. Discuss the three major periods of Roman literature, setting forth their dates, characteristics, leading voices, and the major works. Take one work and show how it embodies the ideals of Roman civilization.
8. Compare and contrast Stoicism and Neo-Platonism, and note how each might appeal to the Roman character.
9. Describe the Roman temple, including its Greek and Etruscan roots. What special building techniques were developed by Roman architects?
10. Discuss the three major phases of Roman sculpture, identifying leading characteristics and giving an example from each phase. What was the relationship of Roman sculpture to that of Greece?
11. What roles did murals and mosaics play in the Roman arts?
12. In what ways have the Romans influenced modern Western civilization?

VIII. MULTIPLE-CHOICE QUESTIONS

1. Generally speaking, the Romans could be characterized as:
   a. imaginative in the arts
   b. both deep and speculative thinkers
   * c. well suited to adapt and borrow from other civilizations (p. 101)
   d. irresponsible

2. The ideal Roman was a(n):
   a. shrewd business type who amassed fortunes
   b. intellectual and philosophical type who spoke against sins
   c. artistic type with a keen and original imagination
   * d. farmer-soldier type who stood ready to protect his home (p. 102)

3. The person or persons who commanded the family and controlled all of its members was:
   a. the mother
   * b. the father (p. 102)
   c. the grandparents
   d. the teenage children

4. A people who influenced the Romans but whose history is not well documented were the:
   a. Greeks
   b. Phoenicians
   * c. Etruscans (p. 104)
   d. Egyptians

5. The date given for the founding of the Roman Republic is:
   a. 753 B.C.
   * b. 509 B.C. (p. 106)
   c. 31 B.C.
   d. 490 B.C.

6. The patricians of Early Republican Rome, like the Archaic Greeks, transformed their political system from:
   * a. a kingship to an oligarchy (pp. 106–108)
   b. an oligarchy to a democracy
   c. a kingship to a democracy
   d. a theocracy to an oligarchy

7. The two major domestic groups who clashed over power in the Early Republic were:
   a. the plebeians and the equestrians
 * b. the patricians and the plebeians (p. 107)
   c. the equestrians and the patricians
   d. the equestrians and the populares

8. One result of struggle between the patricians and the plebeians in the early years of the Roman Republic was:
   a. the installation of a city-state government
   b. overthrow of the patricians
 * c. sharing of the patricians' power with the plebeians (p. 107)
   d. abolition of the Roman Senate

9. Regardless of the political structure of the Roman Republic, the real location of power was:
   a. the army
 * b. the family (pp. 102, 107–108)
   c. the college of priests
   d. the emperor

10. By 264 B.C., the Romans had:
    a. conquered all of the Mediterranean lands
    b. moved their frontier into present-day France
    c. created a democratic government
 * d. brought all of the Italian peninsula under control (p. 108)

11. Rome's chief rival in the Mediterranean during the Middle Republic was:
 * a. Carthage (p. 108)
    b. Egypt
    c. Macedonia
    d. Judea

12. The leader of the Carthaginians during the Second Punic War was:
    a. Cato
 * b. Hannibal (p. 108)
    c. Scipio
    d. Hammurabi

13. Hannibal's military strategy to defeat the Romans was to:
    a. slaughter all the inhabitants of the Italian peninsula
 * b. scorch the earth and devastate the farms (p. 108)
    c. attack Rome and put it under seige
    d. all of the above

14. A new class that appeared on the scene in the late Republic and demanded more political power was the:
    a. plebeian order
    b. farmer-soldiers
 * c. equestrian order (p. 108)
    d. patrician order

15. Which was NOT a cause of the collapse of the Roman Republic?
    a. the rise of the equestrian order
    b. the appearance of an urban underclass
    c. the decline of power among the rich families
 * d. the revolts in the provinces (pp. 108–109)

16. Which was NOT a characteristic of the Roman Republic?
    a. For 400 years it was led fairly effectively by the Senate.
 * b. Economic prosperity bred peaceful class relations. (pp. 107–109)
    c. The army became a very successful fighting machine.
    d. By the Late Republic, Rome dominated the eastern Mediterranean.

17. Under Augustus Caesar, the Roman Empire:
    a. witnessed the abolition of the Senate
    b. returned to the old republican political traditions
    c. experienced years of domestic upheaval
 * d. moved along the path toward an absolute ruler (p. 109)

18. The *Pax Romana* or Roman Peace lasted from:
 * a. 31 B.C. to A.D. 193 (p. 109)
    b. 133 B.C. to 31 B.C.
    c. A.D. 14 to 150
    d. 31 B.C. to A.D. 14

19. Under the *Pax Romana* all of the following occurred EXCEPT:
    a. The economy expanded during most of this period.
    b. The bureaucracy grew throughout the empire.
 * c. The power of the army drastically increased. (p. 111)
    d. The issue of ethnicity faded as most groups became Romanized.

20. One social group that gained more power under Augustus was the:
    a. urban poor
 * b. equestrian order (p. 111)
    c. patrician
    d. farmers

21. One of the important traits of Roman religion was that:
    a. It held firmly to its original practices and refused to accept new ones.
 * b. It accepted other cults, blending them into new ways of worship. (p. 111)
    c. It rejected the Greek deities.
    d. The Roman soldiers remained loyal to the old gods.

22. As Roman religion evolved, it came to be identified with:
    a. a message of social justice
 * b. the worship of the emperor (p.112)
    c. a cult that worshiped trees and rocks
    d. a missionary impulse to spread the worship of Zeus

23. Which would *not* apply to Roman religion?
 * a. Throughout Roman history religion was conducted by priests (pp. 106, 111–112)
    b. Some of the Roman state gods came from the Etruscans.
    c. Some of the Roman state deities were from the Greeks.
    d. The Roman soldiers spread their own religion around the empire.

24. All of these characterized the Latin language EXCEPT:
    a. Latin was well suited for documents and decrees.
 * b. Latin's florid style lent itself to imaginative literature. (p. 112)
    c. Latin became standardized early in the history of the republic.
    d. Latin helped unify the various groups in the empire.

25. Roman writers and artists borrowed most from the:
    a. Etruscans
    b. Egyptians
    c. Nubians
 * d. Greeks (p. 112)

26. Which match between writer and literary genre is correct for the First Literary Period?
    a. Plautus—lyric poetry
 * b. Terence—comic plays (p. 113)
    c. Catullus—epic poems
    d. Lucretius—drama

27. The most influential figure in the First Literary Period was:
    a. Lucretius
    b. Catullus
 * c. Cicero (p. 113)
    d. Vergil

28. The three outstanding literary figures of the Golden Age of Roman literature were:
    a. Vergil, Horace, and Seneca
 * b. Vergil, Horace, and Ovid (p. 114)
    c. Lucretius, Catullus, and Cicero
    d. Vergil, Ovid, and Juvenal

29. The most famous epic poet of Roman literature was:
    a. Ovid
    b. Horace
    c. Homer
 * d. Vergil (p. 114)

30. Vergil wrote an epic poem about:
    a. Achilles' efforts to win the battle of Troy
 * b. the long voyage of Aeneas, a Trojan hero (p. 114)
    c. the exploits of Odysseus
    d. the life of Augustus Caesar

31. *The Aeneid* was written:
    a. to show that the Romans were direct descendants of the Greek gods
 * b. to instill into the Romans the values of a great past (p. 114)
    c. to mark the anniversary of the death of Julius Caesar
    d. to win over the masses to the side of Augustus Caesar

32. The Greek writer who had the most influence on Vergil was:
    a. Sophocles
    b. Hesiod
 * c. Homer (p. 114)
    d. Plato

33. Vergil's poems can be described as:
    a. devices to evoke the rural values of old Rome
    b. celebrations of the farmers in Roman life
    c. prophecies of Rome's great future
 * d. a and b but not c (p. 114)

34. The love poems of Ovid are remembered:
    a. for their tenderness toward women
  * b. for their overt sexuality (p. 114)
    c. for their efforts to raise the level of morality among the Romans
    d. all of the above

35. The Silver Age of Roman literature is called that because:
    a. It lacked the originality of the Golden Age.
    b. It tended to rely on earlier themes and ideas for inspiration.
    c. It emphasized aesthetics rather than morals.
  * d. all of the above (p. 114)

36. The Silver Age produced Rome's greatest historian:
  * a. Tacitus (p. 114)
    b. Ovid
    c. Suetonius
    d. Plutarch

37. Tacitus wrote his historical works:
    a. to win favor from the Emperors
  * b. to trace the decline of political freedom in Rome (p. 115)
    c. to celebrate the great achievements of the *Pax Romana*
    d. to illustrate the rule of powerful and successful emperors

38. The two most influential philosophies during the Roman Empire were:
    a. Stoicism and Cynicism
  * b. Stoicism and Epicureanism (p. 115)
    c. Judaism and Stoicism
    d. Epicureanism and Cynicism

39. Stoicism appealed to the Romans for all of these EXCEPT:
  * a. the clarity of its abstract principles (p. 120)
    b. its emphasis on day-to-day rules by which to live
    c. its stress on duty and honor in one's work
    d. its belief in a hierarchy of gods

40. Marcus Aurelius wrote that a Stoic should:
    a. realize that a well-regulated mind is necessary to survive
    b. retire into one's inner self for comfort
    c. believe in a system of gods and goddesses
  * d. a and b but not c (p. 115)

41. The leader of Neo-Platonism solved the problem of Platonic dualism by:
    a. appealing to the Roman state gods for assistance
    b. calling for the worship of the emperor
  * c. using mystical insight to reach a new vision of truth (p. 117)
    d. a and b but not c

42. All of these describe Roman law EXCEPT:
    a. It was a product of the needs of the state.
    b. It came out of both Greek and Roman thought.
    c. It was identified with the concept of natural law.
  * d. It dealt exclusively with criminal law. (p. 117)

43. Which was a Roman contribution to architecture?
    a. innovations with the rounded arch (groined and barrel vaults and domes)
    b. the discovery of a mixture similar to modern concrete
    c. the combining of the practical with the decorative in public buildings
  * d. all of the above (pp. 117 and 119)

44. The Maison Carrée does NOT have this characteristic:
    a. Greek influence in its post-beam-triangle design
    b. Etruscan influence in its raised platform
  * c. lack of inner sanctum or *cella* (p. 119)
    d. decorated with Corinthian columns

45. Roman Emperors left their mark on the Roman visual arts with:
    a. public forums
    b. triumphal arches
    c. personal statues
  * d. all of the above (pp. 121, 126)

46. Roman portrait sculpture was:
    a. realistic
    b. used to perpetuate the personality of the deceased
    c. used to commemorate their leaders in stone and bronze
  * d. all of the above (pp. 125–131)

47. Roman triumphal arches and victory columns:
    a. are examples of art as propaganda
    b. sent clear messages to the populace about the power of the rulers
    c. emphasized the inescapable presence of the emperor
  * d. all of the above (pp. 129, 131)

48. The last magnificent statue of a Roman ruler during the *Pax Romana* was:
    a. Augustus Caesar in the Prima Porta portrait
    b. Hadrian standing on a column
  * c. Marcus Aurelius on horseback (p. 129)
    d. Titus in a carved relief on the Arch of Titus

49. A frequent subject of Roman painting was:
    a. Greek and Roman myths
    b. religious scenes and ceremonies
    c. landscapes
  * d. all of the above (p. 131)

50. Which is a Roman legacy to Western art and thought?
    a. its law and legal codes
    b. its school curriculum of the arts and sciences
    c. its building forms and techniques
  * d. all of the above (p. 131)

6

JUDAISM AND
THE RISE OF CHRISTIANITY

I. TEACHING STRATEGIES AND SUGGESTIONS

The best introduction to Judaism is through a Historical Overview of the Hebrew people from the earliest times to the destruction of the temple in A.D. 70, surveying cultural milestones and central religious beliefs. The instructor will also find the Reflections/Connections approach helpful, since Jewish religious ideas are so clearly rooted in history; for example, the Jewish belief that God controls history springs from the tradition that God liberated the Hebrew people from bondage in Egypt and gave them a land of their own. Of the central beliefs of Judaism the instructor should focus especially on the commandment to social justice, a belief first expressed by the Jewish prophets. Modern Western ideals of social justice have their roots in this Jewish belief; and no other ancient people, including the Mesopotamians, the Egyptians, the Greeks, and the Romans, had such a concern for the poor, the disadvantaged, and the downtrodden.

The instructor can then approach Christianity through a Historical Overview, laying out the major developments in this religion's evolution from the birth of Christ to A.D. 284. Because Christianity begins as a Jewish sect, the instructor could then use the Diffusion model to show how Jewish beliefs, traditions, and practices were assimilated into the Christian faith. Of central importance in this regard is the Jewish theme of the Suffering Servant (from Isaiah II) that early Christian writers adopted to explain Jesus' suffering and death on the cross. The instructor can also use a Slide Lecture to deal with the art of both Judaism and Christianity. The juxtaposing of the two artistic traditions will also illustrate dramatically how Judaism, because of its prohibition against graven images, differs from the more visually oriented Christian faith. In the Slide Lecture it is important to lay a good foundation for Christian art, since religious themes and ideas will dominate Western art until the coming of the Renaissance in 1400.

Another important topic in this chapter is the beginning of the stormy relationship between Christianity and humanism, the two traditions that make up the most enduring strands in Western civilization. The instructor can use the Comparison/Contrast strategy to deal with this topic, showing how the Christian faith and humanism are similar, yet different, and setting forth the issues that triggered disagreements between them. In addition, using the Reflections/Connections approach, the teacher can show how hostility between Christians and humanists reflected their differing value systems.

II. LECTURE OUTLINE

Non-Western Events

A. Historical Overview
   1. The uniqueness of the contribution of the Jews
   2. The influence of Judaism on Christianity and Islam

B. Judaism
    1. History of the Hebrews, 2000–1500 B.C.   [See Chapter 1 for non-
        a. Nomadic origins   Western developments.]
        b. Abraham
            (1) First introduction to Canaan
            (2) The covenant
            (3) The rite of circumcision
            (4) Belief in an ethical deity with
                ethical principles for the
                faithful
    2. Egypt, exodus, and Moses, 1500–1000 B.C.   [See Chapter 1 for non-
        a. The Egyptian period   Western developments.]
        b. Moses
            (1) The exodus
            (2) Wandering on the Sinai peninsula
            (3) The Mosaic code
                (a) Divinely given
                (b) No distinction between
                    religious and secular
                    offenses
                (c) The Ten Commandments
                (d) The ideal: ethical
                    monotheism
                (e) God or Yahweh
                (f) Other religious practices
            (4) The conquest of Canaan
        c. The Kingdom of Israel, 1000–926 B.C.   [See Chapter 2 for non-
            (1) The reign of Saul   Western developments.]
            (2) The reign of David
                (a) Centralized government
                (b) Economic changes
            (3) The reign of Solomon
                (a) Peace with neighbors
                (b) Expanded trade
                (c) Building program in
                    Jerusalem
                (d) Literature and the arts
        d. The split of Israel into two kingdoms,
           926–722 B.C.   [See Chapter 2 for non-
            (1) The northern kingdom of Israel   Western developments.]
                and the southern kingdom of
                Judah
            (2) The rise of prophets
                (a) Full-fledged monotheism
                (b) The demand for social
                    justice
        e. Defeat and exile: The Babylonian
           Captivity, 722–540 B.C.   [See Chapter 2 for non-
            (1) The destruction of Israel by   Western developments.]
                Assyria
            (2) The conquest of Judah by
                Babylonia
        f. The postexilic period, 540–323 B.C.   [See Chapters 2 and 3 for
            (1) The Persian conquest   non-Western developments.]

(a) Return to Jerusalem
(b) The Second Temple
(c) The beginning of the Diaspora
 (2) The renewed faith
  (a) Zoroastrian influences
  (b) Belief in the end of the world
  (c) Belief in the apocalypse
  (d) The notion of a Messiah
g. The Hellenistic and Roman periods, 323 B.C.–A.D. 284
 (1) The Hellenistic threat to the Jewish way of life
 (2) The Maccabean Jewish state
 (3) The Roman conquest
  (a) Various political strategies for governing
  (b) The Third Temple
  (c) The First Jewish War
  (d) Destruction of the temple
  (e) The second Diaspora

3. The Bible
 a. Evolution of the scriptures
 b. The Septuagint
 c. The parts of the Hebrew Bible
  (1) The Law
   (a) Its books and themes
   (b) Canonization
  (2) The Prophets
   (a) Its themes
   (b) Canonization
  (3) The Writings
   (a) Its themes
   (b) Canonization
 d. Jewish literature outside the canon
  (1) The Apocrypha
  (2) The Pseudepigrapha
 e. The Dead Sea Scrolls
 f. Key ideas of biblical Judaism

4. Early Jewish art and architecture
 a. The effect of the prohibition of graven images
 b. The Ark of the Covenant and other sacred objects
 c. Solomon's Temple
 d. The Second Temple
 e. Hellenistic influences
  (1) The fortress-palace of John Hyrcanus
  (2) The tombs in the Kidron valley
 f. Roman influences
  (1) Herod's fortress-palace at Masada
  (2) The Third Temple

[See Chapters 4 and 5 for non-Western developments.]

C. Christianity, 4 B.C.–A.D. 284 [See Chapter 5 for non-Western developments.]
  1. Historical overview
  2. The life of Jesus Christ and the New Testament
      a. Sources for the life of Jesus
          (1) Biographical summary
          (2) The Gospels
              (a) The synoptic Gospels of Mark, Matthew, and Luke
              (b) The Gospel of John
              (c) The reasons for the various versions
          (3) The Acts of the Apostles
              (a) Relation to Luke's Gospel
              (b) Its purpose
          (4) The seven epistles of Paul
              (a) Record of missionary activities
              (b) The first Christian theology
              (c) Interpretation of the life of Jesus
              (d) Teaching on the resurrection
          (5) The other seven epistles
          (6) The Book of Revelation
              (a) Its relation to Jewish apocalyptic literature
              (b) Its controversial nature
      b. The establishment of the Christian canon
  3. Christians and Jews
      a. Christian borrowings from Judaism
      b. Christian borrowings of Zoroastrian ideas, mediated through Judaism
          (1) Satan as a personification of evil
          (2) Good and bad demons who inhabit human bodies
          (3) Heaven and hell as the twin destinies of humanity
          (4) A divine savior who appears at the end of time
      c. Stormy relations between Jews and Christians
          (1) The Council of Jamnia, A.D. 90, as a turning point
          (2) Causes of tensions between the two religions and their results
  4. Christianity and Greco-Roman religions and philosophies
      a. Christian borrowings from the mystery cults
      b. Christian appropriations from Stoicism and Neo-Platonism

5. Christians in the Roman Empire
   a. Changing attitudes of Romans to Christians
      (1) The early years
      (2) The expansion of Christianity and its separation from Judaism
         (a) Localized, random persecution
         (b) Wide-ranging political assault in the mid-third century A.D.
   b. Christian borrowings from Roman culture
      (1) The Latin language
      (2) The Roman law
      (3) The state administrative structure
      (4) The imperial office
   c. Social patterns of conversion to the late second century A.D.
6. Early Christian literature
   a. Early Roman commentators on the Christian faith
      (1) Celsus
      (2) Galen
   b. The first Christian writers
      (1) Tertullian
         (a) Key ideas
         (b) Uncompromising hostility to humanism
      (2) Origen
         (a) Key ideas
         (b) Harmony with the humanistic legacy
7. Early Christian art
   a. Confusion over the role of art in the early church
   b. The triumph of humanistic values in art
   c. Art in the Roman catacombs
      (1) The symbol of the good shepherd
      (2) The symbol of a communion participant

D. The Legacy of Biblical Judaism and Early Christianity

III. LEARNING OBJECTIVES

To learn:

1. The milestones of Hebrew history from about 2000 B.C. to the destruction of the Third Temple in Jerusalem in A.D. 70

2. The close connection between Hebrew history and the beliefs and practices of Judaism

3. The key ideas of Judaism, including the covenant, Mosaic law, and ethical monotheism

4. The three different temples built by the Jews and the symbolic importance of the temple in the Jewish faith

5. The definition and significance of the Babylonian Captivity

6. The Zoroastrian ideas that became a part of Judaism after the Babylonian exile

7. The threat to Jewish civilization posed by the Hellenistic and Roman conquerors

8. The parts of the Hebrew Bible, their dates of canonization, and their leading themes

9. The impact of the Second Commandment on Jewish art and architecture

10. The achievements of Jewish artists and architects of the biblical period

11. The origins of Christianity in Judaism

12. The sources for the life of Jesus Christ

13. The parts of the specifically Christian scriptures, their date of canonization, and their leading themes

14. The influence of Jewish ideas, beliefs, and practices on the early Christian church

15. The influence of Greco-Roman religions and philosophies and Roman civilization on Christian beliefs and organization

16. The changing attitude of the Roman authorities to the Christian religion

17. The attitudes of Roman writers to early Christianity

18. Tertullian's and Origen's differing views of Greco-Roman civilization and humanism

19. The nature of early Christian art, its themes, its symbols, and its artistic style

20. The historic "firsts" of biblical Judaism that became part of the Western tradition: monotheism; high moral standards for society; social justice for all, including the poor and the powerless; and a canon of scriptures

21. The historic "firsts" of early Christianity that became part of the Western tradition: a belief system that expressed uncompromising hostility to the prevailing culture and the secular state

22. The role of early Christianity in transmitting the heritage of Judaism and Greco-Roman humanism: redirecting Jewish monotheism to an international audience, regardless of racial and ethnic backgrounds; substituting Jesus' golden rule for Judaism's ethical teachings; perpetuating the commandment to give social justice to all; adopting the Jewish canon and enlarging it to include Christian writings; incorporating Greco-Roman subjects, themes, and styles into Christian art; and placing Greco-Roman philosophy in the service of religion

IV. SUGGESTIONS FOR FILMS

The Bible as Literature: Part I—Saga and Story in the Old Testament. Encyclopedia Britannica, 26 min., color.

The Bible as Literature: Part II—History, Poetry, and Drama in the Old Testament. Encyclopedia Britannica, 24 min., color.

Christianity in World History—to 1000 A.D. Coronet, 14 min., color.

The Christians: Faith and Fear. McGraw-Hill, 39 min., color.

The Christians: A Peculiar People, 27 B.C.–A.D. 330. McGraw-Hill, 39 min., color.

Yesterday's Worlds: Treasures from the Land of the Bible. NET, 29 min., color.

V. SUGGESTIONS FOR FURTHER READING

Ausubel, N. *The Book of Jewish Knowledge: An Encyclopedia of Judaism and the Jewish People, Covering All Elements of Jewish Life from Biblical Times to the Present.* New York: Crown, 1964.

Brandon, S.G.F. *The Fall of Jerusalem and the Christian Church: A Study of the Effects of the Jewish Overthrow of A.D. 70 on Christianity.* London: S.P.C.K., 1978.

Cross, F. M. *Canaanite Myth and Hebrew Epic: Essays in the History of the Religion of Israel.* Cambridge: Harvard University Press, 1973.

Eilberg-Schwartz, H. *The Savage in Judaism: An Anthropology of Israelite Religion and Ancient Judaism.* Bloomington: Indiana University Press, 1990.

Gaston, L. *Paul and the Torah.* Vancouver: University of British Columbia Press, 1987.

Gutmann, J. *Sacred Images: Studies in Jewish Art from Antiquity to the Middle Ages.* Northampton, Mass.: Variorum, 1989.

Hoffmann, R. J. *The Origins of Christianity: A Critical Introduction.* Buffalo, N.Y.: Prometheus Press, 1985.

Malina, B. J. *Christian Origins and Cultural Anthropology: Practical Models for Bibilical Interpretation.* Atlanta: John Knox Press, 1986.

Milburn, R.L.P. *Early Christian Art and Architecture.* Aldershot, England: Scolar, 1988.

Murray, C. *Rebirth and Afterlife: a Study of the Transmutation of Some Pagan Imagery in Early Christian Funerary Art.* Oxford, England: B.A.R., 1981.

VI. IDENTIFICATIONS

covenant	canon
Diaspora	Gospels
eschatology	evangelists
apocalypse	theology
Messiah	liturgy
scripture	sarcophagus

VII. DISCUSSION/ESSAY QUESTIONS

1. Show how the beliefs, ideas, and practices of biblical Judaism reflect the early history of the Hebrew people.
2. What was the significance of the development of monotheism by the Hebrew people?
3. Identify the key beliefs of Judaism, and indicate the ones that were later integrated into the Western tradition.
4. What impact ought the Second Commandment to have had on Jewish culture? How do you account for the existence of Jewish art and architecture in biblical times?
5. Discuss the borrowings of early Christianity from Judaism.
6. Identify the key beliefs of Christianity.
7. What impact did Greco-Roman religions and philosophy have on early Christianity?
8. Explain whether the early Christian Church was hostile or friendly to the humanistic tradition of the Greco-Roman world.
9. Discuss the ways that Roman civilization helped to shape the early Christian faith and church.
10. Contrast Tertullian's and Origen's responses to Greco-Roman culture.
11. Discuss the legacy of early Christianity to Western civilization.
12. Discuss early Christian art, its themes, its symbols, and its style. What was the relationship of Christian art to Greco-Roman styles of art?

VIII. MULTIPLE-CHOICE QUESTIONS

1. The beliefs of Judaism helped to shape the religion of:
   a. Buddhism
 * b. Islam (p. 135)
   c. Zoroastrianism
   d. all of the above

2. Christians refer to the Jewish Bible as the:
 * a. Old Testament (p. 135)
   b. New Testament
   c. Torah
   d. Pseudepigrapha

3. The Hebrew people in their early history:
   a. lived as nomads for centuries without a homeland
   b. were outsiders for periods of time in other cultures
   c. had brief control of the promised land of Canaan
 * d. all of the above (p. 135)

4. According to tradition the first patriarch to settle in Canaan was:
   a. Moses
 * b. Abraham (p. 135)

c. Aaron
   d. Adam

5. The word *covenant* means:
    a. promise
    b. life
 * c. contract (p. 135)
    d. bargain

6. The outward sign of the covenant between God and the Hebrews was:
    a. special hair styles for men and women
 * b. the circumcision of all male children (pp. 135–136)
    c. distinctive clothing worn by men and women
    d. all of the above

7. According to the Bible, Moses:
    a. led the Hebrews in the exodus from Egypt
    b. received a law code, including the Ten Commandments, from God
    c. molded his followers into a unified people under a strict ethical code
 * d. all of the above (p. 136)

8. Which of the Ten Commandments had a negative impact on Jewish art?
    a. the First Commandment
 * b. the Second Commandment (p. 144)
    c. the Third Commandment
    d. the Fourth Commandment

9. What made Jewish law different from other ancient law codes?
    a. It claimed to be received from a deity.
    b. It was presented in writing.
 * c. It made no distinction between religious and secular offenses. (p. 136)
    d. all of the above

10. The Ten Commandments condemned:
    a. theft
    b. murder
    c. greed
 * d. all of the above (p. 137)

11. The Jewish name for God may be rendered as:
    a. YHWH
    b. Yahweh
    c. Adonai
 * d. all of the above (p. 136)

12. Which early Hebrew patriarch assumed the name Israel?
    a. Abraham
    b. Moses
    c. Jacob
 * d. Aaron (p. 137)

13. The Hebrews scored what literary achievement during the reign of Solomon?
 * a. the first historical writings (p. 138)
    b. the first written tragedies

c. the first written epics

d. all of the above

14. How did the Hebrew historians differ from the Greek historians?
* a. The Hebrew writers made God the central force in human history, unlike the secular-minded Greek authors. (p. 138)
   b. The Hebrew writers composed oral works, unlike the Greek authors who wrote on scrolls.
   c. The Hebrew writers wrote history in poetic forms, unlike the Greek authors who composed in prose.
   d. all of the above

15. Which event caused the Hebrews to be called Jews?
   a. the exodus from Egypt
   b. the Assyrian conquest of Israel
* c. the rescue of Judah from the Babylonian Captivity (p. 139)
   d. the destruction of the Third Temple in Jerusalem by the Romans

16. All are aspects of the Jewish temple in Jerusalem EXCEPT:
   a. The First Temple was built by Solomon.
   b. Three different temples have been built over the centuries.
   c. The Third Temple was destroyed by the Romans in A.D. 70.
* d. No part of the temple still stands today. (pp. 138–140)

17. From Zoroastrianism, the ancient Jews borrowed the notion of:
   a. ethical monotheism
* b. apocalypse (p. 139)
   c. a chosen people
   d. a universal deity

18. Which Roman monument depicts Roman soldiers carrying off sacred Jewish relics?
   a. the Prima Porta statue of Augustus
   b. the Column of Trajan
* c. the Arch of Titus (p. 140)
   d. the Arch of Constantine

19. All of these apply to the Jewish Bible EXCEPT:
   a. The Law was the first section canonized, in the fifth century B.C.
   b. The Prophets was the second section canonized, in the first century B.C.
   c. The Writings was the third section canonized, in A.D. 90.
* d. The Apocrypha was the fourth section canonized, in A.D. 150. (p. 143)

20. The biblical books of Genesis, Exodus, Leviticus, Numbers, and Deuteronomy constitute the:
   a. Torah
   b. Law
   c. Pentateuch
* d. all of the above (pp. 141–142)

21. The oldest copies of Jewish scriptures were discovered in 1947 and are known as the:
   a. Septuagint
   b. Apocrypha
* c. Dead Sea Scrolls (p. 143)
   d. Pseudepigrapha

22. Hellenistic-style architecture influenced Jewish architecture in:
  * a. the fortress-palace erected by John Hyrcanus, the Maccabean ruler (p. 144)
    b. the Second Temple built in the late sixth century B.C.
    c. the synagogues constructed during the first Diaspora
    d. all of the above

23. All are legacies of biblical Judaism EXCEPT:
    a. the notion of social justice for all people, including the poor and the powerless
  * b. the idea of original sin (p. 143)
    c. the belief in monotheism
    d. the expectation of high moral standards for society

24. The word "diaspora" means:
    a. promise
  * b. dispersion (p. 139)
    c. grief
    d. homeland

25. Which Jewish practice or belief was rejected by the early Christians?
    a. circumcision
    b. the Jewish calendar
    c. prohibition against depicting God or any earthly creatures in art
  * d. all of the above (pp. 147–152)

26. Christianity began in:
    a. Egypt
  * b. Judea (p. 147)
    c. Greece
    d. Italy

27. A major source for the life of Jesus is:
  * a. the Gospels (p. 148)
    b. his autobiography called the *Confessions*
    c. the records of the Roman authorities
    d. all of the above

28. The earliest writings in the New Testament are:
  * a. the letters of Paul (p. 148)
    b. the Gospels
    c. the Book of Revelation
    d. the Acts of the Apostles

29. The Christian Bible does NOT include:
    a. the Book of Revelation
    b. the Torah and the Prophets
  * c. the writings of Origen (pp. 150, 152)
    d. the Acts of the Apostles

30. The writers of the Gospels are called:
    a. Apostles
    b. Disciples
  * c. Evangelists (p. 148)
    d. all of the above

31. The Acts of the Apostles described this turning point in Christian history:
    a. the teaching career of Jesus
    * b. the opening of Christianity to non-Jews (p. 148)
    c. the crucifixion of Jesus
    d. all of the above

32. Paul's letters constitute:
    a. a factual account of the life and teaching of Jesus
    * b. the first Christian theology (p. 148)
    c. an early attempt to patch up differences between Christians and Jews
    d. all of the above

33. Paul's missionary activities resulted in the founding of churches in these places EXCEPT:
    a. Greece
    * b. Egypt (p. 148)
    c. Asia Minor
    d. Italy

34. Paul's interpretation of the life of Jesus was based on the Jewish scripture about:
    * a. the Suffering Servant (p. 148)
    b. Job
    c. David
    d. Moses

35. A key teaching of Paul in his letters was:
    a. the notion that all humans are born with original sin
    b. the belief that Jesus' death atoned for the sins of humankind
    c. the idea that Jesus' resurrection guaranteed everlasting life for others
    * d. all of the above (p. 149)

36. The New Testament is written originally in:
    a. Hebrew
    b. Aramaic
    * c. Greek (p. 150)
    d. Latin

37. This Jewish belief was adopted by the early Christians:
    a. that God's name is Yahweh
    b. that there is only one God
    c. that God demands social justice for all people
    * 4. all of the above (p. 150)

38. This Jewish religious practice was NOT adopted by the early Christians:
    a. the rite of baptism
    * b. the observance of dietary laws (p. 148)
    c. the use of hymns, prayers, and Bible reading as part of the liturgy
    d. the idea of the Sabbath

39. Zoroastrianism influenced Christianity in this way:
    a. the celebration of Easter
    b. the belief that Jesus was born of a virgin
    * c. the concept of Satan as the personification of evil (p. 150)
    d. the idea of the resurrection

40. What Stoic idea was incorporated into early Christianity:
   * a. the universal kinship of humanity (p. 151)
     b. the salvation of the human race through the sacrifice of a savior
     c. the superiority of the spiritual realm to the physical world
     d. all of the above

41. The first wide-ranging persecutions by Romans against the Christians occurred:
     a. during the life of Jesus
     b. in the first century A.D., immediately following Jesus' crucifixion
     c. in the mid-second century A.D.
   * d. in the mid-third century A.D. (p. 151)

42. The earliest converts to Christianity were:
     a. aristocratic men and women
     b. middle-class traders and merchants and their families
   * c. foreign women and slaves (p. 152)
     d. people drawn from every social class

43. This early Christian author helped free Christianity from its Jewish roots and wrote books
     that appealed to Roman intellectuals:
   * a. Origen (p. 152)
     b. Tertullian
     c. Celsus
     d. Galen

44. Tertullian's writings helped to launch this tradition of early Christianity:
     a. hostility to the theater
     b. denunciation of women as sexual temptresses
     c. uncompromising hostility to humanism
   * d. all of the above (p. 152)

45. What Greco-Roman philosophical idea did Origen develop in his Christian theology?
   * a. identifying Jesus with the Stoic notion of the *logos* or reason (p. 152)
     b. using Epicurean arguments to disprove the resurrection of the body
     c. showing Jesus' message to be the same as Aristotle's: moderation
     d. all of the above

46. Early Christian painting and sculpture was used primarily to decorate:
     a. churches and meeting places
   * b. underground burial chambers and tombs (pp. 152–153)
     c. private dwellings
     d. all of the above

47. An early artistic symbol of the Christian faith was:
   * a. the shepherd with his flock as an image of Jesus and the church (p. 153)
     b. a mother with a child as a representation of Mary and Jesus
     c. thirteen male figures around a table as a symbol of the Last Supper
     d. all of the above

48. The most popular image of Jesus in early Christian art was:
     a. as a bearded man
   * b. as a beardless youth (p. 155)

c. as a dying man on a cross
d. as a nude athlete

49. In early Christian art, Jesus is often portrayed in the guise of:
a. the Homeric hero Achilles
b. the tragic hero Oedipus
c. the Greek philosopher Plato
*   d. the Orphic cult leader Orpheus (p. 155)

50. The early Christians:
a. redirected Jewish monotheism to an international audience, regardless of racial and ethnic backgrounds
b. substituted Jesus' golden rule for Judaism's ethical teachings
c. perpetuated the Jewish commandment to give social justice to all
*   d. all of the above (p. 156)

7

LATE ROMAN CIVILIZATION

I. TEACHING STRATEGIES AND SUGGESTIONS

The instructor can treat this chapter using various strategies, for its themes offer a rich assortment of ways to approach the material. The central theme—the death of one civilization and the birth of another—can be taught using the Pattern of Change or the Spirit of the Age model. Another helpful approach could be that of the Case Study, since the long decline of Rome enables the teacher to introduce many topics that relate to the life of any civilization. Specifically, Diocletian's reforms can be used to raise questions about how other states, including the United States, attempt to solve deep-seated social and economic problems with governmental intervention.

A variation on the teaching strategies can be used by formulating a classroom debate over the causes of the fall of the Roman Empire. Aside from the obvious and often-quoted reasons given, the instructor can argue that there was no "fall"; instead it could be argued that this period witnessed the beginning of another era as evidenced by the rise of Christianity, the emergence of new social and political systems among non-Roman peoples, and the appearance of new ways of understanding the world and human nature. This classroom tactic is actually a modification of the Diffusion model. In addition, the instructor could adopt the Comparison/Contrast approach to highlight Christianity's beliefs vis-à-vis other ancient religions and to show why the Christian faith survived and the other cults did not.

One of the most challenging objectives for the instructor is to analyze the transition from Classical humanism to Christian civilization. The Spirit of the Age model might be effective here. The teacher, by using St. Augustine as an example, can also show how attitudes toward the most fundamental issues confronting humans, such as the purpose of life and the meaning of history, were being dealt with in new ways. Furthermore, the instructor can use the Slide Lecture to illustrate changing social attitudes and artistic motives in late Roman civilization.

II. LECTURE OUTLINE

Non-Western Events

A. The Last Days of the Roman Empire
  1. Historical overview
    a. Survey of imperial problems
    b. Phases of late Roman history
  2. Diocletian's reforms and the triumph of Christianity, 284–395
    a. The Great Persecutions and Christian toleration
      (1) Techniques and phases of persecutions

A.D. 285–500

First emperor of northern India, 320

Huns invade Russia and Europe and then withdraw from Europe, 360–470

(2) Constantine and the spread
of Christianity
b. Early Christian controversies
(1) Arianism
(a) The triumph of Bishop
Athanasius
(b) The Nicene Creed
(c) Ulfilas, an Arian bishop
(2) The rise of ascetic movements
(a) Pachomius
(b) Antony
(3) Triumph of Christianity
3. Christian Rome and the end of the
Western Empire, 395–476
a. Invasions by the barbarians
b. Collapse of Roman institutions

B. The Transition from Humanism
to Christian Civilization
1. Literature, theology, and history
a. The decline of secular writing
b. The Fathers of the Church
(1) Ambrose
(a) Writings
(b) Influence
(2) Jerome
(a) Writings
(b) Influence
(3) Augustine
(a) Writings
(b) Influence
c. Church history: Eusebius
(1) New literary genre
(2) Influence
2. The visual arts
a. Late Roman style
b. Architecture
(1) Palaces
(2) Arches
(3) Basilicas
(4) Domed structures
c. Sculpture
(1) Secular developments
(a) Free-standing works
(b) Colossal statues
(c) Reliefs
(d) Stylistic changes
(2) Christian art
(a) Sarcophagus art
(b) Stylistic changes
d. Painting and mosaics
(1) Book illustrations
(2) Mosaics
(a) Subjects and themes

Ch'i dynasty in southern
China, 479–502
Invaders overthrow
northern Indian empire
ca. 484

Kingdom in Ghana

First records of
Japanese history, 400

Expansion of Buddhism
in China
Flowering of Mayan
culture in southern
Mexico, *ca.* 470

Buddhist cave temples
in northern China,
ca. 476
First Shinto shrines
in Japan, 478

        (b)   Contrast with secular art
        (c)   Developments in the Eastern
              Roman Empire

   3. Music
      a. Sacred hymns   Flutes and horns in Peru,
      b. The contributions of Ambrose   *ca.* 475

C. Why Did Rome Fall?
      a. Internal and external pressures
      b. Theories and interpretations

D. The Legacy of Late Roman Civilization

III. LEARNING OBJECTIVES

To learn:

1. The reasons for the crises in the Late Roman Empire and the various solutions applied by the government

2. The phases in the rise of Christianity

3. The controversies within early Christian thought

4. The ideas and contributions of the Church Fathers

5. The central role and importance of St. Augustine in early church history

6. The impact of the new Christian faith on the visual arts, especially in sculpture and painting

7. The various interpretations regarding the collapse of the Roman Empire

8. Historic "firsts" achieved by late Roman civilization: the beginnings of the barbaric kingdoms, the rise of the first Christian state, Christianity as the official religion of Rome, the literary genre of church history, the first Latin Bible, and the writings of the Church Fathers

9. The role of late Roman civilization in transmitting the heritage of earlier times: synthesizing a new civilization from Greco-Roman and Christian elements, fusing Classical values with Christian beliefs in architecture and music, establishing an official church organization, and originating a conception of society in which the Christian church held a pivotal position

IV. SUGGESTIONS FOR FILMS

The Christians: A Peculiar People. McGraw-Hill, 39 min., color.

Decline of the Roman Empire. Coronet, 14 min., color.

In Defence of Rome. McGraw-Hill, 16 min., color.

V. SUGGESTIONS FOR FURTHER READING

Davies, J. G. *The Early Christian Church*. London: Weidenfeld and Nicolson, 1965.

Frend, W. H. *Martyrdom and Persecution in the Early Church: A Study of a Conflict from the Maccabees to Donatus*. Oxford: Blackwell, 1965.

Gough, M. *The Early Christians*. New York: Praeger, 1961.

Kahler, H. *Rome and Her Empire*. London: Methuen, 1965.

MacMullen, R. *Christianizing the Roman Empire, A.D. 100–400*. New Haven: Yale University Press, 1984.

Wilken, R. *The Christians as the Romans Saw Them*. New Haven: Yale University Press, 1984.

VI. IDENTIFICATIONS

symbolic realism	aisles
peristyle	clerestory windows
medallion	atrium
attic	transept
basilica	cruciform
apse	baptistery
nave	impressionistic

VII. DISCUSSION/ESSAY QUESTIONS

1. Compare and contrast the last years of the Roman Republic with the last centuries of the Roman Empire.
2. Discuss the changing policies of the Roman government toward the Christians. Was the issue dividing Romans and Christians political or religious? Explain. How successful were the Roman authorities in dealing with the Christians?
3. What were some of the debates that raged inside the early Christian community? How were they resolved?
4. Do you think that the Roman Empire "fell from within" or was "overwhelmed from the outside"? State your case from either point of view.
5. Note *two* Fathers of the Church, and discuss their contributions to early Christianity.
6. Show how St. Augustine spoke for both the Classical age and the Christian era.
7. Compare and contrast Eusebius's Christian view of history with that of the Greek and Roman historians.
8. What values were reflected in the architecture of late Rome?
9. Discuss the architectural features of the basilica and describe how the Christians adapted this building to their own uses.
10. What were the most lasting contributions of the Romans to Western civilization?

VIII. MULTIPLE-CHOICE QUESTIONS

1. Life in the Late Roman Empire can be described as a time when:
   a. The old Roman values were brought into question.
   b. It appeared that the political and social institutions were unable to change or correct the ills of society.
   c. The emperors offered outstanding leadership.
 * d. a and b but not c (p. 159)

2. This emperor, in the late third century, reformed the Roman Empire:
   a. Commodus
   b. Constantine
 * c. Diocletian (p. 160)
   d. Augustus Caesar

3. One of the major problems facing Diocletian was:
   a. distributing the surplus foods produced by the farmers
 * b. dealing with an unruly army and its many soldiers (p. 159)
   c. deciding how to treat the newly conquered peoples of Italy
   d. defeating the Carthaginians

4. Diocletian's reforms were successful in which of the following areas?
   a. control of the Roman army
   b. containment of the barbarians
   c. restoration of calm to the city of Rome
 * d. all of the above (p. 160)

5. In regard to reforming the government, Diocletian:
   a. split the empire into three separate divisions
   b. divided the empire into two parts
   c. set up a tetrarchy of rulers
 * d. b and c but not a (pp. 160–161)

6. In assessing Diocletian's economic policies, it can be said that:
   a. The Emperor succeeded in laying the foundation for further growth.
 * b. Diocletian could never solve the basic economic problems. (p. 162)
   c. His tax reforms were effective.
   d. He established a new currency that helped trade and commerce.

7. Why did the Romans persecute the Christians?
   a. Christians were split and needed to be brought together.
 * b. Christians refused to worship the Roman gods. (p. 162)
   c. Christians withdrew from Roman society.
   d. Christians sided with Rome's foreign enemies.

8. The persecution of Christians during the first two centuries after the death of Christ can be described as:
   a. very severe and lasting for long periods of time
 * b. occasional and never practiced on an empire-wide scale (p. 162)
   c. continuous following the death of Jesus Christ
   d. led by the chief priests in the mystery cults

9. The Edict of Milan issued in 313:
   a. pardoned all Christians for the their past sins
 * b. permitted Christians to worship openly (p. 162)
   c. demanded that all pagans convert to Christianity
   d. made Christianity the state religion

10. The earliest emperor to convert to Christianity was:
    a. Diocletian
    b. Decius
    c. Julian
  * d. Constantine (p. 162)

11. The founding of Constantinople signified that:
    a. the basis of political power was shifting from the West to the East
    b. Christianity was the official religion of the empire
    c. the city was to become a center of culture and art
  * d. all of the above (p. 163)

12. One of the issues dividing the early Christians was:
    a. the nature of the Virgin Mary
    b. the power of congregations instead of the pope to make decisions
  * c. the divine nature of Jesus (p. 163)
    d. the relationship of the pope to the Roman emperor

13. The early Christians who asserted that Jesus was similar but not identical with God advocated a belief known as:
    a. Athanasium
    b. agnosticism
    c. atheism
  * d. Arianism (p. 163)

14. Much of the debate among the early Christians revealed that:
    a. The Emperor dictated policy within the church.
  * b. Classical thought and Christian faith were often at odds. (p. 163)
    c. Pagan superstition still dominated the Roman mind.
    d. Only minor issues divided the Christian community.

15. Christianity appealed to many individuals because it:
    a. recognized the spiritual worth of the poor
    b. was well organized with control from the leadership in Rome
    c. produced many martyrs who inspired others by their deaths
  * d. a and c but not b (p. 163)

16. The issue of heresy within the Christian church indicated that:
    a. most Christians agreed on dogma and rituals
    b. disagreements were inevitable given that many converts came to Christianity from other religions and with different ideas
    c. Classical thought and Christian beliefs were incompatible
  * d. b and c but not a (p. 163)

17. Roman literature, in the last years of the empire, can be described as:
    a. releasing a new and vital spirit
    b. unable to comprehend the profound changes occurring in society
    c. seeming to care only for the past
  * d. b and c but not a (p. 164)

18. Late Roman Christian authors:
    a. admired Classical writings
    b. adopted the literary styles from Classical literature
    c. preserved many works of Classical literature
  * d. all of the above (p. 167)

19. Three of the most famous Church Fathers were:
    a. Ambrose, Augustine, and Plotinus
    b. Jerome, Augustine, and Constantine
  * c. Ambrose, Jerome, and Augustine (p. 165)
    d. Ambrose, Jerome, and Plotinus

20. Ambrose's leadership in the church was based on:
    a. his service as a capable ecclesiastical administrator
    b. his fusion of Christian and Greco-Roman ideas in his thinking
    c. his contributions as an effective writer of hymns
  * d. all of the above (p. 165)

21. Jerome's most lasting contribution to the church was:
    a. his discovering the True Cross on which Christ was crucified
  * b. his translating of the Bible into Latin (p. 166)
    c. his missionary work among the barbarians
    d. all of the above

22. Augustine:
    a. wrote a monumental work on the causes of the fall of Rome
    b. revealed his innermost thoughts in a confessional work
    c. supported the official point of view in disputes over church dogma
  * d. all of the above (pp. 166–167)

23. Augustine:
    a. had a Classical education
    b. was well acquainted with many philosophies, including Neo-Platonism
    c. converted to Christianity from pagan beliefs
  * d. all of the above (pp. 166–167)

24. In the *City of God*, Augustine asked and answered this question:
    a. Why did God create the world?
  * b. Why does the Roman Empire suffer so much? (p. 167)
    c. Will Rome be powerful again?
    d. Where did evil originate?

25. What event compelled Augustine to write *The City of God*?
  * a. the sack of Rome by the Visigoths (p. 167)
    b. the conquest of Constantinople by the Ottoman Turks
    c. the fall of Athens to the barbarians
    d. the death of Constantine

26. Augustine has been recognized for:
    a. his contributions to pagan philosophy
    b. his reconciling Arianism with Christian thought
  * c. explaining the relationship between God and human beings within the context of history and theology (pp. 166–167)
    d. his identification of happiness as the goal of human life

27. The early church historians believed that:
    a. good would triumph, regardless of the presence of evil in the world
    b. human beings were the primary movers of history
    c. history moved in cycles
  * d. God played the central role in history (p. 167)

28. The first historian of the Christian church was:
    a. Jerome
    b. Augustine
  * c. Eusebius (p. 167)
    d. Constantine

29. Eusebius, in writing his history of the early church:
    a. was inspired by the Greco-Roman historians
    b. sought out sources for his facts
    c. looked back to famous pagan writers like Homer
  * d. all of the above (p. 167)

30. Eusebius's *The History of the Christian Church* should be understood as:
    a. the divine word of God
    b. an attempt to record the formative years of the church
    c. a work that is important for its information even if it is not always presented in an objective way
  * d. b and c but not a (p. 167)

31. Art, in the Late Roman Empire, underwent this change:
    a. Patronage shifted from the emperor to the church.
    b. Classical forms gave way to abstract spiritual qualities.
    c. Artists abandoned Greco-Roman forms.
  * d. all of the above (p. 167)

32. In late Roman times, which Italian city became a center for the new trends in the visual arts?
  * a. Ravenna (p. 167)
    b. Rome
    c. Florence
    d. Milan

33. Ravenna, as the new capital of the Late Roman Empire:
    a. was under constant siege by the barbarians
  * b. reflected Eastern influences in its art styles (p. 167)
    c. was the center of a strong centralized government
    d. was the city in which Augustine was bishop for about 30 years

34. The first Roman emperor to support Christian art and architecture was:
    a. Diocletian
    b. Commodus
  * c. Constantine (p. 168)
    d. Marcus Aurelius

35. Diocletian's Palace on the Dalmatian coast had this aspect:
    a. It was like a Roman camp in its layout and purpose.
    b. It was a tribute to this powerful ruler.
    c. It was intended to impress visitors with the power of Rome.
    *   d. all of the above (p. 168)

36. Which is correct regarding the Arch of Constantine?
    a. It contains scenes that have helped historians understand late Rome.
    b. The arch influenced later builders of trimphant arches.
    c. It showed that Christianity was now the central theme of history.
    *   d. a and b but not c (pp. 168–169)

37. Christians adopted which Roman building type for their churches?
    a. cathedral
    b. forum
    *   c. basilica (p. 171)
    d. amphitheater

38. A typical basilica includes all of these EXCEPT:
    a. It has an oblong hall that is curved on the eastern end.
    b. It contains windows in the upper walls of the central section.
    c. It is usually divided into three areas by columns.
    *   d. Its exterior is decorated with many carvings. (p. 171)

39. The shape of the floor plan of many early Christian churches was the:
    *   a. cruciform (p. 171)
    b. square
    c. rectangle
    d. "X" cross form

40. All of these are correct for the Old St. Peter's Basilica EXCEPT:
    a. It was constructed on the spot where St. Peter was thought to be buried.
    b. Its floor plan was built in the shape of a crucifix.
    *   c. It survived into the twentieth century. (p. 171, caption for Fig. 7.10)
    d. It was dedicated by Constantine.

41. Why was a baptistery built as a separate structure from a church?
    a. It accommodated large crowds at baptisms.
    *   b. Christians felt that those who were not yet baptized should not be allowed in the church
        building. (p. 173)
    c. The baptistery was based on a tradition established by Constantine.
    d. It was the home of the priest.

42. Late Roman secular sculpture can be characterized as:
    a. often monumental in its size
    b. a way to enhance the power and image of the emperor
    c. a device for public propaganda
    *   d. all of the above (pp. 173–174)

43 One of the generalizations that can be made about surviving sculpture from the Late Roman Empire is that:
    a. relief work has nearly disappeared
    b. sculptured statues were smaller than those made in the early empire
  * c. the portraits were more like stereotypes than individuals (p.173)
    d. roman sculptures imitated the Greek Archaic style

44. The leading location of early Christian sculpture is:
  * a. on underground burial vaults or sarcophagi (p. 174)
    b. inside the forums
    c. on the walls of public buildings
    d. within private homes

45. Carvings on Late Roman burial vaults or sarcophagi reveal that:
    a. rich non-Christian Romans wanted to be identified with Classical figures
    b. christians wanted a mixture of Classical and biblical themes and figures
    c. the Christian belief of life after death made the sarcophagus a likely object for art
  * d. all of the above (pp. 174–175)

46. The early Christian artists used many art forms to express their beliefs, including:
    a. mosaics
    b. burial vaults
    c. public statues
  * d. a and b but not c (pp. 174–177)

47. Mosaics became very popular in the churches controlled by:
    a. the newly converted barbarian kings who settled in northern Italy
  * b. the rulers from the eastern regions of the late Roman world (p. 177)
    c. the newly converted invading tribes from Gaul
    d. the rulers in Spain

48. An important hymn writer in the early Christian church was:
    a. Jerome
    b. Augustine
  * c. Ambrose (p. 177)
    d. Plotinus

49. According to the French thinker Montesquieu, Rome fell because:
    a. the barbarians were too powerful to be stopped by the Romans
    b. the population declined
    c. the climate changed and made the Romans lazy
  * d. power ended up in the hands of one person, the emperor (p. 178)

50. Christianity was a major cause for the fall of Rome according to the writings of:
  * a. Edward Gibbon (p. 178)
    b. Montesquieu
    c. Jerome
    d. Ambrose

8

THE SUCCESSORS OF ROME
Byzantium, Islam, and the Early Medieval West

I. TEACHING STRATEGIES AND SUGGESTIONS

The best way to introduce Rome's successors—Byzantium, Islam, and the Early Medieval West—is through a teaching strategy that combines the Patterns of Change method with Historical Overviews. This combined strategy will allow the instructor, using broad strokes, to lay out the origins, major phases and turning points, and characteristics and cultural highlights of the three civilizations and, simultaneously, to show how the Roman heritage was adapted to new conditions in each society. The instructor can also employ the Comparison/Contrast approach to set forth the similarities and differences among these cultures as well as point out the enduring legacies of Byzantium and Islam to the West.

Having briefly surveyed Rome's successors, the instructor can then concentrate on the Early Medieval West, using the Diffusion method to illustrate how Classical, Germanic, and Christian elements were united into a new civilization. With the Patterns of Change model, the instructor can describe how the West was evolving from a relatively simple stage to a more complex model. Shifting to a strategy that blends a Slide Lecture with a Reflections/Connections approach, the instructor can identify the West's major artistic and literary achievements and show how they mirrored developments in political, social, and economic history. In addition, Charlemagne's reign can be treated as a Case Study in which various questions may be raised, such as the validity of monarchy as a form of government, the usefulness of the "Great Man" theory of history, and the viability of the term *Renaissance* as a label for the cultural awakening of this period.

In a concluding lecture for the entire chapter, the teacher could opt for the Spirit of the Age approach, thus raising questions about the *Zeitgiest* of a civilization; that is, in surveying future prospects for all three civilizations from the vantage point of about A.D. 1000, the instructor could speculate on why some civilizations expand and grow, while others stagnate, and a few disappear.

II. LECTURE OUTLINE

Non-Western Events

A. Successors of Rome: Relative Strengths and Weaknesses

B. The Eastern Roman Empire and
    Byzantine Civilization, 476–1453
    1. Shifting fortunes but stable features
    2. History of the Byzantine Empire
        a. Rulers and ruling dynasties
            (1) Justinian
            (2) The Macedonian dynasty and the
                 golden age of Byzantium,
                 867–1081

        (3)   The Comneni dynasty
        (4)   The Paleologian dynasty
   b. Expansions and contractions
   c. Civilizing mission in eastern Europe
   d. Patterns of social change
   e. Surrounded by enemies in later years
3. Byzantine culture: Christianity
and Classicism
   a. Conflict inherited from Rome
   b. The Orthodox religion
       (1)   The office of patriarch
       (2)   Differences between Orthodox
             and Western Christianity
       (3)   Religious disputes
           (a)   Iconoclastic Controversy
           (b)   Other dissension
       (4)   Monasticism
   c. Law
       (1)   Heir to Roman law
       (2)   The Justinian Code
           (a)   Principles
           (b)   Influence
   d. Architecture and mosaics
       (1)   The Byzantine style
           (a)   Elements of Byzantine
                architecture
           (b)   The pendentive
           (c)   The dome
       (2)   Outstanding buildings and their
             characteristics
           (a)   The church of Hagia Sophia,
                Constantinople
           (b)   The church of San Vitale,
                Ravenna
           (c)   The church of Sant'
                Apollinare in Classe
       (3)   Mosaics
           (a)   Contrast with the Roman
                style
           (b)   The portrayals of Justinian
                and Theodora and their
                courtiers
       (4)   Impact of the Iconoclastic
             Controversy
           (a)   Destruction of past art
           (b)   Inauguration of a theological
                art

C. The Islamic World, 600–1517
   1. Overview of Islamic civilization
     a. Meaning of *islam* and *muslim*
     b. Geographic setting
     c. The pre-Islamic Arabs
        (1)   Desert Bedouins

        (2)   Urban Arabs
    d. Jewish and Christian neighbors
2. History of Islam
    a. Life and teachings of Muhammad
        (1)   The Quraish tribe
        (2)   The cities of Mecca and Medina
        (3)   *Jihad* and the expansion of
             Islam
        (4)   The purification of the Kaaba
    b. The Islamic Empire and Muhammad's
       successors
        (1)   Theocracy and the role of the
             Caliph
        (2)   The Abbasid dynasty, the golden
             age of Islam, 754–1258
        (3)   Collapse of the caliphate and
             the rise of mutually hostile
             Islamic states
3. Islamic religious and cultural
   developments
    a. Brilliance of Islamic civilization
        (1)   Brief survey
        (2)   Central role of religion in
             Islamic life
    b. Islamic religion
        (1)   Two central beliefs
        (2)   Relation to Jewish and
             Christian prophetic tradition
        (3)   The Koran
        (4)   The Hadith, or the Tradition
        (5)   Five Pillars of the Faith
             (a)   The affirmation of faith
             (b)   Prayer
             (c)   Fasting
             (d)   Alms-giving
             (e)   Pilgrimage
        (6)   The Shari'a, or holy law
    c. History
        (1)   Various types
        (2)   The pioneering work of
             Ibn Khaldun
    d. Science
        (1)   Link between Roman science and
             medieval Western science
        (2)   Original contributions
             (a)   Medicine
             (b)   Mathematics
        (3)   Adaptations from Hindu science
    e. Art and architecture
        (1)   Complex adaptations of sources
             (a)   Greco-Roman influence
             (b)   Byzantine influence
             (c)   Persian influence

                    (d) Impact of the koranic
                         prohibition against
                         figurative art
          (2) Decorative art
               (a) Arabesques
               (b) Calligraphy
               (c) Mosaics
               (d) Other
          (3) The dominant structure:
               the mosque
               (a) A typical mosque
               (b) The congregational mosque:
                    Ibn Tulun Mosque, Cairo
               (c) The teaching mosque
          (4) Persian miniatures
               (a) Origins
               (b) Characteristics

D. The Early Medieval West   *500–1000*
    1. Explanation of *medieval*
    2. The Early Middle Ages:
        A Romano-Germanic
        Christianized world   T'ang Dynasty in China
        a. Western life after the fall of Rome
        b. Growing stability
            (1) Tribes and kingdoms   Japanese imperial
            (2) The kingdom of the Franks   government
                 (a) The Merovingian dynasty
                 (b) The Carolingian dynasty
            (3) Charlemagne's empire
                 (a) Geographic expansion
                 (b) The coronation in Rome
                 (c) Governmental apparatus
                 (d) Breakup
    3. The political chaos of the ninth and
        tenth centuries and the rise of new
        states
        a. The beginning of modern France:
            Hugh Capet as the king of the
            western Franks
        b. The beginning of modern Germany:
            Otto the Great as emperor of
            the Germans and Saxons
    4. Religion and culture in the   Buddhism introduced into
        Early Middle Ages   Japan, 552–575
        a. Christianity: leadership   Buddhism becomes state
            and organization   religion in Tibet, 632
            (1) The Papacy   Flowering of Buddhist
                 (a) Gregory the Great   civilization in
                 (b) The intractable problem of   China, *ca.* 725
                      secular power over church Introduction of Orthodox
                      affairs   religion into Kiev
            (2) The regular clergy   begins, 988

                    (a) The Benedictine reforms
                    (b) Monastic contributions to
                         cultural life
              b. Literature, history,
                  and learning
                  (1) Scholars and historians   Indian dictionary, 650
                       (a) Boethius   Li Po, the Chinese poet,
                       (b) Gregory of Tours   701–762
                       (c) Bede   Golden age of Chinese
                  (2) The Carolingian Renaissance   poetry, ca. 750
                       (a) Characteristics   Earliest Japanese
                       (b) The palace school   narrative work, 890
                       (c) Alcuin of York   Sixth period of Chinese
                       (d) Einhard   literature, 900–1900
                       (e) Carolingian minuscule   Chinese encyclopedia of
              c. Music   1000 volumes., 978–984
                  (1) Gregorian chants
                  (2) Polyphony
              d. Architecture   Indian stone temples
                  (1) Related to decline in living conditions   Mayan altar with head of
                  (2) Charlemagne's building program   death god, Honduras,
                       (a) Palaces and a royal residence   507
                       (b) Palace chapel in Aachen
              e. Painting: illuminated manuscripts   Earliest Chinese roll
                  (1) Influences and types of books   paintings, 535
                       decorated
                  (2) The Carolingian style   Japanese prints
                  (3) The German Reichnau school

    E. The Legacy of Byzantium, Islam, and the Early Medieval West

III. LEARNING OBJECTIVES

To learn:

1. The successor civilizations to Rome, their major historical periods, their major accomplishments, their adoption of the Roman heritage, and their similarities and differences

2. The strengths of Byzantium that allowed it to survive for more than one thousand years

3. The characteristics of Orthodox Christianity and how it differed from Western Christianity

4. The significance of the Iconoclastic Controversy

5. To recognize visually the Byzantine artistic style and to identify major examples of Byzantine art and architecture

6. Byzantine contributions to the West: the Orthodox church and religion, the Code of Justinian, and elements of Byzantine art and architecture

7. The leading features of the Islamic religion and the role that it plays in Islamic culture

8. The outstanding achievements in Muslim science and mathematics

9. To recognize visually the Islamic artistic style and to identify major examples of Islamic art and architecture

10. The various cultural influences operating in Islamic civilization

11. Islamic contributions to the West: transmission of the basic philosophical and scientific texts from the ancient world; original contributions in algebra and mathematics; transmission of the concept of zero, Arabic numerals, and the pointed arch.

12. The areas in Europe settled by barbarian tribes

13. The stages of the political history of the Frankish kingdom

14. The characteristics and achievements of Charlemagne's reign

15. The structure and organization of the Early Medieval church

16. The accomplishments of the Carolingian Renaissance

17. The characteristics of Early Medieval architecture and painting

18. Historic "firsts" of the Early Medieval West: Benedictine monasticism, earliest successful kingdom in western Europe, the first empire since the fall of Rome, new musical forms, vernacular languages and literature, and the illuminated religious manuscript

19. The role of the Early Medieval West in transmitting the heritage of the Greco-Roman world: revival of learning and scholarship; reshaping the structure of the Christian church; modifying the Latin language; retaining the Classical educational ideal; keeping alive Greco-Roman building and artistic techniques; and, in general, fusing Classical, Christian, and Germanic elements into a new civilization

IV. SUGGESTIONS FOR FILMS

The Byzantine Empire. Coronet, 14 min., color.

Charlemagne and His Empire. Coronet, 14 min., black and white.

The Christians: The Birth of Europe, 410–1084. McGraw-Hill, 39 min., color.

Civilisation: The Frozen World. Time-Life, 52 min., color.

The Fall of Constantinople. Time-Life, 34 min., color.

Islam. McGraw-Hill, 19 min., color.

Islam, the Prophet and the People. Texture Films, 34 min., color.

The Muslim World: Beginnings and Growth. Coronet, 11 min., color.

V. SUGGESTIONS FOR FURTHER READING

Byzantium

Atroshchenko, V. I., and Collins, J. *The Origins of the Romanesque: Near Eastern Influences on European Art, 4th–12th Centuries.* London: Lund Humphries, 1985.

Cameron, A. *Literature and Society in the Early Byzantine World.* London: Variorum, 1985.

Kazhdan, A. P. and Epstein, A. W. *Change in Byzantine Culture in the Eleventh and Twelfth Centuries.* Berkeley: University of California Press, 1985.

Sevcenko, I. *Ideology, Letters and Culture in the Byzantine World.* London: Variorum, 1982.

Wharton, A. J. *Art of Empire: Painting and Architecture of the Byzantine Periphery: A Comparative Study of Four Provinces.* University Park: Pennsylvania State University Press, 1988.

Islam

Crespi, G. *The Arabs in Europe.* New York: Rizzoli, 1986.

Papadopoulo, A. *Islam and Muslim Art.* Translated by R. E. Wolf. New York: Abrams, 1979.

Rodinson, M. *Europe and the Mystique of Islam.* Translated by R. Veinus. Seattle: University of Washington Press, 1987.

Rosenthal, F. *Muslim Intellectual and Social History: A Collection of Essays.* Aldershot, England: Variorum, 1990.

Early Medieval West

Hubert, J., et. al. *The Carolingian Renaissance.* Translated by J. Emmons, S. Gilbert, and R. Allen. New York: Braziller, 1970.

Lopez, R. S. *The Birth of Europe.* New York: Evans-Lippincott, 1966.

McKitterick, R. *The Frankish Kingdoms Under the Carolingians, 751–987.* New York: Longman, 1983.

Musset, L. *The Barbarian Invasions.* University Park: Pennsylvania State University Press, 1975.

Trevor-Roper, H. R. *The Rise of Christian Europe.* London: Thames and Hudson, 1965.

VI. IDENTIFICATIONS

Byzantine style	mosque
Greek cross	minaret
pendentive	miniature
arcade	Gregorian chant
arabesque	ambulatory
calligraphy	illuminated manuscript

VII. DISCUSSION/ESSAY QUESTIONS

1. Discuss the continuities and discontinuities in the Roman legacy as it was adapted to Byzantine civilization.
2. What role did the Orthodox religion play in Byzantine society and culture? Compare and contrast Orthodox religion with the Roman Catholic faith.
3. Select a work of art from the Byzantine period and show how it illustrates the Byzantine artistic style.
4. List and discuss the significance of the legacies of Byzantium to the Western world.
5. Which building most clearly embodies the ideals of Byzantine civilization? Explain.
6. Discuss the continuities and discontinuities in the Roman legacy as it was adapted to Islamic civilization.
7. Describe the Islamic religion. What impact did Islam have on society, politics, art, architecture, and literature?
8. Discuss the part played by Muslim science in the chain of events that led to modern science.
9. What are the two types of mosques? Give an example of each type and list its chief features.
10. Which work of art or building most clearly embodies the ideals of Islamic civilization? Explain.
11. Explain how and why the Franks were able to create a relatively stable political system by 750.
12. Analyze the Christian church's leadership and organization in the Early Middle Ages.
13. What were the major characteristics of the Carolingian Renaissance? Was it a real rebirth of learning or a heroic interlude between two dark periods?
14. Discuss the development of illuminated manuscripts and illustrate their characteristics, using two examples.
15. "The Early Middle Ages laid the foundations for European civilization." Explain.

VIII. MULTIPLE-CHOICE QUESTIONS

1. Byzantine civilization was characterized by all these EXCEPT:
   * a. relatively secure frontiers (p. 181)
   b. Greek as the language of church, state, and culture
   c. exclusive devotion to the Orthodox religious faith
   d. rich and varied urban life, centered in Constantinople

2. During its thousand-year history, the heartland of Byzantium remained:
   a. Bulgaria and Serbia
   * b. Greece and Asia Minor (p. 182)
   c. Egypt and Syria
   d. all of the above

3. Byzantium and the Early Medieval West shared this characteristic:
   a. an economy whose basic source of wealth was agriculture
   b. a society dominated by a feudal aristocracy
   c. a population composed mainly of peasants
   * d. all of the above (pp. 181–182, 198–199)

4. Justinian's reign was noteworthy for:
   a. the reconquest of Italy, southern Spain, and North Africa
   b. a major revision of the Roman law code
   c. the establishment of a second university in Constantinople
   * d. all of the above (p. 182–183)

5. All these peoples were incorporated into the Byzantine empire EXCEPT:
    a. the Bulgarians
*   b. the Russians (p. 184)
    c. the Serbs
    d. the Croats

6. When Constantinople was conquered in 1453, the mantle of leadership of Byzantine civilization was claimed by:
    a. the Bulgarian kingdom
    b. the Ottoman empire
*   c. the Russian state (p. 184)
    d. France

7. Which was a legacy of Byzantium to the West?
    a. Orthodox missionaries introduced civilization and religion to the Slavic peoples of eastern Europe.
    b. The Code of Justinian became the standard legal text studied in medieval Western universities.
    c. Elements of Byzantine art appeared in Renaissance art in Italy.
*   d. all of the above (p. 183, 207)

8. The golden age of Byzantium occurred during the reign of:
    a. Justinian and his dynasty
*   b. the Macedonian dynasty (p. 184)
    c. the Comneni dynasty
    d. the Paleologian dynasty

9. The final conquest of Byzantium was in 1453 by:
    a. the European Crusaders
    b. the Seljuk Turks
*   c. the Ottoman Turks (p. 184)
    d. the Bulgarians

10. Which is a correct distinction between the Western Christian church and the Eastern Orthodox church?
    a. the Western church was ruled by the pope from Rome; the Eastern church was governed by the patriarch of Constantinople.
    b. Latin was the official language in the West, Greek in the East.
    c. Western priests were celibate; Orthodox priests could marry.
*   d. all of the above (p. 185)

11. Which was NOT a consequence of Byzantium's Iconoclastic Controversy?
*   a. After the controversy ended, Byzantine artists were prohibited from portraying the human figure in religious painting. (p. 186)
    b. During the controversy, nearly all religious pictures were destroyed.
    c. The controversy contributed to the widening split between the Western Christian church and the Eastern Orthodox church.
    d. The controversy aligned the emperor, the bishops, the army, and the civil service against the monks.

12. All are features of Byzantine law EXCEPT:
    a. Disputes should be settled by court proceedings.
    b. The individual should be shielded against unreasonable demands of society.

* c. Criminal cases should be adjudicated in trials by a jury of peers. (p. 186)
  d. The limits of a ruler's legitimate power is an issue for courts to determine.

13. Which was an influence on Byzantine architecture?
    a. The Greco-Roman tradition supplied columns, arches, vaults, and domes.
    b. The Oriental tradition contributed rich ornamentation and riotous color.
    c. The Christian tradition supplied subjects for the interior decorations.
* d. all of the above (p. 187)

14. A significant innovation in Byzantine architecture was:
    a. the dome
* b. the pendentive (p. 187)
    c. the pointed arch
    d. the flying buttress

15. The most magnificent church built in the Byzantine world was:
    a. San Vitale in Ravenna
* b. Hagia Sophia in Constantinople (p. 187)
    c. Sant' Apollinare in Classe
    d. Dafni near Athens

16. Which was NOT an aspect of the style of Byzantine mosaics and paintings?
    a. Feet point downward.
    b. Figures are rendered in two dimensions.
* c. Gestures are made expressive. (p. 189)
    d. Figures seem to float in space.

17. Which is an aspect of the church of San Vitale in Ravenna?
    a. It was commissioned by the emperor Justinian.
    b. It is covered with a dome.
    c. It features two impressive mosaics, one of Justinian and his court and the other of his empress, Theodora, and her retinue.
* d. all of the above (pp. 187–189)

18. The word *islam* means:
* a. submission (p. 191)
    b. holy
    c. universal
    d. pure

19. Medieval Islamic civilization did NOT embrace this territory:
    a. southern Spain
* b. France (p. 191)
    c. Sicily
    d. Northern Africa

20. The Islamic faith was born in:
    a. Egypt
* b. the Arabian peninsula (p. 191)
    c. Mesopotamia
    d. Asia Minor

21. The pre-Islamic Arabs trace their ancestry to:
*   a. Abraham and the Hebrew patriarchs (p. 191)
    b. Homer and the Ionian Greeks
    c. Dido and the Carthaginians
    d. Hector and the Trojans

22. The Arab calendar dates from this historic event:
    a. the first vision that Muhammad received from God
*   b. the flight of Muhammad and followers from Mecca to Yatrib (p. 192)
    c. the conquest of Arabia
    d. the death of Muhammad

23. The most sacred shrine in Islamic civilization is:
*   a. the Kaaba in Mecca (p. 192)
    b. the Dome of the Rock, Jerusalem
    c. the Ibn Tulun Mosque, Cairo
    d. the Alhambra, Granada

24. Between 800 and 1100, Arabic scholarship was more advanced than Western scholarship in the area of:
    a. medicine
    b. mathematics
    c. science
*   d. all of the above (p. 192)

25. What are the two central beliefs of the Islamic religion?
    a. "There are two gods, Ahuramazda and Ahriman, and Zoroaster is their prophet."
    b. "There is but one god, Yahweh, and Muhammad is his prophet."
*   c. "There is but one God, Allah, and Muhammad is his prophet." (p. 193)
    d. "There are two Gods, Yahweh and Satan, and Mani is their prophet."

26. Which is NOT a required devotional practice by devout Muslims?
*   a. to confess one's sins to the priest (p. 193)
    b. to pray five times a day facing Mecca
    c. to fast during the lunar month of Ramadan
    d. to give alms to the poor

27. Which of these does NOT have authority over devout Muslims?
    a. the Koran
    b. the Hadith
    c. the Shari'a
*   d. the Muqaddima (p. 192–193)

28. Ibn Khaldun argued that history should have this characteristic:
    a. downplay the role of divine forces
    b. focus on the human motivation to bond with certain groups
    c. study the human desire for improved status
*   d. all of the above (p. 193)

29. In Muslim science:
    a. Scholars translated the Greek scientific texts and preserved them.
    b. Scholars built on the Greek scientific heritage.
    c. Scholars transmitted their scientific knowledge to medieval Christians.
*   d. all of the above (p. 194)

30. Which was NOT an achievement of Muslim science?
    * a. invented the calculus (p. 194)
    b. developed the algebraic system
    c. first made the clinical distinction between measles and smallpox
    d. transformed the Hindu numeration system into the Arabic numerals

31. Which was NOT an influence on Islamic architecture?
    a. the Greco-Roman arcade
    * b. the Egyptian pyramid (p. 194)
    c. the Persian vaulted hall
    d. the Byzantine pendentive

32. The dominant architectural structure in Islam is:
    a. the temple
    b. the fortress-palace
    * c. the mosque (p. 194)
    d. the tomb

33. This type of Islamic art was developed in spite of the Koran's prohibition against figurative art:
    a. arabesque
    * b. Persian miniature (p. 197)
    c. calligraphy
    d. all of the above

34. A characteristic feature of an Islamic mosque is:
    a. a nearby minaret for prayer calls
    b. an open courtyard
    c. rich decorations of mosaics, Oriental carpets, and calligraphic friezes
    * d. all of the above (p. 195)

35. Life in the West after the collapse of Rome can be characterized as:
    a. based on farming
    b. exhibiting a low standard of living for the bulk of the population
    c. having a restricted economy based on barter
    * d. all of the above (p. 198)

36. Select the INCORRECT match-up of tribe and place of final settlement:
    a. Visigoths in Spain
    b. Vandals in North Africa
    * c. Saxons in Italy (p. 198)
    d. Burgundians in southern France

37. The first important ruler among the Franks was:
    a. Pepin
    b. Charlemagne
    * c. Clovis (p. 198)
    d. Charles Martel

38. Charlemagne was able to keep control of his kingdom:
    a. through a relatively efficient bureaucracy
    b. with the help of the church
    c. by means of a powerful army
    * d. all of the above (p. 199)

39. Pope Gregory the Great made all of these contributions EXCEPT:
 * a. He crowned the Frankish king as the new Emperor. (p .200)
    b. He sent missionaries to England.
    c. He wrote hymns and music for church ceremonies.
    d. He reformed the clergy.

40. In the *Consolation of Philosophy*, Boethius:
    a. argued that life is unfair
    b. described his search for happiness
    c. denounced Christianity
 * d. a and b but not c (p. 202)

41. The Carolingian Renaissance can be described as:
    a. the most important intellectual movement between the collapse of Rome and the learning revolution of the twelfth century
    b. an educational reform movement
    c. led by the best minds at the court of Charlemagne
 * d. all of the above (p. 202)

42. The leading intellectual who was primarily responsible for the founding of Charlemagne's palace school was:
    a. Einhard
    b. Ethelred
    c. Bede
 * d. Alcuin (p. 202)

43. Einhard's biography of Charlemagne:
    a. presents a firsthand account of the life of this great man
    b. was modeled on the writings of Roman historians, like Suetonius
    c. reflects the author's admiration for his subject
 * d. all of the above (p. 202)

44. The new Carolingian minuscule accomplished all of these EXCEPT:
    a. It made documents and other written materials more accessible to the educated.
    b. It created a writing form of capital and small letters.
 * c. It inaugurated a series of literary works that lasted for a century. (p. 202, caption for Fig. 8.20)
    d. It cut down on the number of errors that monks might make in recopying documents.

45. Gregorian chants, which were developed in the Early Middle Ages, were:
    a. named for their inventor, Pope Gregory the Great
    b. used in the ceremonies of the church
    c. sung by male voices only
 * d. all of the above (pp. 202–203)

46. Charlemagne's Palace Chapel can be characterized as:
    a. looking essentially the same today as it did when first constructed
    b. serving as the principal site of the emperor's ceremonies
    c. showing the influence of Islamic architecture
 * d. a and b but not c (pp. 203–205)

47. Charlemagne's Palace Chapel:
    a. symbolized the ruler's earthly power
    b. was constructed to impress those who stood within its walls

    c.   became a sacred place for later ceremonies, such as coronations

*   d.   all of the above (pp. 203–205, caption for Fig. 8.21)

48. Illuminated manuscripts had this purpose:
*   a.   to decorate sacred writings and Bibles (p. 205)
     b.   to impress the masses with the power of the emperor
     c.   to transmit secret messages among the monkish scribes
     d.   to educate the illiterate

49. Illuminated manuscripts had this characteristic:
     a.   Their decorative schemes became more complex over the years.
     b.   They were filled with Christian symbols.
     c.   They allowed artists to express both their devotion to God and their artistic talents.
*   d.   all of the above (p. 205)

50. By the end of the Early Medieval period, the West could be characterized as:
     a.   a fusion of Classical, Germanic, and Christian elements
     b.   only indirectly affected by events in Byzantium and Islam
     c.   profoundly affected by Christianity, both as a religion and a way to organize society
*   d.   all of the above (p. 206)

9

THE HIGH MIDDLE AGES
The Christian Centuries

I. TEACHING STRATEGIES AND SUGGESTIONS

The High Middle Ages can be introduced with a Standard Lecture that gives a Historical Overview, setting forth the key historical and cultural milestones of this period. After this opening, either of two approaches may be used to teach the section on feudalism. One approach is the Patterns of Change model, which will allow the instructor to analyze the origins of feudalism and trace its development from its simple beginning to its later, more complex stages. A second strategy is to focus on the feudal monarchies, using a Comparison/Contrast approach to point out their similarities and differences. Whichever approach is used, the instructor should underscore the idea that the papal monarchy functioned just like a secular monarchy in the High Middle Ages.

Another major theme in the High Middle Ages is Christianity, which may be approached in two ways. A variation on the Reflections/Connection model can be adopted to show the relationships between the church and other medieval institutions (political, social, and economic) as well as the way that Christian values helped to shape standards of public and private morality. Second, the Patterns of Change model can be applied to demonstrate the fluctuating fortunes of the church. As part of this presentation on the church, the instructor can also discuss institutions in general, dealing with such features of institutional development as life cycles, purposes for seeking power, and innate contradictions.

Scholasticism can also be treated with the Patterns of Change model. For almost the first time since teaching the Classical period, the instructor has enough material to delve into the personalities of many key figures being studied, including Peter Abelard, Peter Lombard, and Thomas Aquinas. The teacher can also apply the Diffusion model to show the significant impact of Arab artists and intellectuals on Christian civilization. In light of the contemporary debate about opening the canon of Western culture, it is important to stress the role of the Arabs in the development of medieval Christian science, architecture, and literature.

The teacher can use the Reflections/Connections model to show influences—particularly those of feudalism and the church—on the medieval arts and humanities. With the Diffusion model, the instructor can set forth the shift from the monastic, feudal culture of the first half of this period to the courtly, urban culture of the second half; in literature, this shift is represented by the change from the *chansons de geste* to romances, from monkish poets to the secular Dante; and, in theology, by the change from Abelard to Thomas Aquinas. In addition, the instructor, employing the Patterns of Change approach, can trace the evolution of architecture from the Romanesque to the Gothic; and a Slide Lecture or films can illustrate the two artistic styles. As a conclusion to the High Middle Ages, the instructor can use the Spirit of Age approach to demonstrate the medieval synthesis that embraced Dante's *Divine Comedy*, the Gothic cathedrals, Thomist philosophy, and scholastic reasoning.

II LECTURE OUTLINE

A. Historical Overview
   1. Major events of the High Middle Ages
   2. The medieval synthesis
   3. The two phases of the era

B. Feudalism
   1. The feudal system and feudal society
      a. Origins of feudalism
      b. Characteristics of feudalism
      c. Spread of feudalism
      d. Chivalric code
         (1) Impact on men
         (2) Impact on women
   2. Peasant life
      a. Serfdom
      b. Daily routines
   3. The rise of towns
      a. Rise in population and migrations
      b. Town life
         (1) At odds with feudal system
         (2) Work and commerce
            (a) Trade routes
            (b) Role of women
   4. The feudal monarchy
      a. The French monarchy
         (1) The Capetian kings
         (2) Institutional developments
      b. The English monarchy
         (1) Norman England
         (2) Conflicts between kings and barons
      c. The Holy Roman Empire
         (1) Lay investiture
         (2) Failure to centralize
      d. The Papal monarchy
         (1) Reform movements
         (2) Powerful popes

C. Medieval Christianity and the church
   1. Structure and hierarchy
   2. Christian beliefs and practices
      a. Church as way to salvation
      b. Rituals and ceremonies
         (1) Inseparable from doctrine
         (2) Seven sacraments
   3. Religious orders and lay piety
      a. Monasteries and nunneries
      b. Mendicant orders
      c. The Albigensians

Non-Western Events

1000–1300

Mayan civilization at a secondary height, fused with Toltec elements, eleventh and twelfth centuries
Inca civilization, 1000–1500
In China, Sung dynasty 960–1279; Mongol (Yüan) dynasty, 1279–1368
Shogunate in Japan, 1192
Bantu, Arab, and Indian cultures blend in Swahili civilization on eastern African coast, 1100–1500
Decline of kingdom of Ghana, 1224
In India, Turkish Sultanate, Delhi, 1206–1526
Explosive powder used in weapons in China, 1150
Marco Polo in China, 1275–1292

Neo-Confucianism, 1130–1200
Zen Buddhism in Japan, 1200
Expansion of Islam, 1000–1500
Rumi, Persian poet, founder of the Order of Dancing Dervishes, d. 1273

D. The Age of Synthesis: Equilibrium between the Spiritual and the Secular
   1. Learning and Theology
      a. Cathedral schools and the development of scholasticism
         (1) Curriculum
         (2) Scholasticism: aims and methods
      b. Peter Abelard
         (1) Life and ideas
         (2) Realism and Nominalism
      c. The rise of the universities
      d. Intellectual controversy and Thomas Aquinas
         (1) Averroists vs. traditionalists
         (2) Thomas Aquinas
             (a) Thomistic theology
             (b) Thomistic summaries
             (c) Influence of Aquinas
   2. Literature
      a. Monastic and feudal writing
         (1) Goliards and poetry
         (2) *Chanson de geste:* the *Song of Roland*
      b. Vernacular and courtly writing
         (1) Troubadors and courtly romances
         (2) Chrétien de Troyes
      c. Dante
         (1) Life and works
         (2) *Divine Comedy*
   3. Architecture and art
      a. Romanesque churches and related arts
         (1) Origins and evolution of churches
             (a) Floor plan and decorations
             (b) Vézelay
         (2) Illuminated manuscripts
      b. Gothic churches and related art
         (1) Origins and evolution
             (a) Early Gothic style, 1145–1194: Notre Dame, Paris
             (b) High Gothic Style, 1194–1300: Amiens and Chartres
         (2) Illuminated manuscripts
   4. Music
      a. Innovations on the Gregorian chants
      b. Liturgical drama
      c. Secular music

E. The Legacy of the Christian Centuries

Avicenna, Arab philosopher, d. 1037
Averroes, Arab philosopher, 1126–1198

Maimonides, Jewish philosopher, 1135–1204

Omar Khayyám, d. 1123, the Persian poet, author of the *Rubáiyát*
Saadi, Persian poet, 1193–1292
Chinese drama developed, 1235

Chinese landscape painting at its height, 1141–1279
Sanjusangendo Temple, Kyoto, Japan, 1266

Buddhist art in Burma
In Japan, Toshiro starts porcelain manufacture, 1227
"Ying Tsao Ea Shih", a building manual, 1103
Rajarani Temple, Bhubanesvara, Orissa, 1098

III. LEARNING OBJECTIVES

To learn:

1. The origins, evolution, and spread of feudalism

2. The impact of the chivalric code on feudal society and how it helped shape relationships between men and women

3. The rise, characteristics, and impact of courtly love

4. The nature of peasant life

5. The way of life in medieval towns

6. The similarities and differences among the feudal monarchies

7. The reasons for the successes and failures of feudal monarchies, including the papacy

8. How the church maintained its dominance of society and culture

9. The origins and influence of the new monastic orders

10. The sources of the heresies and the fate of the Albigensians

11. The nature and characteristics of scholasticism

12. The issues involved in the medieval intellectual debates and how they were resolved

13. The medieval synthesis of Thomas Aquinas

14. The characteristics of monastic writing and a representative example of this literary genre

15. Examples of feudal writing and its themes

16. The characteristics of courtly romances and examples of this literary genre

17. The importance of Dante and examples of his writings, in particular the structure and meaning of the *Divine Comedy*

18. The development of Romanesque architecture and its main features

19. The transition from the Romanesque to the Gothic style

20. The Gothic cathedral styles, including different phases with examples, chief features, and decorative principles

21. The role, evolution, and impact of music in the High Middle Ages

22. Historic "firsts" achieved in the High Middle Ages that became legacies for later Western developments: the writings of Dante; the theology of Thomas Aquinas, or Thomism; Romanesque and Gothic artistic styles; the epic, the romance, and the chivalric tale; courtly love with its

shared social roles for men and women; the legends of King Arthur and the Knights of the Round Table; the basic theoretical system for composing music; and the love song

23. The role of the High Middle Ages in transmitting the heritage from earlier civilizations: redefining the liberal arts curriculum within the context of Catholic faith; rediscovering ancient Classical philosophy and science from Muslim scholars; and reviving Aristotelianism and the rationalist tradition and integrating it with the teachings of the Christian faith

IV. SUGGESTIONS FOR FILMS

Art of the Middle Ages. Encyclopedia Britannica, 30 min., color.

Chartres Cathedral. Encyclopedia Britannica, 30 min., color.

Civilisation: The Great Thaw. Time-Life, 50 min., color.

The Medieval Mind. Encyclopedia Britannica, 26 min., color.

Medieval Times: The Role of the Church. Coronet, 14 min., color.

Middle Ages: Rise of Feudalism. Encyclopedia Britannica, 20 min., color.

V. SUGGESTIONS FOR MUSIC

German Plainchant & Polyphony. Schola Antiqua. Elektra/Nonesuch H–71312; 71312–4 (cassette).

Gregorian Chant. Deller Consort. Harmonia Mundi 234.

The Memory of Thomas à Becket. [12th-century Mass]. Schola Hungarica. Hungaroton SLPD–12458 (D); MK–12458 (CD).

The Play of St. Nicholas. [12th–century liturgical drama]. New York Ensemble for Early Music. Musicmasters 20001X; 20001 W (cassette).

Songs of Chivalry. Martin Best Medieval Ensemble. Nimbus NI–5006 (CD).

Troubadours, Trouveres and Minnesingers (Songs and Dances of the Middle Ages). Augsburg Ensemble for Early Music. Christophorus CD–74519 (CD).

VI. SUGGESTIONS FOR FURTHER READING

Baldwin, M. W. *The Medieval Church.* Ithaca, N.Y.: Cornell University Press, 1953.

Branner, R. *Gothic Architecture.* New York: G. Braziller, 1961.

Brooke, C., *The Structure of Medieval Society.* London: Thames and Hudson, 1971.

Contamine, P. *War in the Middle Ages.* Oxford: Basil Blackwell, 1984.

Grabar, A., and Nordenfalk, C. *Romanesque Painting.* London: Skira, 1958.

Kirshner, J., and Wemple, S. *Women of the Medieval World.* Oxford: Basil Blackwell, 1985.

Martindale, A. *Gothic Art.* London: Thames and Hudson, 1967.

Southern, R. W. *Western Society and the Church in the Middle Ages.* Baltimore: Penguin Books, 1972.

VII. TERMS FOR IDENTIFICATION

chivalric code	tympanum
friars	narthex
cathedral	ribbed vault
scholasticism	pier
Realism	flying buttress
Nominalism	choir
via media	rose window
goliard	blind arcade
chanson de geste	gargoyle
vernacular language	gallery
canzone	*Rayonnant*
troubador	tracery
romance	trope
terza rima	liturgical drama
Romanesque style	polyphony
Gothic style	organum
bay	motet

VIII. DISCUSSION/ESSAY QUESTIONS

1. Discuss the origins of feudalism and its impact on society.
2. What was the chivalric code, and how did it manifest itself in feudal society?
3. Discuss the separate roles that men and women played in the feudal aristocracy, and describe how these roles affected their relationships with each other.
4. Compare and contrast the life of a peasant on a manor with that of a town merchant.
5. Discuss the characteristics of medieval secular monarchy (France, England, and the Holy Roman Empire), and note some common problems and issues and how they dealt with them.
6. Compare and contrast the papal monarchy with the medieval secular monarchies.
7. Show how the medieval church was both helped and hindered by its institutional organization.
8. Discuss the impact of new religious orders and the lay piety movements on the medieval church.
9. What is meant by the term *medieval synthesis*? Show how this term applies, or does not apply, to medieval society and culture.
10. What is meant by the term *scholasticism*? What does the style of scholastic reasoning reveal about the nature of the medieval mind?
11. Explain the differences between Realism and Nominalism. Who were the major supporters and what were their basic arguments for each of these philosophical positions?
12. How did Thomas Aquinas reconcile faith and reason?
13. Summarize the ideas in Aquinas's thought.
14. What was Thomas Aquinas's most important contribution? Explain.
15. What were the main themes in the *Song of Roland?* How did these themes express the ideals of feudalism?
16. Discuss the origins and characteristics of courtly romances.
17. Discuss the main allegorical and theological features of Dante's *Divine Comedy.* Explain how this work summarizes medieval thought.

18. Identify the major characteristics and features of Romanesque architecture, and show how they are evident in the church at Vézelay.
19. How does Notre Dame cathedral, Paris, manifest the Early Gothic style?
20. Describe the High Gothic style and show how Amiens cathedral is representative of this style.
21. Trace the evolution of music in the High Middle Ages and describe its use by the church.
22. Name at least three legacies from the High Middle Ages, and show how they are still part of the Western tradition.

IX. MULTIPLE-CHOICE QUESTIONS

1. The High Middle Ages are usually dated from:
   a. 400–700
   b. 700–1000
 * c. 1000–1300 (p. 209)
   d. 1300–1500

2. The feudal system rested primarily on:
   a. economic coercion by the wealthy
   b. the moral foundations of the church
 * c. personal loyalty and kinship (p. 209)
   d. the lingering influence of Charlemagne's kingdom

3. Feudalism evolved into a set of relationships between:
   a. lords and peasants
   b. lords and clerics
 * c. lords and vassals (p. 210)
   d. popes and kings

4. The obligations of vassalage included which of the following?
   a. responsibilities for both lords and vassals
   b. military service from the vassal
   c. military protection from the lord
 * d. all of the above (p. 210)

5. The role of aristocratic women in feudal society can be described as :
   a. being treated in reality somewhat differently from the ideal
   b. being praised in poems and stories
   c. being recognized as equal to men
 * d. a and b but not c (p. 211)

6. Which would *not* describe the life of a peasant?
   a. Peasants worked hard but found some relief on Holy Days.
   b. Peasant families found it difficult to move from the manor.
 * c. Peasant life was the same all across Europe. (p. 211)
   d. Life improved for some after more efficient farming methods were introduced.

7. During the High Middle Ages the population in Europe:
   a. declined
   b. remained stationary
   c. grew at a slow rate
 * d. nearly doubled (p. 212)

8. Townspeople protected themselves from the feudal system:
    a. by forming alliances with the Muslims
    b. by creating self–governing towns with charters
    c. by forming guilds to regulate and to improve the local economy
*   d. b and c but not a (p. 212)

9. One of the outgrowths of the feudal system was:
    a. the creation of Christendom
*   b. the feudal monarchy (p. 213)
    c. the unification of Europe
    d. the further fragmentation of feudalism

10. The French feudal monarchy began under this dynasty:
    a. the Bourbons
*   b. the Capetians (p. 214)
    c. the Normans
    d. the Hohenstaufens

11. Am important event in medieval England was:
*   a. the granting of the Magna Carta (p. 215)
    b. the Irish invasion of England
    c. the coming to power of Henry VIII
    d. a and c but not b

12. The leader of the Normans who invaded England in 1066 was:
    a. Ethelred the Unready
*   b. Duke William (p. 214)
    c. King John
    d. Edward the Confessor

13. The lay investiture controversy centered on the question:
    a. of who possessed the power to control the fief—the lord or vassal
*   b. of whether local lords or the church should appoint certain bishops to their office (p. 215)
    c. of when a vassal should become a lay leader
    d. of whether or not it was legal to give fiefs to subvassals

14. The major church reform that began in the tenth century started at:
    a. the castle of Louis the Pious
*   b. the monastery at Cluny (p. 215)
    c. Rome under Pope Zacharius
    d. the church at Vézelay

15. The most powerful pope in the High Middle Ages was:
    a. Gregory VII
    b. Boniface VIII
    c. Urban II
*   d. Innocent III (p. 216)

16. Christian beliefs and ceremonies were derived from:
    a. the biblical scriptures
    b. the writings of church fathers and later commentaries
    c. past traditions and practices
*   d. all of the above (p. 217)

17. The Christian practices of confession and penance meant that:
    a. A sinner could sin without fear of punishment.
  * b. A sinner could be absolved from sins and penalties could be erased. (p. 218)
    c. A sinner would be allowed into heaven.
    d. b and c but not a

18. The new religious orders founded during the Middle Ages:
    a. were originally created to work among the urban poor
    b. had the goal of expanding the papacy
    c. became involved in higher education
  * d. a and c but not b (pp. 218–219)

19. Medieval culture was influenced by:
    a. European peoples across national boundaries
    b. the Classical world's arts and thought
    c. Muslim civilization
  * d. all of the above (p. 219)

20. Before the medieval universities appeared, most education was associated with:
    a. cathedral schools usually run by the bishops
    b. monastic schools operated by monks
    c. surviving schools from the time of Charlemagne
  * d. all of the above (pp. 219–220)

21. Medieval church schools can be described as:
    a. relying heavily on the local lords for financial help
    b. being founded to train young men for the church
    c. having a curriculum based on the seven liberal arts
  * d. b and c but not a (p. 220)

22. Scholasticism's primary task was:
    a. to reconcile the state *versus* church controversy
  * b. to bring Aristotle's ideas into accord with Christian doctrine (p. 220)
    c. to reconcile Platonism with Christian beliefs
    d. to discover new areas of knowledge

23. Peter Abelard's theological goal was:
    a. to undermine the morals of his day
  * b. to use reason to reconcile differences between Church doctrine and biblical writings (pp. 221)
    c. to attack church dogma
    d. to find proofs for the existence of God

24. The debate between the Realists and Nominalists:
    a. was settled by a church council in 1215
  * b. centered on the issue of universals (p. 221)
    c. arose from attempts to reconcile Arabic thought and Christian beliefs
    d. was fought between the papacy and scholarly monks

25. The Nominalists believed that universals:
    a. were real and actually existed
  * b. existed only in the mind as useful devices to identify and categorize things (p. 221)
    c. were planted in the mind by God
    d. had existence only in an invisible world of Truth

26. The Realists:
    a. were influenced by Plato
    b. thought that universals were only words and had no independent existence
    c. believed that abstractions or ideas existed as universals
 * d. a and c but not b (p. 221)

27. The Greek philosopher whose works became the heart of Scholasticism was:
    a. Protagoras
 * b. Aristotle (p. 220)
    c. Zeno
    d. Empedocles

28. The writings of Aristotle came to the West by way of:
    a. Arabic scholars
    b. Byzantine monks
    c. Jewish intellectuals
 * d. a and c but not b (p. 221)

29. Thomas Aquinas in his writings about faith and reason:
    a. adopted the same position as the medieval thinker Bonaventure
 * b. tried to reconcile Aristotelian thought and Christian doctrine (pp. 221–222)
    c. agreed with Averroes's teachings
    d. rejected Abelard and his tradition

30. Thomism might best be described as:
    a. a thought process that reconciled Greek and Arabic philosophy
 * b. a synthesis of the faith *versus* reason debate (p. 222)
    c. a failure to reconcile the dispute between the popes and the secular monarchs
    d. a last effort in philosophy to prove the existence of God

31. Thomas Aquinas, in addition to writing on philosophical and theological topics, also:
    a. addressed himself to such issues as the best form of government
    b. dealt with economic problems
    c. supported a new system for choosing the popes
 * d. a and b but not c (p. 222)

32. The *goliards* are best known for their:
    a. lectures in the universities
 * b. songs and poems performed at aristocratic courts (p. 222)
    c. contributions to the faith *versus* reason debate
    d. a and c but not b

33. The *chanson de geste* is a literary genre known as:
    a. a morality play
    b. a mystery drama
    c. a sonnet
 * d. an epic poem (p. 222)

34. Which medieval ideal is found in *The Song of Roland?*
    a. allegiance to the chivalric code
    b. support for Christianity against Islam
    c. loyalty to one's king
 * d. all of the above (pp. 222–223)

35. The *chansons de geste* were replaced after about 1150 by:
    a. secular plays
 * b. courtly romances (p. 224)
    c. religious dramas
    d. romantic novels

36. The most popular subject of medieval romances focused on:
    a. King Henry II and his wife Eleanor
 * b. King Arthur and his knights (p. 224)
    c. the Capetian dynasty
    d. ancient Greek myths

37. The life of Dante can be best summarized as:
    a. a life of a monastic intellectual
    b. a life of political turmoil
    c. a life of fame but of disappointment too
 * d. b and c but not a (pp. 224–225)

38. In the *Divine Comedy* Dante recounts:
    a. in allegorical terms the experience of all human beings
    b. the claim that both reason and faith are needed to understand God
    c. in poetic form many theological arguments of his day
 * d. all of the above (pp. 224–225)

39. Besides Dante himself the two main figures in the *Divine Comedy* are:
    a. Ganelon and Roland
 * b. Vergil and Beatrice (p. 225)
    c. Thomas Aquinas and the Virgin Mary
    d. Plato and Aristotle

40. The rhyme scheme of the *Divine Comedy* is:
 * a. *terza rima* (p. 225)
    b. *bel canto*
    c. rhymed couplets
    d. fourteen-line sonnet form

41. In its complex structure the *Divine Comedy* is the equivalent of a:
 * a. Gothic cathedral (*passim*)
    b. Romanesque church
    c. religious crusade
    d. chivalric tale

42. The dominant visual art of the medieval ages was:
 * a. architecture (p. 225)
    b. fresco painting
    c. portrait painting
    d. sculpture

43. The arts in the High Middle Ages:
    a. were treated separately, each being judged by different standards
    b. were dominated by painting
 * c. were subservient to religion and had no independent status (p. 225)
    d. were used to entertain the public

44. Romanesque architecture can be characterized as:
   a. growing out of the basilica tradition
   b. appearing to be a spiritual fortress in an unsettled time
   c. reflecting the needs of monastic life
 * d. all of the above (pp. 225–226)

45. Romanesque sculpture was:
   a. a teaching device to carry the Christian message to the illiterate
   b. primarily a decoration for churches
   c. seldom copied from Greco-Roman models
 * d. all of the above (p. 227)

46. The Gothic cathedral was identifiable by its:
 * a. flying buttresses, ribbed vaulting, stained glass windows (pp. 230–231)
   b. ribbed vaulting, rounded arches, thick walls
   c. flying buttresses, domed ceiling, many statues
   d. ribbed vaulting, stained glass windows, and simple decorations

47. Who originated the Gothic architectural style?
   a. Peter Abelard
 * b. Suger of St. Denis (p. 230)
   c. Olaf of St. Gall
   d. St. Bonaventure

48. Notre Dame cathedral, Paris, exhibits which characteristic(s) of Gothic art?
   a. the ideal of harmony
   b. integration of sculptural details with building units
   c. an enormous choir
 * d. all of the above (pp. 231–235)

49. In contrast to the Early Gothic, High Gothic architecture:
   a. had more elaborate sculptural decorations
   b. was taller
   c. was noted for its pointed spires
 * d. all of the above (p. 237, caption for Fig. 9.27)

50. Developments in Gothic music included:
   a. the appearance of the motet
   b. the spread of secular music
   c. the creation of the first symphony orchestra
 * d. a and b but not c (p. 239)

10

THE LATE MIDDLE AGES
1300–1500

I. TEACHING STRATEGIES AND SUGGESTIONS

The instructor can introduce the Late Middle Ages with a Standard Lecture that is organized as a Historical Overview, presenting the major milestones in the cultural sphere as well as the key political, economic, and social developments. With a Pattern of Change approach, the instructor can show the changes that occurred as High Gothic gave way to Late Gothic civilization; and a Slide Lecture can illustrate the accompanying stylistic shifts in the arts and architecture. In addition, the instructor can use the Reflections/Connections strategy to demonstrate that the change from High Gothic to Late Gothic was rooted in the period's multiple calamities.

Besides constituting the final phase of medieval civilization, the late medieval period also marks the first stirrings of the modern world. The best way to deal with this topic is to use a blend of the Spirit of the Age approach with the Comparison/Contrast technique, setting forth the death of the Middle Ages as the modern world struggles to be born. In this combined approach the instructor should concentrate on three major aspects of the emerging modern world: first, the shift from the medieval ideal of a unified Christian Europe to the modern reality of a system of rival states; second, a decline in the power of the church coupled with the rise of secular consciousness; and, third, the appearance of the painter Giotto, who set art on its modern path. A Slide Lecture is essential for understanding the radical nature of Giotto's artistic achievements. If circumstances allow, the instructor can organize a Discussion on the Late Middle Ages as a transition period, encouraging students to consider what has been gained and lost by the shift from medieval to modern times.

II. LECTURE OUTLINE

Non-Western Events

A. Historical Overview

1300–1500

  1. The "calamitous" fourteenth century
  2. Breakup of the unique culture of the High Middle Ages

B. Hard Times Come to Europe
  1. Ordeal by plague, famine, and war
    a. The plague
      (1) Its pattern and the death toll
      (2) Types of plague
      (3) Impact on culture
    b. Famine
      (1) Patterns
      (2) Impact on society

Indian famine, 1335–1342
Bubonic plague originates
  in India, 1332
Inca civilization,
  1000–1500
Bantu, Arab, and Indian
  cultures blend in
  Swahili civilization

c. War
   (1) Patterns
   (2) Impact on society and economics
2. Depopulation, rebellion, and industrialization
   a. Depopulation
      (1) Reasons
      (2) Impact on society and economics
   b. Rebellion
      (1) Patterns
      (2) Impact on society
   c. Industrialization
      (1) Textiles
      (2) The rise of the "putting out system"
      (3) New industries
3. The secular monarchies
   a. France
      (1) Wars with England and Burgundy
      (2) Rise of modern France
   b. England
      (1) Wars with France
      (2) The emergence of a strong Parliament
      (3) The Tudor dynasty
   c. The spread of the French-English ruling style
4. The papal monarchy
   a. An age of decline
      (1) Dislocation
         (a) The Avignon papacy
         (b) Impact on the church
      (2) Schism
         (a) The Great Schism
         (b) Impact on the church
         (c) How settled
      (3) The conciliar movement
   b. Restoration of papal power in about 1450

C. The Cultural Flowering of the Late Middle Ages
1. Breakdown of the medieval synthesis
2. Religion
   a. Absence of monastic reform
   b. Lay piety
      (1) The beguines and beghards
      (2) The *devotio moderna*
      (3) The flagellants
   c. Heresies
      (1) John Wycliffe
      (2) Jan Hus
   d. The Inquisition
   e. Witchcraft

on eastern African coast, 1100–1500
In India, Turkish Sultanate, Delhi, 1206–1526
In Japan, dual rule between the civil (ornamental) power of the emperor and the military (actual) power of the Shogun, 1192–1867; Muromachi Period (Ashikaga Shogunate), 1392–1572; rise of daimyo ("Great Names"), 1300–1500
Muberak (1316–1320), last of the Khilji rulers of Delhi
Gharzi Khan, Sultan of Delhi, in 1320 became first of the Tughlak dynasty
The Aztecs found Mexico City in 1327
Civil War in Japan against Hojo regents
Tamerlaine begins conquest of Asia in 1363
In China, Mongol (Yüan) dynasty, 1279–1368; Ming dynasty, 1368–1644
Egypt ruled by Mameluke Sultans, former Turkish slaves, 1250–1517

3. Theology, philosophy, and science
   a. The *via antiqua* versus the *via moderna*
      (1) The attack on Thomism after the death of Thomas Aquinas
      (2) The followers of Thomas Aquinas: the *via antiqua*
         (a) John Duns Scotus
         (b) Failure in the short run
      (3) The opponents of Thomas Aquinas: the *via moderna*
         (a) William of Ockham
         (b) Victory in the short run
   b. Developments in science
      (1) High Gothic forerunners
         (a) Robert Grosseteste
         (b) Roger Bacon
      (2) Nicholas Oresme
4. Literature
   a. Forces transforming literature
      (1) Rising literacy and shift to vernacular
      (2) The invention of movable type
   b. Northern Italian literature
      (1) Italian city-states in transition
      (2) Francesco Petrarch
         (a) A dedicated Classicist
         (b) *Secretum, My Secret*
      (3) Giovanni Boccaccio
         (a) A representative of the new secular age
         (b) *The Decameron*
   c. English literature
      (1) Evolution of common language
      (2) William Langland
      (3) Geoffrey Chaucer
         (a) Representative of the new secular age
         (b) *The Canterbury Tales*
5. Art and architecture
   a. Characteristics of the Late Gothic style
   b. Late Gothic architecture
      (1) The Flamboyant style on the continent
      (2) The Perpendicular style in England
      (3) The Italian Gothic
   c. Late Gothic sculpture
      (1) Italy
         (a) Foreshadowing of the Renaissance
         (b) Giovanni Pisano

Chinese encyclopedia in 22,937 volumes, begun in 1403

Hafiz, Persian poet, d. 1389

Restoration of the Great Wall of China, 1368
Development of Middle and Upper Mississippi phases of Mound Builders, North America, after 1400
Great Temple of the Dragon, Peking, 1420
The Golden Pavilion (Kiukakuji), Kyoto, 1397

                (2)   Burgundy
                      (a)   The Burgundian setting
                      (b)   Claus Sluter
            d.   Late Gothic painting and the rise of
                 new trends
                (1)   Radical changes
                (2)   Illuminated manuscripts
                      (a)   Secular influences
                      (b)   The Limbourg brothers
                (3)   New trends in Italy   Ni Tsan, Chinese poet
                      (a)   Giotto   and painter,
                      (b)   The new style   1301–1374
                (4)   Flemish painting
                      (a)   The Burgundian setting
                      (b)   Characteristics
                      (c)   Jan van Eyck

   D.   The Legacy of the Late Middle Ages

III. LEARNING OBJECTIVES

To learn:

1.   The calamities that occurred in the fourteenth century and the impact they had on society and culture

2.   To recognize visually Late Gothic art and architecture and to identify their leading characteristics

3.   To understand the foundations of the modern world that were laid in this period

4.   To trace the decline of the papacy from its pinnacle of power and prestige in 1200 to its nadir during the Great Schism, ended in 1417

5.   The lay movements and heresies that arose at the same time as the decline in the prestige and power of the papacy

6.   The theological struggle between the *via antiqua* and the *via moderna* and its outcome

7.   The significant developments in late medieval science

8.   The highlights of late medieval literature, especially the writings of Petrarch, Boccaccio, and Chaucer

9.   Giotto's achievements and their significance for later painters

10.   The contributions of the Flemish painters

11.   Historic "firsts" of the Late Middle Ages that became part of the Western tradition: the growth of the middle class as a dominant force in society, the emergence of secular rulers ready to curb church power, the birth of the tradition of common people challenging aristocratic control of culture and society, the release of a powerful secular spirit, and the invention of the technique of oil painting

12. The role of the Late Middle Ages in transmitting the heritage of earlier civilizations: continuing development of vernacular literature, separating Greco-Roman philosophy from Christian theology, freeing the practice of painting from its bondage to architecture, making painting the leading artistic medium, and reviving the realistic tradition in painting that stretched back to ancient Greece

IV. SUGGESTIONS FOR FILMS

Art Portrays a Changing World: Gothic to Early Renaissance. Alemann Films, 17 min., color.

Chaucer's England. Encyclopedia Britannica, 30 min., color.

Faith and Fear. CRM/McGraw-Hill, 40 min., color [Reaction to the Black Death].

Giotto and the Pre-Renaissance. Universal Educational and Visual Arts, 47 min., color.

Joan of Arc. Learning Corporation of America, 26 min., color.

Medieval England: the Peasants' Revolt. Learning Corporation of America, 31 min., color.

V. SUGGESTIONS FOR FURTHER READING

Becker, M. B. *Civility and Society in Western Europe, 1300–1600.* Bloomington: Indiana University Press, 1988.

DuBoulay, F.R.H. *An Age of Ambition: English Society in the Late Middle Ages.* London: Nelson, 1970.

Duby, G. *History of Medieval Art, 980–1440.* New ed. New York: Skira/Rizzoli, 1986.

Mâle, E. *Religious Art in France: The Late Middle Ages: a Study of Medieval Iconography and its Sources.* Translated by M. Mathews. Princeton: Princeton University Press, 1986.

Mollat, M. *The Popular Revolutions of the Late Middle Ages.* Translated by A. L. Lytton-Sells. London: Allen & Unwin, 1973.

Snyder, J. *Medieval Art: Painting-Sculpture-Architecture, 4th–14th Century.* New York: Abrams, 1989.

Swaan, W. *The Late Middle Ages: Art and Architecture from 1350 to the Advent of the Renaissance.* London: P. Elek, 1977.

VI. TERMS FOR IDENTIFICATION

devotio moderna	Flamboyant
via antiqua	Perpendicular
via moderna	fan vault
Late Gothic style	Italo-Byzantine

VII. DISCUSSION/ESSAY QUESTIONS

1. What natural and human calamities occurred during the fourteenth century? Discuss the impact of these misfortunes on society and culture.
2. In what way were the foundations of the modern world laid in the Late Middle Ages?
3. Describe the decline of the church and especially its ruling hierarchy, the papacy, during the Late Middle Ages. How did this religious decline affect the age's culture and society?
4. Discuss the issues and personalities involved in the theological struggle between the *via antiqua* and the *via moderna*. What was the outcome of this theological controversy? What was the significance of this controversy for the future?
5. Discuss medieval contributions to science.
6. How was literature being changed by new forces in the Late Middle Ages? Show specifically how those forces affected the works of the Italian writers Petrarch and Boccaccio and the English writers Langland and Chaucer.
7. Identify the characteristics of Late Gothic architecture. Take a building from this period and show how it embodies this style.
8. Identify the characteristics of Late Gothic sculpture. Choose a work by Pisano or Sluter and show how it expresses this style.
9. In what way did Giotto "rescue and restore" painting in the fourteenth century? Compare and contrast a painting by Giotto with one by his contemporary Cimabue in order to demonstrate the nature of Giotto's achievement.
10. Discuss the contributions of Burgundian artists in the fifteenth century, concentrating on the works of the Limbourg brothers, Jan van Eyck, and Claus Sluter.
11. What is the most significant legacy of the Late Middle Ages to the modern world? Explain.

VIII. MULTIPLE-CHOICE QUESTIONS

1. Which development signaled the breakup of the High Middle Age's unique blend of the spiritual with
   the secular?
   a. warfare among the rival Christian states of Europe
   b. separation of theology and philosophy
   c. decline in the power and prestige of the church
   * d. all of the above (p. 243)

2. A fourteenth-century calamity was:
   a. the onset of the plague
   b. an extended period of economic depression
   c. an era of urban riots and peasant unrest
   * d. all of the above (p. 243)

3. The "Black Death" of the fourteenth century was:
   a. AIDS
   b. tuberculosis
   * c. bubonic plague (p. 245)
   d. smallpox

4. As a result of the devastating plague, the leading image in late medieval art and literature became:
   * a. the Dance of Death (p. 245)
   b. the Final Judgment
   c. the Garden of Eden
   d. the Fountain of Youth

5. Who tried to carve out a "middle kingdom" between France and Germany?
   a. the Kings of England
 * b. the Dukes of Burgundy (p. 245)
   c. the Counts of Champagne
   d. the Ottoman Turks

6. A consequence of the demographic crisis of the fourteenth century was:
   a. a sharp decrease in the density of the rural population
   b. the rise of new economic centers in Bohemia, Poland, Hungary, Scandinavia, and Portugal
   c. the decline of manorialism in western Europe
 * d. all of the above (p. 246)

7. An important technological innovation in the Late Middle Ages was:
   a. the wheel
   b. the steam engine
 * c. movable type (p. 246)
   d. all of the above

8. The Hundred Years' War was fought between:
 * a. France and England (p. 246)
   b. Italy and Germany
   c. Spain and Portugal
   d. the Netherlands and Scandinavia

9. The court of the Burgundian dukes was located in:
   a. Amsterdam
   b. Paris
   c. Brussels
 * d. Dijon (p. 247)

10. How were England and France similar in 1500?
    a. Each had a national assembly that represented various interests.
    b. Each had a strong centralized government.
    c. Each had an efficient national bureaucracy.
 * d. all of the above (p. 247)

11. During most of the fourteenth century the popes ruled the church from:
    a. Rome
 * b. Avignon (p. 247)
    c. Milan
    d. Madrid

12. Papal power in the Late Middle Ages was weakened by:
    a. the Avignonese papacy
    b. the Great Schism
    c. the conciliar movement
 * d. all of the above (p. 248)

13. What was the Great Schism?
 * a. the 40-year period when there were two and sometimes three popes, each claiming papal authority (p. 248)
    b. the 70-year period when the popes ruled from Avignon
    c. the split in the church when the Orthodox separated from the Roman Catholics
    d. the division in the church between Protestants and Catholics, started by Martin Luther

14. Late medieval religion was characterized by all of these EXCEPT:
    a. the rise of lay piety
  * b. the development of new monastic orders (p. 248–249)
    c. the emergence of new heresies
    d. the spread of anticlerical feelings

15. An example of lay piety in the late medieval church was:
    a. the beguines and beghards
    b. the Brethren and Sisters of the Common Life
    c. the Friends of God
  * d. all of the above (pp. 248–249)

16. John Wycliffe:
    a. advocated the abolition of church property
    b. urged the subservience of the church to the state
    c. denied papal authority
  * d. all of the above (pp. 249–250)

17. This medieval religious heresy became a vehicle for Czech nationalism:
    a. the Wycliffite
  * b. the Hussite (p. 250)
    c. the Waldensian
    d. the Albigensian

18. All are correct for the Inquisition EXCEPT:
    a. It was a church court.
  * b. It was founded to deal with the Wycliffite heresy. (p. 250)
    c. It flourished mainly in Spain and Italy.
    d. It was used to rid the church of heresy and witchcraft.

19. In late medieval theology, the *via antiqua:*
    a. supported the beliefs of Thomas Aquinas
    b. urged that faith and reason be combined in order to reach divine truth
    c. was championed by Duns Scotus
  * d. all of the above (pp. 250–251)

20. In late medieval theology, the *via moderna:*
    a. urged the combination of faith and reason
    b. ignored reason altogether and concentrated on faith
  * c. advocated the complete separation of faith and reason (p. 250)
    d. supported the system of Thomas Aquinas

21. The leading advocate of the *via moderna* was:
    a. John Wycliffe
    b. Duns Scotus
  * c. William of Ockham (pp. 250–251)
    d. Robert Grosseteste

22. Ockham's contribution to philosophy was that he:
    a. originated a closely reasoned style of argument called Ockham's razor
    b. helped to separate theology and philosophy
    c. contributed to the triumph of Nominalism in the universities
  * d. all of the above (p. 251)

23. This medieval thinker pioneered the experimental system in science:
* a. Roger Bacon (p. 251)
   b. William of Ockham
   c. Duns Scotus
   d. Nicholas Oresme

24. This late medieval thinker questioned the then-prevailing view that the earth did not move:
   a. Jan Hus
   b. William of Ockham
   c. Duns Scotus
* d. Nicholas Oresme (p. 251)

25. A change in literature during the Late Middle Ages occurred because:
   a. The invention of movable type gave birth to printed books.
   b. Vernacular literature began to replace literature written in Latin.
   c. The rich middle class started to supplant the nobility as audience and patrons.
* d. all of the above (pp. 251–252)

26. The inventor of movable type was:
   a. Lorenzo Valla
   b. Pico della Mirandola
   c. Nicholas Oresme
* d. Johann Gutenberg (p. 252)

27. Petrarch and Boccaccio were both citizens of:
   a. Rome
   b. Venice
* c. Florence (p. 252)
   d. Milan

28. Petrarch's *My Secret* has all these aspects EXCEPT:
   a. It is written in the form of a dialogue.
   b. It has a religious theme.
   c. It features a conversation between St. Augustine and Petrarch.
* d. It was originally composed in Latin. (p. 252)

29. The plague had this impact on medieval culture:
   a. It gave rise to the flagellants.
   b. It provided the setting for *The Decameron*.
   c. It led to the image of the Danse Macabre.
* d. all of the above (pp. 249, 253, and caption for Fig. 10.2)

30. The author of *The Decameron* was:
   a. Petrarch
* b. Boccaccio (p. 253)
   c. Langland
   d. Chaucer

31. *The Decameron* helped bring into existence:
   a. the modern novel
* b. the modern short story (p. 253)
   c. the modern verse-drama
   d. the modern comic play

32. The most original developments in late medieval literature occurred in:
    a. France and western Germany
    b. Scandinavia and eastern Europe
  * c. England and northern Italy (p. 252)
    d. Spain and southern Italy

33. This work reflected the social tensions caused by the 1381 Peasants' Revolt:
    a. Petrarch's *My Secret*
    b. Boccaccio's *Decameron*
  * c. Langland's *Vision of Piers Plowman* (p. 253)
    d. Chaucer's *Canterbury Tales*

34. Chaucer's poetry was written for:
  * a. the royal court of the king of England (p. 253)
    b. London's rich middle class
    c. the noble court of the Duke of Norfolk
    d. the ecclesiastical court of the Archbishop of Canterbury

35. The poetry of Chaucer, a commoner, caused him to be honored by being:
    a. elevated to the nobility
    b. made a member of the Order of the Garter
  * c. buried in Westminster Abbey (p. 253)
    d. all of the above

36. What is the setting for *The Canterbury Tales*?
    a. a castle outside Canterbury
  * b. a pilgrimage to Canterbury (p. 253)
    c. a harem at Canterbury
    d. a monastery at Canterbury

37. In literary form, Chaucer's *Canterbury Tales* most closely resembles:
  * a. Boccaccio's *Decameron* (p. 253)
    b. Petrarch's *My Secret*
    c. Langland's *Vision of Piers Plowman*
    d. Dante's *Divine Comedy*

38. Chaucer's Canterbury pilgrims:
    a. are drawn exclusively from the upper classes
    b. are drawn exclusively from the lower classes
  * c. represent all walks of medieval society (p. 253)
    d. represent idealized portraits of medieval types

39. Which type of tale was included in Chaucer's *Canterbury Tales*?
    a. fabliau
    b. romance
    c. beast fable
  * d. all of the above (p. 253)

40. The Wife of Bath is a famous character in:
    a. Petrarch's *My Secret*
    b. Boccaccio's *Decameron*
    c. Langland's *Vision of Piers Plowman*
  * d. Chaucer's *Canterbury Tales* (p. 253)

41. The hallmark of Late Gothic builders was:
    a. to return to the basics of the Gothic style
    b. to treat in a balanced manner the Gothic style's fundamental elements
    * c. to push the Gothic style to extravagant limits (p. 254)
    d. to continue the aesthetic goals of the High Gothic style

42. Late Gothic architecture was characterized by:
    a. ever greater heights for buildings
    b. elaborate decoration
    c. delicate, lacy details
    * d. all of the above (p. 254)

43. Late Gothic architecture in France culminated in the:
    * a. Flamboyant style (p. 254)
    b. Perpendicular style
    c. Exuberant style
    d. Vertical style

44. Late Gothic architecture in England is called:
    a. the Flamboyant style
    * b. the Perpendicular style (p. 254)
    c. the Exuberant style
    d. the Vertical style

45. A unique feature of England's Late Gothic architecture was:
    a. calligraphic ornamentation
    * b. fan vaulting (p. 254)
    c. circular towers
    d. all of the above

46. Late Gothic sculpture and painting was characterized by:
    a. athletic bodies
    * b. willowy, swaying bodies (p. 254)
    c. abstract designs
    d. primitive effects

47. This artwork was commissioned by a person or persons associated with the Dukes of Burgundy:
    a. Sluter, *The Well of Moses*
    b. the Limbourg brothers, *Très Riches Heures du Duc de Berry*
    c. van Eyck, *Arnolfini Wedding Portrait*
    * d. all of the above (pp. 259, 260, 265)

48. This artist turned painting in a new direction, one that led to the Renaissance:
    a. the Limbourg brothers
    b. Cimabue
    * c. Giotto (p. 261)
    d. Jan van Eyck

49. What was Giotto's achievement in painting?
    a. a three-dimensional art
    b. full expression of human emotions
    c. naturalistic treatment of figures
    * d. all of the above (p. 261)

50. Fifteenth-century Flemish art was primarily concerned with:
 * a. symbolic realism (p. 264)
    b. psychological truth
    c. abstract purity
    d. idealized perfection

11

THE EARLY RENAISSANCE
Return to Classical Roots
1400–1494

I. TEACHING STRATEGIES AND SUGGESTIONS

The teacher can begin the section on the Early Renaissance with a Standard Lecture using either the Diffusion or the Pattern of Change approach to show the connections and discontinuities between this first modern period and the Middle Ages. At the same time, a general survey can be made between these two cultural periods, contrasting the religious, corporate-minded Middle Ages with the secular, individualistic Renaissance. Because the nature of the Renaissance is such a hotly debated topic, the instructor may want to help students sort through the rival interpretations summarized in the textbook; these interpretations can also be used as the basis for a more general discussion on the nature of historical writing, such as what motivates historians and why they do not always agree.

The teacher will be able to use fifteenth-century Italy as a Case Study to show the interrelationship of politics, diplomacy, economics and war—a recurring theme in history. The Reflections/Connections model will work well in illustrating that in Early Renaissance Florence the brilliant developments in the arts were directly tied to political changes, economic prosperity, and ambitious families.

Various paths may be followed in the lectures on Early Renaissance intellectual and artistic developments. The Pattern of Change model can be applied to the arts and ideas by tracing their evolution over the century. Innovations in education can be contrasted with medieval education, using the Comparison/Contrast approach. The arts can be illustrated with visual aids—slides, films or both—and should probably be presented as an evolution in techniques, local traditions, and generational differences while underscoring the revival of Greco-Roman Classicism. The instructor might want to use the "Great Individual" argument in discussing the lives and contributions of such key figures as Donatello, Brunelleschi, or Leonardo da Vinci. A final lecture can deal with two topics: first, using a Spirit of the Age approach, the underlying unity of the cultural developments in the Early Renaissance; and, second, using a Diffusion approach, the impact that this age had on subsequent periods, including our own.

II. LECTURE OUTLINE

	Non-Western Events
A. The Renaissance: Schools of Interpretation	*1400–1494*
1. Burckhardt and his critics	Middle and Upper
2. Phases of the Renaissance	Mississippi phases
	of Mound Builders, 1400
B. Early Renaissance History and Institutions	Timur, Mongol leader,
1. Italian city-states during the Early	invades Turkey, 1402
Renaissance	Mughal Dynasty in
a. Wars, alliances, treaties	India, 1483–*ca.* 1750

        b. Trade and commerce
        c. The role of the family
    2. Florence, the center of the Renaissance
        a. Phases of governments
        b. The Medici family
    3. The resurgent papacy, 1450–1500
        a. Popes caught up in pursuit of power
        b. Patrons of Renaissance culture
        c. Three powerful popes

C. The Spirit and Style of the Early
    Renaissance
    1. Humanism, scholarship, and
        schooling
        a. Humanistic studies
            (1) Textual criticism
            (2) Civic humanism
        b. Educational reform and curriculum
    2. Thought and philosophy
        a. Platonism in Florence
            (1) Ficino
            (2) Pico della Mirandola
        b. Relation to Classicism
    3. Architecture, sculpture, and painting
        a. Artistic ideals and innovations
            (1) Classical influences
            (2) Late medieval influences
            (3) Types of perspectives
            (4) Secular values in art
        b. Architecture
            (1) Brunelleschi
            (2) Alberti
        c. Sculpture
            (1) Donatello
            (2) Ghiberti
        d. Painting
            (1) Changes and innovations in
                 painting
            (2) Masaccio
            (3) Fra Angelico
            (4) Piero della Francesca
            (5) Botticelli
            (6) Leonardo da Vinci
    4. Music
        a. Influences on Renaissance music
        b. The leading composers
            (1) John Dunstable
            (2) Josquin des Prez

D. The Legacy of the Early Renaissance

West African
    civilizations,
    1400–1470
Aztecs expand empire in
    Mexico, 1427
Portuguese slave trade
    in west Africa, 1441

Inca rule founded in Peru
    1438
End of Byzantine Empire,
    and Constantinople
    becomes capital of
    the Ottoman Empire,
    1453
Ivan III of Moscow weds
    Sophia Paleologus, the
    niece of the last
    Byzantine emperor, 1472

Sultan Mohammed II's
    mosque in
    Constantinople, 1463
Tomb of Timur in
    Samarkand, 1406
Great Temple of the
    Dragon, Peking, 1420
Jamma Musjid Mosque of
    Husain, Jaunpur, 1438
Santa Sophia church
    converted into a
    mosque, 1453

III. LEARNING OBJECTIVES

To learn:

1. The various schools of interpretation of the Renaissance

2. The phases of fifteenth-century Italian politics and diplomacy

3. The phases of Italian economic trends during the fifteenth century

4. The role of Florence as the center of the Early Renaissance

5. The impact of the Medici family in Florentine history

6. The nature of the Renaissance papacy, its leaders, and their contributions

7. The characteristics of the Early Renaissance

8. The characteristics and evolution of Renaissance humanism

9. The development of Renaissance scholarship and learning, including its leaders and their contributions

10. The characteristics of Early Renaissance architecture, including the chief architects, their innovations, examples of their works, and their influence

11. The nature of Early Renaissance sculpture, including its origins, the major sculptors, and their influence

12. The characteristics of Early Renaissance painting and its impact on later styles, with references to specific painters and their innovations

13. To compare and contrast selected works of Early Renaissance architecture or sculpture or painting, noting the artists, what influenced them, and their contributions

14. The changes in music—types of works and new techniques and other innovations

15. The cultural changes in the areas of the arts and how these changes, including the revival of Classicism, affected the arts until modern times

16. Historic "firsts" of Early Renaissance civilization that became part of the Western tradition: textual criticism and realistic painting based on mathematical perspective

17. The role of Early Renaissance civilization in transmitting the heritage of earlier civilizations: rediscovering Classical art styles and redefining them, reviving Greco-Roman humanism and restoring it to the primary place in the educational curriculum, reinvigorating humanistic studies, freeing painting and sculpture from their tutelage to architecture in imitation of the Classical tradition, and making skepticism a central part of the consciousness of the educated elite as had been characteristic of ancient Greece and Rome

IV. SUGGESTIONS FOR FILMS

Civilisation: Man the Measure of All Things. Time-Life, 52 min., color.

I, Leonardo da Vinci. McGraw-Hill, 52 min., color.

Renaissance: Its Beginnings in Italy. Encyclopedia Britannica, 26 min., black and white.

Renaissance and Resurrection. ABC News, 55 min., color.

The Spirit of the Renaissance. Encyclopedia Britannica, 31 min., color.

V. SUGGESTIONS FOR LISTENING

The Castle of Fair Welcome. [15th-century courtly songs]. The Gothic Voices. Hyperion CDA-66194.

Josquin des Prez. *La Deploration sur la mort de Johannes Ockeghem.* New London Chamber Choir. Amon Ra CDSAR-24.

————. *Missa Gaudeamus.* Capella Cordina. Lyr. 7265.

Guillaume Dufay. *Hymns (with Introductory Gregorian Chants from the Cambrai Antiphonal).* Schola Hungarica. Hungaroton HCD-12951.

John Dunstable. *Motets.* Hilliard Ensemble. Angel CDC-49002.

————. *Sacred and Secular Music.* Ambrosian Singers. EA S-36E.

Medieval English Music [from the 14th and 15th centuries]. Hilliard (Vocal Ensemble). Harmonia Mundi HMA-190.1153.

VI. SUGGESTIONS FOR FURTHER READING

Burke, P. *Culture and Society in Renaissance Italy 1420–1540.* New York: Scribner, 1972.

Gilmore, M. P. *The World of Humanism, 1453–1517.* New York: Harper Torchbooks, 1952.

Goldthwaite, R. A. *The Building of Renaissance Florence: An Economic and Social History.* Baltimore: Johns Hopkins University Press, 1980.

Jensen, D. *Renaissance Europe: Ages of Recovery and Reconciliation.* Lexington, Mass.: D. C. Heath, 1981.

Klopisch-Zuber, C. *Women, Family and Ritual in Renaissance Italy.* Chicago: University of Chicago Press, 1985.

Mattingly, G., ed. *Renaissance Profiles.* New York: Harper Torchbooks, 1961.

Rice, E. F. *The Foundations of Early Modern Europe, 1460–1559.* New York: Norton, 1970.

VII. TERMS FOR IDENTIFICATION

Renaissance
studia humanitatis
Neo-Platonism
Early Renaissance style
perspective

vanishing point
pilaster
relief
chiaroscuro
sfumato
a capella

VIII. DISCUSSION/ESSAY QUESTIONS

1. Discuss the various schools of interpretation of the Renaissance. Which is the most valid? Explain.
2. Trace military and diplomatic developments in the Italian peninsula from 1400 to 1494. What impact did these events have on society and culture?
3. What changes occurred in the Italian economy during the fifteenth century? Describe the social impact of these changes.
4. Summarize the major stages of Florentine political history from 1300 to 1494 and discuss the Medici family's role in events.
5. Identify three Early Renaissance popes and explain their contributions to this cultural movement.
6. What were the intellectual characteristics of the Early Renaissance? How did these ideas manifest themselves in painting, sculpture, architecture, and literature?
7. What is meant by "humanistic studies"? What are its origins? How did this new learning take root in Italy?
8. Was there a radical break between the Early Renaissance and the Middle Ages? Explain your answer.
9. What influence did fifth-century B.C. Athens have on fifteenth-century Florence?
10. Discuss the impact of Neo-Platonism on the Italian Renaissance. Who was the major voice of this movement? What were his contributions?
11. "Pico della Mirandola is the personification of Early Renaissance thought and life." Write a defense of this cultural generalization.
12. How did Brunelleschi change the direction of architecture during the Early Renaissance? Use one of his buildings in your discussion.
13. Explain the role of Classical ideals in Alberti's aesthetic code.
14. Show how Donatello used Classicism to revive sculpture in the Early Renaissance.
15. Discuss the contributions of the painter Masaccio to the Early Renaissance, and use at least one of his works in your essay to illustrate his innovations.
16. What was Botticelli's contribution to Early Renaissance painting? Compare and contrast his style with that of Masaccio.
17. How is Leonardo da Vinci the ideal "Renaissance Man"?
18. What brought about the changes that led to Renaissance music? Was interest in Classicism involved? Who are the leading composers of the Early Renaissance, and what are their contributions?
19. Are you a "child of the Renaissance"? Explain your answer.

IX. MULTIPLE-CHOICE QUESTIONS

1. Historians of the Renaissance:
   a. agree about the general nature of the movement
   b. agree that the movement made a complete break with the Middle Ages
   * c. have recently concluded that it was a very complex cultural movement with attendant social and political changes (p. 273)
   d. accept Burckhardt's interpretation

2. The Peace of Lodi signed in 1454:
   a. was forced on the Italian city-states by the papacy
   b. brought on several decades of peace in the peninsula
   c. created a balance of power among the city-states
   * d. b and c but not a (p. 274)

3. The most significant consequence of Renaissance warfare was:
   a. the introduction of cannon
   b. the use of mercenary soldiers
   c. the creation of alliances
   * d. the development of diplomacy as an alternative to war (pp. 275–276)

4. The center of the Early Renaissance was:
   a. Venice
   b. Rome
   * c. Florence (pp. 277–278)
   d. Siena

5. The Medici family in Florence can be described as:
   a. a family that used its wealth to back the pope
   * b. a family with a keen political sense and a love of the arts (pp. 277–278)
   c. a family led by men more interested in war than in peace
   d. a family dominated by women more interested in peace than in war

6. At the height of the Florentine Renaissance the Medici family and Florence were controlled by:
   a. Cosimo
   * b. Lorenzo the Magnificent (p. 277)
   c. Piero
   d. Giuliano

7. The late fifteenth-century popes:
   a. started reforms to raise the morals of the clergy
   b. opposed the conciliar movement in order to keep power in their hands
   c. were patrons of Renaissance culture
   * d. b and c but not a (p. 278)

8. The Early Renaissance pope most attuned to Classical learning was:
   * a. Pius II (p. 278)
   b. Nicholas V
   c. Sixtus IV
   d. Alexander VI

9. The Early Renaissance borrowed from:
   a. medieval architecture
   b. Classical sculpture and architecture
   c. the writings of Petrarch
   * d. b and c but not a (pp. 278–279)

10. A major source of artistic patronage in the Early Renaissance was:
    a. the entrepreneurial nobility
    b. the wealthy middle class
    c. high church officials
    * d. all of the above (p. 279)

11. The Early Renaissance can best be described as:
    a. a period that made a complete break with the Middle Ages
    b. an age of great scientific advances
  * c. an age when emerging secular values threatened long-accepted religious beliefs (p. 279)
    d. a stagnant period with little cultural innovation

12. Early Renaissance scholars were especially attracted to:
    a. the philosophy of Aristotle
    b. the ideas of the Stoics
  * c. the writings of Cicero (p. 279)
    d. Greek dramas

13. The term *humanistic studies* means:
    a. practical guidelines for taking care of the socially disadvantaged
    b. Latin literature and language
    c. learned inquiries regarding morals, grammar, history, and rhetoric
  * d. b and c but not a (p. 279)

14. The earliest humanistic scholars were:
    a. educated in various languages, especially Latin and Greek
    b. trained to compare texts in order to determine their authenticity
    c. convinced that language and writing changed as society changed
  * d. all of the above (p. 279)

15. Textual criticism resulted in:
    a. the examination of many medieval documents
    b. the uncovering of forgeries, such as the Donation of Constantine
    c. the affirmation of an error-free Bible
  * d. a and b but not c (p.279)

16. The early humanists thought that an educated person:
  * a. ought to spend time in government service (p. 279)
    b. ought to live in isolation from society
    c. ought to live solely for personal pleasure
    d. ought to take orders in the church

17. One of the most successful Early Renaissance schools:
    a. was located in Florence
    b. was situated in Mantua
    c. stressed the importance of developing both the mind and the body
  * d. b and c but not a (p. 280)

18. The founding patron of the Platonic Academy in Florence was:
    a. Lorenzo ("the Magnificent") de' Medici
  * b. Cosimo de' Medici (p. 280)
    c. Giuiano de' Medici
    d. Piero de' Medici

19. Ficino, the leader of the Platonic Academy in Florence, contributed which of the following:
    a. a reconciliation of Platonic thought and Christian beliefs
    b. a new interpretation of the concept of love
    c. a furthering of individualism
  * d. all of the above (p. 280)

20. Early Renaissance Neo-Platonism:
    a. was essentially the same as late Roman Neo-Platonism
    b. could not be made compatible with Christianity
  * c. taught that Platonic love was superior to erotic love (p. 280)
    d. failed to capture the attention of many thinkers and artists

21. Pico della Mirandola was:
    a. a wealthy and persuasive young man
    b. a scholar trained in philosophy, language, and history
    c. a modest individual who refused to speak out for his beliefs
  * d. a and b but not c (p. 280)

22. Underlying much of Pico della Mirandola's writing was the assumption that:
    a. all people share basic truths
    b. Christianity is only part of a totality of truthful knowledge
    c. the individual is of primary importance
  * d. all of the above (pp. 280–281)

23. Central to the thought of Pico della Mirandola was the belief:
  * a. that individuals can raise or lower themselves (p. 281)
    b. that all human beings are morally imperfect
    c. that all human beings must trust in God's mercy for salvation
    d. b and c but not a

24. The visual arts of the Classical era had a strong impact on Early Renaissance Italy because:
  * a. In Italy the ruins of ancient Rome survived. (pp. 281–282)
    b. The Italians often traveled to nearby Greece for study.
    c. The church in Italy kept the Classical tradition alive.
    d. The Italian monasteries were built in a Classical style.

25. The visual arts of the Early Renaissance:
    a. followed the Classical ideals of balance and harmony
    b. encouraged the separation of sculpture and painting from architecture
    c. aimed for a realism similar to Classical art
  * d. all of the above (p. 292)

26. This fourteenth-century painter inspired Early Renaissance artists:
    a. Cimabue
  * b. Giotto (p. 282)
    c. Masaccio
    d. Pisano

27. Linear perspective:
    a. was developed by Brunelleschi
    b. is a way to create a sense of three dimensions on a two-dimensional surface
    c. is a mathematically based procedure for giving depth to painting
  * d. all of the above (p. 282)

28. A principle of Alberti's theory of art was:
    a. that painters are creators in much the same way as God
    b. that paintings should present a noble subject to enlighten the viewer
    c. that the Classical tradition is outdated and should be discarded
  * d. a and b but not c (pp. 282–283)

29. Brunelleschi's most lasting work is:
    a. the dome on the Santa Croce church
*   b. the dome on the Florentine cathedral (p. 284)
    c. the bell tower next to the Florentine cathedral
    d. the city hall of Florence

30. Brunelleschi solved the problem of the dome for the Florentine cathedral by:
    a. constructing a dome of wedged stones as in the Pantheon in Rome
*   b. employing sets of diagonal ribs based on the pointed arch (p. 284)
    c. using reinforced rods and a new type of concrete
    d. borrowing the Classical post-and-lintel model

31. In building the Pazzi chapel, Brunelleschi:
    a. put a Gothic spire on the chapel
    b. turned to Gothic sculpture for decorations
*   c. adhered to Classical design and proportions (pp. 284–285)
    d. copied the basilica floor plan

32. This architect also wrote a treatise on painting:
*   a. Alberti (p. 285)
    b. Masaccio
    c. Lorenzo Valla
    d. Ficino

33. Donatello can be described as a sculptor:
    a. influenced by late Gothic art
    b. indebted to realism
    c. influenced by Classical ideals
*   d. b and c but not a (p. 285)

34. In his sculpture of *David*, Donatello was able to:
    a. capture the sense of a young man in a pensive mood
    b. portray the latent power of the male figure
    c. imitate the mysticism of Gothic sculpture
*   d. a and b but not c (p. 286, caption for Fig. 11.10)

35. Donatello's *Gattamelata* is significant because it:
    a. is the first successful equestrian statue since Roman times
    b. expresses the boldness and power of an actual soldier
    c. portrays a realistic face, even to the point of ugliness
*   d. all of the above (p. 286, caption for Fig. 11.12)

36. Ghiberti's panels for the east doors of the Florentine Baptistery:
    a. show his debt to Classicism
    b. depict scenes from the Old Testament
    c. are known as the "Gates of Paradise"
*   d. all of the above (p. 288, caption for Fig. 11.14)

37. In comparison to the changes occurring in architecture and sculpture, those that transpired in painting were:
*   a. more radical and far reaching (p. 289)
    b. less innovative

c. about the same in terms of styles and techniques
d. less influential on later artistic developments

38. Masaccio's paintings were influenced by the perspectival experiments of:
    a. Botticelli, the painter
  * b. Brunelleschi, the architect (pp. 283–290)
    c. Pico della Mirandola, the philosopher
    d. Cosimo de' Medici, the patron of arts

39. In *The Holy Trinity*, Masaccio:
    a. used linear perspective
    b. painted a light source to illuminate the figures
    c. made the scene realistic despite its mystical subject
  * d. all of the above (p. 290)

40. An innovation in Masaccio's painting, *The Tribute Money*, was:
    a. depicting each figure in precise, mathematical space
    b. using chiaroscuro
    c. portraying human figures realistically, fully modeled in the round
  * d. all of the above (p. 290)

41. Fra Angelico painted with a sense of the new style as evidenced:
    a. by his treatment of realistic space
    b. by his ability to capture the feelings of his subjects
    c. by his use of drab colors
  * d. a and b but not c (pp. 290–291)

42. Piero della Francesca's painting of *The Flagellation*:
    a. was influenced by Fra Angelico
    b. uses linear perspective
    c. has an odd displacement of the human figures
  * d. all of the above (pp. 291–292)

43. Botticelli's early paintings were influenced by:
    a. Aristotelianism
  * b. Neo-Platonism (p. 292)
    c. Epicureanism
    d. Stoicism

44. In Botticelli's early paintings he sometimes:
    a. allegorized pagan myths
    b. introduced female nudes
    c. made Venus the subject of his art
  * d. all of the above (p. 292)

45. Which is correct for Botticelli's *The Birth of Venus?*
    a. It appears flattened with little sense of perspective.
    b. Its theme is the birth of love.
    c. It unites the images of water, baptism, and rebirth.
  * d. all of the above (p. 293, caption for Fig. 11.3)

46. Leonardo da Vinci is called a Renaissance Man because:
    a. He was a model of courtly behavior.
  * b. He was intellectually curious about nearly every subject. (pp. 294–295)

    c.   He was deeply influenced by Neo-Platonism.

    d.   He was a strict Classicist.

47. A distinctive aspect of Leonardo's *The Virgin of the Rocks* was:

    a.   its depiction of a religious subject in a very natural setting

    b.   its pyramidal arrangement of the three figures

    c.   its use of vibrant colors

*   d.   a and b but not c (p. 295)

48. Innovations in Early Renaissance music came from the influence of:

    a.   rediscovered Classical compositions

*   b.   the seductive harmonics of English music (p. 295)

    c.   the tradition of Byzantine music

    d.   the use of mathematical proportion in composition

49. The Franco-Netherlandish school of music is remembered for:

    a.   its blending of the English style with North European and Italian traditions

    b.   its Latin Masses

    c.   its a capella singing

*   d.   all of the above (p. 295)

50. Josquin des Prez, the composer:

    a.   matched the sounds with words of the texts

    b.   created expressive music

    c.   composed with major and minor scales

*   d.   all of the above (p. 295)

12

THE HIGH RENAISSANCE
AND EARLY MANNERISM
1494–1564

I. TEACHING STRATEGIES AND SUGGESTIONS

The period 1494–1564 embraces two different but related cultural styles: the High Renaissance and Early Mannerism. To introduce this complex period the instructor can begin with a Standard Lecture organized as a Historical Overview that stresses, in particular, the critical events of the 1520s as a watershed, including Luther's break with the church and the sack of Rome by the Emperor Charles V's troops. The instructor can then shift to a Comparison/Contrast approach to show the similarities and differences between the two cultural styles, the humanistically oriented High Renaissance and the antihumanistically inclined Early Mannerism. A Slide Lecture is indispensable for helping students to distinguish between the two styles in art and architecture. A Music Lecture would also be appropriate to show developments in music, although there was no radical break between Early Renaissance and High Renaissance music, and Mannerism as a term in music is meaningless.

Having established the identifying characteristics of the High Renaissance and Early Mannerism, the instructor can then focus on these contrasting styles. The best approach is to use the Reflections/Connections strategy in order to demonstrate how each cultural style was affected by its historical setting. The Pattern of Change method can also be used to illustrate how the High Renaissance evolved out of the Early Renaissance. In addition, the instructor should highlight the influence of ancient Classicism on the High Renaissance—the most Classical period in Western civilization after fifth-century B.C. Greece. For this purpose the instructor's best approach is the Diffusion model, setting forth how Classical ideals were reborn and revised in High Renaissance Italy.

A good way to conclude this unit is with a Case Study strategy. With this strategy the instructor can challenge the students to ponder the peculiar fate of Classical ages in Western culture; these ages—such as fifth-century B.C. Greece, early sixteenth-century Italy, and late eighteenth-century France—were remarkably brief in duration and were followed by periods of upheaval that sharply repudiated Classical ideals.

II LECTURE OUTLINE

Non-Western Events

A. Period of Genius
1. Key writers and artists
2. The High Renaissance
   a. Characteristics
   b. Centered in Rome
3. Early Mannerism
   a. Antihumanistic vision
   b. Characteristics

1494–1564
In China, Ming dynasty,
   1368–1644
In Japan, Sengoku
   ("Country at War")
   period, 1500–1600
West African empire of
   Songhay, 1464–1591

B. The Rise of the Modern Sovereign State
  1. Emergence of unified, stable kingdoms
    a. The balance of power principle
    b. Overview of France's and Spain's involvement in international affairs
      (1) Characteristics of a typical sovereign state
      (2) The decline of the feudal nobility
      (3) French and Spanish wars
  2. The struggle for Italy, 1494–1529
    a. Charles VIII's determining role
    b. Louis XII's and Francis I's continued aggression
    c. Charles V and the first Hapsburg-Valois war
    d. The independence of Venice
  3. Charles V and the Hapsburg Empire
    a. Hapsburg-Valois struggles, 1530–1559
    b. Charles V, a ruler of paradox and irony
    c. The lands of Charles V
    d. The abdication of Charles V and the division of the Hapsburg inheritance
      (1) Ferdinand and the German-Austrian Hapsburg territories
      (2) Philip and the Spanish-Hapsburg territories

C. Economic Expansion and Social Development
  1. Period of increasing prosperity
    a. Recovery from plague years
    b. Commercial shift from Mediterranean to the Atlantic coast
  2. Population growth
  3. Prosperity and attendant problems
  4. Delayed impact of new raw materials
  5. Introduction of slavery to Europe's colonies in the New World

D. From High Renaissance to Early Mannerism
  1. Definition of High Renaissance style
    a. Inspired by ancient Classicism
      (1) Humanistic
      (2) Secular
      (3) Idealistic
    b. Relationship to Early Renaissance style
    c. Central role of Rome and the popes
  2. Definition of Mannerism
    a. Inspired by the religious crisis and the sack of Rome, 1527

In India, Turkish Sultanate at Delhi, 1206–1526; Mughal Dynasty, 1483–ca. 1750

The Portuguese sailor Vasco da Gama discovers sea route to India, 1498

In Ottoman Empire, Selim I, 1512–1520; Suleiman "the Magnificent," 1520–1566

Cortes destroys Aztec state and takes control of Mexico, 1520

Portuguese settlement of Brazil, 1530

Pizarro executes the Inca of Peru, 1533

Buenos Aires founded by Pedro de Mendoza, 1536

Bogotá founded by Jiminez de Quesada, 1538

Antonio da Mota enters Japan as first European, 1542

Japanese pirates besiege Nanking, 1555

Spaniards build Manila, 1564

Slave trade in New World, 1509

Chocolate brought from Mexico to Spain, 1520

Silver mines of Potosi, Bolivia, discovered, 1544

Silver mines of Zaatear, Mexico, mined by Spanish, 1548

Tobacco in Spain, 1555

In Japan, No "dance-drama" at zenith, 1400–1600

Height of Ottoman civilization under Suleiman "the Magnificent," 1520–1566

b. Reaction against Classical ideals
   (1) Antihumanistic
   (2) Odd perspectives in painting
   (3) Twisted figures placed in bizarre poses in sculpture
   (4) Architecture that tries to surprise
   (5) Negative view of human nature

3. Literature
  a. High Renaissance
   (1) Castiglione and the court of Urbino
   (2) *The Book of the Courtier*
    (a) The ideal gentleman
    (b) The ideal lady
  b. Early Mannerism
   (1) Machiavelli and the republic of Florence
   (2) *The Prince*
    (a) Negative view of human nature
    (b) A treatise on "how to govern"

4. Painting
  a. Primary art form of the age
  b. Leonardo da Vinci
   (1) *The Last Supper*
    (a) Description
    (b) Characteristics
   (2) *Mona Lisa*
    (a) Description
    (b) Characteristics
  c. Michelangelo
   (1) His aesthetic creed
   (2) The Sistine Chapel ceiling frescoes: High Renaissance
    (a) Description
    (b) Characteristics
   (3) *The Last Judgment* fresco: Early Mannerist
    (a) Description
    (b) Characteristics
  d. Raphael
   (1) His aesthetic creed
   (2) *The School of Athens*
    (a) Description
    (b) Characteristics
   (3) *Sistine Madonna*
    (a) Description
    (b) Characteristics
  e. The Venetian School: Titian
   (1) The Venetian tradition
   (2) *Martyrdom of St. Lawrence*

Wang Yang-ming, Chinese philosopher, 1472–1528
University of Lima founded, 1551
An Aztec dictionary published, 1555
Hsu Wei's *Ching P'Ing Mei*, first classic Chinese novel, 1560

Kano Motonobu, Japanese court painter, 1476–1559
In Japan, Zen landscape painting at its height, fifteenth and sixteenth centuries

    (a) Description
    (b) Characteristics
   f. The School of Parma: Parmigianino
    (1) His aesthetic ideal
    (2) *Madonna with the Long Neck*
     (a) Description
     (b) Characteristics
 5. Sculpture
   a. Introduction: Michelangelo
   b. *Pietà*, 1498–1499, High Renaissance
    (1) Description
    (2) Characteristics
   c. *David*, High Renaissance
    (1) Description
    (2) Characteristics
   d. *Pietà*, before 1555, Early Mannerist
    (1) Description
    (2) Characteristics
 6. Architecture
   a. Bramante
    (1) His aesthetic code
    (2) The Tempietto, High Renaissance
     (a) Description
     (b) Characteristics
   b. Michelangelo
    (1) His aesthetic code
    (2) St. Peter's Basilica, High
      Renaissance
     (a) Description
     (b) Characteristics
   c. Andrea di Pietro, called Palladio
    (1) Aesthetic code
    (2) The Villa Capra, or the Villa
      Rotonda—Early Mannerist
     (a) Description
     (b) Characteristics
 7. Music
   a. Josquin des Prez and the High
     Renaissance musical style
   b. Adrian Willaert
   c. The invention of families of
     instruments called consorts

Suleiman's Mosque in
Constantinople,
1550–1556

E. The Legacy of the High Renaissance and Early
Mannerism

III. LEARNING OBJECTIVES

To learn:

1. The leading characteristics of the High Renaissance and Early Mannerism and to distinguish
   between the two cultural and artistic styles

2. The prominent role played by Classicism in the High Renaissance and Early Mannerism

3. How the High Renaissance and Early Mannerism reflected their historic settings

4. The determining role played by events of the 1520s in shaping the Mannerist outlook

5. The sources of the Hapsburg-Valois wars

6. The dominant control exercised by France and Spain over international affairs in this period

7. The pivotal part played by the popes in the High Renaissance

8. That Venice, of all Italy's states, remained free of foreign control or influence after 1530

9. That a commercial revolution shifted economic power from the Mediterranean to Europe's North Atlantic coast in this period

10. The achievements of Machiavelli and Castiglione in literature

11. The major contributions in painting of Leonardo, Michelangelo, Raphael, Titian, and Parmigianino

12. The major achievements in architecture of Michelangelo and Palladio

13. The characteristics of the High Renaissance musical style and the achievements of its leading composers, Josquin des Prez and Adrian Willaert

14. The historic "firsts" of the High Renaissance and Early Mannerism that became part of the Western tradition: the golden age of European painting, sculpture, and architecture; the beginning of modern political thought; the origins of the modern secular state; the birth of etiquette for ladies and gentlemen; and the rise of the belief that free expression is both a social and a private good

15. The role of the High Renaissance and Early Mannerism in transmitting the heritage of the past: reviving and updating Classical ideals in the High Renaissance arts and humanities; pushing Classical principles in new and unorthodox directions while continuing to copy Classical forms in Early Mannerism; and persisting in the trend to secularism that had begun in the Late Middle Ages

IV. SUGGESTIONS FOR FILMS

Civilisation: The Hero as Artist, BBC/Time-Life, 52 min., color.

I, Leonardo da Vinci. McGraw-Hill, 52 min., color.

Michelangelo: The Last Giant. McGraw-Hill, 68 min., color.

Michelangelo: The Medici Chapel. West, 22 min., color.

Music and Art: Italy and Music and the Court: The German Court of Maximilian I (Music and the Renaissance Series). Indiana University, 30 min. each, black and white.

V. SUGGESTIONS FOR LISTENING

Josquin des Prez. *Chansons.* Ensemble Clement Janequin & Ensemble les Eléments. Harmonia Mundi HMC-901279

———. *Mass, "Hercules Dux Ferraiae."* New London Chamber Choir. Amon Ra CDSAR-24.

———. *Motets.* Chapelle Royale Chorus. Harmonia Mundi HM-901243.

———. *Missa, "La sol fa re mi."* The Tallis Scholars. Gimell CDGIM-009.

Music in the Age of Leonardo da Vinci. Ensemble Claude-Gervaise. Musica Viva MVCD-1022.

Adrian Willaert. *Motets.* Boston Camerata Motet Chorus. Elektra/Nonesuch H-71345.

VI. SUGGESTIONS FOR FURTHER READING

Koenigsberger, H. G., Mosse, G. L., and Bowler, G. G. *Europe in the Sixteenth Century.* 2nd ed. London: New York: Longman, 1989.

Mellafe, R. *Negro Slavery in Latin America.* Translated by J.W.S. Judge. Berkeley: University of California Press, 1975.

Mitchell, B. *Rome in the High Renaissance: The Age of Leo X.* Norman: University of Oklahoma Press, 1973.

Pope-Hennessy, J. W. *Italian High Renaissance and Baroque Sculpture.* Oxford: Phaidon, 1986.

Reese, G. *The New Grove High Renaissance Masters: Josquin, Palestrina, Lassus, Byrd, Victoria.* New York: Norton, 1984.

Skinner, Q. *Machiavelli.* New York: Hill and Wang, 1981.

Smart, A. *The Renaissance and Mannerism in Northern Europe and Spain.* New York: Harcourt Brace Jovanovich, 1972.

Woodhouse, J. R. *Baldesar Castiglione: A Reassessment of The Courtier.* Edinburgh: Edinburgh University Press, 1978.

VII. TERMS FOR IDENTIFICATION

High Renaissance	Pietà
Mannerism	scenographic
machiavellianism	consort
putti	

VIII. DISCUSSION/ESSAY QUESTIONS

1. Compare and contrast the High Renaissance and Early Mannerism as cultural styles.
2. Show how Machiavelli's *Prince* and Castiglione's *Book of the Courtier* embody the styles of the High Renaissance and Early Mannerism, respectively.

3. Discuss the different roles played by Classicism in the High Renaissance and Early Mannerism.
4. What were some of Michelangelo's contributions to painting, sculpture, and architecture? Show how his genius helped to define both the High Renaissance and Early Mannerism.
5. What were the causes of the Hapsburg-Valois wars, and what was the final outcome of this bloody struggle?
6. How did historic events in the 1520s contribute to the rise of Mannerism?
7. Compare and contrast the architectural ideal of Michelangelo with that of Palladio.
8. Describe the sound of High Renaissance music. Who were the leading composers in this style, and what were some of their principal achievements?
9. Select a painting, a sculpture, and a building from both the High Renaissance and Early Mannerism and compare and contrast them, with the goal of setting forth the distinguishing characteristics of these two artistic styles.
10. What was the single most important development in this period? Explain.

IX. MULTIPLE-CHOICE QUESTIONS

1. The cultural center of the High Renaissance was:
* a. Rome (p. 299)
  b. Florence
  c. Venice
  d. Parma

2. The leading patrons of the High Renaissance were:
  a. the rich middle class
* b. the popes (p. 299)
  c. the nobles
  d. the monks and nuns

3. Which Classical ideal was revived and revised in the High Renaissance?
  a. rational design
  b. beauty
  c. simplicity
* d. all of the above (p. 299)

4. The High Renaissance begins with:
  a. the Peace of Lodi
* b. the invasion of Northern Italy by France's king, Charles VIII (p. 299)
  c. the death of Leonardo da Vinci
  d. the Treaty of Cambrai

5. A political development between 1494 and 1564 is:
  a. the emergence of the modern sovereign state
  b. the birth of the concept of the balance of power
  c. France's and Spain's domination of continental affairs
* d. all of the above (p. 299)

6. Between 1494 and 1564 Europe's international political life was dominated by:
  a. England and the Netherlands
* b. France and Spain (p. 300)
  c. Italy and Greece
  d. Scandinavia and Russia

7. What was a consequence of the sack of Rome in 1527?
   a. It cast doubt on Rome's ability to control Italy.
   b. It ended papal patronage of the arts for almost a decade.
   c. It contributed to the rise of Mannerism.
 * d. all of the above (pp. 301–302)

8. Which Italian state maintained its independence from foreigners throughout the 1500s?
 * a. Venice (p. 302)
   b. Florence
   c. Rome
   d. all of the above

9. A cause of the Valois-Hapsburg wars was:
   a. The Valois kings felt encircled by Hapsburg power.
   b. The Hapsburgs thought the French king stood in the way of their dream of a united Christendom.
   c. Each state wanted to maintain the balance of power.
 * d. all of the above (p. 303)

10. Which treaty finally brought the Hapsburg-Valois wars to a close?
    a. the Peace of Lodi
    b. the Treaty of Cambrai
 * c. the Treaty of Cateau-Cambrésis (p. 303)
    d. the Peace of Augsburg

11. Charles V's territories included all of these EXCEPT:
    a. Spain and Austria
    b. Burgundy and the Low Countries
    c. most of South and Central America
 * d. Scandinavia and Finland (p. 303)

12. On Charles V's abdication his vast holdings were:
    a. inherited by his son Philip
 * b. divided between his brother (the German-Austrian inheritance) and his son (the Spanish territories) (p. 304)
    c. parceled out among a wide number of enemies
    d. taken over by the Valois dynasty

13. Between 1494 and 1564 a revolution occurred that shifted the center of commerce from the Mediterranean to:
    a. the Black Sea
 * b. the Atlantic coast (p. 304)
    c. the Baltic Sea
    d. the German Rhineland

14. Which is a socioeconomic development in this period?
    a. The importation of South American gold and silver fueled an upward price revolution.
    b. Europeans established slavery in their colonies in the New World.
    c. The opening phase of commercial capitalism laid the foundation for Europe's future economic expansion.
 * d. all of the above (pp. 304–305)

15. The High Renaissance style cultivated the image of:
*   a. heroism (p. 305)
    b. piety
    c. suffering
    d. all of the above

16. High Renaissance literature was based on:
    a. the concept that life has a basic secular purpose
    b. the ideal that human nature is inherently rational and good
    c. the belief that social values are created by people of good sense
*   d. all of the above (p. 306)

17. The Mannerist viewpoint was anti-Classical in its:
    a. belief that human nature is weak or evil
    b. rejection of the principle that art should imitate nature
    c. support for an art of odd perspectives that called attention to the artist's technical effects
*   d. all of the above (p. 306)

18. The Classical principle of idealism may be seen in:
    a. the body of David in Michelangelo's sculpture of that name
    b. the portrait of the gentleman and lady in Castiglione's *Book of the Courtier*
    c. the treatment of space in Raphael's *School of Athens*
*   d. all of the above (pp. 307, 315, 318)

19. The subject of Castiglione's *Book of the Courtier* is:
    a. diplomacy
*   b. etiquette (p. 306)
    c. aesthetics
    d. love

20. Castiglione's model courtier was:
    a. educated in the humanities
    b. skilled in horsemanship and swordplay
    c. trained in painting and sculpture
*   d. all of the above (p. 307)

21. Castiglione's model lady was described as:
    a. a good mother
    b. an excellent housekeeper
*   c. a charming hostess (p. 307)
    d. all of the above

22. Castiglione argued that in social relations:
    a. Men and women should be ruled by Platonic love.
    b. Women should be educated equally with men.
    c. Women should be kept on a pedestal as the civilizing influence on men.
*   d. all of the above (p. 307)

23. "Machiavellianism" means:
    a. "Handsome is as handsome does."
*   b. "The end justifies any means." (p. 308)
    c. "Love God and do as you please."
    d. "Still waters run deep."

24. Machiavelli dedicated *The Prince* to this ruler, who he hoped would become his patron:
    a. Cesare Borgia, the illegitimate son of Pope Alexander VI
    b. Leo X, the Medici pope
* c. the Medici prince who governed Florence (p. 308)
    d. Charles V, the Holy Roman emperor

25. Machiavelli's *Prince* reflected the author's:
* a. anguish at Italy's domination by foreigners (p. 308)
    b. experience as a courtier of Charles V, Holy Roman emperor
    c. background as a Venetian official
    d. all of the above

26. Machiavelli's political advice to rulers was to:
    a. follow the Bible in the conduct of government
* b. practice conscious duplicity in all matters (p. 308)
    c. be virtuous and upright in all relationships
    d. all of the above

27. This writer laid the foundation for modern political theory:
    a. Castiglione
* b. Machiavelli (p. 307)
    c. Palladio
    d. Aretino

28. This Classical value was evident in High Renaissance painting:
    a. harmonious colors
    b. serene faces
    c. realistic space and perspectives
* d. all of the above (p. 308)

29. An Early Mannerist painting was:
    a. Leonardo's *Mona Lisa*
    b. Michelangelo's *Creation of Adam*
* c. Parmigianino's *Madonna with the Long Neck* (p. 316)
    d. Raphael's *Sistine Madonna*

30. Which is a Classical aspect of Leonardo's *Last Supper?*
    a. the realistic space and perspective
    b. the balanced composition with six disciples flanking Jesus
    c. the restrained expression of emotions
* d. all of the above (pp. 308–309)

31. The subjects of Michelangelo's Sistine Chapel ceiling frescoes were based on:
    a. biblical narrative
    b. Neo-Platonist phiiosophy
    c. Classical allusions
* d. all of the above (pp. 311–312)

32. A Neo-Platonic influence on Michelangelo's Sistine chapel ceiling frescoes was:
    a. the portrayal of the pagan sibyls
    b. the use of geometric shapes
    c. the depiction of Adam half-awakened and reaching to God
* d. all of the above (p. 312 and caption for Fig. 12.7)

33. A Mannerist effect in Michelangelo's *Last Judgment* fresco was:
    a. the elongated bodies with heads reduced in size
    b. the expressive faces
    c. a chaotic surface appearance with bodies swirling around the central image of Jesus
    * d. all of the above (p. 314)

34. Raphael is acknowledged as the supreme painter of:
    a. psychological truth
    * b. ordered space (p. 315)
    c. scientific accuracy
    d. expressive faces

35. Which High Renaissance master painted a likeness of Castiglione, author of *The Book of the Courtier?*
    a. Leonardo da Vinci
    b. Michelangelo
    * c. Raphael (p. 316)
    d. Titian

36. Venetian art was famous for its tradition of:
    a. sensual surfaces
    b. rich colors
    c. theatrical lighting
    * d. all of the above (p. 316)

37. The outstanding Venetian painter between 1494 and 1564 was:
    a. Correggio
    * b. Titian (p. 316)
    c. Parmigianino
    d. Caravaggio

38. What is the subject of a "pietà" scene?
    * a. the Virgin Mary and the dead Christ (p. 317)
    b. the crucifixion of Jesus flanked by two other crucified persons
    c. the birth of Jesus with angels and shepherds
    d. the journey of Jesus into Jerusalem, riding a donkey

39. A Classical aspect of Michelangelo's statue of *David* was:
    a. the graceful contrapposto
    b. the heroic nudity
    c. the athletic, muscular body
    * d. all of the above (p. 318)

40. The founder of High Renaissance architecture was:
    * a. Bramante (p. 320)
    b. Leonardo da Vinci
    c. Raphael
    d. Alberti

41. Bramante's Tempietto, or Little Temple, expresses this Classical ideal:
    a. Ornamentation is restricted to a few architectural details.
    b. Its proportions are computed using ancient mathematical formulas.
    c. It functions like a work of sculpture, being placed on a pedestal with steps.
    * d. all of the above (p. 320)

42. Michelangelo's outstanding architectural monument is:
    a. the plan of the Tempietto, Rome
  * b. the dome of St. Peter's Basilica, Rome (p. 321)
    c. the dome of the Florentine cathedral
    d. the Villa Capra, or the Villa Rotonda

43. What unifying agent was used by Michelangelo to give a harmonious appearance to the exterior of St. Peter's Basilica?
    a. stained glass windows
    b. flying buttresses
  * c. Corinthian columns (p. 321)
    d. statues of saints

44. What is the basic plan of the Villa Rotonda?
    a. a Roman rectilinear temple raised on a pedestal
  * b. four identical wings surrounding a domed central area (p. 322)
    c. a meandering shape determined by the eccentric topography of the site
    d. a circular temple covered by a dome

45. Who designed the Villa Capra, or Villa Rotonda?
    a. Alberti
    b. Bramante
    c. Michelangelo
  * d. Palladio (p. 321)

46. Which national school dominated High Renaissance music?
    a. the English
  * b. the Franco-Netherlandish (p. 322)
    c. the Italian
    d. the German

47. What musical innovation occurred in the High Renaissance?
    a. the birth of the orchestra
    b. the development of opera
  * c. the invention of families of instruments, called consorts (pp. 323–324)
    d. the emergence of the piano

48. High Renaissance music was characterized by:
    a. multiple voices, usually two to six
    b. a capella singing
    c. clearly sung texts
  * d. all of the above (p. 322)

49. The dominant composer in this period was:
  * a. Josquin des Prez (p. 322)
    b. Gabrieli
    c. Willaert
    d. Byrd

50. An enduring legacy of this period to the Western tradition was:
    a. a new code of etiquette for gentlemen and ladies
    b. the belief that free expression is both a private and a social good
    c. the beginning of the modern secular state
  * d. all of the above (p. 324)

13

THE RELIGIOUS REFORMATIONS, NORTHERN HUMANISM, AND LATE MANNERISM
1500–1603

I. TEACHING STRATEGIES AND SUGGESTIONS

The instructor, again, can choose from several teaching models—the Comparison/Contrast, the Diffusion, or the Spirit of the Age—for the first lecture. The Comparison/Contrast approach is probably the most effective, comparing and contrasting the Italian Renaissance with northern humanism and then contrasting the Italian Renaissance with the religious reformations. Other teaching strategies can include using the Pattern of Change model to explain the causes of the Protestant and Catholic reformations and the Case Study approach to draw parallels between the Reformation and later reform movements, such as the Enlightenment or the American Great Awakening.

The teacher can apply the Comparison/Contrast model in analyzing the topics of the Protestant order and the Counter–Reformation. The Diffusion model can then be used to treat Northern Humanism, showing how it grew out of Italian Humanism and took on its own characteristics; the Reflections/Connections approach can establish the historical framework for the presentations on literature, thought, the arts, and music. A Music Lecture can illustrate the music of this period, particularly the music of Palestrina, the central figure of the Catholic Reformation. Late Mannerism in literature and the visual arts can be explained with the Pattern of Change strategy, showing the evolution from Early Mannerism into more and more complex forms. Another option is to teach Late Mannerism using the Reflections/Connections model to demonstrate how the values and beliefs of the Reformation, the Counter-Reformation, and Northern Humanism were expressed in literature and the visual arts.

II. LECTURE OUTLINE

Non-Western Events

A. Overview of Mannerism and the Religious Reformations

1500–1603

B. The Breakup of Christendom: Causes of the Religious Reformations
  1. Conditions in the church
  2. Situation in Germany
  3. The Protestant order
     a. Luther's revolt

Abkar, the Great Mughal, *1556–1605*
Ashikaga Shogunate, in Japan, 1392–1568; "Country at War" Period, *1500–1600;* Tokugawa

            (1) The Ninety-Five Theses
            (2) Luther's beliefs
            (3) Social and political implications
                 of Luther's revolt
            (4) Luther's Bible
        b. The reforms of John Calvin
            (1) Calvin's beliefs
            (2) Impact of Calvin's beliefs
                 on society
            (3) The success of Calvinism
        c. The reform of the English Church
    4. The Counter-Reformation
        a. The reformed papacy
        b. New monastic orders
        c. The Council of Trent
    5. Warfare as a response to
        religious dissent, 1520–1603
        a. Charles V and the Religious Peace of Augsburg
        b. Spain's bid for power

C. Northern Humanism
    1. Characteristics of the movement
    2. Northern Humanists: Rabelais and
        Erasmus

D. Late Mannerism
    1. Characteristics of Late Mannerism
    2. Mannerist literature in
        northern Europe
        a. Michel de Montaigne
        b. William Shakespeare, *Hamlet*
    3. Mannerist painting in
        northern Europe
        a. Albrecht Dürer
        b. Mathias Grünewald
        c. Pieter Bruegel the Elder
    4. Mannerist painting in Spain:
        El Greco
    5. Italian culture, 1564–1603
        a. Late Mannerist painting
            in Italy: Tintoretto
        b. Late sixteenth-century music
            in Italy

E. The Legacy of the Religious Reformations,
    Northern Humanism, and Late Mannerism

Shogunate, 1603–1867
Growth of black
    slave trade in Africa,
    1500–1800
Suleiman I, the
    Magnificent, of
    Turkey
Spanish conquest of
    Mexico, 1522
Spanish conquest of
    Peru, 1537
Jesuit missionaries
    active in China and
    Japan, 1550–1650

Aztec dictionary
    published, 1555
Hsu Wei, *Ching P'Ing
    Mei,* first classic
    Chinese novel, 1560

Beginning of Kabuki
    theater in Japan
Osaka Castle in Japan,
    1583

III. LEARNING OBJECTIVES

To learn:

1. The causes of the Protestant Reformation

2. The political conditions in Germany and the Holy Roman Empire in the early sixteenth century

3. The major phases of the life of Martin Luther and the events in Germany during his early years

4. The basic beliefs and tenets of Lutheranism

5. The impact of Luther's revolt on social and political movements

6. The major phases of and influences on John Calvin's life

7. The basic beliefs and ideas of Calvinism

8. The impact of Calvinism on social and political developments

9. The causes of the rise of the Church of England

10. The results and impact of the religious changes in England

11. The causes of the Counter-Reformation

12. The leaders and contributions of the reformed papacy

13. The origins, development, and results of the founding of new Catholic monastic orders and, in particular, the Jesuits

14. The central issues of and their outcome at the Council of Trent

15. The major phases and results of the Wars of Religion

16. The characteristics of Northern Humanism, its literary leaders, and their contributions

17. The role played by Erasmus in Northern Humanism and the Protestant Reformation

18. The characteristics of Late Mannerist literature, its leading writers, and their contributions

19. The major phases of the life of William Shakespeare, his types of plays, and the themes and ideas in *Hamlet* that express the ideas of Mannerism

20. The nature of Late Mannerist painting, its major painters, and representative examples of this style

21. The nature of Italian culture in the late sixteenth century and representative examples as expressed in painting and music

22. The historic "firsts" of the age of the Reformations, northern humanism, and Late Mannerism that became part of the Western tradition: the end of the dream of a united European Christendom and the division of Europe between Protestantism and Roman Catholicism, the first European explorations and overseas colonies, beginning of the modern sovereign state and the rivalry among these new political entities, formulation of distinct cultural attitudes between Protestants and Roman Catholics, and the establishment of the commercial theater as a legitimate art form

23. The role of this age in transmitting the heritage of earlier ages: continuing the basic ideas and values of Renaissance humanism as modified by Northern Humanism, furthering the concept of the worth of the individual, making religious differences and preferences the basis of intolerance and persecutions, and adapting Renaissance styles in literature and the visual arts into Late Mannerism

IV. SUGGESTIONS FOR FILMS

Civilisation: Protest and Communication. Time-Life, 52 min., color.

John Calvin. University of Utah, Educational Media Center, 29 min., color.

Martin Luther and the Protestant Reformation. Time-Life, 30 min., black and white.

The Reformation. McGraw-Hill, 52 min., color.

The Reformation: Age of Revolt. Encyclopedia Britannica, 24 min., color.

V. SUGGESTION FOR MUSIC

Palestrina, Giovanni. *Missa de Beata Virgine.* Ugrin, Jeunesses Musicales Chorus. Hungaraton HCD-12921.

———. *Missa Papae Marcelli.* Phillips, The Tallis Scholars. Gimell CDGIM-339.

———. *Stabat Mater.* Brown, Pro Cantione Antiqua. MCA Classics MCAD-25191 (CD); MCAC-25191 (digital).

Shakespeare Songs and Consort Music. Deller Consort. Harmonia Mundi HMC-202; HMA-190.202 (CD).

VI. SUGGESTIONS FOR FURTHER READING

Bainton, R. *Erasmus of Christendom.* New York: Scribner's, 1969.

Bousma, W. *John Calvin.* Oxford: Oxford University Press, 1987.

Davis, R. *The Rise of the Atlantic Economies.* London: Weidenfeld and Nicolson, 1973.

Dickens, A. G. *Reformation and Society in Sixteenth Century Europe.* New York: Harcourt, Brace & World, 1966.

———. *The Counter-Reformation.* London: Thames and Hudson, 1968.

Elliott, J. H. *Europe Divided: 1559–1598.* New York: Harper Torchbooks, 1968.

Grimm, H. *The Reformation Era 1500–1650.* New York: Harper & Row, 1973.

Wright, A. D. *The Counter-Reformation.* New York: St. Martin's, 1984.

VII. IDENTIFICATIONS

Reformation	Jesuits
Counter-Reformation	Christian humanism
Lutheranism	revenge tragedy
Calvinism	Late Mannerism
Puritanism	madrigal
Anglicanism	

VIII. DISCUSSION/ESSAY QUESTIONS

1. Discuss the causes of the Protestant Reformation, noting the "internal" conditions of the church and the "external" situation in Germany.
2. In what ways did the life of Martin Luther contribute to his break with the Catholic church?
3. Show how the quarrel over indulgences triggered the Protestant Reformation.
4. Discuss the major beliefs of Lutheranism and note their impact on nonreligious issues.
5. Explain the basic ideas of Calvinism and show how they affected societies where large numbers of Calvinists were citizens.
6. What were the causes and major phases of the English Reformation?
7. Trace the Catholic church's response to the rise of Protestantism. How successful was the church in its early encounters with the new movement?
8. Discuss the origins and beliefs of the Society of Jesus.
9. How did the sixteenth-century reforms of the Catholic church lay the foundations for the church until the twentieth century?
10. Outline the major phases of warfare in the sixteenth century and explain their consequences for politics and culture.
11. What were the basic characteristics of Northern Humanism and how did it differ from Italian Humanism?
12. Why is Erasmus called the "prince of humanists"? Discuss his beliefs as they were manifested in his writings.
13. How are Montaigne and Shakespeare representative of Late Mannerist literature?
14. Discuss the phases of Shakespeare's life. How are his insights into human nature expressed in *Hamlet?*
15. Discuss the impact of the Protestant Reformation on north European painting and note the works of two artists affected by this movement.
16. How were the themes of Late Mannerism and the Protestant Reformation manifested in the painters in northern Europe?
17. Relate the impact of the Counter-Reformation on El Greco and discuss this impact as revealed in his paintings.
18. How did the Counter-Reformation affect Italian painting and music in the late sixteenth century?
19. Compare and contrast the religious reformations with the Renaissance.
20. How did the rise of the sovereign state affect politics, warfare, and culture in sixteenth-century Europe?
21. What were the long-range consequences of the religious reformations for European society and its values?
22. What were the most important legacies of Northern Humanism and Late Mannerism to the Western humanistic traditions?

IX. MULTIPLE-CHOICE QUESTIONS

1. During the sixteenth century Europe witnessed which of the following:
   a. the breakup of the Catholic church
   b. the establishment of Christendom
   c. the beginnings of sovereign nations
   * d. a and c but not b (p. 329)

2. As the Protestants and Catholics went their separate ways in the sixteenth century, they tended to rally around which of the following sets of leaders?
   a. Protestant King John and Catholic Queen Anne
   * b. Protestant Queen Elizabeth and Catholic Philip II (p. 329)
   c. Protestant King Henry VIII and Catholic Emperor Charles V
   d. Protestant Queen Mary and Catholic Philip II

3. The disintegration of the Catholic church can be attributed to which of these broader movements:
    a. the growing corruption within the church
    b. the impact of humanism and humanistic studies
    c. the rise of sovereign states
  * d. all of the above (p. 331)

4. Among the problems confronting the Catholic church were:
    a. the moral weakness of papal leadership
    b. the rise of anticlericalism
    c. the continued issues raised during the Great Schism
  * d. all of the above (p. 331)

5. The two European states that were beginning to free themselves from papal control at the beginning of the sixteenth century were:
    a. Spain and France
  * b. England and France (p. 331)
    c. England and Germany
    d. France and Germany

6. What best characterizes the conditions in Germany prior to the Protestant Reformation?
    a. The area was politically united but lacked a strong national leader.
  * b. Local princes resented the power of the church and its economic holdings in the area. (p. 343)
    c. The Holy Roman Emperor was supported by the local German princes.
    d. a and b but not c

7. The European leader who possessed much land but could not rule it effectively was:
  * a. Emperor Charles V (p. 331)
    b. Emperor Frederick of Saxony
    c. Queen Elizabeth
    d. Pope Julius II

8. Regarding the coming of the Protestant Reformation and the political situation in Europe, it happened when:
    a. The towns and the rural areas were at peace.
  * b. The new nation-states and church clashed. (p. 331)
    c. The feudal lords and the serfs were at odds.
    d. The towns and feudal lords fought one another.

9. The one event that upset Luther and ultimately launched the Protestant Reformation was:
    a. the collection of Peter's Pence in his town
    b. the appointing of the Bishop of Mainz by the local prince
  * c. the selling of indulgences in Germany (p. 331)
    d. the crowning of the Duke of Saxony by the Pope

10. An indulgence is defined as:
    a. a grant from the Pope for a Christian to indulge in sinful living
  * b. a pardon that reduced the time spent for doing penance (p. 331)
    c. the taking of the Holy Eucharist while in a state of sin
    d. the sale of a church office

11. Luther attacked the sale of indulgences in his:
  * a. Ninety-Five Theses (p. 331)
    b. *Address to the Christian Nobility of the German Nation*
    c. treatise on free will
    d. translation of the Bible

12. In his search for answers to his sense of sin, Luther finally found the solution through:
    a. the preachings of the local bishop
    * b. the biblical passage on the power of one's faith (p. 332)
    c. the forgiving quality of the clergy
    d. the use of the seven sacraments

13. Which of the following characterizes Luther's beliefs?
    a. The Bible was all that was necessary to gain Christian truths.
    b. Relics should not be worshiped.
    c. He rejected the concept of purgatory.
    * d. all of the above (p. 332)

14. The impact of Luther's revolt can be summarized as:
    a. having no effect outside of religious circles
    * b. giving hope to many of the lower classes that their plight might improve (pp. 333)
    c. inspiring monks to remain in monasteries and to purify their personal lives
    d. affecting the commercial community in most German towns

15. Central to John Calvin's beliefs was:
    a. the concept of free will
    b. the importance of relics
    * c. the doctrine of predestination (p. 334)
    d. the efficacy of the sacraments

16. Calvin's concept of predestination meant that:
    a. Each priest had the power to save his congregation.
    b. Every believer who took the sacraments was saved.
    * c. Only God knew who was saved or not saved. (p. 334)
    d. All Christians were predestined to die and go to purgatory.

17. Closely associated with Calvinism was the belief:
    a. that everyone who made money would end up in hell
    b. that hard work would result in worldly success
    c. that worldly success indicated that God approved of you
    * d. b and c but not a (p. 334)

18. Calvin's ideas attracted many followers in all of these countries EXCEPT:
    a. Scotland
    b. the Netherlands
    * c. Spain (p. 334)
    d. England

19. In England, the event that set off the Reformation was:
    a. the burning of Lutheran missionaries by Catholic priests
    * b. Henry VIII's desire to divorce Catherine (p. 334)
    c. Parliament's plan to confiscate church property
    d. the rumors of scandalous living among the monks and nuns

20. The Counter-Reformation was successful because of which of the following:
    a. the feeling among many Protestants that they had made an error in leaving the church and should return to Catholicism
    b. a line of vigorous and dedicated popes
    c. the rise of new monastic orders, such as the Jesuits
    * d. b and c but not a (pp. 335)

21. The success of the Society of Jesus can be explained, in part, by:
    a. the zeal and leadership of its founder, Loyola
    b. the dedication and discipline of its members
    c. the support given the order by the papacy
  * d. all of the above (p. 336)

22. The Council of Trent is remembered for its:
    a. willingness to compromise with the Protestants
    b. determination to rid the church of its worst abuses
    c. clarification and reaffirmation of dogma and rituals
  * d. b and c but not a (p. 336)

23. When the Protestants and Catholics failed to resolve their differences they:
    a. called on Greek Orthodox church leaders to help settle their disputes
  * b. turned to warfare and alliances (p. 337)
    c. declared a twenty-year truce
    d. decided that both sides could settle down and live in peace

24. In comparing Christian humanism with Renaissance thought, which of the following is correct?
    a. Both upheld rationalism and respected Classical literature.
    b. Both concentrated primarily on secular matters.
    c. Christian humanists were more concerned with religious issues.
  * d. a and c but not b (p. 338)

25. Christian humanists:
    a. were convinced that the early church was the model to be imitated
    b. felt that relics and sacred objects were overemphasized in ceremonies
    c. wanted to place Christ and his teachings at the center of their faith
  * d. all of the above (p. 338)

26. As part of their goals, the Christian humanists wanted to:
    a. establish schools for the urban classes
    b. work with the papacy and monks
  * c. make sure that the translations of early Christian writings were correct (p. 338)
    d. prove the correctness of papal policies

27. Who of the following was NOT a Northern Humanist:
    a. Rabelais
    b. Erasmus
  * c. Ignatius Loyola (pp. 336 and 338–339)
    d. Thomas More

28. In describing Erasmus's life, it can be said that:
    a. He lived the life of a devout and pious monk.
    b. He traveled to many royal and ecclesiastical courts.
    c. He was educated in both humanism and Christian thought.
  * d. b and c but not a (p. 338)

29. Erasmus, in his *Praise of Folly*, attempted to:
    a. defend the Catholic church against its critics
    b. satirize many individuals and institutions of his day
    c. expose much of the hypocrisy of the church
  * d. b and c but not a (p. 339)

30. The fate of Erasmus was:
    a. that he founded Protestantism
    *   b. that he alienated both the Catholics and the Protestants (p. 339)
    c. that in defending the Catholics he lost the support of the Protestants
    d. that he became a wandering scholar without credibility.

31. The issue that divided Erasmus and Luther was the:
    a. use and efficacy of the seven sacraments
    b. importance of the role of the clergy
    *   c. question of free will and predestination (p. 339)
    d. question of salvation and forgiveness of sin

32. In his *Essays*, Montaigne viewed the world and human nature:
    a. with an optimistic outlook, for he had faith in fellow human beings
    b. without any hope, since all humans were sinners
    *   c. with some hope for survival, but his skepticism prevented him from having too much faith (p. 340)
    d. through the eyes of conventional Christian beliefs

33. The English, under Elizabeth I, can be described as:
    a. enjoying a period of relative peace regarding religious differences
    b. being a nation beginning to find its national sense of identity
    c. reaching new heights in the verbal arts, in particular in the theater
    *   d. all of the above (pp. 335 and 340)

34. What was the state of the theater during the Middle Ages?
    a. It was popular throughout most of the period.
    b. It consisted largely of morality and mystery plays.
    c. It offered Christian messages to audiences.
    *   d. b and c but not a (pp. 340–341)

35. Shakespeare wrote which type of play?
    a. comedies
    b. tragedies
    c. historical plays
    *   d. all of the above (pp. 341–342)

36. What are the characteristics of a Renaissance revenge tragedy?
    a. It concentrates on a murder that must be avenged.
    b. It introduces a ghost who urges the revenge.
    c. It is filled with suspense and violence.
    *   d. all of the above (p. 342)

37. *Hamlet* is representative of Mannerist literature in which of the following ways?
    a. The main character Hamlet is seen from several different perspectives.
    b. The moody Hamlet often seems to change his personality.
    c. Hamlet seems to have a low opinion of himself and most of his fellow humans.
    *   d. all of the above (pp. 342)

38 What was the impact of the Protestant Reformation on painting and sculpture?
    a. The Protestants supported elaborately decorated churches.
    b. The arts suffered as many Protestants saw art as idol worship.
    c. Some works of art were destroyed as a result of the actions of Protestant zealots.
    *   d. b and c but not a (p. 342)

39. Albrecht Dürer, in his self-portraits, seemed to be:
    a. fully aware of his own importance
    b. bordering on the sacrilegious with his Christlike self-portraits
    c. rather mystical in his approach
  * d. all of the above (p. 343, caption for Fig. 13.9)

40. Besides paintings, Dürer also is known for his:
  * a. engravings (p. 343)
    b. sculptures
    c. bronze castings
    d. architectural designs

41. The themes of the *Isenheim Altarpiece* included which of the following?
    a. the symbols of the Christian faith, such as the sacrificial lamb
    b. the horror and anguish of the fate of Jesus
    c. the belief that humanity is basically good
  * d. a and b but not c (pp. 344–345)

42. Pieter Bruegel's paintings were:
    a. products of the Catholic Reformation
  * b. efforts to capture the ordinary lives of peasants (p. 345)
    c. works that reflected the values of the Renaissance
    d. judged to be lewd and immoral in his day

43. The most representative Mannerist artist in Spain who captured the spirit of the Catholic Reformation was:
    a. Velázquez
    b. Goya
  * c. El Greco (p. 346)
    d. Dali

44. The major influences on El Greco's paintings were:
    a. a Mannerist sensibility
    b. the works of Michelangelo
    c. the tradition of Venetian art
  * d. all of the above (p. 346)

45. A central characteristic of El Greco's painting style was:
    a. his ability to render landscapes that were true to life
  * b. his sense of mysticism and religious feeling (p. 346)
    c. his portrayal of human effort as a noble task
    d. a and c but not b

46. In his portraits El Greco seemed to:
    a. capture the personality of his subject
    b. often go beyond the surface and depict the real person
    c. flatter his subject
  * d. a and b but not c (p. 348)

47. The Council of Trent:
    a. affected the visual arts by decreeing that paintings should be simple and direct so the illiterate could understand them
    b. wanted music and the arts to be part of the church's efforts to win over the uneducated
    c. decreed that indecent paintings should be altered for modesty's sake
  * d. all of the above (p. 348)

48. Tintoretto, in his *Last Supper:*
    a. slavishly copied Leonardo da Vinci's arrangement of the figures
    b. wanted to emphasize the rationality of the Christian faith
  * c. appealed to human feelings, not to reason (p. 349, caption for Fig. 13.16)
    d. a and c but not b

49. As music evolved in the late sixteenth century:
    a. Sound began to dominate the words.
    b. The Catholic church decreed that music should emphasize the melodies.
  * c. It became more simple in many ways. (pp. 349–350)
    d. a and b but not c

50. What type of song was most expressive of late-sixteenth-century music?
    a. Gregorian chant
    b. *canzone*
    c. motet
  * d. madrigal (p. 350)

14

THE BAROQUE AGE
Glamour and Grandiosity, 1603–1715

I. TEACHING STRATEGIES AND SUGGESTIONS

The instructor can begin the Baroque Age with a Standard Lecture, using a Historical Overview to summarize the historical and cultural events that determined the shape of this glamorous epoch. The lecture should stress the central role played in continental politics and culture by Roman Catholic rulers and patrons, particularly the Italian popes and the French king Louis XIV, perhaps the most powerful Western monarch ever. The instructor can then adopt a Comparison/Contrast approach to show how political and cultural developments in Protestant Europe, notably in England and the Netherlands, differed from those in the Catholic world, though there were some similarities. It is necessary to describe these contrasting developments in some detail because from this background arose three variations on the international Baroque: the Florid Baroque, the French Baroque, and the Protestant Baroque.

The arts and architecture are the supreme expressions of Baroque taste; hence the best approach to the three separate and distinct manifestations of the Baroque style is through a series of Slide Lectures built around a Comparison/Contrast strategy. A film on the Baroque arts and architecture would also help students understand the nuances of this international style. The Comparison/Contrast strategy can also be employed to deal with Baroque literature, especially the works of Roman Catholic France and Protestant England. In addition, a Music Lecture can be used to introduce students to opera, a major innovation of the Baroque era, and to Bach and Handel, two Baroque composers who rank among the West's musical immortals.

A summary lecture will probably be needed to draw the diverse aspects of this sprawling age together. To this end the instructor can choose a Spirit of the Age approach to demonstrate the unity beneath the period's often tumultuous events. And that unifying idea can be expressed as follows: the Baroque writers and artists, sensing themselves adrift in an ever-changing universe, created a style that mirrored their age's expanding horizons and territorial expansion.

II. LECTURE OUTLINE

Non-Western Events

A. Brief Historical Overview
   1. Stylistic meaning
   2. Baroque *versus* Mannerism
   3. Turbulent events
   4. Scientific discoveries

B. Absolutism, Monarchy, and the Balance of Power

1603–1715
In India, Mughal
   Dynasty, 1483–ca. 1750
In China, Ming Dynasty,
   1368–1644; Manchu
   Dynasty, 1644–1912

In Japan, the Tokugawa
   Shogunate, 1603–1867;

1. Rise of absolutism
   a. The emergence of a system of sovereign states
   b. The five great military states and the balance of power
      (1) Kingship
      (2) Bureaucracies
      (3) Diplomacy and warfare
      (4) Standing armies
2. France: the supreme example of absolutism
   a. Henry IV
   b. Louis XIII
      (1) Cardinal Richelieu
      (2) Cardinal Mazarin
   c. Louis XIV
      (1) Public style and policies
      (2) Self-glorification
3. England: from monarchy to republic to limited monarchy
   a. James I
   b. Charles I and civil war
   c. The Commonwealth
   d. The Restoration: Charles II and James II
   e. Glorious Revolution: William and Mary
4. Warfare in the Baroque period: maintaining the balance of power
   a. Role of warfare in power configuration
   b. The Thirty Years' War, 1618–1648
      (1) Religious consequences
      (2) International consequences
      (3) The new role of France
   c. The wars of Louis XIV, 1665–1713
      (1) Summary of four wars
      (2) Results

C. The Baroque: Variations on an International Style
   1. Origins and development
      a. Meaning
      b. Variations
   2. The Florid Baroque
      a. The Council of Trent and the seventeenth-century popes
         (1) Dominance of religious values
         (2) The aesthetic program
      b. Architecture
         (1) The church of St. Peter's, Rome
            (a) Maderno's nave and façade
            (b) Bernini's colonnade
         (2) Impact of this style

Japanese isolation, 1637–1854
British East India Co. chartered, 1600
Maratha Confederacy in India, 1650–1760
Downfall of African kingdoms of Kongo and Ngola, 1665–1671
British Royal Africa Co. chartered, 1672
Portuguese dominance of African east coast city-states, 1505–1650
Growth of African slave trade, 1500–1800
Rise of Asante empire in Africa, based on Gold Coast trade, 1700–1750
Jesuit missionaries active in China and Japan, 1550–1650
Spaniards founded Santa Fe, New Mexico, 1605
English founded Jamestown, Virginia, 1607
Jesuit state of Paraguay established, 1608
Tea trade begins between China and Europe, 1609
In India, Jahangir 1605–1627; Shah Jahan 1627–1658; Aurangzeb 1658–1707

In 17th-century Japan, decline of daimyo class, revival of Shintoism
Mitsui family's trading and banking house founded, Japan, 1673

Shah Jahan builds Taj Mahal, 1632–1647
Golden Temple of the Sikhs, Amritsar, India, 17th century

c. Sculpture
   (1) Reintegration of sculpture with architecture
   (2) Bernini
       (a) Decorations for St. Peter's: the baldacchino
       (b) *The Ecstasy of St. Teresa*
d. Painting
   (1) Reintegration of painting with architecture
   (2) Caravaggio
       (a) Style characteristics
       (b) *The Martyrdom of St. Matthew*
   (3) The illusionistic ceiling fresco
       (a) Description
       (b) Pozzo, *Allegory of the Missionary Work of the Jesuits*
   (4) Velázquez
       (a) Style characteristics
       (b) *Las Meninas*, or *The Maids of Honor*
   (5) Rubens
       (a) Style characteristics
       (b) *The Landing of Marie de' Medici at Marseilles*

3. The French Baroque
   a. Definition of style
   b. Architecture
      (1) The patronage of Louis XIV
      (2) The redesign of Versailles Palace
   c. Painting
      (1) Influence of Classicism and Caravaggio
      (2) Poussin
          (a) Characteristics
          (b) *Et in Arcadia Ego*

4. The Protestant Baroque
   a. Painting
      (1) The setting in the Calvinist Netherlands
          (a) Rembrandt
          (b) Vermeer
      (2) The setting in Anglican England
          (a) Characteristics
          (b) Van Dyck
   b. Architecture
      (1) Characteristics
      (2) Wren

5. Literature
   a. Drama as enduring legacy
      (1) Drama and epic
      (2) Characteristics of the literary Baroque

Great Mosque at Lahore, late 17th century
Pagoda at Nikko, Japan, 1636
Edo (Tokyo) becomes capital of Tokugawa Shogunate after 1603

By 1600, more than 300,000 Christian converts in Japan; a Christian rebellion in 1637 led to a war in which the Christian communities were exterminated
In 1680, Emperor K'ang Hsi founds factories for development of art industries in China
In 1678, first chrysanthemums arrive in Holland from Japan

Tulsi Das, Hindu poet, 1532–1623
Poems of Basho (pseudonym of Matsuo Munefusa), 1644–1694,

    b. The French Baroque
      (1) Characteristics
      (2) Tragedy
        (a) Corneille
        (b) Racine
      (3) Comedy: Molière
    c. The English Baroque
      (1) The epic
      (2) Milton
        (a) Background
        (b) *Paradise Lost*

6. Music
    a. Trends
    b. The development of opera
      (1) Monteverdi and Italian opera
      (2) Popularization
      (3) French opera: Lully
    c. Climax of Baroque music, after 1715
      (1) Bach in Germany
      (2) Handel in England

D. The Legacy of the Age of the Baroque

III. LEARNING OBJECTIVES

To learn:

1. The major historical developments that occurred in the Baroque period and how they helped shape the dominant cultural style

2. The impact of the balance of power principle on international affairs in the Baroque period

3. The leading characteristics of secular monarchies in the seventeenth century

4. To trace the development of absolutism in France and the defining role played by Louis XIV in shaping the French Baroque

5. To trace the development of limited monarchy in England and the defining role played by England in shaping the Protestant Baroque

6. The characteristics of the variations on the Baroque style and how each reflected its historical setting, such as how the French Baroque reflected French court society, how the Florid Baroque reflected papal court circles, and how the Protestant Baroque reflected English and Dutch society

7. The role of the wars of Louis XIV in establishing the primacy of French culture on the continent

8. How the church of St. Peter's, Rome, expressed the Florid Baroque building style

9. The leading artists and architects of the Florid Baroque, the French Baroque, and the English Baroque—and their contributions

10. How Versailles Palace expressed the French Baroque building style

11. The characteristics, major figures, and chief literary genres of Baroque literature and the differences and similarities between the French and the English Baroque

12. The four chief trends operating in Baroque music

13. The reason that opera is the quintessential symbol of the Baroque

help popularize haiku poetry, Japan
In 1684, Takemoto Gidayu begins puppet theater "Joruri" in Tokyo
In 1686, *Shusse Kagekiyo*, famous puppet play by Monzaemon, performed in Tokyo

14. The sources and early developments of opera

15. The contributions of the Baroque composers Bach and Handel

16. The historic "firsts" of the Baroque Age that became part of the Western tradition: the system of great states governed by a balance of power, France and England's dominance of culture and politics, the concept and practice of "world war," mercantilism, the illusionistic ceiling fresco, opera, and oratorio

17. The role of the Baroque Age in transmitting the heritage of the past: redirecting Classical ideals into the grandiose and exuberant Baroque style; giving permanent stamp to the religious division of Westerners into Protestant and Catholic camps; bringing the monarchical tradition to its height in France; launching the trend toward rule by the people in the limited monarchy that developed in England; and carrying Western values to overseas colonies

IV. SUGGESTIONS FOR FILMS

The Age of Absolute Monarchs in Europe. Coronet, 14 min., black and white.

Bernini's Rome. Teaching Films: Indiana University, 30 min., black and white.

Civilisation: Grandeur and Obedience. 52 min., BBC/Time-Life, color.

Civilisation: The Light of Experience. BBC/Time-Life, 52 min., color.

Johann Sebastian Bach. International Film Bureau, 27 min., color.

The Restoration and the Glorious Revolution. Coronet, 11 min., color.

Rubens. International Film Bureau, 27 min., color.

The Sun King. Indiana University, 30 min., black and white.

Unquiet Land: Civil War in England. Universal Studio's Educational and Visual Arts Division, 25 min., black and white.

V. SUGGESTIONS FOR MUSIC

Bach, Johann Sebastian. *The Art of the Fugue.* Hill, harpsichord. Music & Arts CD-279.

————. *Bach's Greatest Hits.* Leonhardt Ensemble. Pro Arte CDM-801.

————. *Brandenburg Concerti (6).* Orchestra of the Age of Enlightenment. Virgin Classics VCD 7 90747-2.

Handel, George Frederic. *Giulio Cesare in Egitto.* Popp, Ludwig, Wunderlich, Nocker, Berry, Leitner, Bavarian Radio Symphony and Chorus. Melodram 37059.

————. *Messiah.* Te Kanawa, Gjevang, Lewis, Howell, Solti, Chicago Symphony and Chorus. London 414396-2 LH2 (cassette); 414396-2 LH2 (CD); 414396-1 (digital).

————. *Water Music: Suite.* Van Beinum, Concertgebouw Orchestra. Philips 420857-2 PM.

Monteverdi, Claudio. *Il Combattimento di Tancredi e Clorinda.* Clemencic, Clemencic Consort. Harmonia Mundi HUA-190.986.

———. *L'Incoronazione di Poppea.* Donath, Soderstrom, Berberian, Esswood, Harnoncourt, Vienna Concentus Musicus. Teldec 35247 ZC.

VI. SUGGESTIONS FOR FURTHER READING

Anthony, J. R. *The New Grove French Baroque Masters: Lully, Charpentier, Lalande, Couperin, Rameau.* London: Macmillan, 1986.

Berger, R. W. *In the Garden of the Sun King: Studies on the Park of Versailles Under Louis XIV.* Washington, D.C.: Dumbarton Oaks Research Library and Collection, 1985.

Grafton, A. *Defenders of the Text: The Traditions of Scholarship in an Age of Science, 1450–1800.* Cambridge, Mass: Harvard University Press, 1991.

Magnuson, T. *Rome in the Age of Bernini.* Atlantic Highlands, N.J.: Humanities Press, 1982.

Mainstone, M. *The Seventeenth Century.* Cambridge, England: Cambridge University Press, 1981.

Maiorino, G. *The Cornucopian Mind and the Baroque Unity of the Arts.* University Park: Pennsylvania State University Press, 1990.

Munck, T. *Seventeenth Century Europe: State, Conflict, and the Social Order in Europe, 1598–1700.* New York: St. Martin's, 1990.

Roston, M. *Milton and the Baroque.* Pittsburgh: University of Pittsburgh Press, 1980.

Skrine, P. *The Baroque: Literature and Culture in Seventeenth-Century Europe.* New York: Holmes & Meier, 1978.

VII. IDENTIFICATIONS

Baroque	Protestant Baroque style
Florid Baroque style	virtuoso
baldacchino	opera
illusionism	*bel canto*
French Baroque style	oratorio

VIII. DISCUSSION/ESSAY QUESTIONS

1. Identify the three variations on the international Baroque style, discuss their characteristics, and show how each style variation reflected its historical setting.
2. Discuss political developments in Europe during the Baroque Age, and show what impact they had on the evolution of the Baroque cultural style.
3. Compare and contrast political developments in England and France in the Baroque Age, and explain how they affected the distinctive cultural style of each country.
4. What influence did religion have on the Baroque style? What values in Protestantism and Catholicism made for different developments?

5. Explain the relationship of the Baroque style to the Renaissance style.
6. What Classical features and ideals survived in the Baroque style? Where was Classicism the strongest in Baroque culture? Why?
7. How did the Council of Trent affect the ideals of the Baroque arts and architecture?
8. Compare and contrast the Baroque buildings of St. Peter's, Rome, and Versailles Palace.
9. What new musical form developed in the Baroque period? Why is this new form so expressive of Baroque cultural values?
10. What were the basic trends in music during the Baroque period?
11. Compare and contrast the Florid Baroque painting styles of Rubens and Caravaggio.
12. Show how the Palace of Versailles is a fitting symbol of the French Baroque.
13. Discuss Baroque artistic developments in the Netherlands, and show how they were related to conditions in the Dutch, Calvinist republic.
14. What are the characteristics of Baroque literature? What literary forms flourished during the Baroque era? Compare and contrast literary developments in England and France during this period.
15. Who are the two best-known Baroque composers, and what are their major contributions to Western music?
16. What are the four chief legacies of the Baroque age to the Western tradition?

IX. MULTIPLE-CHOICE QUESTIONS

1. The term *baroque* probably derives from the Portuguese word *barocco* meaning:
* a. an irregular pearl (p. 353)
  b. a sinking boat
  c. a labyrinthine palace
  d. a concave mirror

2. The Baroque love of vast, expanding horizons reflected the seventeenth century's:
  a. new discoveries in astronomy
  b. race among the European states for overseas empires
  c. movement of Western peoples to the New World
* d. all of the above (p. 353)

3. European politics in the seventeenth century was characterized by all of these EXCEPT:
  a. a system of sovereign states
  b. a balance of power among England, France, Austria, Prussia, and Russia
* c. the Italian city-states as the center of political life (pp. 353–355)
  d. absolutist monarchies

4. The most spectacular advocate of Absolutism in the Baroque Age was:
  a. James I of England
* b. Louis XIV of France (pp. 354–355)
  c. Charles II of England
  d. Henry IV of France

5. A characteristic of seventeenth-century sovereign states was:
  a. bureaucracies staffed by university-trained career officials
  b. a permanent diplomatic corps
  c. a standing army funded from governmental revenues
* d. all of the above (p. 355)

6. The founder of the Bourbon dynasty in France was:
* a. Henry IV (p. 355)
  b. Louis XIII

    c.   Louis XIV
    d.   Louis XV

7. Louis XIV's reign was characterized by:
    a.   a glorification campaign of the ruler as the Sun King
    b.   intolerance toward religious minorities
    c.   rich patronage of the academies that were emerging at the time
*   d.   all of the above (pp. 356–357)

8. Louis XIV's economic policy was called:
    a.   *laissez faire*
*   b.   mercantilism (p. 357)
    c.   the guild system
    d.   capitalism

9. The founder of England's Stuart dynasty was:
*   a.   James I (p. 357)
    b.   Charles I
    c.   Charles II
    d.   James II

10. What caused monarchical power to be limited in early seventeenth-century England?
    a.   The nobility made common cause with middle-class members of parliament.
    b.   The parliament considered itself the king's partner in government.
    c.   Many in the Anglican majority shared the purifying zeal of the Calvinist minority.
*   d.   all of the above (p. 357)

11. During the course of the seventeenth century, England:
    a.   had a civil war that toppled the monarchy
    b.   became a short-lived republic called the Commonwealth
    c.   underwent a bloodless coup known as the Glorious Revolution
*   d.   all of the above (pp. 357)

12. By 1715 the principle that government should rest on the consent of the governed was successfully established in:
    a.   France
*   b.   England (pp. 357–358)
    c.   Prussia
    d.   all of the above

13. The Thirty Years' War was fought largely in:
    a.   France
    b.   Italy
*   c.   Germany (p. 358)
    d.   Bohemia

14. Which country profited most from the Thirty Years' War?
    a.   Germany
    b.   Brandenburg-Prussia
*   c.   France (p. 358)
    d.   Denmark

15. The War of the Spanish Succession:
    a. was the first of the "world war" type
    b. won England advantages that enabled it to become the world trade leader in the eighteenth century
    c. gave France the national boundaries that still exist today
  * d. all of the above (pp. 358–359)

16. The Baroque ideal was:
    a. repose
  * b. exuberance (p. 359)
    c. a single, static perspective
    d. a design complete in itself

17. The Florid Baroque:
  * a. was a product of the Counter-Reformation (p. 359)
    b. was aristocratic and courtly
    c. had a strong Classical dimension
    d. was centered in the Netherlands

18. The French Baroque:
    a. was dominated by Roman Catholic religious ideals and themes
  * b. followed strict rules of design (p. 359)
    c. was middle class and respectable
    d. was characterized by extravagance and profusion

19. The Protestant Baroque:
    a. was aristocratic and courtly
  * b. was simple and restrained (p. 360)
    c. was centered in Italy and Spain
    d. was dominated by Christian themes

20. The supreme expression of Florid Baroque architecture is:
    a. St. Paul's cathedral, London
    b. the Palace at Versailles
  * c. St. Peter's church, Rome (p. 360)
    d. Villa Rotondo, Vicenza

21. Bernini was either the architect or the sculptor of each of these EXCEPT:
    a. the colonnade for St. Peter's, Rome
    b. the baldacchino in St. Peter's, Rome
  * c. the Palace at Versailles (pp. 361–62)
    d. *The Ecstasy of St. Teresa*

22. A Baroque aspect of the colonnade for St. Peter's, Rome, is:
    a. the line of statues above the colonnade
    b. the curving arms of the colonnade
    c. the keyhole-shaped space of the colonnaded area
  * d. all of the above (p. 361)

23. Caravaggio's painting style is characterized by:
    a. antinaturalism
 * b. dramatic use of chiaroscuro (p. 364)
    c. simplicity
    d. serenity

24. A new art form in the Baroque era was:
    a. in art, the illusionistic ceiling fresco
    b. in music, the opera
    c. in music, the oratorio
 * d. all of the above (pp. 365, 376–378)

25. Pozzo's *Allegory of the Missionary Work of the Jesuits* illustrates the Baroque love of:
 * a. infinite space (p. 365)
    b. repose
    c. serenity
    d. antinaturalism

26. A Baroque theme in Velázquez's painting *Las Meninas,* or *The Maids of Honor,* is:
 * a. the interplay of space and illusion (p. 367)
    b. the love of infinite space
    c. the intersection of the supernatural and the natural
    d. all of the above

27. Rubens's paintings are known for their:
    a. disciplined order
 * b. ripe sensuality (p. 367)
    c. calm beauty
    d. domestic tranquility

28. Rubens was:
    a. official court painter to the French court
    b. influenced by Caravaggio's use of chiaroscuro and Titian's mastery of gorgeous color
    c. commissioned to paint a cycle of paintings glamorizing the life of Queen Marie de' Medici
 * d. all of the above (p. 367)

29. The dominant influence on the French Baroque was:
    a. Gothic civilization
 * b. Classical tradition (p. 368)
    c. Byzantine culture
    d. Christian doctrine

30. Versailles' decorations were intended to identify King Louis XIV with:
    a. Jesus Christ
    b. the Roman leader, Julius Caesar
 * c. the Greek god, Apollo (caption for Fig. 14.11)
    d. the French ruler, Charlemagne

31. Versailles Palace is Baroque in:
    a. the great size of the central structure
    b. the monumentality of the setting with support structures, all placed in a vast park
    c. the grandiose decorative plan
 * d. all of the above (p. 368)

32. The outstanding representative of French Baroque art is:
    a. Rubens
  * b. Poussin (p. 369)
    c. Vermeer
    d. Velázquez

33. Poussin's art is renowned for its:
  * a. detached style (p. 369)
    b. lively manner
    c. urban scenes
    d. middle-class values

34. The Netherlands in the seventeenth century was:
    a. ruled by a well-to-do middle class
    b. dominated by the sober values of the Calvinist religion
    c. regarded briefly as one of Europe's great powers
  * d. all of the above (p. 370)

35. Dutch art in the seventeenth century reflected:
    a. the sober values of the Calvinist religion
    b. the civic ideals of their society
    c. the fluctuations of the art market
  * d. all of the above (p. 370)

36. The outstanding artist of the Protestant Baroque is:
    a. Poussin
    b. Rubens
  * c. Rembrandt (p. 370)
    d. Van Dyck

37. Rembrandt's painting style was typified by all of these EXCEPT:
  * a. portrayal of figures modeled on ancient statuary (p. 371)
    b. use of dramatic chiaroscuro
    c. forceful expressiveness
    d. ability to depict the full range of human moods and emotions

38. The Dutch painter Vermeer specialized in:
    a. still lifes
    b. landscapes and seascapes
  * c. domestic genre scenes (p. 373)
    d. portraits

39. Painting in seventeenth-century England:
    a. reflected the fluctuation of the local art market
  * b. was controlled by the courtly but restrained taste of the aristocracy (p. 373)
    c. responded to the demands of middle-class patrons for a civic-minded art
    d. had religious themes as the dominant subject

40. The outstanding architect of the Protestant Baroque was:
    a. Maderno
    b. Bernini
    c. Hardouin-Mansart
  * d. Wren (p. 374)

41. The inspiration for the dome of St. Paul's cathedral, London, was:
   a.   the dome of the Pantheon, Rome
   b.   the dome of Santa Sophia, Constantinople
* c.   the dome of St. Peter's, Rome (p. 374)
   d.   the dome of San Vitale, Ravenna

42. Baroque literature had significant expressions in this literary genre:
   a.   tragedy
   b.   comedy
   c.   epic
* d.   all of the above (pp. 374–375)

43. The zenith of Baroque drama was reached:
   a.   at the papal court in Rome
* b.   at the court of King Louis XIV in Versailles (p. 375)
   c.   in the commercial theaters of Amsterdam in the Netherlands
   d.   at the court of King Charles II in London

44. French drama in the seventeenth century:
   a.   was expected to observe the unities of time, place, and action
   b.   was supposed to use elevated language and focus on universal problems
   c.   was controlled by strict rules laid down by the French Academy
* d.   all of the above (p. 375)

45. Racine's tragedies were NOT characterized by:
   a.   penetrating psychological insights
   b.   a study of sex as a motive for action
* c.   occasional comic scenes to give relief to the dramatic tension (pp. 375–376)
   d.   lofty language

46. Comic plays were the specialty of:
   a.   Racine
   b.   Corneille
* c.   Molière (p. 376)
   d.   Milton

47. The Baroque literary work *Paradise Lost* is:
* a.   a Christianized epic (p. 376)
   b.   a satirical epic based on a trivial episode in middle-class life
   c.   a continuation of Homer's *Odyssey*, picking up the story where the original work ended
   d.   a historical epic based on the English Civil War

48. A trend in seventeenth-century music was:
   a.   major or minor tonality as a central feature of music
   b.   exaggerated expressiveness
   c.   virtuoso performances
* d.   all of the above (p. 376)

49. The first great composer of opera was:
* a.   Monteverdi (p. 376)
   b.   Bach
   c.   Handel
   d.   Lully

50. An outstanding development in Baroque music was:
   a. the French operas of the Italian composer Lully
   b. the London operas of the German composer Handel
   c. the sacred music of Bach
 * d. all of the above (pp. 377–378)

15

THE BAROQUE AGE II
Revolutions in Scientific and Political Thought, 1600–1715

I. TEACHING STRATEGIES AND SUGGESTIONS

The instructor can introduce this second unit on the Baroque Age with a Standard Lecture blended with a Spirit of the Age approach, underscoring the distinguishing characteristics of the period's art styles as previously set forth in Chapter 14. This first lecture on Chapter 15 should emphasize two new revolutionary themes: radical changes in science and political theory. As background to these two revolutions, the teacher can employ one of several teaching models: the Diffusion, the Pattern of Change, the Comparison/Contrast, or, again, the Spirit of the Age. The instructor should then concentrate on the Scientific Revolution, since its changes had the more radical impact of the two intellectual movements. Perhaps the best approach is to do a comparison and contrast, showing the extraordinary differences between seventeenth-century and medieval science. The Pattern of Change model can then be used for the two sections of this chapter that are closely connected: the actual scientific discoveries *and* the remnants of magical thinking that survived even in the minds of the scientists themselves. The Pattern of Change method is also useful for setting forth the stage-by-stage developments in astronomy, physics, medicine, and chemistry. Either the Diffusion or the Reflections/Connections approach will work in assessing the impact of science on philosophy and the ironic aspects of the Scientific Revolution.

To introduce the revolution in political thought, the teacher can use a Standard Lecture with a Reflections/Connections slant, since all of the political thinkers were clearly influenced by the politics of their day. The Diffusion model is the most appropriate for examining the topic of European exploration and expansion. As a conclusion for this unit, the instructor can use a Spirit of the Age approach to explain how the revolutions in science and political thinking forever altered Western values and attitudes.

II. LECTURE OUTLINE

Non-Western Events

A. The Themes of the Baroque Age

1603–1715

B. The Background of the
   Scientific Revolution
   1. Geocentrism: Aristotle
      and Ptolemy
   2. Empiricism, inductive
      and deductive reasoning

Tartars of Manchu invade
   China, 1616–1620
Ming dynasty ends and
   Manchu dynasty begins
   in China, 1644

C. The Scientific Revolution:
Discoveries and Theories

D. The Magical and the Practical in
the Scientific Revolution
1. The paradox in the movement
2. The role of technology
3. Astronomy and physics: from
Copernicus to Newton
a. Nicolas Copernicus: a
heliocentric universe
b. Johannes Kepler: the
three planetary laws
c. Galileo Galilei: revelations
about the heavens and
discoveries about motion
d. Isaac Newton: gravity and synthesis
4. Medicine and chemistry
a. Ancient and medieval opinions
b. Andreas Vesalius: early
discoveries about the circulatory
system
c. William Harvey: the circulatory
system explained
d. Marcello Malpighi: identification of
capillaries
e. Robert Boyle: beginnings of chemistry
5. The impact of science on philosophy
a. Francis Bacon: explaining the new
learning
b. René Descartes: skepticism and the
dualism of knowledge
c. Pascal: uncertainty and faith
6. Ironic aspects of the Scientific
Revolution
a. Work of a minority
b. Christian faith, superstition,
and mysticism

E. The Revolutions in Political Thought
1. Impact of changing political systems
2. Natural law and divine right:
Grotius and Bossuet
a. Hugo Grotius: natural law and
international law
b. Bishop Bossuet: divine right and
God's plans
c. Absolutism and liberalism:
Hobbes and Locke
(1) Thomas Hobbes's *The Leviathan*
(2) John Locke's *Second Treatise
on Civil Government* and *An
Essay Concerning the Human
Understanding*

Manchus conquer Formosa,
1683

Taj Mahal built by Shah
Jahan, 1628–1650
Making of the Peacock
Throne, *ca* 1650
Dalai Lama's residence in
Lhasa, Tibet

Book on Chinese
inventions

Mexico Cathedral
finished

Kabuki theater in Japan

Two schools of Japanese
painting united, 1702
Blue mosque,
Constantinople

F. European Exploration and Expansion
    1. Into the Americas, Africa, and the Far East
    2. Roles of various European nations in discoveries and settlements

Translation of *Popul Vah*, the sacred book of the Quiche Indians of Guatemala, 1701–1721

G. Responses to the Revolutions in Thought
    1. The spread of ideas
        a. Academies
        b. Fontenelle: popularizing science
        c. Bayle: classifying knowledge
    2. Impact on the arts
        a. Baroque painting
        b. Literature and drama

Kao-ts'en, *Autumn Landscape*, famous Chinese india-ink drawing, 1672

H. The Legacy of the Revolutions in Scientific and Political Thought

III. LEARNING OBJECTIVES

To learn:

1. The foundations of Western science prior to the seventeenth century, in particular the contributions of Aristotle and Ptolemy in formulating the geocentric system

2. The general nature of the Scientific Revolution

3. The magical and practical elements at work in the Scientific Revolution

4. The discoveries of Copernicus, Kepler, Galileo, and Newton and their contributions to the rise of modern astronomy and physics

5. The discoveries of Vesalius, Harvey, Malpighi, and Boyle and their contributions to the rise of modern medicine and chemistry

6. The impact of seventeenth-century science on philosophy

7. The ideas and contributions of Francis Bacon

8. The ideas and contributions of René Descartes and his impact on Western philosophy

9. Pascal's basic beliefs and their influence on Western thought

10. The ironic aspects of the Scientific Revolution

11. The impact of seventeenth-century political events on political thought

12. The definition, origins, and basic concept of natural law and Hugo Grotius's interpretation of the term

13. The definition, origins, and basic concepts of divine right and Bishop Bossuet's interpretation of the term

14. The meaning of political absolutism and Thomas Hobbes's explanation of the theory

15. The origins and definition of political liberalism and John Locke's interpretation of the theory

16. What is meant by the social contract and the ways it may be used to justify a civil society

17. John Locke's theory of the origin of ideas and its influence on modern psychology

18. The early explorations of Europeans, the expansion of European peoples and culture abroad, and the effect of these developments on western Europe

19. The methods of spreading the ideas of the Scientific Revolution and the implications of those ideas for politics and culture

20. The impact of the Scientific Revolution on the arts

21. Historic "firsts" of the seventeenth-century revolutions in scientific and political thought that became part of the Western tradition: the heliocentric system; Newtonian physics and astronomy; Harvey's explanation for the circulation of the blood; new habits of scientific thought, including empiricism and the inductive method; social contract theory; the beginnings of both modern authoritarian and liberal thought; and the opening phase of European expansion and influence around the world

22. The role of this period in transmitting the heritage of earlier civilizations: reshaping medieval science to conform to the new scientific discoveries and ways of thinking; reviving, for the first time since the fall of Rome, skepticism and intellectual restlessness; and reinterpreting medieval Christian political thought along secular lines

IV. SUGGESTIONS FOR FILMS

Ascent of Man: The Majestic Clock Work. Time-Life, 52 min., color.

Ascent of Man: The Starry Messenger. Time-Life, 52 min., color.

The Light of Experience. Time-Life, 52 min., color.

Galileo, the Challenge of Reason. Learning Corporation of America, 26 min., color.

Newton: The Mind that Found the Future. Learning Corporation of America, 21 min., color.

Science and Society. McGraw-Hill, 18 min., color.

Vesalius: Founder of Modern Anatomy. Yale Medical School, 13 min., color.

William Harvey and the Circulation of the Blood. International Film Bureau, 33 min., color.

V. SUGGESTIONS FOR FURTHER READING

Ashcraft, R. *Revolutionary Politics and Locke's Two Treatises of Government.* Princeton: Princeton University Press, 1986.

Brown, K. C. *Hobbes: Studies by L. Strauss and others.* Oxford, Blackwell, 1965.

Jacob, M. C. *The Cultural Meaning of the Scientific Revolution.* New York: Knopf, 1988.

Kuhn, T. *The Structure of Scientific Revolutions.* 2nd. ed. Chicago: University of Chicago Press, 1970.

Webster, C. *The Great Instauration: Science, Medicine, and Reform.* London: Duckworth, 1975.

Westfall, R. S. *The Construction of Modern Science: Mechanisms and Mechanics.* New York: Wiley, 1971.

VI. IDENTIFICATIONS

geocentrism
empiricism
inductive reasoning
deductive reasoning
heliocentrism

Scientific Revolution
social contract
liberalism
tabula rasa
virtuoso

VII. DISCUSSION/ESSAY QUESTIONS

1. Show that the Scientific Revolution was both an outgrowth and a rejection of Aristotelian cosmology.
2. Define the term *geocentrism*, and note how the discoveries and ideas of Aristotle and Ptolemy were illustrative of this concept.
3. What is meant by the term *Scientific Revolution* and what areas of study did it encompass?
4. Discuss the paradoxes and the causes that gave rise to the Scientific Revolution.
5. Discuss the ideas of Copernicus, Kepler, Galileo, and Newton and their contributions to astronomy and physics. How did their discoveries threaten the existing view of the universe? What was the outcome of their work in science?
6. Define the Newtonian system and explain how it replaced the medieval world view.
7. What contributions did Vesalius, Harvey, and Malpighi make to the study of the human body?
8. What role did Francis Bacon play in the rise of modern thought and what has been his impact on modern thought?
9. Discuss René Descartes's most important contributions to Western philosophy and assess their value to modern thought.
10. In what ways did Pascal's ideas question the Scientific Revolution?
11. Discuss the ironic aspects of the Scientific Revolution and show how it was both medieval and modern.
12. Define "natural law," and demonstrate how it was manifested in the writings of Grotius.
13. What were the major arguments of Bishop Bossuet in his defense of divine right?
14. How did English politics influence Hobbes's political thinking? What impact has *The Leviathan* had on modern political theory?
15. Define the term "social contract" and illustrate how Hobbes and Locke used this term in their writings on political thought.
16. Show the influence of John Locke's political theories on the founders of the United States.
17. Explain how Locke's theory of knowledge has influenced modern psychology.
18. Identify the overseas areas settled by Europeans during the seventeenth century and discuss the impact of these settlements at home and abroad.
19. How were the discoveries and ideas of the Scientific Revolution disseminated to educated Europeans?
20. In what ways did Bayle's *Dictionary* conflict with accepted approaches to learning, and how did it affect literature?
21. Discuss the impact of the Scientific Revolution on Baroque art.
22. Do you think that the Scientific Revolution was more important than the Renaissance and the Reformation? Defend your position. Explain the impact of all three movements on Western thought.
23. How did the Scientific Revolution affect the rise of skepticism in Western thought?
24. Discuss some of the short-term and long-range effects of European explorations and settlements on modern times.

VIII. MULTIPLE-CHOICE QUESTIONS

1. In the late seventeenth century, Western thought reached a "crisis of conscience" that can be characterized as:
   a. a time when advanced thinkers accepted the notion of original sin
   b. an age when progressive scholars began to think in terms of natural law
   c. a period when mathematics became an accepted tool for problem solving
   * d. b and c but not a (p. 381)

2. The intellectual tradition of Aristotelian physics and astronomy:
   a. was passed from Greek to Roman to Arabic civilizations before it reemerged in the West in the High Middle Ages
   b. asserted that the sun was the center of the universe
   c. reasoned that the planets moved in circular orbits
   * d. a and c but not b (p. 381)

3. The Egyptian scholar Ptolemy:
   a. rejected Aristotle's model of the universe
   * b. modified Aristotle's model with new mathematical calculations (p. 382)
   c. was forced to denounce his findings before religious authorities
   d. b and c but not a

4. How did Western scholars in the Middle Ages explain the universe?
   a. They accepted the Ptolemaic model.
   b. They concluded that the Unmoved Mover was God.
   c. They accepted the church's teaching that the earth was made of corrupt materials.
   * d. all of the above (p. 382)

5. Which culture modified and improved the Ptolemaic system before it was transmitted to the West?
   a. the Egyptian
   * b. the Muslim (p. 382)
   c. the Byzantine
   d. the Judaic

6. Aristotle's explanation of motion was challenged in the fourteenth century by scholars at the university of:
   a. Bologna
   b. Alexandria
   * c. Paris (p. 382)
   d. Oxford

7. Which of the following developments began to undermine Aristotelianism in the Middle Ages?
   a. the direct observation of nature
   b. the use of empiricism
   c. the application of inductive reasoning
   * d. all of the above (p. 382)

8. A feature of the Scientific Revolution was:
   a. new discoveries in astronomy and biology
   b. a radically changed perspective about the physical world
   c. the beginning of the separation of philosophy and theology
   * d. all of the above (pp. 382–383)

9. Which is a correct statement about the Scientific Revolution?
   a. Early modern scientists built on the work of medieval thinkers.
   b. Many of the early modern scientists were Neo-Platonists and were thus led to emphasize mathematical reasoning.
   c. Late medieval technology had little impact on the new learning.
 * d. a and b but not c (p. 383)

10. Neo-Platonism affected the rise of modern science by:
   a. rejecting all of the Christian points of view
 * b. emphasizing the power of mathematics (p. 383)
   c. denying mystical properties to the sun
   d. denying the existence of a greater power than humans

11. A positive influence on the course of the Scientific Revolution was:
 * a. technology (p. 383)
   b. religious faith
   c. rich capitalists
   d. universities

12. The triumph of heliocentrism over geocentrism, from Copernicus to Newton, required how many years?
 * a. 150 years (p. 384)
   b. 50 years
   c. 100 years
   d. 10 years

13. The central issue between geocentrism and heliocentrism was:
   a. which theory had the greatest quantity of data
   b. which theory was supported by the Church
 * c. which theory was simpler (p. 384)
   d. which theory was more complex

14. Copernicus's explanation of the universe can be described as:
   a. a brand-new idea
 * b. a revival of an ancient Greek theory (p. 384)
   c. a system compatible with medieval Christian theology
   d. a revival of an ancient Babylonian theory

15. How did religious leaders react to Copernicus's theory?
   a. It was fully accepted by both Catholics and Protestants.
 * b. The Catholics, after an initial acceptance, later rejected it, whereas the Protestants, lacking a centralized authority, were forced to accommodate themselves to his thinking. (p. 385)
   c. It was accepted by the Catholics but rejected by the Protestants.
   d. It was rejected by the Catholics and the Protestants for more than 200 years.

16. This sixteenth-century astronomer amassed a huge collection of celestial observations that aided later astronomers:
   a. Isaac Newton
   b. Plotinus
 * c. Tycho Brahe (p. 385)
   d. William of Ockham

17. Kepler's major contribution to the Scientific Revolution was:
   a. the invention of the telescope
 * b. the discovery of three key planetary laws (p. 385)

c.   a convincing explanation of gravity

d.   a treatise on terrestial motion

18.   A consequence of Kepler's scientific research was that:

a.   His startling discoveries made further investigations unnecessary.

b.   The sun-centered universe could now be understood in mathematical terms.

c.   There was a regularity in the operation of the universe.

*   d.   b and c but not a (p. 385)

19.   Galileo's important discoveries were influenced by his:

a.   determination to win favor with the church

b.   reliance on the theory of Ptolemy

*   c.   use of the new technological invention, the telescope (p. 385)

d.   dependence on the writings of Thomas Aquinas

20.   Galileo's celestial observations proved:

a.   that the moon was full of craters and had a rough surface

b.   that Jupiter has moons or satellites

c.   that the sun is not the center of the universe

*   d.   a and b but not c (p. 385)

21.   Besides astronomical research, Galileo also contributed to:

a.   the science of anatomy

*   b.   the overturning of Aristotle's theory of motion (p. 385)

c.   the modern explanation for the circulation of the blood

d.   the modern view that the body is composed of tiny cells

22.   Regarding Galileo's astronomical writings, the Catholic church:

a.   readily accepted them as confirming biblical scripture

b.   agreed with his findings after summoning a church council

*   c.   arrested Galileo and threatened to torture him (p. 386)

d.   ignored him although it declared his ideas to be unacceptable

23.   Whose scientific research finally confirmed the truth of the Copernican system?

a.   Galileo

b.   Kepler

*   c.   Newton (p. 386)

d.   Leibniz

24.   Newton's outstanding contribution to the Scientific Revolution was the mathematical basis for:

*   a.   the law of gravity (p. 386)

b.   the law of inertia

c.   the theory of opposites

d.   the theory of relativity

25.   What did the English poet Alexander Pope mean when he wrote: "God said, 'Let Newton be!'and All was *Light*"?

a.   that Newton had discovered how electricity operated

b.   that Newton had discovered the source of light

*   c.   that Newton had shed light on the mysteries of nature (p. 387)

d.   that Christians would now be able to follow God's light

26.   Besides being a pioneer of modern science, Newton was also:

a.   a religious person who never doubted the existence of God

b.   a scholar not fully liberated from medieval habits of thought

c. a Christian who wanted to be remembered for his religious writings
* d. all of the above (p. 387)

27. Prior to modern times scientists had difficulty studying the human body because of:
   a. the church's prohibition against dissection of corpses
   b. the medical schools' reliance on animal dissection as the basis for its knowledge of human bodies
   c. the authoritative position in medical circles of the Greek thinker Galen, whose writings were riddled with errors
* d. all of the above (p. 387)

28. The earliest research into the true origins of the circulation of blood began at this university by this scientist:
* a. at the University of Padua by Vesalius (p. 387)
   b. at the University of Paris by Harvey
   c. at the University of Bologna by Malpighi
   d. at Oxford University by William of Ockham

29. William Harvey and Isaac Newton both:
   a. spent time doing careful research before publishing their findings
   b. used mathematics to prove their theories
   c. made important discoveries in celestial physics
* d. a and b but not c (p. 387)

30. Robert Boyle made this contribution to modern chemistry:
   a. He was the first thinker to make chemistry a separate study from other researches.
   b. He used the inductive method to learn about the chemical properties of a substance.
   c. He united alchemy with chemistry.
* d. a and b but not c (pp. 387–388)

31. Francis Bacon's success as a popularizer of the Scientific Revolution was a direct result of:
   a. his clear and precise writing style
   b. his complete reliance on the experimental method
   c. his belief in progress
* d. all of the above (p. 388–389)

32. The scientific work of René Descartes resulted in the development of:
   a. calculus
* b. analytical geometry (p. 389)
   c. logarithms
   d. irrational numbers

33. In outlining his steps to gain knowledge, Descartes:
   a. used deductive logic and reasoning
   b. appealed to the irrational drives in the mind
   c. applied a mathematical approach, especially geometry
* d. a and c but not b (p. 389)

34. Descartes, in his search for the truth:
   a. never doubted the existence of God
   b. maintained that his body was always present
* c. concluded that he existed because his mind questioned (p.389)
   d. a and b but not c

35. What is meant by Descartes's dualism?
   a. Everything comes in pairs.
 * b. The mind and body are separate. (p. 390)
   c. Only by dividing objects into two parts can they be understood.
   d. Human beings have both a human and animal nature.

36. This thinker questioned the benefits of the Scientific Revolution:
 * a. Blaise Pascal (p. 390)
   b. Francis Bacon
   c. René Descartes
   d. Thomas Hobbes

37. Pascal believed that:
   a. Mathematics is a useful tool for understanding the world.
   b. The human passions are helpful in understanding God.
   c. God's existence can be proven by using the laws of probability.
 * d. all of the above (p. 390)

38. Which was NOT an ironic aspect of the Scientific Revolution?
 * a. The discoveries were made by a scientific elite, but the populace quickly adopted the new findings. (p. 390)
   b. The discoveries were outgrowths of practical studies and not the result of an attempt to reconstruct the universe.
   c. The scientists produced a model of the universe that was fully secular, but they were all Christians who accepted the existence of God.
   d. The scientists overturned earlier scientific thinking, but they still shared ideas and perceptions rooted in medieval thought.

39. Seventeenth-century political thought was influenced by:
   a. the wars of Louis XIV
   b. the English Civil War
   c. the rise of the early modern state
 * d. all of the above (p. 391)

40. Seventeenth-century political thinkers borrowed ideas from:
   a. the Bible and other religious writings
   b. the period's scientific discoveries
   c. the writings of Byzantine scholars
 * d. a and b but not c (p. 391)

41. An influence on Grotius's political ideas was:
   a. his personal experiences during the Thirty Years' War
   b. his travels and observations as an ambassador
   c. his education and reading in ancient philosophy
 * d. all of the above (p. 391)

42. Grotius founded his political theories on his belief in:
   a. original sin
 * b. natural law (p. 391)
   c. divine right
   d. the social contract

43. Bishop Bossuet favored the notion of the divine right of kings, because:
    a. God gave certain men the power to rule.
    b. Kings act as God's agent on earth.
    c. When a ruler goes against God's plan, the subjects may legitimately rebel.
  * d. a and b but not c (pp. 391–392)

44. Hobbes reasoned that the best form of government is a(n):
    a. constitutional monarchy limited by the doctrine of natural rights
  * b. absolutist state with the ruler completely controlling the people (p. 392)
    c. enlightened aristocracy in which the best people rule
    d. democracy where there is rule of the people, by the people, and for the people

45. Hobbes's legacy to modern political thought was an idealized model of:
    a. self-government
  * b. absolutism (p. 392)
    c. liberalism
    d. socialism

46. Locke believed:
    a. that a social contract is necessary to form a civil society
    b. that humans have reason and are basically decent
    c. that private property has to be protected in the civil society
  * d. all of the above (p. 393)

47. Locke argued that the social contract was:
    a. an ironclad agreement that cannot be broken
    b. simply an arrangement whereby the citizens give the rulers the right to govern but not the power to ignore their demands
    c. arranged so that the populace still possesses its sovereignty
  * d. b and c but not a (p. 393)

48. As seventeenth-century Europeans began to move overseas:
    a. They increased continental rivalries.
    b. They opened new trade opportunities for their home societies.
    c. They initiated the slave trade out of Africa.
  * d. all of the above (p. 393)

49. Bayle's *Historical and Critical Dictionary* can be described as:
    a. an encyclopedic work arranged in systematic form
    b. a controversial publication that often challenged Christian beliefs
    c. a book that supported prevailing institutions and traditional ideas
  * d. a and b but not c (p. 395)

50. How did the Scientific Revolution affect the arts?
    a. It had no impact at all.
    b. The new science became a prominent theme in Baroque art.
  * c. Baroque artists and writers became highly analytical, an influence from the new science. (p. 397)
    d. Baroque artists and writers, reacting against the Scientific Revolution, adopted religious themes in their works.

16

THE AGE OF REASON
1700–1789

I. TEACHING STRATEGIES AND SUGGESTIONS

The instructor can begin the Age of Reason with a Historical Overview that describes the West in 1700, treating such matters as the politics (kingship, absolutist or limited), economics (mercantilism), society (aristocratic and hierarchical), religion (state churches and legalized intolerance), education (piecemeal, random, and elitist), and culture (Baroque and soon to be Rococo). This summary will enable students to better understand the program of the Physiocrats and particularly the *philosophes* who wanted radical changes in Western society and culture. The instructor can next introduce the Enlightenment, using a Spirit of the Age approach that sets forth this cultural movement's goals and guiding ideals, including scientific methodology, mathematical reasoning, and healthy skepticism. The instructor, using the Pattern of Change approach, can briefly describe the influences that helped to shape the Enlightenment mentality, specifically the Scientific Revolution, Greco-Roman Classicism, and the Renaissance. A handout listing key figures by country and the major contribution of each is a good device for demonstrating to students that the Enlightenment was truly an international movement as well as for familiarizing them with the leading *philosophes* and their achievements.

The instructor can use a Standard Lecture to establish the Enlightenment's historical setting, focusing briefly on major historical events affecting the great powers (England, France, Prussia, Austria, and Russia) and to a lesser extent the almost-great powers (the Netherlands, Portugal, and Spain) and showing especially the differences between England with its limited monarchy and growing middle class and France with its absolute monarchy and its resurgent aristocracy. This information is vital for students, since these events were determining factors in the rise of the Rococo and Neoclassical styles. With the Reflections/Connections approach, the instructor can then show how the Rococo reflected the French and, to a lesser extent, the Austrian aristocracy and how, in England, it led to a backlash by Hogarth, who ridiculed the excesses of this style in his satiric paintings. Similarly, it can be shown how the Neoclassical style was in part a response to the *philosophes'* criticism of eighteenth-century politics and culture and how, after appearing in about 1770, this style was quickly adopted by progressive spirits across the West. The instructor can employ Slide Lectures blended with a Comparison/Contrast approach to set forth the differences between the Rococo and Neoclassical styles. The Comparison/Contrast approach can also be used to treat literary developments in France and England, and a Music Lecture is essential to illustrate the riches of Rococo and Neoclassical music.

An excellent conclusion can be achieved using a Historical Summary—following the topics laid down in the opening lecture—to describe the agenda of the *philosophes* in 1789, touching on such matters as politics (government by the consent of the governed), economics (*laissez faire*), society (natural rights, including freedom and equality), religion (Deism, natural religion, and religious tolerance), education (the universal panacea as a problem solver), and culture (Neoclassicism). Time permitting, the instructor can conduct a Discussion, encouraging students to identify those aspects of contemporary life that are direct outgrowths of Enlightenment habits of thought, such as representative government, public school systems, free trade, and religious freedom. The instructor can also show that contemporary rights movements, such as those for African-Americans, women, the disabled, and gays, have their roots in the struggle for rights that began as an academic discussion by the *philosophes* in the Enlightenment.

II. LECTURE OUTLINE

A. Historical Overview
    1. Four trends of
        the age
        a. Concentration of political power in
            the great states
        b. The resurgence of the aristocracy
        c. The political eminence of the middle
            class
        d. The Enlightenment
    2. Reaction against the Baroque
        a. The Rococo style
        b. The Neoclassical style

B. The Enlightenment
    1. Influences
        a. Greco-Roman world
        b. The Renaissance
        c. The Scientific Revolution
    2. Its geographic boundaries
    3. The *philosophes* and their program
        a. Definition of the *philosophes*
        b. Representative thinkers
        c. Their ideals
        d. Their program
    4. Deism
        a. Metaphor of a clockwork universe
        b. Impact
    5. The *Encyclopédie*
        a. Origins
        b. The project
        c. The editorship of Diderot
    6. The Physiocrats
        a. Definition
        b. Critique of mercantilism
        c. Their doctrines
        d. Adam Smith and his advocacy of a
            free-market economy

C. The Great Powers during the Age of Reason
    1. Less turbulent than 1600s
    2. Society: continuity and change
        a. Growing urbanization of society
        b. Continuation of a traditional,
            hierarchical society
        c. Subordinate role for women
        d. Conditions of black slaves in Europe's
            overseas colonies

1700–1789
In India, Mughal
Dynasty, 1483–ca. 1750;
    regime of British
    East India company,
    1757–1858
In China, Manchu
    Dynasty, 1644–1912;
    greatest extent of
    Manchu empire, 1760
In Japan, the Tokugawa
    Shogunate, 1603–1867

Japanese isolation,
    1637–1854
In China, K'ang Hsi,
    Manchu emperor,
    1661–1722; institutes
    competitive civil
    service examinations;
    a Chinese version of
    an enlightened despot
Chinese Emperor Ch'ien
    Lung, 1736–1796—a
    patron of Jesuit
    painters and
    architects; height of
    Manchu civilization but
    also the beginning of
    the dynasty's decline
In China, emergence of
    secret societies, like
    the White Lotus, that
    are hostile to the
    Manchu dynasty
Tibet brought into
    Chinese orbit, 1720

In 1763, France cedes its
    lands in Canada and
    India to Britain
In 1800, Edo (Tokyo) had
    a population 1 million,
    making it probably the
    largest city in the
    world at the time
Literacy rate in Japan

3. Absolutism, limited monarchy, and enlightened despotism
   a. Last great age of kings
   b. France: the successors to the Sun King
      (1) Louis XV and Louis XVI
         (a) Gathering sense of drift
         (b) Society and culture
         (c) Decline abroad
         (d) Domestic problems at home
      (2) France at a crossroads in 1789
   c. Great Britain and the Hanoverian kings
      (1) The ideal state of the *philosophes*
      (2) The early Hanoverians: George I and George II
      (3) George III
         (a) Restoration of kingly power
         (b) The American Revolution
   d. Enlightened despotism in central and eastern Europe
      (1) Survey of the lesser states of Europe
      (2) Prussia: Frederick II
         (a) His reforms
         (b) Commitment to Enlightenment values
      (3) Austria: Maria Theresa and Joseph II
         (a) Their reforms
         (b) Their contrasting involvement with Enlightenment ideas
      (4) Russia: Peter the Great and Catherine the Great
         (a) Their reforms
         (b) Relationship to the Enlightenment

D. Cultural Trends in the Eighteenth Century: from Rococo to Neoclassical
   1. The Rococo style in the arts
      a. The origin of the Rococo
      b. Its geographical boundaries
      c. Rococo painting
         (1) Watteau
            (a) Style characteristics
            (b) *Departure from Cythera*
            (c) *The Sign for Gersaint's Shop*
         (2) Boucher
            (a) Style characteristics
            (b) *Nude on a Sofa*

during the Tokugawa Shogunate was highest in Asia, 45% for males, 15% for females

In Africa, between 1730 and 1800, the states of Lunda, Luba, Oyo, Benin, and Asanta prospered and became empires; collapse of Kongo, Ngola, and Mwenemutapa, largely a result of contacts with Europeans

Revival of Islam in West Africa after 1725

Kumasi, the capital of Asante in Africa, called a "garden city" by foreigners

Asante civilization in Africa at its zenith, 1721–1750

Dahomey, an African state built on the slave trade, the most rigidly controlled state of the 18th century

In 1728, the Portuguese were driven from their stronghold in Mombassa, Africa, by a combined African-Arab army

Reduction of slavery in China, 1730

Baal Shem, 1699–1760, founds Jewish sect of Chassidim in Carpathia

In China, the visual arts flourish during the Manchu Dynasty

Chinese fashions exported to Europe, including Chinese-style gardens, pagodas, pavilions, lacquer, sedan chairs, incense, and porcelain

Translations of Chinese thought and literature by Jesuits make their way into the West

Hokusai, 1760–1849,

                   (3) Vigée-Lebrun
                       (a) Style characteristics
                       (b) Portrait of Marie
                           Antoinette
                   (4) Fragonard
                       (a) Style characteristics
                       (b) *The Swing*
               c. Rococo interiors
                   (1) Aspects of the style
                   (2) Boffrand and the
                       "Salon de la Princesse"
                       in the Hotel
                       de Soubise, Paris
                   (3) Neumann and the Kaisersaal in
                       the Residenz, Würzburg
               d. The English response
                   (1) Style characteristics
                   (2) Hogarth
                       (a) The art market
                       (b) *Marriage à la Mode* series
       2. The challenge of Neoclassicism
           a. Origins
           b. Neoclassical painting
               (1) Vien and the *Académie de
                   France* in Rome
               (2) David
                   (a) Style characteristics
                   (b) *Oath of the Horatii*
                   (c) *The Death of Socrates*
           c. Neoclassical architecture
               (1) Adam
                   (a) Style characteristics
                   (b) Kenwood House, London
               (2) Soufflot
                   (a) Style characteristics
                   (b) The Pantheon, Paris
       3. Political philosophy
           a. Background
           b. Alternatives to absolutism
               (1) Montesquieu and *The Spirit of
                   the Laws*
               (2) Rousseau and *The Social Contract*
       4. Literature
           a. Mission: to liberate consciousness
           b. French writers: the development of
               new forms
               (1) Montesquieu: *The Persian Letters*
               (2) Rousseau: *The Confessions*
               (3) Voltaire
                   (a) *Essay on Customs*
                   (b) *Candide*
           c. Neoclassicism and English literature
               (1) The English setting
               (2) Pope

Japanese artist famous for wood block prints and landscapes

Harunobu, 1724–1770, the earliest master of the multicolored print in Japan

Sharaku, Japanese wood block artist, late 18th century, noted for caricatures of actors

In Asante, earrings, anklets, pendants, and armbands fashioned from gold and bronze

Utamaro, Japanese painter, 1753–1806

Philadelphia Museum founded, 1773

Okyo, Japanese painter, 1733–1795

In 1715, the Jesuit missionary Castiglione arrives in China, influences Chinese painting

In China, the Summer Palace of Emperor Ch'ien Lung, designed by Jesuits

Emerald Buddha Chapel, Bangkok, Thailand, 1785

In China, revival of Neo-Confucianism; study of mathematics, astronomy, and geography increases; dictionaries compiled

Compilation of Chinese literature and history made for Emperor Ch'ien Lung, numbering 36,000 volumes; in this reign also appeared *Dream of the Red Chamber*, China's greatest novel

Rise of the Kabuki drama, a popular

(a) His style
(b) *Essay on Man*
(3) Gibbon: *History of the Decline and Fall of the Roman Empire*
d. The rise of the novel
(1) Characteristics
(2) Samuel Richardson
(a) Theme: love between the sexes
(b) *Pamela,* or *Virtue Rewarded*
(c) *Clarissa*
(3) Henry Fielding
(a) Theme: satiric adventures
(b) *Tom Jones*
e. Music
(1) Rococo music
(a) *Style galant*
(b) The harpsichord and the pianoforte
(c) Couperin
(d) Rameau
(2) Classical music
(a) Characteristics
(b) The sonata form and its impact
(c) Haydn
(d) Mozart

form of entertainment for middle- and lower-class patrons Yokai Yagu, Japanese poet, 1702–1783

Ballad opera, "Flora," first musical theater in North America at Charleston, S.C., 1735
First public concert in Philadelphia, 1757

E. The Legacy of the Enlightenment

III. LEARNING OBJECTIVES

To learn:

1. The goals and the ideals of the Enlightenment as well as the leading *philosophes* and their contributions to this cultural movement

2. The influences on the Enlightenment, especially Greco-Roman Classicism, the Scientific Revolution, and the Renaissance

3. The meaning and significance of Deism and its relationship to the Scientific Revolution

4. The role played by the *Encyclopédie* in the Enlightenment

5. The reasons that both the Physiocrats and Adam Smith encouraged *laissez-faire* economics instead of mercantilism

6. The condition of Europe in 1700 and the historical changes that occurred between 1700 and 1789, particularly in England, France, Prussia, Austria, and Russia (the great powers) and to a lesser extent in the Netherlands, Spain, and Portugal (the almost-great powers)

7. How the Rococo style reflected its origins in France and Austria, where aloof aristocracies dominated society, and how, in England, Hogarth satirized this style in paintings that appealed to middle-class patrons

8. How the Neoclassical style was, in part, a rebellion against the frivolity of the Rococo style and, in part, a reflection of devotion to Greco-Roman values, especially love of country and virtuous behavior

9. How seventeenth-century England and France, two of the age's leading political powers, represented two contrasting approaches to monarchy and the impact this difference had on artistic and literary developments

10. The characteristics of the Rococo, along with leading exponents of this style and their contributions

11. The characteristics of Neoclassicism, along with leading exponents of this style and their contributions

12. The new ideas that originated in the political philosophy of Montesquieu and Rousseau and their later influence

13. The characteristics and leading composers of Rococo music

14. The defining role played by Haydn and Mozart in originating Classical-style music and their major contributions to this style

15. The historic "firsts" of the Age of Reason that became part of the Western tradition: the emergence of the middle class as a potent force for change; the literary form of the novel; in music, the sonata form and the symphony; a democratizing tendency in culture; a progressive view of history; the principle of government by consent of the governed; and the beliefs that the least amount of state interference in the lives of citizens is best and that all people are created equal

16. The role of the Age of Reason in transmitting the heritage of the past: making the idea of absolutist government an indefensible concept, renewing democratic ideals, reviving and adapting Classical principles and forms to new conditions in the Neoclassical arts and architecture and Classical music, making the civilization of Rome and its fate a comparative model for Western states, continuing the new science and applying its methodology and principles to the Enlightenment, and modifying the Baroque into the Rococo style

IV. SUGGESTIONS FOR FILMA

Catherine the Great: A Profile in Power. BBC/Time-Life, 72 min., black and white.

The Christians: Politeness and Enthusiasm (1689–1791). McGraw-Hill, 45 min., color.

Civilisation: The Light of Experience.: The Smile of Reason. BBC/Time-Life, 52 min. each, color.

The Market Society and How It Grew. NET, 2 parts, 29 min. each,. black and white.

Voltaire Presents Candide: An Introduction to the Age of Enlightenment. Encyclopedia Britannica.34 min., color.

V. SUGGESTIONS FOR MUSIC

Couperin, François. *Concerts Royaux (4).* Claire, See, Moroney, Ter Linder, Harmonia Mundi. 901151 [CD].

Haydn, Franz Joseph. *Quartets (6) for Strings, Op. 50.* Juilliard String Quartet. CBS M2K-42154 [CD].

————. *The Seasons (Oratorio).* Mathis, Jerusalem, Fischer-Dieskau, Marriner, St. Martin's Academy & Chorus. Philips 411428-2 PH2 [CD].

————. *Symphonies (104).* Marriner, St. Martin's Academy. Philips 6768003 PSI.

Mozart, Wolfgang Amadeus. *Don Giovanni.* Arroyo, Te Kanawa, Freni, Burrows, Wixell, Ganzarolli, Davis, Royal Opera. Philips 6707022 2.

————. *Piano Music.* Barenboim. Angel CDC-47384 [CD].

————. *Mozart's Greatest Hits.* Cleveland Orchestra. CBS MLK-39436 [CD].

Rameau, Jean Philippe. *Les Boreades (suite); Dardanus (suite).* Bruggen, Orchestra of the 18th Century. Philips 420240-2 PH.

————. *Les Indes Galantes: Airs et Danses.* Herreweghe, Chapelle Royale Orchestra. Harmonia Mundi 1028.

VI. SUGGESTIONS FOR FURTHER READING

Anderson, M. S. *Europe in the Eighteenth Century, 1713–1783.* 3d ed. New York: Longman, 1987.

Black, J. *Eighteenth-Century Europe, 1700–1789.* New York: St. Martin's, 1990.

Braham, A. *The Architecture of the French Enlightenment.* London: Thames and Hudson, 1980.

Hulme, P., and Jordanova, L. *The Enlightenment and Its Shadows.* New York: Routledge, 1990.

Jones, S. *The Eighteenth Century.* New York: Cambridge University Press, 1985.

McLeish, K. *Listeners' Guide to Classical Music: An Introduction to the Great Classical Composers and Their Works.* Harlow, Eng.: Longman, 1986.

Porter, R. *The Enlightenment.* Atlantic Highlands, N.J.: Humanities Press, 1990.

Sewter, A. C. *Baroque and Rococo Art.* London: Thames and Hudson, 1972.

VII. IDENTIFICATIONS

Enlightenment
philosophes
Deism
Physiocrats
Rococo style
fête galante
rocaille
Neoclassical style

style galant
pianoforte
Classical style (in music)
sonata form
symphony
concerto
sonata
scherzo

VIII. DISCUSSION/ESSAY QUESTIONS

1. Discuss the Enlightenment, identifying its goals, ideals, leading figures, and enduring contributions to the Western tradition.
2. Show how the Greco-Roman world, the Scientific Revolution, and the Renaissance affected the Enlightenment.

3. How did the *philosophes* avoid censorship in their public criticisms of eighteenth-century politics and culture?
4. Define Deism. What were its intellectual origins?
5. Compare and contrast the economic theories of the Physiocrats and Adam Smith.
6. Summarize historical developments in England, France, Prussia, Austria, and Russia—the great powers—and discuss how these developments helped to shape arts and architecture, literature, and political theory of the Age of Reason.
7. Identify the characteristics and leading figures of the Rococo style of art. Explain Hogarth's negative response to the Rococo style.
8. What is enlightened despotism? Where and why did it develop in the eighteenth century? Discuss the successes and failures of this political system.
9. Using a specific painting from each style, compare and contrast the Rococo with the Neoclassical artistic style.
10. What influences helped to bring about the Neoclassical style? What are its characteristics?
11. Why did most of the *philosophes* reject absolutism and support an alternative form of government? Discuss the alternative types of government preferred by Montesquieu and Rousseau.
12. Compare and contrast the literary contributions of Montesquieu, Rousseau, Voltaire, Gibbon, and Alexander Pope to the Enlightenment.
13. Discuss the rise of the novel in eighteenth-century England. What conditions encouraged its development, who were the first novelists, and what were their themes?
14. What innovations occurred in music during the Age of Reason?
15. How does Classical music differ from Rococo music? Explain the role played by the sonata form in the evolution of the Classical style.
16. Discuss the contributions of Haydn and Mozart to Classical music.
17. In what way did the Enlightenment lay the foundations of the modern world?
18. What are the three most significant developments in the Age of Reason? Explain.

IX. MULTIPLE-CHOICE QUESTIONS

1. The Enlightenment style of thinking favored:
   a. scientific methodology
   b. mathematical reasoning
   c. healthy skepticism
   * d. all of the above (p. 401)

2. Which was NOT a trend during the Age of Reason?
   a. growing concentration of power in the great dynastic states
   * b. decline in the power of the aristocracy (p. 401)
   c. growing political and cultural eminence by the middle class
   d. unfolding of the cultural movement known as the Enlightenment

3. The Rococo style reflected:
   * a. the lighthearted pursuits of the French aristocracy (p. 401)
   b. the sober values of the Dutch middle classes
   c. the religious doctrines of the papacy
   d. the formal needs of the Spanish royal court

4. Classical values in the eighteenth century were expressed in:
   a. the piano music of Mozart
   b. the poems of Alexander Pope
   c. the painting style of David
   * d. all of the above (pp. 401, 418, 424)

5. The Enlightenment owed intellectual debts to all of these EXCEPT:
    a. the discoveries of the Scientific Revolution
    b. the secular values of the Greco-Roman world
    c. the humanism of the Renaissance
  * d. the religious doctrines of Christianity (pp. 401–402)

6. The Enlightenment was most influential in:
    a. Italy and Germany
    b. Scandinavia and Russia
  * c. France and Great Britain (p. 404)
    d. Spain and Portugal

7. The European state with the least censorship in the Enlightenment was:
    a. France
    b. Spain
  * c. the Netherlands (p. 404)
    d. Russia

8. The *philosophes* called for all of these reforms EXCEPT:
    a. religious toleration
    b. public education
  * c. women's suffrage (p. 404)
    d. abolition of slavery

9. A central tenet of Deism is that:
    a. Jesus Christ is the savior of humanity.
  * b. God created the universe and set the laws of nature in motion and thereafter never again
        interfered in human and natural affairs. (p. 404)
    c. God answers all human prayers.
    d. all of the above

10. The *Encyclopédie* was:
    a. edited by Diderot
    b. a monumental work in 17 volumes and 11 books of plates
    c. the outstanding voice of the *philosophes*
  * d. all of the above (p. 405)

11. Another name for *laissez-faire* economics is:
    a. the guild system
  * b. free trade (p. 406)
    c. mercantilism
    d. a government-run system

12. Laissez-faire economics was advocated by:
    a. the Physiocrats
    b. Adam Smith
    c. the entrepreneurs who made the Industrial Revolution
  * d. all of the above (p. 406)

13. During the Age of Reason, which class bore the heaviest tax burden?
    a. the aristocracy
    b. the middle class
  * c. the peasants (p. 406)
    d. the urban working class

14. The states of the West in the eighteenth century were characterized by:
    a. religious intolerance
    b. slavery in the colonies overseas
    c. a traditional, hierarchical social system
    * d. all of the above (pp. 406–407)

15. France's decline in the Age of Reason was symbolized by:
    a. the loss of colonies in both North America and India to Britain in 1763
    b. the inability of the king to reform the state because of the power of the nobility
    c. the failure of the tax system to provide adequate state revenues
    * d. all of the above (p. 408)

16. The founder of the Hanoverian Dynasty in Britain was:
    a. Anne
    * b. George I (p. 409)
    c. George II
    d. George III

17. This state, as a limited monarchy, became the ideal model for many *philosophes:*
    * a. Great Britain (p. 409)
    b. France
    c. Sweden
    d. Spain

18. The outstanding example of enlightened despotism in the Age of Reason was:
    * a. Austria under Joseph II (p. 410)
    b. Russia under Peter the Great
    c. France under Louis XVI
    d. Great Britain under George I

19. The originator of the Rococo style was:
    a. Hogarth
    * b. Watteau (p. 410)
    c. Fragonard
    d. Boucher

20. The painter Watteau specialized in this subject:
    a. domestic interiors
    * b. aristocratic entertainments (p. 410)
    c. portraits
    d. still lifes

21. A feature of Watteau's *Departure for Cythera* was:
    a. the air of melancholy
    b. mythological allusions
    c. erotic undercurrent
    * d. all of the above (p. 411)

22. This painter's works were famous for their outspoken sexuality:
    a. Watteau
    b. Hogarth
    * c. Boucher (p. 412)
    d. David

23. The dominant subject of Vigée-Lebrun in her paintings was:
 * a. society portraits (p. 412)
   b. aristocratic entertainments
   c. mythological scenes
   d. historical events

24. A prominent design element in Rococo interiors was the use of:
   a. mirrors
   b. *rocaille*
   c. chandeliers
 * d. all of the above (p. 414)

25. A splendid example of a Rococo interior is:
   a. the Library of Kenwood House, London
 * b. the "Salon de la Princesse" in the Hôtel de Soubise, Paris (p. 415)
   c. the Hall of Mirrors in Versailles Palace
   d. the auditorium of the Pantheon, Paris

26. What innovation is associated with Hogarth's art?
   a. He is the originator of the Neoclassical style.
 * b. He is the first artist to run off multiple engravings of his paintings to reach a larger audience.
        (p. 415)
   c. He established the subject of the *fête galante.*
   d. all of the above

27. Hogarth's *Marriage à la Mode* series:
   a. is anti-Rococo in style
   b. is a satirical view of a loveless marriage made for money
   c. appealed to the values of England's Protestant middle class
 * d. all of the above (pp. 415–416)

28. The origins of Neoclassicism are associated with:
   a. the archeological excavations at Pompeii
   b. the publication of Stuart and Revett's *The Antiquities of Athens*
   c. the birth of art history in the writings of Winckelmann
 * d. all of the above (pp. 416–417)

29. The principal exponent of Neoclassical painting was:
   a. Hogarth
   b. Watteau
 * c. David (p. 417)
   d. Fragonard

30. Neoclassicism was characterized by:
   a. frivolous subjects
 * b. disciplined perspective (p. 418)
   c. weightless floating images
   d. all of the above

31. Neoclassical architecture relied on:
   a. the Classical orders
   b. architectural detail rather than sculptural decoration
   c. the ideals of proportion and simplicity
 * d. all of the above (pp. 418–419)

32. In politics, Voltaire:
    a. was a democrat
  * b. supported enlightened despotism (p. 421)
    c. advocated absolutism
    d. was an exponent of socialism

33. Rousseau's democratic ideas reflected his origins as a citizen of:
    a. the nation-state of England
    b. the world
  * c. the city-state of Geneva (pp. 421–422)
    d. the Holy Roman Empire

34. Montesquieu's most enduring idea in *The Spirit of the Laws* is:
    a. Governments should be based on the consent of the governed.
    b. Governments are created to protect property.
  * c. Separation of powers prevents governments from becoming tyrannical. (p. 422)
    d. Natural rights are inalienable.

35. In *The Social Contract* Rousseau advocated the idea:
    a. that the people collectively personify the state
    b. that obedience to the laws of the state makes the citizens moral
    c. that the state grants civil rights to its citizens
  * d. all of the above (p. 422)

36. Montesquieu's *Persian Letters:*
    a. were cleverly written to avoid censorship
    b. satirized French institutions and customs
    c. launched a new literary genre, the letters of a "foreign" traveler who voices social criticism
  * d. all of the above (p. 422)

37. This eighteenth-century literary work foreshadowed the Romantic sensibility of the nineteenth century:
    a. Montesquieu's *Persian Letters*
  * b. Rousseau's *Confessions* (p. 422)
    c. Voltaire's *Candide*
    d. Pope's *Essay on Man*

38. Voltaire's chief aim in *Candide* was to satirize:
  * a. the philosophy of optimism (p. 423)
    b. the institution of monarchy
    c. the practice of arranged marriages
    d. the legal system of France

39. English Neoclassical writers and their readers shared these values:
    a. lightheartedness and love of luxury
    b. formality and courtliness
  * c. good taste and moral and religious values (p. 424)
    d. free-spiritedness and unconventionality

40. Pope's optimism in *Essay on Man* was satirized by:
    a. Montesquieu in the *Perisian Letters*
  * b. Voltaire in *Candide* (p. 424)
    c. Gibbon in *History of the Decline and Fall of the Roman Empire*
    d. Rousseau in the *Confessions*

41. Gibbon's *History of the Decline and Fall of the Roman Empire:*
    a. appealed to the Age of Reason's Classical interests
    b. echoed the *philosophes'* skepticism about the Christian faith
    c. reflected the Enlightenment's belief that history should be philosophy teaching through example
    * d. all of the above (p. 424)

42. What new literary form was developed in the Age of Reason?
    * a. the novel (p. 424)
    b. the epic
    c. the sonnet
    d. the philosophic dialogue

43. Eighteenth-century novelists generally wrote about:
    a. famous historical events
    b. legends or fables
    * c. true-to-life individuals (p. 424)
    d. glamorous personages

44. English novelists used this technique to make their works realistic:
    a. They focused on the lives of ordinary men and women.
    b. They followed their characters over the course of minutely observed time.
    c. They used a narrative voice that was appropriate to the setting.
    * d. all of the above (p. 425)

45. Samuel Richardson's novel *Pamela* has this theme:
    * a. a sentimental domestic drama (p. 425)
    b. a robust world of comedy and adventure
    c. a tragic situation confronting aristocratic lords and ladies
    d. a mythological story about fatal passion

46. The new power of the middle classes was reflected in the appearance of:
    a. the English novel
    b. the paintings of Hogarth
    c. most of the writings of the *philosophes*
    * d. all of the above (*passim*)

47. The plot of Fielding's *The History of Tom Jones* is:
    a. a sentimental domestic drama
    * b. a robust comedy and adventure tale (p. 425)
    c. a tragic situation brought on by fate
    d. a legendary tale of a famous highwayman

48. The perfect instrument for Rococo music was:
    a. the violin
    b. the trumpet
    * c. the harpsichord (p. 425)
    d. the organ

49. The music of Couperin is a perfect counterpart to:
    a. the paintings of David
    b. the poems of Alexander Pope
    * c. the art of Watteau (p. 424)
    d. the architecture of Robert Adam

50. Classical music was characterized by its:
    a. emphasis on form and structure
    b. widespread reliance on the sonata form
    c. use of clear, simple harmonies
  * d. all of the above (pp. 425–426)

17

REVOLUTION, REACTION,
AND CULTURAL RESPONSE
1760–1830

I. TEACHING STRATEGIES AND SUGGESTIONS

The instructor will be challenged to keep this complicated chapter's central threads together, to focus on the main themes of several complex movements, and to connect the material institutions with the intellectual developments and artistic trends. One or possibly two Standard Lectures may be necessary to set the stage for this period. The Historical Overview can be used to introduce the period in the first lecture; the instructor can then employ the Diffusion model to show what precipitated the three "revolutions"—namely, the American, the French, and the Industrial revolutions, specifically posing the question of how much impact the Enlightenment had on the two political upheavals.

A good approach to the Industrial Revolution is to adopt the Pattern of Change method; and the two political revolutions can be presented with the Case Study or the Comparison/Contrast model. However, the instructor should seriously consider giving a brief Historical Overview in order to lay out in a straightforward manner the origins, phases, and outcome of the French Revolution. To supplement the lecture on the French Revolution, it is recommended that the textbook's Table 17.1, entitled Shifts in the French Government, be copied and distributed in class; this table will help to keep this period's complex details from becoming overwhelming for students. The section in the textbook entitled "Reaction, 1815–1830" should not be scanted when dealing with the topics in this chapter, since it establishes the groundwork for many of the themes that are taken up in the next chapter.

The Reflections/Connections model should be the most effective in setting the themes, trends, and works identified with Neoclassicism and Romanticism. The paintings and architecture of Neoclassicism and Romanticism should be explained by means of Slide Lectures. The origins and causes of Romanticism can be explored with the Reflections/Connections model or the Spirit of the Age approach—the latter being more appropriate perhaps since Hegel, the author of this idea, is treated in this chapter. The instructor, using a Music Lecture, can show how the roots of Romantic music reach back to the Rococo and Classical styles.

Since Chapter 17 is so pivotal to the narrative of Western history and so central to *The Western Humanities*, a concluding lecture on the legacy of this period is necessary both as a summary and as an introduction to the nineteenth century, which will be covered in Chapters 18 and 19.

II. LECTURE OUTLINE

Non-Western Events

1760–1830
In China, Manchu
Dynasty, 1644–1912

A. General Characteristics of the
1760–1830 Period

B. The Industrial Revolution
   1. Industrialization in England
      a. Conditions and causes
      b. Changes in cotton manufacturing
      c. Social changes
   2. Classical economics: the rationale
      for industrialization
      a. Adam Smith: *Wealth of Nations*
      b. Thomas Malthus: *Essay on the
         Principle of Population*
      c. David Ricardo: *Principles of Political
         Economy and Taxation*

C. Political Revolutions, 1780–1814
   1. The American Revolution
      a. Causes and phases
      b. Results of the revolution
   2. The French Revolution
      a. Causes and phases
      b. The Napoleonic era

D. Reaction, 1815–1830
   1. Assessment of the results of the
      revolutions
   2. Reform and restoration across
      Europe

E. Revolutions in Art and Ideas: From
   Neoclassicism to Romanticism
   1. Comparison and contrast of the
      two movements
   2. Neoclasssical painting and
      architecture after 1789
      a. Jacques–Louis David
      b. Jean–Auguste–Dominique Ingres
      c. Thomas Jefferson
   3. Classicism in Literature after 1789
   4. Romanticism: its spirit
      and expression
      a. Causes and characteristics of
         Romanticism
      b. The Romantic movement in literature
         (1) *Sturm und Drang:* Goethe as a
             young writer
         (2) English Romanticism
             (a) Wordsworth
             (b) Coleridge
         (3) Goethe: *Faust*
         (4) Lord Byron: *Don Juan*
      c. Romantic painting
         (1) John Constable
         (2) J.M.W. Turner
         (3) Casper David Friedrich
         (4) Francisco Goya

In Japan, Tokugawa
Shogunate,
1603–1867
In India, British East
India Company,
1757–1858
Sayyid Said, ruler of
Zanzibar and Muscat,
1804–1856
Shaka, King of the
Zulu, 1818–1828
Decline of Mughal Empire
in India, 1700–1800
Indian adventurer Hyder
Ali conquers parts of
India, *ca.* 1760
Abdul Hamid I as Sultan
of Turkey, 1774
Toussaint–L'Ouverture
leads slave revolt in
Santo Domingo, 1802
Revolts for independence
in Central and South
America, 1810–1830

Society to found Liberia
for free U. S. blacks,
1820

Emerald Buddha Chapel
in Bangkok, 1785
Height of Manchu
civilization in China
in reign of Ch'ien
Lung, 1736–1796

Katsushika Hokusai,
Japanese painter,
1760–1849

Suzuki Harunobu,

      (5)   Théodore Géricault
      (6)   Eugène Delacroix
    d. German Idealism
      (1)   Immanuel Kant
      (2)   F.W.J. von Schelling
      (3)   G.F.W. Hegel
    e. The birth of Romantic music
      (1)   Ludwig van Beethoven
      (2)   Franz Schubert
      (3)   Hector Berlioz

Japanese painter, 1724–1770

Okyo, Japanese painter, 1733–1795

F.   The Legacy of the Age of Revolution and Reaction

III. LEARNING OBJECTIVES

To learn:

1. Why the 1760–1830 period was so revolutionary and what it produced
2. The characteristics and causes of the Industrial Revolution
3. Why the Industrial Revolution occurred first in England
4. How the Industrial Revolution changed English society
5. The arguments put forward by the Classical economists regarding the nature of the economy and why these arguments seemed to justify the first phases of the Industrial Revolution
6. The causes, phases, and results of the American Revolution
7. The causes, phases, and results of the French Revolution
8. How and why Napoleon rose to power and what he accomplished
9. How Europe reacted to the French Revolutions from 1815 to 1830
10. The characteristics of Neoclassicism, its major painters, and their contributions
11. The impact of Neoclassicism on American architecture
12. The characteristics and origins of Romanticism
13. How Romanticism was manifested in literature, who were its major writers, and what were their works
14. The role that Goethe played in Romanticism and his influences on later writers
15. How Romanticism was expressed in the visual arts, who were its major artists, and what are key examples of their works
16. The artistic contributions of Francisco Goya
17. The nature of German Idealism and its major voices
18. The origins and nature of Romantic music, its chief composers, and their contributions
19. Historic "firsts" of this period that became part of the Western tradition: the Industrial Revolution, the American Revolution, the French Revolution, Classical economics, states based on natural rights theory, a revolutionary tradition, militant nationalism, and Romanticism
20. The role of this period in transmitting the heritage of earlier civilizations: continuing the Neoclassical style, particularly developing an enduring type of public building style; restoring the idea of democracy, which had been in disrepute since fifth-century B.C. Athens, and giving it

a modern interpretation; furthering the Renaissance idea of free expression; and reviving beliefs and ideals of the medieval period

IV. SUGGESTIONS FOR FILMS

The Ascent of Man: The Drive for Power. Time–Life, 52 min., color.

Bernstein on Beethoven: Ode to Joy from the Ninth Symphony. BFA Educational Media, 27 min., color.

Civilisation: Heroic Materialism. Fallacies of Hope. Time–Life, 52 min. each, color.

English Literature: Romantic Period. Coronet, 14 min., color.

The French Revolution. Coronet, 17 min., color.

The Industrial Revolution in England. Encyclopedia Britannica, 26 min., black and white.

Napoleon: The Making of a Dictator. Learning Corporation of America, 27 min., color.

Seeds of the Revolution: Colonial America 1763–75. Graphic Curriculum, 24 min., color.

Spirit of Romanticism. Encyclopedia Britannica, 27 min., color.

Thomas Jefferson's Monticello. Comco Productions/Paramount, 24 min., color.

V. SUGGESTIONS FOR MUSIC

Beethoven, Ludwig van. *Symphony No. 3 in E Flat, Op. 55, "Eroica."* Mehta, New York Philharmonic. CBS IM–35883 [digital]; MK–35883 [CD].

————. *"Leonore" Overture No. 3 and Symphony No. 5.* Boult, London Promenade Orchestra. Vanguard CSRV–190 [cassette].

————. *Beethoven's Greatest Hits.* Various orchestras and performers. CBS MLK–39434 [CD].

Berlioz, Hector. *Symphonie fantastique, Op. 14.* Muti, Philadelphia Orchestra. Angel DS–38210 [Digital]; CDC–47278 [CD]; 4DS–32810 [cassette].

————. *Requieum, Op. 5.* Burrows, Bernstein, French National Radio Orchestra. CBS M2–34202.

————. *Harold in Italy, for viola and orchestra, Op. 16.* Christ, Maazel, Berlin Philharmonic and Chorus. DG 415109–2 GH [CD].

Schubert, Franz. *Songs.* Ameling, w. Baldwin. Etcetera ETC–1009; ARN–268006 [CD].

————. *Symphony No. 8 in b, D. 759, "Unfinished."* Marriner, St. Martin's Academy. Philips 412472–2 PH [CD].

————. *Octet in F for Strings and winds, D. 803, Op. 166.* Scott, Heller, Jolley, Genualdi, Falimir, Tenenbaum, Wiley, and Lloyd. Marlboro Recording Society MRSCD–18 [CD].

VI. SUGGESTIONS FOR FURTHER READING

Bergeron, L. *France Under Napoleon.* Princeton: Princeton University Press, 1981.

Brion, M. *Art of the Romantic Era.* London: Thames and Hudson, 1966.

Eitner, L.E.A. *Neoclassicism and Romanticism 1750–1850: Sources and Documents.* Englewood Cliffs, N.J.: Prentice–Hall, 1970.

Hampson, N. *A Social History of the French Revolution.* London: Routledge and Kegan Paul, 1963.

Honour, H. *Romanticism.* New York: Harper & Row, 1979.

Klingender, F. D. *Art and the Industrial Revolution.* New York: Shocken Books, 1970.

Rosenblum, R. *Transformations in Late Eighteenth–Century Art.* Princeton: Princeton University Press, 1967.

Sutherland, D. *France 1789–1815: Revolution and Counter–revolution.* New York: Oxford University Press, 1986.

VII. IDENTIFICATIONS

Romanticism
Sublime
Sturm und Drang
Faustian

program music
art song (*lied*)
idée fixe

VIII. DISCUSSION/ESSAY QUESTIONS

1. Discuss the reasons why the Industrial Revolution occurred first in England and describe its impact on English society.
2. Summarize early developments in the Industrial Revolution, using the situation in cloth manufacturing as your example.
3. Show how the writings of Adam Smith, Thomas Malthus, and David Ricardo could be used to justify the Industrial Revolution.
4. What were the causes of the American Revolution, what were the goals of the revolt, and how successful were the American colonists in achieving their goals?
5. Some historians claim that the French Revolution has been the most important political event in the modern world. Explain why this may or may not be true.
6. Discuss the events leading up to the French Revolution, and describe the events of the first year of the revolution.
7. What were the major phases of the French Revolution from 1789 to 1799? How successful were the French in accomplishing their goals of 1789?
8. Why had events come "full circle" with the rise of Napoleon?
9. Napoleon called himself "a child of the Enlightenment." Did his domestic program reflect Enlightenment values? Explain.
10. Discuss the various European responses in the years between 1815 and 1830 to the ideals and goals of the French Revolution and Napoleon.
11. What were the roots of Neoclassicism, how would you define the term, and how did the paintings of David and Ingres express Neoclassicism?
12. Show how David's career as a painter reflected the changing political climate in France.

13. Discuss the impact of Neoclassicism on American building styles.
14. Discuss the origins of Romanticism and identify its chief characteristics.
15. What was the *Sturm und Drang* movement? Discuss its relationship to Romanticism.
16. What contributions did Wordsworth, Coleridge, and Lord Byron make to Romantic literature?
17. Goethe has often been cited as the central figure in the Romantic movement. Why?
18. How were the themes of Romanticism expressed in the paintings of Constable, Turner, and Friedrich?
19. How does Goya fit into Romanticism? Discuss at least two of his works to justify your position.
20. Compare and contrast the art styles of Géricault and Delacroix, using a painting by each artist in your discussion.
21. What is meant by German Idealism and how was it expressed in the philosophy of Kant?
22. Discuss the role of Hegel in the evolution of nineteenth–century European thought.
23. What were the origins of Romantic music? How do Beethoven's musical works express the Romantic style?
24. Which event of the 1760–1830 period has had the most important effect on your life? Justify your answer.
25. What were the "good" and "bad" results of the French Revolution?
26. In what ways is Romanticism still a part of our lives today?

IX. MULTIPLE-CHOICE QUESTIONS

1. The time period between 1760 and 1830 can be described as:
   a. an age when the ways of creating wealth began to change
   b. a period marked by complacency
   c. an era when the middle class began to challenge the aristocracy
   * d. a and c but not b (p. 431)

2. One of the major events that changed agricultural production in England in the eighteenth century was:
   a. the back–to–the–farm movement
   * b. the enclosure acts (pp. 431–432)
   c. the three–field system
   d. the use of manufactured fertilizers

3. Why did the Industrial Revolution begin in England?
   a. England's colonial empire was a ready source for raw materials.
   b. A rise in the population created a new pool of labor.
   c. A minimum of internal tariffs and custom duties allowed goods to be shipped from one place to another.
   * d. all of the above (pp. 431–432)

4. The English Industrial Revolution began in these two industries:
   a. coal mining and shoe manufacturing
   * b. textiles and coal mining (p. 432)
   c. textiles and chinaware
   d. iron casting and bridge building

5. Which development(s) occurred in the English cloth–making industry at the start of the Industrial Revolution?
   a. As one invention was made, others followed in another part of the process of making cloth.
   b. Laborers had to conform to the way the machines operated.
   c. Factories had to be built near sources of power, such as a river.
   * d. all of the above (p. 432)

6. The writings of these economists seemed to justify the Industrial Revolution:
*   a. the Classical economists (p. 433)
    b. the Utopian economists
    c. the Marxist economists
    d. the Federal economists

7. Adam Smith in his *Wealth of Nations:*
    a. dealt mainly with agriculture and commerce, not manufacturing
    b. emphasized the concept of enlightened self–interest
    c. called for the intervention of governments to control their economies
*   d. a and b but not c (p. 433)

8. Malthus's "law" of population meant that:
    a. The future is inevitably brighter than the past.
    b. Wages inevitably fall behind prices.
*   c. Population growth will inevitably outstrip food production leading to natural calamities, such as famines, plagues, and wars. (p. 433)
    d. Populations remain fairly stable in industrial states, because of the widespread use of birth control measures.

9. The economic conclusions reached by Malthus and Ricardo:
    a. led many to believe that the workers deserved what they got
    b. indicated that there were laws in the operation of the economy
    c. forecast a rise in the standard of living for the working class
*   d. a and b but not c (p. 433)

10. What was the major issue dividing England and her American colonies in 1776?
    a. cultural differences
    b. class conflicts
*   c. taxes and the cost of upkeep of the colonies (p. 433)
    d. the slave trade

11. When did the American colonists first join together?
    a. at the time of the first battle of the Revolution
*   b. when the Continental Congress was convened (p. 433)
    c. when the British declared war
    d. after the Declaration of Independence was signed

12. What was an outcome of the American Revolution?
    a. All citizens were granted the right to vote.
    b. The United States became the most democratic government since ancient Athens.
    c. The United State became an example for other peoples to follow in their struggle for freedom.
*   d. b and c but not a (p. 434)

13. A characteristic of France when Louis XVI became king was:
    a. class hatred between the aristocracy and the wealthy middle class
    b. a bankrupt economy with a large national debt
    c. an unfair tax system
*   d. all of the above (p. 434)

14. The major accomplishment of the French Revolution's first phase was:
    a. the end of the class system in France
    b. the triumph of the workers
    * c. the creation of a limited constitutional monarchy (p. 435)
    d. the right to vote being given to women citizens

15. What caused the French Revolution to enter a new phase in 1792?
    a. Louis XVI proved untrustworthy and ineffective.
    b. Some segments of French society wanted more radical reforms.
    c. Class feelings were still running high.
    * d. all of the above (p. 435)

16. The French Revolution's second phase can be described as a time of:
    a. domestic tranquility
    b. control by the radicals
    c. foreign wars
    * d. b and c but not a (p. 435)

17. A major domestic reform made by Napoleon was:
    a. a refurbished public educational system
    b. an accord with the Catholic church
    c. a stabilized economy
    * d. all of the above (p. 436)

18. In foreign affairs Napoleon:
    a. succeeded in setting up client kingdoms across Europe
    b. convinced other European states that he wanted peace
    * c. failed to liberate oppressed people (p. 436)
    d. proved to be an inept military leader

19. Which is correct regarding changes in Europe between 1789 and 1815?
    a. The French succeeded in exporting their revolution to other countries.
    b. Many of Napoleon's reforms remained in place after his fall from power.
    c. Europe's leaders tried to prevent revolutionary ideas from infecting their own citizenry.
    * d. b and c but not a (pp. 437–438)

20. Why did France's revolutionary leaders favor Neoclassicism?
    a. They liked its subjects, which focused on patriotism.
    b. They identified with the noble qualities of the ancient Greco–Roman world.
    c. They thought that its style was morally uplifting and aesthetically satisfying.
    * d. all of the above (p. 438)

21. In the painting *The Death of Marat*, David:
    a. created a realistic work
    b. captured a specific moment in history
    c. portrayed the ideals of the French Revolution by glamorizing one of its martyrs
    * d. all of the above (p. 439 and caption for Fig. 17.4)

22. David's painting called *The Coronation* can be described as:
    * a. a work of political propaganda (p. 439)
    b. a sentimental interpretation of an event
    c. an exact portrayal of what happened at the coronation
    d. the best group portrait of the era

23. Who introduced the Neoclassical style to the United States?
    a. George Washington
    b. Benjamin Franklin
  * c. Thomas Jefferson (p. 443)
    d. James Madison

24. Which is correct regarding Jefferson's design for Monticello?
    a. The design was influenced by Palladio, the Italian architect.
    b. The design expresses the ideals of the ruling middle class.
    c. The design reflects the new Romantic style.
  * d. a and b but not c (p. 443)

25. Romanticism:
    a. grew out of a rejection of the Enlightenment's ideas
    b. looked to nature and the Middle Ages for inspiration
    c. reflected, in part, the revolutionary values of the French Revolution
  * d. all of the above (p. 443)

26. Romanticism viewed nature as:
    a. a resource to be exploited
    b. a power that overawed the individual
    c. God
  * d. b and c but not a (p. 443)

27. How did the Romantics interpret the French Revolution?
    a. They envisioned it as the wave of the future.
    b. They were appalled at its extreme violence.
    c. They thought that its ideals were too abstract.
  * d. all of the above (pp. 443–444)

28. Romantic writers and artists expressed:
  * a. an admiration for nonconformity (p. 444)
    b. a deep respect for the middle class
    c. a yearning to be part of the aristocracy
    d. a preference for the Classical world

29. The country that could best claim to be the home of Romanticism was:
    a. England
    b. France
  * c. Germany (p. 444)
    d. Italy

30. The *Sturm und Drang* movement:
    a. started in Germany
    b. revolted against Classicism
    c. glorified the lives of peasants
  * d. all of the above (p. 444)

31. Goethe's novel entitled *The Sorrows of Young Werther* was:
    a. one of the opening works of the Romantic movement
    b. a work filled with emotionalism
    c. a work that illustrated how an individual might be crushed by society
  * d. all of the above (p. 445)

32. English Romanticism was launched by the writings of:
 * a. Wordsworth and Coleridge (p. 445)
   b. Keats and Shelley
   c. Goethe and Lessing
   d. Lord Byron and Dickens

33. The poems in Wordsworth's *Lyrical Ballads:*
   a. were written in a Classical style
   b. celebrate the joy and pleasure of ordinary events
   c. show that nature and humans have an intimate relationship
 * d. b and c but not a (p. 445)

34. Goethe's hero Faust:
   a. symbolized the universal rebel, willing to do anything to discover the spiritual meaning of life
   b. was filled with intellectual restlessness
   c. underwent a series of sordid adventures, including murder and seduction
 * d. all of the above (p. 445)

35. Lord Byron personifies the Romantic ideal because:
   a. He was a rebel against middle–class respectability.
   b. His poetry expressed the Romantic spirit.
   c. He died as a hero in a noble cause.
 * d. all of the above (p. 445)

36. A theme of Romantic painting was:
   a. quiet pastoral scenes
   b. scenes of country folk and peasants
   c. scenes depicting nature's awesome aspects
 * d. all of the above (p. 446)

37. In his paintings Constable:
   a. depicted the play of sunlight
   b. made the ever–changing sky a major focus of his work
   c. preferred simple scenes of nature lacking dramatic details
 * d. all of the above (p. 446)

38. Which painter's treatment of color later influenced the Impressionists?
 * a. Turner (pp. 446–447)
   b. Ingres
   c. Goya
   d. Friedrich

39. The painter who established the Romantic style in Germany was:
   a. Millet
   b. Delacroix
 * c. Friedrich (p. 448)
   d. Biedermeier

40. In his paintings Goya expressed:
   a. a love of nature that he identified with God
   b. a nightmarish vision of the world
   c. a growing despair over the fate of his beloved Spanish homeland
 * d. b and c but not a (p. 448)

41. Goya's etchings entitled *Caprices:*
    * a. express his most personal feelings (p. 449)
      b. have optimistic themes
      c. portray idealized subjects
      d. all of the above

42. Géricault's painting of *The Raft of the Medusa* portrayed the theme of:
      a. the breakdown of civilization
      b. the power of the sea
      c. the human struggle to survive
    * d. all of the above (p. 451 and caption for Fig. 17.18)

43. Delacroix's painting entitled *Liberty Leading the People:*
      a. combines realism and allegory
      b. made France's tricolor flag the focal point
      c. was an embarrassment to France's bourgeois monarchy
    * d. all of the above (pp. 452–453 and captions for Figs. 17.20 and 17.21)

44. Delacroix's *Liberty Leading the People* was inspired by:
      a. the Revolution of 1789
      b. the defeat of Napoleon in 1815 and the restoration of the Bourbons
    * c. the July Revolution of 1830 (p. 452)
      d. the French revolutionary tradition

45. German Idealism is:
      a. a revival of ancient Platonism
    * b. a philosophic alternative to religion (p. 454)
      c. a philosophy based on atheism
      d. a system of thought based on materialism and determinism

46. All of the following are ideas of Hegel EXCEPT:
      a. History evolves through a dialectical process.
      b. The goal of the World Spirit is freedom.
    * c. Individuals have significant roles in the struggle for freedom. (p. 455)
      d. Conflict and strife are essential for historical growth.

47. Hegel's ideas influenced:
      a. conservatives, who adopted his theory of a strong centralized state
      b. Marxists, who borrowed his concept of the dialectic
      c. democrats, who shared his views on the role of the people in history
    * d. a and b but not c (p. 455)

48. How did the middle class influence late-eighteenth-century music?
      a. the rise of public concerts and performances with admission fees and paid performers
      b. more accessible music to serve the tastes of the new audiences
      c. music written to be performed in homes on the inexpensive musical instruments that were now available
    * d. all of the above (p. 455)

49. Which of these is correct about Beethoven and his music?
    a. His life passed through several stages that were mirrored in his search for new forms of music.
    b. He personified the new breed of musician, supporting himself with concerts, lessons, and sales of his music.
    c. His works represented both the culmination of Classical music and the introduction of Romantic music.
  * d. all of the above (p. 455)

50. All of these are innovations of Romantic music EXCEPT:
    a. program music
    b. the art song
    c. the use of choral music within the symphonic form
  * d. the sonata (pp. 455–456)

18

THE TRIUMPH
OF THE BOURGEOISIE
1830–1871

I. TEACHING STRATEGIES AND SUGGESTIONS

The instructor can introduce the Age of the Bourgeoisie, 1830–1871, with a Historical Overview that summarizes this epoch's key historical developments and, with a Pattern of Change approach, can set forth the accompanying stylistic evolution from the dominant Romantic and Neoclassical styles to the new style of Realism. Turning to a Reflections/Connections approach, the instructor can show how Neoclassicism and Romanticism mirrored historical events prior to 1848, the year of European-wide revolutions and a watershed year, and how Realism expressed the changed situation thereafter. A Slide Lecture combined with a Comparison/Contrast approach can show the changes in the arts and architecture. Special emphasis should be given to the painter Manet, because his "art for art's sake" dictum opened the door to the radical changes that produced modern art. A Music Lecture can illustrate the transformation in music, although Romantic music remained dominant throughout the era. A Standard Lecture organized on the Comparison/Contrast model can demonstrate the literary changes taking place, as Romantic writing gave way to Realism. And a Standard Lecture can be used to explain the contributions in philosophy, religion, and science. The instructor can conclude this series of presentations with a Spirit of the Age approach, emphasizing the role played by the ruling middle class, liberalism, and science in shaping mid-nineteenth-century culture.

II. LECTURE OUTLINE

Non-Western Events

A. Historical Overview
   1. The legacy of the American and
      French revolutions
   2. The plight of the proletariat
   3. Summary of stylistic developments

B. The Political and Economic Scene:
   Liberalism and Nationalism
   1. Liberalism
      a. Definition
      b. Ideals and influence
   2. Nationalism
      a. Definition
      b. Ideals and influence to 1848

1830–1871
In India, British East
   India company rules to
   1858 when power passes
   to the British crown
   (raj), 1858–1947

First telegraph in India
   in 1853
In China, Manchu
   Dynasty, 1644–1912
In Japan, the Tokugawa
   Shogunate, 1603–1867;
   opening of Japan,
   1854; Meiji Dynasty,

3. The revolutions of 1830 and their aftermath
   a. The July uprising in France and the bourgeois monarchy
   b. The failed revolutions in central and southern Europe
4. The revolutions of 1848
   a. Background
   b. The axis of revolution: Paris through Berlin to Vienna
   c. The failed revolutions and the rise of *Realpolitik*
5. European affairs in the grip of *Realpolitik*
   a. The lessons of *Realpolitik*
   b. Limited reforms in France and Great Britain
      (1) France
         (a) Napoleon III maneuvers to power
         (b) Benign despotism
      (2) Great Britain
         (a) Electoral reforms
         (b) Economic prosperity
   c. Wars and unification in central Europe
      (1) Power struggle between Austria and Prussia
      (2) The Bismarck era and the unification of Germany
      (3) The unification of Italy
6. Civil War in the United States
   a. Sectional tension
   b. The slavery question
   c. Civil War, abolition of slavery, and reconstruction
7. The spread of industrialism
   a. The European continent
   b. England: phase two
   c. Travel, communications, and raw materials
   d. The Crystal Palace: the first world's fair
   e. The Suez Canal: a short water route to Asia
   f. Condition of the workers
   g. Increased suffrage

C. Nineteenth-Century Thought
   1. Philosophy
      a. The liberal tradition and the socialist challenge
      b. Liberalism redefined

1868–1912; end of feudalism, 1871
In Africa, Sayyid Said, ruler of Zanzibar and Muscat, 1804–1856; Moshesh, King of Basutoland, 1824–1868; British consulates in coastal states, 1830–1860; exploration of interior continent, 1830–1875; decline of slave trade, 1840–1863
France seizes Algeria, 1830
Ecuador breaks away from Colombia and becomes a republic, 1830
Porfirio Diaz, Mexican statesman, 1830–1915
Exportation of nitrates from Chile begins, 1830–
Mehemet Ali in 1833 founds the dynasty that rules Egypt until 1952

Abolition of slavery in British Empire, 1833

Prince Matsukata, Japanese stateman, 1835–1924
Texas wins independence from Mexico, 1836; joins United States in 1845
Boer farmers found Natal, Transvaal, Orange Free State in Africa, 1836

Rabindranath Tagore, Indian philosopher and poet, 1861–1941

              (1) Jeremy Bentham: Utilitarianism
              (2) John Stuart Mill
         c. Socialism
              (1) The utopian socialists
                   (a) Owen, Saint-Simon, Fourier
                   (b) Failed experiments
              (2) The Marxists
                   (a) Marx and Engels
                   (b) Dialectical materialism
                   (c) Formation of international
                        socialist organization
                   (d) Little influence before 1871
    2. Religion and the challenge of science
         a. The higher criticism
         b. Science
              (1) Geology discredits the
                   biblical view of creation
              (2) Biology questions the divine
                   image of human beings
              (3) Pasteur: the germ theory of
                   disease
              (4) Chemistry: advances in
                   atomic theory,
                   anesthetics, and surgery

D. Cultural Trends: from Romanticism to Realism
    1. Order and escape
         a. Neoclassicism and Romanticism adopted
              by the middle class
              (1) Art becomes routinized
              (2) The development of "official art"
         b. The challenge of Realism
              (1) Rejection of Neoclassicism
                   and Romanticism
              (2) Art with a moral point of view,
                   focused on ordinary people
              (3) Influences on Realism
    2. Literature
         a. Overview
              (1) Romanticism: free will
              (2) Realism: deterministic
         b. The height of English and French
              Romanticism
              (1) Hugo
                   (a) *Hernani*
                   (b) *Les Misérables*
              (2) The Brontë sisters
                   (a) Emily Brontë, *Wuthering
                        Heights*
                   (b) Charlotte Brontë, *Jane Eyre*
         c. Realism in French and English novels
              (1) Balzac and *The Human Comedy*
              (2) Flaubert and *Madame Bovary*
              (3) The English Realists

In China, Taiping reform
program ("Heavenly
Peace") advocates
examinations based on
the Bible instead of
Chinese classics, equal
distribution of land,
property rights for
men and women, common
granary, 1853–1864

Ando Hiroshige, Japanese
painter, 1797–1858;
publishes series of
color prints "Fifty-
three Stages of the
Tokaido," 1832
Paris world's fair
introduces Japanese
art to the West, 1867

Sequoya, Cherokee leader,
creates Cherokee
alphabet, 1770–1843
Mori Ogai, Japanese poet,
translator of *Faust*,
1860–1921
Japanese literature after
1868 influenced by
the Realist literary
style of the West

            (a) Characteristics
            (b) Dickens
            (c) Gaskell
            (d) Evans (George Eliot)
        d. The Russian Realists
            (1) Characteristics
            (2) Tolstoy
            (3) Dostoyevsky
    3. Art and architecture
        a. Neoclassicism and Romanticism after
            1830
            (1) Ingres
                (a) A power in official art
                (b) *The Turkish Bath*
            (2) Delacroix
                (a) Color theories
                (b) *The Abduction of Rebecca*
            (3) Romantic architecture
                (a) Characteristics
                (b) Barry and Pugin's Houses of
                     Parliament, London
        b. The rise of Realism in art
            (1) Background
            (2) Courbet
                (a) *A Burial at Ornans*
                (b) *Interior of My Studio*
            (3) Daumier
                (a) Satirical subjects
                (b) *Le Ventre Législatif (The
                     Legislative Belly)*
                (c) *Third Class Carriage*
            (4) Millet
                (a) The Barbizon school
                (b) *The Sower*
                (c) *The Gleaners*
            (5) Manet
                (a) *The Salon des Refusés* (Salon of the Rejects)
                (b) *Le Déjeuner sur l'Herbe
                     (Luncheon on the Grass)*
                (c) His radical aesthetic
    4. Photography
        a. Historical background
            (1) Daguerre
            (2) Fox Talbot
            (3) Photography as art
        b. Matthew Brady
    5. Music
        a. Changes in Romantic music;
            adherence to Classical forms
        b. Romantic music: opera
            (1) Middle class audiences and
                 their impact
            (2) Verdi
                (a) His style

By 1850, East Africa is
most important source
of world's ivory and
illicit slaves

A. Carlos Gomez,
Brazilian composer,
1839–1896

                    (b) *Rigoletto* and other operas
              (3) Wagner
                    (a) Aesthetic goals
                    (b) *The Ring of the Nibelung*
        c. Romantic music: orchestral and chamber
            works
              (1) Changes under Romanticism
              (2) Brahms

  E. The Legacy of the Bourgeois Age

III. LEARNING OBJECTIVES

To learn:

  1. The defining events of the Age of the Bourgeoisie

  2. The characteristics of the reigning styles of Neoclassicism and Romanticism and how they
      reflected events to 1848, along with the characteristics of Realism and how it was a product of the
      post-1848 period

  3. The roles played by the middle class and the ideologies of liberalism and nationalism in shaping
      politics and culture during this era

  4. The significance of the revolutions of 1830 and their aftermath

  5. How the revolutions of 1848 were a watershed in politics and culture

  6. The cultural importance of the Civil War in the United States

  7. The impact of industrialism on history and civilization

  8. The challenge to religion by the conclusions of higher criticism and the advances in science

  9. The major contributions of science to an understanding of the universe

  10. The dialectic between liberalism and socialism, with special attention to Marxism and its origins

  11. The changed nature of Neoclassicism and Romanticism in the Age of the Bourgeoisie

  12. The characteristics of the Romantic novel, along with the leading writers and examples of their
       novels

  13. The characteristics of the Realist novel, along with the leading writers and examples of their
       novels

  14. To compare and contrast the Neoclassical style of Ingres with the Romantic style of Delacroix

  15. The significance of the official Salon in helping to shape Romantic and Neoclassical art prior to
       1871

  16. The characteristics of Realism in art along with the leading advocates and examples of
       significant works

  17. That Manet laid the groundwork for modern painting

  18. That photography was developed and became a new art form during this period

  19. The characteristics of Romantic music in this era

  20. The impact of the bourgeoisie as patrons of opera

  21. That Verdi and Wagner dominated opera although with contrasting musical styles

22. That Brahms was the leader of the conservative school against the followers of Wagner

23. Historic "firsts" of the Age of the Bourgeoisie that became part of the Western tradition: the Realist style of the arts, architecture, and literature; the germ theory of disease; anesthesias; advances in surgery; the pasteurization process; Marx's analysis of history; Darwin's theory of evolution; Pasteur's work in immunology and microbiology; the camera; the art of photography; the high-tech tradition; "art for art's sake" credo; higher criticism; and socialism

24. The role of the Age of the Bourgeoisie in transmitting the heritage of earlier civilizations: reviving Gothic architecture as the Neo-Gothic; continuing Neoclassicism in art and Romanticism in the arts and music; meeting the challenges to religious beliefs posed by scientific discoveries; perpetuating Romantic music, especially in the operas of Wagner that pushed this style to the limit; updating liberalism and moving toward democracy; turning nationalism toward greater militancy; maintaining the revolutionary tradition begun in the American and French revolutions; bringing the ancient institution of slavery to an end; and intensifying industrialism

IV. SUGGESTIONS FOR FILMS

Balzac. Radim, 23 min., black and white.

Bismarck: Germany from Blood and Iron. Learning Corporation of America, 30 min., color.

Civilisation: The Fallacies of Hope. BBC/Time-Life, 52 min., color.

Early Victorian England and Charles Dickens. Encyclopedia Britannica, 30 min., color.

Karl Marx: The Massive Dissent. Films, Inc., 57 min., color.

Les Misérables. Indiana University Audio-Visual Center, 54 min., black and white.

Nationalism. Encyclopedia Britannica, 20 min., black and white.

The Victorian Period. Coronet, 14 min., color.

V. SUGGESTIONS FOR MUSIC

Brahms, Johannes. *Symphonies (4).* Vienna Philharmonic. DG 423053-1 GH4 [digital].

———. *Quartets (3) for Strings.* Juilliard String Quartet. CBS M2K-45154 [CD].

———. *Brahms's Greatest Hits.* Vienna Symphony et. al. Pro Arte CDM-823 [CD].

Verdi, Giuseppi. *Otello.* Freni, Malagu, Vickers, Bottion, Senechal, Glossop, van Dam, Karajan, Berlin Philharmonic. Angel CDMB-69308 [CD].

———. *Requiem Mass.* Amara, Forrester, Tucker, London, Ormandy, Philadelphia Orchestra. Odyssey Y2-35230.

———. *Rigoletto.* Cotrubas, Obraztsova, Domingo, Cappuccilli, Giulini, Vienna Philharmonic and State Opera. DG415288-1 GH3 [Digital]; 415288-2GH2 [CD].

Wagner, Richard. *Der Ring des Nibelungen (orchestral excerpts).* New York Philharmonic. CBS MK-37795 [CD].

———. *Tristan: Prelude and Liebestod.* Bernstein, New York Philharmonic. CBS MS-7141.

———. *Wagner's Greatest Hits.* Philadelphia Orchestra et. al. CBS MLK-39438 [CD].

VI. SUGGESTIONS FOR FURTHER READING

Bierman, J. *Napoleon III and His Carnival Empire.* New York: St. Martin's, 1988.

Clark, K. *The Romantic Rebellion: Romantic Versus Classic Art.* New York: Harper & Row. 1986.

Chamberlin, J. E., and Gilman, S. L., eds. *Degeneration: The Dark Side of Progress.* New York: Columbia University Press, 1985.

Fortescue, W. *Revolution and Counter-Revolution in France, 1815–1852.* New York: Blackwell, 1988.

Hamerow, T. S. *The Birth of a New Europe: State and Society in the Nineteenth Century.* Chapel Hill: University of North Carolina Press, 1983.

Needham, G. *19th Century Realist Art.* New York: Harper & Row. 1988.

Reynolds, D. M. *The Nineteenth Century.* New York: Cambridge University Press, 1985.

Schenk, H.G.A.V. *The Mind of the European Romantics: An Essay in Cultural History.* London: Constable, 1966.

Stonyk, M. *Nineteenth-century English Literature.* New York: Schocken Books, 1984.

Tipton, F. B., and Aldrich, R. *An Economic and Social History of Europe, 1890–1939.* Baltimore: Johns Hopkins University Press, 1987.

Whittall, A. *Romantic Music: A Concise History from Schubert to Sibelius.* London: Thames and Hudson, 1987.

Winch, D. *The Emergence of Economics as a Science, 1750–1870.* London: Collins, 1971.

VII. IDENTIFICATIONS

Utilitarianism	aria
socialism	recitative
higher criticism	libretto
evolution	music drama
Realism	*leitmotif*

VIII. DISCUSSION/ESSAY QUESTIONS

1. Discuss the major historical and cultural events between 1830 and 1871 and show how they influenced the arts and humanities, particularly the Neoclassical and Romantic styles before 1848 and the Realist style thereafter.
2. Explain the significance of the 1848 revolutions and how they represented a turning point in nineteenth-century culture and politics.
3. What impact did the middle class and its ideology of liberalism have on nineteenth-century politics and culture? Explain the changed nature of liberalism in the mid-nineteenth century.
4. Define nationalism. Show how this ideology influenced culture and politics in this epoch.
5. Define *Realpolitik*. How did *Realpolitik* influence politics after 1848? What caused *Realpolitik* to develop?

6. What were the causes and the outcome of the American Civil War? Explain this war within the context of general trends in the West during the nineteenth century.
7. Discuss industrial developments in this era. What impact did these changes have on culture, particularly on political philosophy?
8. "The 1851 Exhibition in the Crystal Palace, London, was a fitting symbol of the Age of the Bourgeoisie." Explain.
9. Summarize the key ideas in Marxism. Explain the sources of Marx's philosophy of history.
10. What scientific advances were made between 1830 and 1871? What impact did these advances have on the development of cultural styles?
11. Discuss Romantic literature, focusing on the major characteristics and the leading authors and their contributions.
12. Compare and contrast Realist literature with Romantic fiction.
13. Discuss the impact of the Royal Academy of Painting and Sculpture on art during the Age of the Bourgeoisie. Define "official art."
14. Who founded Realist art? Why? What are the characteristics of Realism? Who are the leading Realist painters?
15. What was Manet's innovation that laid the foundations of modern art? Explain.
16. What new art form was invented during this era? Explain its significance.
17. How did Romantic music change during this Age of the Bourgeoisie? What forces were operating on music and causing it to change?
18. Compare and contrast the contributions of Verdi and Wagner to Romantic opera.
19. Discuss the role of Brahms in the history of Romantic music.

IX. MULTIPLE-CHOICE QUESTIONS

1. Between 1830 and 1871 European culture and politics was dominated by:
   a. the aristocracy
 * b. the wealthy bourgeoisie (p. 461)
   c. the working class
   d. the church

2. A basic principle of nineteenth-century liberalism was that:
 * a. The individual should be free from external control. (p. 461)
   b. Wealth and power should be distributed fairly in society.
   c. The state is a divine institution.
   d. all of the above

3. In nineteenth-century Europe, liberalism was most successful in:
   a. Italy
   b. Russia
 * c. France (p. 461)
   d. Germany

4. Nineteenth-century nationalism:
   a. overlooked class divisions
   b. stressed the concept that all members of a nation are brothers and sisters
   c. focused on the common language and heritage of an ethnic group
 * d. all of the above (p. 463)

5. A consequence of the 1830 revolutions was:
 * a. the end of the Bourbon monarchy in France and the installation of the bourgeois King Louis Philippe (p. 463)
   b. the expulsion of Metternich in Austria and the setting up of a revolutionary assembly

c.   the unification of Italy
d.   all of the above

6.   A consequence of the revolutions of 1848 was:
     a.   the end of the bourgeois monarchy in France and the installation of the Second Republic with Louis-Napoleon as president
     b.   the failure to achieve any meaningful reforms outside of France
     c.   the beginning of an age of *Realpolitik*
*   d.   all of the above (p. 464)

7.   *Realpolitik*, between 1850 and 1871, had a powerful impact on:
*   a.   the unification campaign in Germany (p. 464)
     b.   the electoral changes in Great Britain
     c.   the economic policies of Napoleon III in France
     d.   all of the above

8.   Who engineered the unification of Germany?
     a.   Cavour
     b.   Disraeli
*   c.   Bismarck (p. 466)
     d.   Metternich

9.   Italy in 1871 was unified around this small Italian state:
     a.   the Venetian republic
     b.   the duchy of Tuscany
*   c.   the kingdom of Sardinia (p. 466)
     d.   the kingdom of the Two Sicilies

10. The American Civil War had the immediate consequence of:
     a.   ending regional tensions
*   b.   abolishing slavery (pp. 467–468)
     c.   industrializing the national economy
     d.   resolving racial problems

11. By 1871 the right to vote was guaranteed to:
     a.   women in England
*   b.   working-class men in England and America (pp. 470)
     c.   lower middle-class men in Austria and Germany
     d.   all of the above

12. By 1871 the West was linked together by:
     a.   thousands of miles of rail line covering the European continent, America, and England
     b.   transatlantic telegraph cables between western Europe and America
     c.   an international banking system
*   d.   all of the above (pp. 468–469)

13. All were aspects of the Great Exhibition of 1851 staged in the Crystal Palace, London, EXCEPT:
     a.   It was the first world's fair.
*   b.   The building was constructed in the reigning Neo-Gothic style. (p. 469)
     c.   The exhibition confirmed Britain's status as the world's dominant industrial power.
     d.   The exhibition displayed the newest inventions and the latest machine-made goods.

14. Between 1830 and 1871 industrialization:
     a.   sparked the rapid growth of cities in Britain, France, and Belgium
     b.   resulted in the creation of vast slums for poor and ill-trained workers

c. created breeding grounds for class hatred and socialist ideas

*   d. all of the above (p. 470)

15. The seeds of World War I were sown by:
    a. the opening of the Suez Canal in 1869
    b. Britain's introduction of free trade in 1846
*   c. Prussia's humiliating defeat of France in 1870–1871 (p. 466)
    d. the unification of Italy in 1871

16. At the heart of nineteenth-century liberalism was a belief in:
    a. government control
*   b. free expression for the individual (p. 470)
    c. state-funded welfare
    d. all of the above

17. The founder of Utilitarianism was:
*   a. Jeremy Bentham (p. 470)
    b. John Stuart Mill
    c. Robert Owen
    d. Charles Fourier

18. Bentham believed that society should be based on "utility," meaning:
    a. natural rights
*   b. "the greatest happiness for the greatest number" (p. 470)
    c. God's law
    d. tradition

19. A leading nineteenth-century Utilitarian was:
    a. Robert Owen
    b. Friedrich Engels
*   c. John Stuart Mill (p. 470)
    d. Napoleon III

20. John Stuart Mill advocated:
    a. free expression so long as no person was physically harmed
    b. voting rights for women
    c. religious toleration
*   d. all of the above (p. 470)

21. Utopian socialists, in general:
    a. supported the bourgeois values of thrift and hard work as ways for workers to improve their condition
*   b. urged reform of the ills of industrial society based on the experience of model communities (p. 471)
    c. advocated violent overthrow of existing governments
    d. agreed with liberal principles

22. A leading utopian socialist was:
    a. Friedrich Engels
*   b. Comte de Saint-Simon (p. 471)
    c. Jeremy Bentham
    d. all of the above

23. Marx's dialectical reasoning was based on the philosophy of:
*   a. Hegel (p. 471)
    b. Burke
    c. Kant
    d. Fichte

24. Marx theorized that history is propelled by:
    a. individual greed
*   b. class conflict (p. 471)
    c. God
    d. chance events

25. A key idea in Marxism is that:
    a. The middle class will bring forth its own gravediggers, the proletariat.
    b. The proletariat will eventually install a classless society.
    c. Government, law, the arts, and the humanities reflect the values of a particular ruling class.
*   d. all of the above (p. 471)

26. "Higher criticism" refers to the nineteenth-century intellectual movement in which scholars:
    a. focused exclusively on literary texts while ignoring their historical settings
*   b. studied the Bible not as a divinely inspired book incapable of error but simply as a set of writings susceptible to varied interpretations (p. 471)
    c. analyzed all writings, secular and sacred, in accordance with Marxist theory
    d. applied linguistic theory to literature to show that all texts are the same

27. Whose researches in geology cast doubt on the biblical story of creation?
*   a. Charles Lyell (pp. 471–472)
    b. Charles Darwin
    c. Louis Pasteur
    d. John Dalton

28. Between 1830 and 1871 all of these scientific advances were made EXCEPT:
    a. Data were collected showing that modern plants and animals had evolved from simpler forms through a process of natural selection.
    b. The germ theory of disease was established.
*   c. The interior structure of the atom was mapped out. (p. 472)
    d. Chloroform and other anesthesias were introduced.

29. In science Charles Darwin:
    a. established the germ theory of disease
*   b. marshalled data to support the theory of evolution (p. 472)
    c. introduced the anesthesia called chloroform
    d. formulated the periodic table of the elements

30. In science Pasteur:
*   a. established the germ theory of disease (p. 472)
    b. marshalled data to support the theory of evolution
    c. introduced the anesthesia called chloroform
    d. formulated the periodic table of the elements

31. Between 1830 and 1871 Romantic art became:
    a. spectacular and showy
    b. respectable and inoffensive
    c. sentimental and moralistic
  * d. all of the above (p. 472)

32. Which development contributed to the rise of Realism?
    a. Bismarck's political policies
    b. Darwinian science
    c. the invention of the camera
  * d. all of the above (p. 473)

33. A leading French Romantic writer was:
    a. Honoré de Balzac
  * b. Victor Hugo (p. 474)
    c. Gustave Flaubert
    d. George Eliot

34. Romantic novelists concentrated on:
    a. scientific accuracy
    b. ordinary people without idealizing them
  * c. the feelings of their characters (p. 574)
    d. the social and economic forces that determined the lives of their characters

35. Realistic novelists:
    a. depicted the lives of ordinary men and women
    b. wrote without romanticizing their characters
    c. described the human world with scientific accuracy
  * d. all of the above (p. 574)

36. Romanticism may be seen in Emily Brontë's *Wuthering Heights:*
    a. in the ghostly apparitions and graveyard scenes
    b. in the tale of mismatched soulmates
    c. in the unconventional hero Heathcliff
  * d. all of the above (p. 574)

37. French Realists, unlike English Realists, often wrote about:
  * a. sexual issues (p. 475)
    b. middle-class hypocrisy
    c. the ills of a materialistic society
    d. the lives of ordinary men and women

38. The English Realist with the largest audience was:
    a. Charlotte Brontë
  * b. Charles Dickens (p. 475)
    c. George Eliot
    d. Elizabeth Gaskell

39. An innovation of Dostoevsky, the Russian Realist, was:
    a. a first-person narrative style
    b. stream-of-consciousness writing
  * c. the anti-hero type (p. 475)
    d. the socialist novel

40. The leading Neoclassical painter between 1830 and 1871 was:
    a. Delacroix
  * b. Ingres (p. 476)
    c. Courbet
    d. Manet

41. All of these are products of the Romantic style EXCEPT:
  * a. Ingres's *The Turkish Bath* (pp. 476, 478, 485)
    b. Delacroix's *The Abduction of Rebecca*
    c. Barry and Pugin's Houses of Parliament, London
    d. Verdi's *Rigoletto*

42. The founder of Realism in painting was:
    a. Delacroix
    b. Ingres
  * c. Courbet (p. 478)
    d. Manet

43. Courbet's painting called *Interior of My Studio:*
    a. was rejected by the Salon jury
    b. portrays realistic contemporary figures
    c. visually summarizes the painter's approach to art up until this time
  * d. all of the above (p. 473)

44. The key element in Daumier's approach to painting was:
    a. a love of exotic scenes
    b. a fascination with fiery action
  * c. a satirical eye (p. 473)
    d. a feeling for the geometry underlying nature

45. The painter Millet:
    a. was a member of the Barbizon school
    b. made the rural folk and their labors his primary subject
    c. painted pastoral scenes without idealizing or romanticizing them
  * d. all of the above (p. 481)

46. In what sense was Manet the first modern painter?
    a. He opened the door to abstraction.
  * b. He originated the tradition of "art for art's sake." (p. 483)
    c. He paved the way for Expressionism.
    d. He pioneered the Cubist style.

47. Romantic music was characterized by:
    a. frequent use of minor keys
    b. unique styles expressive of composers' individual feelings
    c. themes drawn from folk songs, national anthems, and ethnic dance rhythms
  * d. all of the above (p. 484)

48. The composer of the opera *Rigoletto* was:
  * a. Verdi (p. 485)
    b. Puccini
    c. Wagner
    d. Brahms

49. Wagner's contribution to opera did NOT include:
    a. a new style of opera that fused all of the arts together
    b. the use of *leitmotifs* as identifying musical phrases for characters, things, or ideas
  * c. a performance style that alternated arias with recitatives (p. 485)
    d. the composing of a type of music with a continuously flowing melodic line

50. Which composer was the leader of the traditionalists who opposed the music of Wagner?
    a. Verdi
    b. Schubert
  * c. Brahms (p. 485)
    d. Chopin

19

THE AGE OF EARLY MODERNISM
1871–1914

I. TEACHING STRATEGIES AND SUGGESTIONS

Since Chapter 19 covers a shorter time period relative to most chapters in *The Western Humanities*, the instructor can omit the usual introduction (the Standard Lecture with a Historical Overview) and begin lecturing on the topics and themes of the period of Early Modernism. The Spirit of the Age teaching strategy can be used for the opening lecture to describe the characteristics of Modernism, with the emphasis on Early Modernism. It is extremely important to point out the distinction between the Modernist cultural style and the phenomenon known as "modern life," since both were emerging during this period. There are three major topics in this chapter, the Second Industrial Revolution, the emergence of militant nationalism, and the rise of imperialism; and the Comparison/Contrast approach can be used to discuss them, showing how they evolved from earlier versions in the late eighteenth century. Another teaching strategy is to adopt the Case Study method to draw connections between the nationalism and militarism of Early Modernism and contemporary manifestations of these same phenomena.

After having established the historical background and the chief traits of Early Modernism, the teacher can then use the Reflections/Connections teaching strategy, blended with a Slide Lecture and a Music Lecture, to set forth the leading developments in philosophy, literature, science, and the arts and explain their interrelationship with the wider culture. The instructor should explain carefully the various movements during this time, such as Expressionism, abstraction, and Cubism, since they set the stage for twentieth-century civilization and many of them continue today, even if in a diluted or barely recognizable form.

As a concluding lecture, the instructor can set the stage for the next chapter, which deals with the twentieth century's two world wars, by focusing on the West's long slide into war despite its efforts to maintain the peace.

II. LECTURE OUTLINE

Non-Western Events

1871–1914

A. Characteristics of Early Modernism

B. Europe's Rise to World Leadership
    1. The Second Industrial Revolution
       and the making of the
       phenomenon of modern life
        a. Differences between the First
          and Second Industrial Revolutions

In Japan, feudalism
    ended, 1871; the
    Constitution of 1885
    sets up a
    constitutional
    monarchy

        (1)   Urbanism
        (2)   The middle class
        (3)   The working class
        (4)   The changing role of women
  2. Responses to industrialism:
      politics and crises
      a. Domestic policies in the heavily
          industrialized West: Germany,
          France, Great Britain, and the U.S.
      b. Domestic policies in central and
          eastern Europe: Italy, Austria
          Hungary, and Russia
  3. Imperialism and international relations
      a. The scramble for colonies:
          Africa and the Far East
      b. World War I: causes

C. Early Modernism
  1. Philosophy and psychology
      a. Nietzsche
      b. Freud
      c. Jung
  2. Literature
      a. Naturalistic literature
        (1)   Zola
        (2)   Ibsen
        (3)   Chekhov
      b. Decadence in literature
        (1)   Huysmans
        (2)   Wilde
        (3)   Proust
      c. Expressionist literature
        (1)   Strindberg
        (2)   Kafka
  3. The advance of science
      a. Mendel
      b. The Curies
      c. Roentgen
      d. Planck
      e. Bohr
      f. Einstein
  4. The Modernist revolution in art
      a. Impressionism
        (1)   Monet
        (2)   Renoir
        (3)   Cassat
        (4)   Morisot
      b. Post-Impressionism
        (1)   Seurat
        (2)   Cézanne
        (3)   Gauguin
        (4)   van Gogh
      c. Fauvism, Cubism, and Expressionism
        (1)   Matisse

End of involuntary
    servitude in sub-
    Suharan Africa,
    1901–1910
Bank of Japan founded,
    1882
First Indian National
    Congress, 1886
In Japan, samurai revolt
    in 1877; first general
    election in 1890
Russo-Japanese War,
    1904–1905
Boxer Rebellion, 1900
Young Turks Revolt, 1908
Revolution in China, 1911

In Japan, *Journal of
    the Enlightenment,*
    a journal dedicated to
    progressive reform,
    established in 1874 but
    suppressed in 1876;
    literature flourishes,
    often influenced by
    Western writers;
    newspapers of high
    quality appear
Rabindranath Tagore,
    Nobel laureate in
    literature, 1913
Olive Schreiner, *The
    Story of an African
    Farm,* 1883
Kiyoshi Shiga, a Japanese
    scientist isolates
    dysentery bacillus,
    1898
Baha'u'llah, 1817–1892,
    Iranian founder of
    Baha'ism, a widespread
    modern religion
Coomaraswamy, 1877–1947,
    Sri Lankan art
    historian who portrayed
    Indian art as spiritual
    in contrast to post-
    Renaissance art in the
    West

Gauguin settles in
    Tahiti, 1891

        (2) Picasso
        (3) Kandinsky
   d. New directions in sculpture and
      architecture
        (1) Rodin
        (2) Sullivan
        (3) Wright
   e. Music: from Impressionism to jazz
        (1) Debussy
        (2) Schoenberg
        (3) Stravinsky
        (4) Joplin

D. The Legacy of Early Modernism

III. LEARNING OBJECTIVES

To learn:

1. The major characteristics of "modern life" and Early Modernism, 1871–1914

2. The causes and nature of the Second Industrial Revolution and its effect on society—in particular, on women

3. How the heavily industrialized nations reacted to the Second Industrial Revolution

4. The social and economic policies of central and eastern Europe, 1871–1914

5. The characteristics, origins, and results of late-nineteenth-century imperialism

6. The long-range and immediate causes of World War I

7. The directions of late-nineteenth-century philosophy and specifically the philosophy of Nietzsche

8. The ideas and achievements of Sigmund Freud

9. The ideas and contributions of Carl Jung

10. In Early Modernist literature, the meaning of Naturalism, Decadence, and Expressionism, the major voices, and representative writings

11. Innovations in science, the discoverers, and their long-range significance

12. The ideas of Albert Einstein and their implications

13. The origins and characteristics of Impressionism, its most important artists, representative paintings, and its influence on later schools of art

14. The Post-Impressionists, representative paintings, and their impact

15. The nature of Fauvism, Cubism, and Expressionism; the leading artists and representative works in each of these styles; and the three movements' influence on later styles

16. Late-nineteenth-and early-twentieth-century trends in sculpture and architecture, the major sculptors and architects, and representative works

17. Developments in music, including innovations, new schools, leading composers, and representative works

18. Historic "firsts" during the period of Early Modernism that became part of the Western tradition: imperialism and colonial empires; Western dominance of the non-Western world through goods,

ideas, and values; anti-imperialistic attitudes outside of the West; a new stage of industrialism in the West and the beginning of industrialism outside of the West; Early Modernism, (1) in art, Impressionism, Post-Impressionism, Cubism, Fauvism, and Expressionism, along with the Post-Impressionist trends of Expressionism, abstraction, and primitivism and fantasy, (2) in literature, Naturalism, Decadence, and Expressionism, (3) in sculpture, the eclectic style of Rodin, (4) in architecture, functionalism and the Organic style, and (5) in music, Impressionism, Expressionism, and jazz; Nietzsche's philosophy; Freudian psychology; Jungian psychology; and psychoanalysis

19. The role of Early Modernism in transmitting the heritage of earlier civilizations: intensifying militant nationalism, absorbing and adjusting to new developments in industrialism, continuing advances in science, increasing the spread of public education, continuing the trend to a secularized culture, reinterpreting Romanticism

IV. SUGGESTIONS FOR FILMS

Europe, the Mighty Continent. Time-Life, thirteen films on Europe from 1900 to the present, 52 min. each, color.

Imperialism and European Expansion. Coronet, 13 min., black and white.

Impressionists. Universal Educational and Visual Arts, 42 min., color.

Nationalism. Encyclopedia Britannica, 20 min., black and white.

Paris, 1900. Brandon, MacMillan, 81 min., black and white.

Pioneers of Modern Painting. International Film Bureau, 40 min., color.

The Post-Impressionists. International Film Bureau, 25 min., color.

What Is Impressionism? [On music]. Columbia Broadcasting System. 52 min., black and white.

V. SUGGESTIONS FOR MUSIC

Debussy, Claude. *Danses sacrée et profane, for Harp and Orchestra. (1904).* Tietov, Slatkin, St. Louis Symphony. Telarc DG-10071 [digital]; CD-80071 [CD].

————. *La mer (1903–1905).* Ashkenazy, Cleveland Orchestra. London 417488-1 LH [digital]; 417488-2 LH [CD]

————. *Prélude à l'après-midi d'un faune (1892–1894).* Rubinstein. RCA 5670-2-RC [CD].

Schoenberg, Arnold. *Verklärte Nacht, Op. 4 (1899).* Boulez, Ensemble Intercontemporain, CBS IM-39566 (Digital); MK-39566 [CD]; IMT-39566 [cassette].

————. *Pierrot Lunaire, Op. 21 (1912).* DeGaetani, Weisberg, Contemporary Chamber Ensemble. Elektra/Nonesuch H-71309; 71251-4 [cassette].

————. *Quartet No. 2 in f sharp for Soprano and Strings, Op. 10 (1907–1908).* Beardslee, Sequoia Quartet. Elektra Nonesuch D-79005; D1-79005 [cassette].

Stravinsky, Igor. *Petrushka (1911).* Mehta, New York Philharmonic. CBS MK-35823 [CD]; IMT 35823 [digital].

———. *Le Sacre du Printemps (1913).* Karajan, Berlin Philharmonic. DG 423214-2 GMW [CD].

———. *Fireworks, Op. 4 (1908).* Dutoit, Montreal Symphony. London 414409-1 LH [digital]; 414409-2 LH [CD].

VI. SUGGESTIONS FOR FURTHER READING

Callen, A. *Techniques of the Impressionists.* London: Orbis, 1982.

Canaday, J. *Mainstreams of Modern Art.* 2nd ed. New York: Holt, Rinehart and Winston, 1981.

Gilbert, F. *The End of the European Era, 1890 to the Present.* New York: Norton, 1970.

Hobsbawn, E. *The Age of Empire, 1875–1914.* New York: Pantheon, 1987.

LaFore, L. *The Long Fuse: An Interpretation of the Origins of World War I.* New York: Lippincott, 1965.

Pollard, S. *European Economic Integration, 1815–1970.* London: Thames and Hudson, 1974.

Poole, P. *Impressionism.* London: Thames and Hudson, 1967.

Rewald, J. *Post-Impressionism from Van Gogh to Gauguin.* 3rd ed. New York: Museum of Modern Art, 1978.

Wohl, R. *The Generation of 1914.* Cambridge: Harvard University Press, 1979.

VII. IDENTIFICATIONS

Modernism	Pointillism
avant-garde	Fauvism
Naturalism	Cubism
Decadence	collage
Expressionism	atonality
abstraction	syncopation
Impressionism	ragtime
Post-Impressionism	blues

VIII. DISCUSSION/ESSAY QUESTIONS

1. Define Early Modernism and give *two* examples of Early Modernism as found in literature and the arts.
2. What is meant by the Second Industrial Revolution? What were its phases, and how did it affect European society?
3. In what ways did the Second Industrial Revolution affect the role of women in the European social system?
4. Compare and contrast the ways the heavily industrialized nations responded to the Second Industrial Revolution.
5. What were the patterns of industrial growth in central and eastern Europe, and how did the countries in those regions deal with the economic changes between 1871 and 1914?
6. Describe the nature of late-nineteenth-century imperialism and briefly identify which European nations claimed what territories around the world.
7. Discuss the fundamental causes of World War I and also the more immediate events that led up to the outbreak of the war. Do you think that the war could have been avoided? Explain.

8. What beliefs of Western thought were questioned by the Early Modernists? How were these doubts manifested in literature and the arts?
9. Define the word *avant-garde* and discuss what role it played in late-nineteenth-century Western literature and art.
10. Discuss the ideas of Friedrich Nietzsche and assess the influence of his ideas in the modern world.
11. Discuss Sigmund Freud's explanation of human behavior, especially focusing on his conclusions regarding human happiness.
12. What is meant by "psychoanalysis"? Describe Freud's role in the development of this technique.
13. Discuss Early Modernist literature, focusing on the styles of Naturalism, Decadence, and Expressionism. Identify at least *two* representative works from each style in your essay.
14. Assess the advancements made in biology, chemistry, and physics between 1871 and 1914, identifying the major participants and their contributions.
15. Show that Impressionism was both an outgrowth *and* a reaction to earlier Western styles of art.
16. Demonstrate the characteristics of Impressionism, using the paintings of Monet, Renoir, Cassatt, and Morisot as the basis of your discussion.
17. What is meant by Post-Impressionism? Who were its leading painters? Show how their works expressed this style.
18. Compare and contrast Fauvism, Cubism, and Expressionism, noting the leading artists in each style and their representative works.
19. Define Cubism in painting and assess its impact on modern art.
20. Briefly discuss the major trends in sculpture and architecture during Early Modernism.
21. Describe Impressionist music. Who were its chief innovators? What are the names of representative Impressionist works?
22. Discuss the origins of jazz and the work of Scott Joplin.
23. Write an essay in which you explain how militant nationalism, imperialism, and militarism affected historical and cultural events during Early Modernism.
24. How has the late-nineteenth-century *avant-garde* affected Western values?

IX. MULTIPLE-CHOICE QUESTIONS

1. Modernism was a cultural movement that:
   a. marked the end of the Middle Ages
 * b. rejected both Greco-Roman Classicism and the Judeo-Christian tradition (p. 489)
   c. began with the Renaissance
   d. all of the above

2. Three major forces that helped shape events between 1871 and 1914 were:
   a. Christianity, feudalism, manorialism
   b. war, famine, plague
 * c. imperialism, militarism, nationalism (p. 489)
   d. overpopulation, pollution, class violence

3. Europe between 1871 and 1914:
   a. moved closer to political unity
 * b. was increasingly involved in internal disputes (p. 489)
   c. came increasingly under the influence of American culture
   d. launched a moral crusade against Modernism

4. The Second Industrial Revolution was powered by this new form of energy:
   a. steam
   b. water
 * c. electricity (p. 490)
   d. nuclear energy

5. Under Early Modernism, many Europeans moved to the cities because:
* a. Urban jobs paid better than those in the country. (p. 491)
  b. The cities promised free social benefits to their citizens.
  c. City life was more spiritual than isolated rural areas.
  d. Urban school systems were better than those in the countryside.

6. Life in the growing late-nineteenth-century cities was:
  a. much better for the middle class than the working class
  b. a place for some women to find new jobs and opportunities
  c. lived at a slower pace than in the countryside
* d. a and b but not c (pp. 492–493)

7. How did the Second Industrial Revolution affect women in industrialized states?
  a. It opened up new employment opportunities in teaching, nursing, business offices, and retailing.
  b. It led to more education for women in jobs requiring special skills.
  c. It encouraged women to unite in campaigns to revise property and divorce laws.
* d. all of the above (p. 493)

8. What weakened the appeal of liberalism in the Early Modernist period?
  a. Liberalism's opposition to social welfare programs made the movement's ideas unattractive to workers who wanted more state services.
  b. Liberalism's promise that free trade would lead to a harmoniously working economy was proved untrue.
  c. Socialism offered more benefits to the workers than did liberalism with its emphasis on *laissez faire* and individualism.
* d. all of the above (p. 493)

9. The German Empire under Bismarck was dominated by:
  a. liberals and socialists
* b. the landed aristocrats (p. 493)
  c. Roman Catholics
  d. all of the above

10. France in the 1890s was devastated by the scandal called:
* a. the Dreyfus Affair (pp. 493, 495)
  b. the Boulanger crisis
  c. the *Action Français* Affair
  d. the XYZ Affair

11. Unlike Germany and France, Great Britain during the 1871–1914 period:
  a. was beset with violence at home
  b. saw the rise of militant socialist parties
* c. reformed the living conditions of the poor (p. 495)
  d. witnessed the decline of its middle class

12. The United States between 1871 and 1914:
  a. was dominated by its wealthy Northeast region
  b. was a haven for millions of immigrants, mainly from eastern and southern Europe
  c. finally overcame the racial problems that had remained unresolved after the Civil War
* d. a and b but not c (p. 495)

13. The quintessential city symbolic of Modernism during this period was:
    * a. Vienna (p. 495)
    b. Budapest
    c. Rome
    d. Prague

14. As the Industrial Revolution came to Russia:
    a. The standard of living improved for all classes.
    b. Agriculture expanded and became a vital source of wealth.
    * c. The government became more oppressive and dictatorial. (p. 495)
    d. The leaders kept the country out of war so the economy could grow.

15. Late-nineteenth-century imperialism occurred because:
    a. The industrialized nations needed new markets for their products.
    b. Surplus capital, generated by profits, needed to be reinvested.
    c. New, cheap sources were needed for raw materials.
    * d. all of the above (p. 496)

16. Europe's division of Africa included:
    a. the taking of Central Africa by Great Britain
    b. the taking of North Africa by Germany
    * c. the taking of parts of North Africa and West Africa by France (p. 496)
    d. the taking of South Africa by Belgium

17. Before World War I, how significant was imperialism as a cause of war?
    a. It had no impact.
    * b. It heightened tensions but did not lead directly to war. (p. 497)
    c. It led directly to warfare in Europe among the great powers.
    d. It lessened tensions among the great powers as all were united by the bond of imperialism.

18. The immediate cause of World War I was a quarrel between:
    a. Germany and Russia
    b. France and Germany
    * c. Austria and Serbia (p. 497)
    d. Austria and Russia

19. A key idea of Nietzsche's was that:
    a. All Western philosophies are false.
    b. There are no moral certainties.
    c. Christianity is a slave morality.
    * d. all of the above (p. 497)

20. Nietzsche's life and thought are ironical in what ways?
    a. Despite his anti-Christian views, many Christians admired him.
    * b. Although he was an opponent of a strong German state, his writings were taken up by the Nazis, who advocated a unified Germany. (p. 499)
    c. A popular thinker during his lifetime, Nietzsche ceased to have any influence after World War II
    d. all of the above

21. Nietzsche and Freud:
    a. supported the traditional values of Western thought
    b. found fault with middle-class morality
    c. explored beneath the surface motives of human behavior to find the underlying truth
    * d. b and c but not a (pp. 497, 499)

22. Freud thought that human personality:
    a. was shaped by the environment
    b. was determined by what God had implanted in each person
    * c. was the product of an inescapable struggle between inborn instincts and a culturally based conscience (p. 499)
    d. was free and spontaneous and could change at will

23. Freud's research led him to emphasize:
    a. the innermost thoughts of his patients
    b. the dreams of his patients
    c. the sexual history of his patients
    * d. all of the above (p. 499)

24. The three styles of Early Modern literature are:
    a. Realism, Impressionism, Romanticism
    * b. Naturalism, Decadence, Expressionism (p. 499)
    c. Functionalism, Organicism, Constructivism
    d. Fauvism, Cubism, Surrealism

25. How do Zola's novels express Naturalism?
    a. They explore serious social issues.
    b. They use accurate details to describe society and nature.
    c. They are always set in the countryside.
    * d. a and b but not c (p. 500)

26. Ibsen's *A Doll's House* is written in which style?
    * a. Naturalism (p. 500)
    b. Decadence
    c. Expressionism
    d. Realism

27. The hero in Huysmans' *À rebours* expresses what Decadence means by:
    * a. cultivating unfashionable and exotic pleasures (p. 501)
    b. embracing materialism
    c. escaping to a tropical island
    d. becoming a devotee of mass culture

28. An example of Decadence in literature is:
    a. Kafka's *The Trial*
    * b. Wilde's *The Portrait of Dorian Gray* (p. 501)
    c. Ibsen's *A Doll's House*
    d. Zola's *Germinal*

29. An example of Expressionism in literature is:
    a. Chekhov's *The Three Sisters*
    b. Wilde's *The Portrait of Dorian Gray*
    c. Proust's *Remembrance of Things Past*
    * d. Strindberg's *The Dream Play* (p. 503)

30. The most famous Expressionist in Early Modernist literature was:
    * a. Kafka (p. 503)
    b. Strindberg
    c. Zola
    d. Wilde

31. Kafka's novel *The Trial* has this Modernist theme:
    a. a person brought to a tragic end for having broken the universe's moral code
    b. a person overwhelmed by the spiritual forces of Nature
    * c. a person victimized by forces beyond control (p. 503)
    d. a person forced to choose between conscience and the laws of the state

32. The first female scientist to win the Nobel Prize for science was:
    a. Mary Baker Eddy
    * b. Madame Curie (p. 503)
    c. Dorothy Richardson
    d. Mrs. Emmeline Pankhurst

33. Max Planck is credited with:
    a. discovering X-rays
    * b. establishing the quantum theory of radiation (p. 503)
    c. formulating the theory of dominant and recessive genes
    d. explaining the behavior of electrons at the subatomic level

34. Niels Bohr:
    a. established the quantum theory of radiation
    b. proved that the Newtonian system was still valid
    * c. explained the behavior of electrons at the subatomic level (p. 504)
    d. discovered X-rays

35. Einstein's theoretical work in physics did all EXCEPT:
    a. eventually lead to the overthrow of Newtonian concepts of space and time
    b. assert that the only absolute in the universe is the speed of light
    c. prove that there are no absolutes in space and time
    * d. overturn what Bohr had proposed (p. 504)

36. Which was an innovation of the Impressionist painters?
    a. They painted spontaneously, not working deliberately from careful study.
    b. They painted out of doors, not in their studios.
    c. They concentrated on the play of light, not caring about precise forms.
    * d. all of the above (p. 504)

37. The Impressionists were influenced by:
    a. the Barbizon school
    b. the Romantic school
    c. the Neoclassical school
    * d. a and b but not c (pp. 504–505)

38. The first critics of Impressionist painting:
    a. praised the new style as representing a turning point in art
    * b. ridiculed the new style as being messy and slapdash (p. 505)
    c. ignored the new style, hoping it would go away
    d. greeted it with faint praise, seeing little difference between it and Romantic painting

39. Monet's painting style can be described as depicting:
    a. a carefree view of the world
    b. a subtle sense of light and shadows
    c. the artist's appreciation of science in art
    * d. all of the above (p. 505)

40. Renoir's painting style can be described as:
    a. pioneering the tradition that led to Cubism
    * b. moving beyond Impressionism to a greater concentration on form (p. 505)
    c. experimenting constantly with various styles
    d. restoring Classical principles to art

41. All of these are significant Impressionist painters EXCEPT:
    a. Mary Cassatt
    b. Berthe Morisot
    c. Auguste Renoir
    * d. Vincent van Gogh (pp. 507–509)

42. The leading painters of Post-Impressionism were:
    a. Monet, Renoir, Morisot
    * b. Cézanne, Gauguin, van Gogh (pp. 507–509)
    c. Picasso, Matisse, Braque
    d. Courbet, Manet, Millet

43. Cézanne's painting pointed the way to the twentieth century's:
    a. primitive-like art
    * b. abstract art (pp. 507–509)
    c. Expressionist art
    d. Surrealist art

44. Van Gogh launched the Post-Impressionist trend in painting called:
    a. abstraction
    b. fantasy
    * c. Expressionism (p. 510)
    d. Primitivism

45. The leading painters in Paris on the eve of World War I were:
    a. Malevich and Kandinsky
    * b. Matisse and Picasso (p. 511)
    c. Mondrian and van Dongen
    d. Giacometti and Boccioni

46. What is the significance of Picasso's *Les Demoiselles d'Avignon?*
    a. It foreshadowed later developments, especially nonobjective art.
    b. It opened the door to influences from non-Western art.
    c. It was the prelude to Cubism.
    * d. all of the above (p. 513)

47. The artist and school identified with the breakthrough to pure abstract art were:
    a. Matisse and Fauvism
    * b. Kandinsky and *Der Blaue Reiter* (p. 515)
    c. Picasso and Cubism
    d. Monet and Impressionism

48. Which architect coined the phrase "form follows function"?
    * a. Louis Sullivan (p. 517)
    b. Frank Lloyd Wright
    c. Auguste Rodin
    d. Georges Seurat

49. A characteristic of Expressionist music is:
    a. music that sounds discordant and even disturbing
    b. a text that is reflected expressively in the musical sounds
    c. music scored without a designated key
    * d. all of the above (pp. 518–519)

50. The roots of jazz stretch back to:
    a. ragtime and blues
    b. West African and African–Caribbean rhythms
    c. European harmony
    * d. all of the above (p. 519)

20

THE AGE OF THE MASSES
AND THE ZENITH OF MODERNISM
1914–1945

I. TEACHING STRATEGIES AND SUGGESTIONS

The instructor can introduce the Age of the Masses and the Zenith of Modernism with a Historical Overview that focuses on the two world wars, the Great Depression, and totalitarianism; and then, using a Reflections/Connections approach, can show how these developments were reflected in the reigning Modernist style. For example, unbridled warfare and its threat contributed to the prevailing mood of pessimism; economic depression encouraged assaults on capitalism and led to the introduction of socialist and protest themes in literature and art; and the growth of Nazism in Germany caused the flight of *avant garde* intellectuals and artists to freer countries and, in Germany, to the replacement of innovative, difficult art with a sentimental, easily accessible style. The Historical Overview should also focus on the rise of the masses and their impact on culture and politics, both positively and negatively. With a Standard Lecture, the instructor can set forth the intellectual and scientific advances made in this era. A Slide Lecture, blended with a Pattern of Change approach, can illustrate artistic developments and, at the same time, demonstrate how Modern art shifted from its Early to its High phase. A Music Lecture can show similar changes in Modernist music. A Pattern of Change approach can also illuminate the literary changes taking place in High Modernism.

A good conclusion to this section is to summarize the West's and the world's situation in 1945, making the point that many of the dilemmas then are the same as those that are now being resolved in the 1990s, such as the Soviet Union *versus* the United States, totalitarianism *versus* liberal, democratic governments, communism *versus* capitalism, anti-Semitism *versus* Jewish assimilation, and art for art's sake *versus* art with a social conscience. With a Discussion, the instructor can ask students to consider whether and how these issues are being resolved.

II. LECTURE OUTLINE

Non-Western Events

1914–1945
Chinese republic, 1912–1949; Yüan Shih-k'ai, first president, 1912–1916; the era of warlords, 1916–1928; Nationalist regime under Chiang Kai-shek, 1928–1949
Sun Yat-sen, Chinese

A. Wars, Depression, and the
Rise of the Masses

B. The Collapse of Old Certainties and the
Search for New Values
1. Historical overview
a. Liberalism under fire
b. The world in 1945
c. The view from the United States

2. World War I and its aftermath
   a. The Central Powers
   b. The Allied Powers
   c. The events of spring, 1917
      (1) The United States joins the Allies
      (2) Revolution in Russia, which becomes the Soviet Union
   d. The Versailles Treaty
   e. Postwar developments to 1930
      (1) Prosperity in Britain, France, and the United States
      (2) Contrasting events in Germany and Austria
      (3) Stock market crash, 1929
3. The Great Depression of the 1930s
   a. Attempts to restore the economy
      (1) France, Great Britain, and the United States
      (2) Germany
   b. Prosperity in Japan
4. The rise of totalitarianism
   a. Background
      (1) The defeat of democratic hopes after Versailles
      (2) Definition of totalitarianism
   b. Russian communism
      (1) Lenin's revision of Marxism
      (2) Conditions in the Soviet Union
      (3) Bolshevik revolution
      (4) The struggle for power after Lenin's death
      (5) The Stalin era
   c. European fascism
      (1) Definition and characteristics
      (2) Mussolini and Italy, the first fascist state
      (3) Hitler and the Nazis in Germany
      (4) Franco and Spain
5. World War II: origins and outcome
   a. Origins
      (1) The Versailles Treaty
      (2) The Great Depression
      (3) Nationalistic feelings
   b. The course of the war
   c. The Holocaust
      (1) Jews
      (2) Gypsies, homosexuals, and others

C. The Zenith of Modernism
   1. Background
      a. *Avant-garde* developments

revolutionary leader, 1866–1925
In Japan, a liberal-leaning regime, 1914–1936; Manchuria invaded and becomes Japanese puppet state of Manchukuo, 1932; triumph of militarism, 1936; invasion of China, 1937
First dictatorship of President Vargas in Brazil, 1930–1945
In India, the British raj, 1858–1947; intensification of Indian nationalism, 1919–1947; Amritsar massacre, 1919
In Mexico, land distribution under President Cardenas, 1934–1940
In 1930s China, rise of communist revolutionary group led by Mao Zedong, 1893–1973; between 1934 and 1935 the Chinese communists make the "Long March" to avoid extinction by the Nationalists
China's capital moved to Chungking, 1937
2 million people killed in Mexican revolution, 1910–1917; the Constitution of 1917 becomes basis of a reformist, democratic state; nationalization of oil fields, 1930s
In Argentina, 1930 coup leads to a military-based regime; growth of local fascist movement during World War II

In China, the "May Fourth Movement" launched in 1919, protesting

b. Mass culture
  (1) Definition
  (2) Features
  (3) The defining role of the United States
  (4) Relation to Modernism

2. Experimentation in literature
  a. The novel
    (1) Stream-of-consciousness writing
    (2) Joyce's *Ulysses*
    (3) Woolf's *To the Lighthouse* and other works
    (4) Hemingway's *The Sun Also Rises*
    (5) Faulkner's Yoknapatawpha novels
    (6) Lawrence's *Lady Chatterley's Lover*
    (7) Orwell: a writer for all seasons
  b. Poetry
    (1) Yeats
    (2) Eliot
    (3) Hughes and the Harlem Renaissance
  c. Drama
    (1) Brecht and "epic theater"
    (2) Cocteau
    (3) O'Neill

3. Philosophy and science: the end of certainty
  a. Idealist philosophy replaced
  b. The logical positivist school: Wittgenstein
  c. The existentialist school
    (1) Heidegger
    (2) Sartre
  d. Physics
    (1) Einstein and the general relativity theory
    (2) Heisenberg's uncertainty principle
    (3) Opening of the nuclear age

4. Art, architecture, and film
  a. Painting
    (1) Abstraction
      (a) Malevich and Suprematism
      (b) Mondrian and *De Stijl*
      (c) Picasso's *Guernica*
    (2) Primitivism and fantasy
      (a) Duchamps and Dada
      (b) Surrealism: Dali and Klee

Marginal notes:

corruption of Chinese society and culture

Cat Country, a popular Chinese novel, 1932

Tagore's *The Home and the World*, 1919

Mori Ogai, 1860–1922, a founder of modern Japanese literature

Lu Xun, 1881–1936, Chinese short-story writer; *Call to Arms*, a collection of stories, 1923

1945 Nobel Prize for Literature to Gabriela Mistral, Chilean poet

Juan Zorrila, Uruguayan poet, 1857–1931

Tsukiji little theater opens in Tokyo, beginning of Japanese modern theater, 1924

Shintoism abolished in Japan, 1945

Indian physicist C. V. Raman receives Nobel Prize, 1930

Hideyo Noguchi, Japanese bacteriologist, 1876–1928

South African microbiologist Max Theiler develops a yellow fever vaccine, 1930

Exhibition of Chinese art at Burlington House, London, 1935

            (3) Expressionism
                 (a) Beckmann
                 (b) Matisse
        b. Architecture
            (1) The Bauhaus
            (2) The International Style
        c. Film
            (1) Film *versus* movies
            (2) Griffith
            (3) Eisenstein
            (4) Developments in Hollywood
            (5) Welles
        d. Music: atonality, Neoclassicism,
            American idioms
            (1) Schoenberg and serial music
            (2) Stravinsky and Neoclassicism
            (3) American music
                 (a) Ives
                 (b) Copland
                 (c) Jazz

    D. The Legacy of the Age of the Masses and
        Modernism

In Africa, the longest bridge in the world opened over the Lower Zambesi, 1935

III. LEARNING OBJECTIVES

To learn:

1. The characteristics of Modernism and how this style reflected the era's historical events

2. The key historical happenings between 1914 and 1945

3. How liberalism altered during this period and the causes of these changes

4. The history of World War I, including its causes, major events, turning point, and peace settlement, along with its consequence for politics and culture

5. The nature of the Great Depression and its impact on culture and politics

6. About totalitarianism, its definition, its two major types, communism and fascism, and how this authoritarian form of government affected politics and culture during this period

7. The history of World War II, including its causes, major events, turning point, and outcome

8. The historical and cultural situation in 1945

9. About mass culture, its defining characteristics, origins, and relationship to technology and how it affected the course of Modernism

10. The dominant role of the United States in the emerging worldwide mass culture

11. The innovations in the novel, particularly the introduction of stream-of-consciousness technique

12. The leading Modernist novelists, representative works, and literary characteristics

13. The chief Modernist poets, representative works, and style characteristics

14. The principal Modernist dramatists, their innovations, representative works, and literary style

15. The advance in philosophy, notably the founding of logical positivism and existentialism and the influences of these schools of thought on the wider culture

16. The leading scientific developments and how they both influenced and reflected events in politics and culture

17. The major trends in Modernist painting, the leading artists in each trend, and representative works

18. How the Bauhaus was the most significant development in architecture during this period

19. About International Style architecture, its chief exponents, and a representative building

20. How film became an art form in this period and how film differs from movies

21. The impact of artistic and literary refugees from Europe's totalitarian regimes on the free societies in which they sought sanctuary

22. The dominant schools of music in this era, the leaders of the two schools, and representative compositions

23. About the rise of American music with a distinctive style, the leading American composers, and representative works

24. Historic "firsts" of the Age of the Masses that became part of the Western tradition: nuclear power and nuclear weapons, a first modern instance of genocide, the highest standard of living in history for the most people, democracy for millions of citizens, polarization between mass and high culture, film as an art form, American dominance of worldwide mass culture, two superpowers instead of a multipolar arrangement, America as the world's industrial leader, Einstein's general theory of relativity, Heisenberg's uncertainty principle, and stream-of-consciousness writing

25. The role of the Age of the Masses and High Modernism in transmitting the heritage of earlier civilizations: keeping Classical influences alive in Neoclassical music, continuing the tradition of world wars begun in the Baroque era, reviving absolutist forms of government in totalitarianism, updating artistic trends that began in Post-Impressionism, and perpetuating Modernism in general and giving it a pessimistic focus

IV. SUGGESTIONS FOR FILMS

The A-Bomb Dropped on Japan. Fleetwood, 4 min., black and white.

And the World Listened: Winston Churchill. University of Wisconsin. 28 min., black and white.

Bolshevik Victory. Films, Inc., 20 min., black and white.

Europe, the Mighty Continent: This Generation Has No Future. Time-Life, 52 min., color.

Expressionism. International Film Bureau, 26 min., color.

Germany—Dada. University Educational and Visual Arts, 55 min., color.

The Great War—Fifty Years After. NBC, 25 min., color.

Igor Stravinsky. Carousel, 42 min., black and white.

Lenin and Trotsky. CBS, 27 min., black and white.

Nazi Concentration Camps. National Audio-Visual Center, 59 min., black and white.

The Spanish Turmoil. Time-Life, 64 min., black and white.

Surrealism. International Film Bureau, 24 min., color.

Twisted Cross [The rise of Nazism]. McGraw-Hill, 55 min., black and white.

The World at War Series. [1933 to a reunion of WWII veterans]. Heritage Visual Sales, 26 parts, 51 min. each, color.

V. SUGGESTIONS FOR MUSIC

Schoenberg, Arnold. *Concerto for Piano & Orchestra, Op. 42 (1943).* Fellegi, Ferencsik, Budapest Symphony. Hungaroton SLPX-12021.

———. *Moses und Aron (1930–1932).* Bonney, Zakai, Langridge, Mazura, Haugland, Solti, Chicago Symphony and Chorus and Glen Ellyn Children's Chorus. London 414264-1 LH2 [digital]; 414264-2 LH2 [CD].

———. *Concerto for Cello (1932–1933).* Yo-Yo Ma, Ozawa, Boston Symphony. CBS IM-39863 [digital]; MK-39863 [CD].

Stravinsky, Igor. *Oedipus Rex (1927).* Norman, Moser, Nimsgern, Bracht, Davis, Bavarian Radio Symphony & Chorus. Orfeo S-071831 A [digital]; C- 071831 [CD].

———. *Pulcinella. (1920; rev. 1949).* Murray, Rolfe Johnson, Estes, Boulez, Ensemble Intercontemporain. Erato ECD-88107 [CD].

———. *Symphony in C (1940); Symphony in Three Movements (1945); Symphony of Psalms (1930).* Stravinsky, CBC Symphony. CBS MK-42434 [CD].

Ellington, Duke. *Sophisticated Ellington.* (Rec. 1927–1966). RCA CPL2-4098E; CPK2-4098 [cassette].

———. *This Is Duke Ellington.* (1927–1945). RCA VPM-6042 [mono].

———. *The Symphonic Ellington.* (Rec. *circa* 1950). Trend 529 [mono].

VI. SUGGESTIONS FOR FURTHER READING

Detwiler, B. *Nietzsche and the Politics of Aristocratic Radicalism.* Chicago: University of Chicago Press, 1990.

Goldwater, R. J. *Primitivism in Modern Art.* Enl. ed. Cambridge, Mass.: Belknap, 1986.

Hunter, S. and Jacobus, J. *Modern Art: Painting, Sculpture, Architecture.* 2nd ed. Englewood Cliffs, N.J.: Prentice-Hall, 1985.

Kitchen, M. *Europe Between the Wars: A Political History.* London: Longman, 1988.

Lee, S. J. *The European Dictatorships, 1918–1945.* New York: Methuen, 1987.

Lipsey, R. *An Art of Our Time: The Spiritual in Twentieth-Century Art.* New York: Random House, 1988.

Mayo, A. J. *The Persistence of the Old Regime.* New York: Pantheon Books, 1981.

Monaco, P. *Modern European Culture and Consciousness, 1870–1980.* Albany: State University of New York Press, 1983.

Muller, K. J. *The Army, Politics and Society in Germany, 1933–1945: Studies in the Army's Relation to Nazism.* Manchester: Manchester University Press, 1987.

Neret, G. *The Arts of the Twenties.* Trans. by T. Higgins. New York: Rizzoli, 1986.
Timms, E., and Collier, P., eds. *Visions and Blueprints: Avant-Garde Culture and Radical Politics in Early Twentieth-Century Europe.* New York: Manchester University Press, 1988.

VII. IDENTIFICATIONS

mass culture
stream of consciousness
epic theater
logical positivism
existentialism
Suprematism
Constructivism
Socialist Realism

De Stijl
Dada
Surrealism
International Style
serial music
twelve-tone scale
Neoclassicism

VIII. DISCUSSION/ESSAY QUESTIONS

1. Explain how the impact of events between 1914 and 1945, including the world wars, the Great Depression, the rise of totalitarianism, and the growth of the masses, influenced developments in High Modernism.
2. How did historical events affect the political and economic principles of liberalism between 1914 and 1945? Show how and why different patterns emerged in various regions of the West.
3. Discuss World War I, its causes, major events, turning point, and peace settlement. What impact did the war and its aftermath have on politics and culture?
4. Discuss World War II, its causes, major events, turning point, and peace settlement. Summarize the situation in the West and the world in 1945.
5. Describe conditions in the Great Depression, focusing on the countries that suffered most and least. What impact did economic failure have on the era's politics and culture?
6. Define totalitarianism. Compare and contrast the two types of totalitarian governments that arose after 1917. What were the origins of these governments, their accomplishments, and their failures? What part, if any, did these totalitarian regimes have on the outbreak of World War II?
7. Discuss the impact of totalitarianism on politics and culture between 1917 and 1945.
8. Select the artistic or literary work that best symbolizes the Age of the Masses, and justify your selection.
9. Define mass culture. What were its contributions between 1914 and 1945? Discuss the complex relationship between mass and high culture during this epoch.
10. Discuss literature in the High Modernist era, setting forth the major writers (novelists, poets, and dramatists) and representative works of each. Compare and contrast their characteristics within the context of the Modernist style. What part did stream-of-consciousness writing have on developments in the novel?
11. What two schools dominated philosophy during this era? What was the goal of each school, and who were its leaders? How did these developments in philosophy mirror events in the wider culture?

12. Discuss the scientific advances made between 1914 and 1945. Show what relationship, if any, these advances had to the era's politics and culture.
13. What Post-Impressionist trends dominated painting during this period? In each trend, identify the leading artists, a representative work of each, and characteristics of each painter's individual style.
14. Discuss developments in film during the Age of the Masses.
15. What impact did intellectual and artistic refugees from totalitarian regimes have on the states in which they sought sanctuary?
16. Discuss High Modernist music, concentrating on the two dominant schools, their leaders, and their differing styles.
17. What were the unifying characteristics of High Modernism, as seen in the arts, literature, philosophy, and music of the Age of the Masses?
18. "American music found its distinctive voice in the Age of the Masses." Explain.

IX. MULTIPLE-CHOICE QUESTIONS

1. The "masses" refers to:
   a. the aristocracy
   b. the wealthy middle class
 * c. the lower-middle and working class (p. 523)
   d. the peasants

2. The rise of the masses contributed to:
   a. the birth of mass culture
   b. fresh forms of popular entertainment
   c. a negative backlash among "serious" writers and artists
 * d. all of the above (p. 523)

3. How was liberalism challenged between 1914 and 1945?
   a. The two world wars undercut liberalism's promise of peace.
   b. The Great Depression called into question free-trade policies.
   c. The Holocaust raised doubts about human morality.
 * d. all of the above (pp. 523–524)

4. All of these characterized the West in 1945 EXCEPT:
   a. The nuclear age had been inaugurated.
   b. The United States was now the world's leading power.
 * c. International affairs continued to be dominated by five sovereign states. (p. 524)
   d. The West was now divided between liberal regimes in western Europe and totalitarian states in central and eastern Europe.

5. The Treaty of Versailles signed after World War I:
   a. established the League of Nations
   b. was based on U.S. President Wilson's plan
   c. sowed the seeds of World War II by its treatment of Germany
 * d. all of the above (p. 525)

6. The Spring 1917 events that helped determine the outcome of World War I were:
 * a. the Russian revolution and the entry of the U.S. into the war on the side of the Allies (p. 525)
   b. the Germans' unrestricted submarine warfare and the entry of Italy into the war on the side of the Allies
   c. the harsh armistice terms offered by the Allies and the entry of Turkey into the war on the side of the Central Powers
   d. all of the above

7. Germany between the Versailles Treaty and the rise of Hitler was governed from:
   a. Berlin
   b. Bonn
 * c. Weimar (p. 526)
   d. Potsdam

8. Because of the Great Depression Britain and France in the 1930s did all EXCEPT:
   a. introduce paper money systems
 * b. become socialist societies (p. 527)
   c. abandon the gold standard
   d. move toward government-controlled economies

9. The first totalitarian state in Europe was:
   a. Spain
   b. Italy
 * c. Russia (p. 528)
   d. Germany

10. Lenin and Marx agreed about all of these ideas EXCEPT:
    a. Economic conditions determine the course of history.
    b. History leads inevitably to a communist society.
 * c. A dedicated elite is necessary to initiate revolutionary change. (p. 528)
    d. The goal of history is a society run by and for the workers.

11. A characteristic of the Soviet Union under Stalin was:
    a. a slave-labor system called Gulags
    b. a series of five-year plans
    c. rigid control of all forms of cultural expression
 * d. all of the above (p. 528)

12. Fascism supported:
    a. the supremacy of individual expression
 * b. the fusion of the people into a whole (p. 529)
    c. representative democracy
    d. free enterprise

13. A European fascist leader(s) in the 1930s:
    a. Hitler in Germany
    b. Mussolini in Italy
    c. Franco in Spain
 * d. all of the above (pp. 529–530)

14. The causes of World War II did NOT include:
 * a. France's dissatisfaction with its treatment at the Versailles Peace Conference in 1919 (p. 530)
    b. Germany's aggressive policies in central Europe in the 1930s
    c. Japan's invasions of Manchuria and China in the 1930s
    d. German nationalistic feelings about recovering "lost" German lands and peoples

15. The Holocaust:
    a. reflected Germany's anti-Semitic attitudes
    b. expressed Germany's nationalistic feelings
    c. resulted in the deaths of six million Jews and millions of other groups considered undesirables
 * d. all of the above (p. 531)

16. Mass culture tends to be:
    a. inexpensive
    b. mass-produced
    c. easily accessible
 * d. all of the above (p. 532)

17. Mass culture, between 1914 and 1945, did NOT reflect:
    a. the tastes of the lower middle and working class
 * b. the spirit of skepticism and experimentation (p. 532)
    c. the growth of industrialized society
    d. the development of new technologies

18. The leading symbol of America's dominance of worldwide mass culture was:
    a. Igor Stravinsky
    b. Babe Ruth
 * c. Walt Disney (p. 532)
    d. Louis Armstrong

19. A literary innovation of the Modernist novel was:
 * a. stream-of-consciousness writing (p. 532)
    b. fixed realism
    c. an omniscient narrator
    d. all of the above

20. Which novel reflected the author's debt to popular hardboiled detective fiction of the 1930s?
    a. Joyce's *Ulysses*
    b. Woolf's *To the Lighthouse*
 * c. Hemingway's *The Sun Also Rises* (p. 533)
    d. Faulkner's *The Sound and the Fury*

21. This novel was a satire on Stalinist Russia:
    a. Woolf's *Mrs. Dalloway*
 * b. Orwell's *Animal Farm* (p. 534)
    c. Lawrence's *Lady Chatterley's Lover*
    d. Hemingway's *The Sun Also Rises*

22. What Modernist symbol was intended to reflect the hollowness of contemporary life?
    a. Yeats' Byzantium
 * b. Eliot's waste land (p. 534)
    c. Hughes's river
    d. Faulkner's Yoknapatawpha County

23. Langston Hughes's poetry reflected:
    a. the values of the late Roman poets
 * b. his anguish as a black man in a white world (p. 534)
    c. his hatred of totalitarian governments
    d. all of the above

24. The Harlem Renaissance was an outgrowth of:
    a. the growing popularity of jazz
    b. the *avant-garde* cult of primitivism
    c. the population shift of American blacks from the rural south to northern cities
 * d. all of the above (p. 534)

25. What type of theater was developed by Bertolt Brecht?
* a. epic theater (p. 535)
  b. modernized Greek classics
  c. tense family dramas
  d. absurdist plays

26. Cocteau's drama *The Infernal Machine* is a Modernist version of the story of:
  a. Orestes
* b. Oedipus (p. 536)
  c. Orpheus
  d. Odysseus

27. This author's philosophy helped to lay the groundwork for logical positivism:
* a. Wittgenstein (p. 537)
  b. Heidegger
  c. Sartre
  d. Heisenberg

28. Existentialism is concerned primarily with:
  a. defining terms
  b. clarifying statements
* c. authenticity (p. 537)
  d. spiritual values

29. A key value in Sartrean existentialism is:
  a. human freedom
  b. individual responsibility
  c. personal choice
* d. all of the above (p. 537)

30. Heisenberg's uncertainty principle:
  a. states that absolute certainty is impossible in subatomic physics
  b. means that with their instruments scientists inescapably interfere with the accuracy of their studies of atomic structure
  c. is based on the inability of physicists to identify both an electron's exact location and its path at the same time
* d. all of the above (p. 538)

31. The scientist who headed the team that built the first atomic bomb was:
  a. Einstein
  b. Heisenberg
  c. Planck
* d. Oppenheimer (p. 538)

32. The prevailing style of Soviet art between 1917 and 1922 was called:
  a. Cubism
  b. Futurism
* c. Constructivism (p. 538)
  d. Surrealism

33. Malevich's style of painting reflected his:
  a. Christian concept that Christian mysticism is superior to Marxist materialism
  b. belief that the feelings are supreme over every other element of life
  c. notion that art should be nonobjective and nonrepresentational
* d. all of the above (p. 538)

34. The *De Stijl* movement was led by:
    a. Picasso
  * b. Mondrian (p. 541)
    c. Matisse
    d. Malevich

35. All of these are correct statements about Picasso's *Guernica* EXCEPT:
    a. It is a protest against Franco's unbridled warfare.
    b. It is executed in a modified Cubist style.
  * c. Its vivid colors express the artist's rage. (p. 541)
    d. It is a visual symbol of the era's conflict between totalitarianism and human freedom.

36. Dada artists were famous for their:
  * a. outrageous acts (p. 543)
    b. spiritual values
    c. humanistic beliefs
    d. pure abstraction

37. Surrealist art was inspired by the theory of:
    a. Marx
  * b. Freud (p. 543)
    c. Einstein
    d. Heisenberg

38. The most influential exponent of Dada was:
    a. Picasso
  * b. Duchamp (p. 543)
    c. Malevich
    d. Mondrian

39. A leading Surrealist was:
    a. Beckmann
    b. Matisse
  * c. Dali (p. 543)
    d. all of the above

40. The Bauhaus:
    a. was the leading art institute in Germany between 1919 and 1933
    b. brought together artists, craftspeople, and architects
    c. developed a spartan (all white) type of interior decoration
  * d. all of the above (p. 546)

41. Matisse's art in the 1930s is noted for its:
    a. social protest themes
  * b. expressiveness (pp. 544–545)
    c. religious values
    d. pure abstraction

42. This artist's paintings reflected his hatred of Nazism:
    a. Mondrian
    b. Malevich
    c. Matisse
  * d. Beckmann (p. 545)

43. International Style architecture was characterized by:
* a. sleek exteriors (p. 546)
  b. the Classical orders
  c. Gothic towers
  d. ornamented façades

44. The Russian director Eisenstein pioneered this film technique:
  a. the close-up
* b. the montage (p. 547)
  c. cross-cutting
  d. the hand-held camera

45. Moviemaking between 1914 and 1945 was changed by:
  a. the three-color cinematography process
  b. the addition of sound
  c. the flight of talented German filmmakers to Hollywood
* d. all of the above (p. 547)

46. Between 1914 and 1945 the composer Schoenberg:
  a. was the leader of the atonal school of music
  b. pioneered serial music
  c. composed with a twelve-tone scale
* d. all of the above (p. 548)

47. Between 1919 and 1945 the Neoclassical school of music was led by:
  a. Ives
* b. Stravinsky (p. 548)
  c. Copland
  d. Harris

48. Between 1914 and 1945 a distinctive American style of music was developed by:
  a. Aaron Copland
  b. Duke Ellington
  c. Ella Fitzgerald
* d. all of the above (p. 549)

49. Stravinsky's music between 1919 and 1945 was characterized by all of these EXCEPT:
* a. serial composition (p. 548)
  b. complex rhythmic patterns
  c. Classical operatic forms inspired by Pergolesi and Mozart
  d. small orchestras and musical structures based on Baroque models

50. Mass culture influenced Modernism in:
  a. Copland's incorporation of jazz elements into his serious music
  b. Cocteau's use of film in the production of *The Infernal Machine*
  c. Hemingway's adoption of a popular detective fiction style in *The Sun Also Rises*
* d. all of the above (pp. 533, 536, 549)

21

THE AGE OF ANXIETY AND BEYOND
1945–

I. TEACHING STRATEGIES AND SUGGESTIONS

Because of the press of time, the instructor often must either omit or condense material at the end of the term. The tendency, therefore, is to rush through the last class lectures without much thought to the teaching model. Yet, these last lectures sometimes demand the most care in determining teaching strategies. The instructor should not fall into the trap of simply giving an encyclopedic listing of events and names just in order to "cover" the material in the final chapter. A minimum of three lectures should be scheduled for the last chapter.

Since the time frame in Chapter 21 is approximately fifty years, the instructor need not begin with the standard Historical Overview but can open the final set of lectures with either the Spirit of the Age or the Comparison/Contrast approach regarding Late Modernism and Post-Modernism. The Pattern of Change model and/or the Diffusion model can then be used effectively with two major topics: first, the distinctions between Late Modernism and Post-Modernism and, second, the globalization of culture, particularly under Post-Modernism. In the closing lecture, the instructor can use the Reflections/Connections approach to make some educated guesses about the future of the emerging global culture. Such remarks must, of necessity, be guarded and can touch on such matters as impending directions of political, social, and economic trends; the projected influence of such trends on intellectual, literary, and artistic developments; and, finally, the continuing relationship between the world today and the civilizations of Mesopotamia and Egypt where Western civilization arose almost five thousand years ago.

II. LECTURE OUTLINE

Non-Western Events

A. Characteristics of the Age of Anxiety and Beyond: Late Modernism and Post-Modernism

1945–
In Japan, Showa Period, Hirohito, 1926-1989; Western-style constitution, 1946

B. From a European to a World Civilization
   1. The era of the superpowers, 1945–1970
      a. Postwar recovery and the new world order
         (1) Divisions and alliances in western Europe and around the globe

Arab League founded, 1945

In China, in 1949, the Nationalist regime is overthrown and replaced by communism, under Mao Zedong,

                (2) The Soviet Union   1949–1976
                (3) The United States
        b. The Cold War   "Quotations of Chairman
                (1) Division of East and West   Mao," 1966
                     in Europe   Riots in Johannesburg
                (2) Spreads to other parts   against apartheid, 1950
                     of world   Cuban revolution, 1959
                (3) Military conflicts and   Organization of African
                     international tensions   Unity, 1963
        c. Emergence of the Third World
                (1) The end of colonialism
                (2) New states and new economic
                     systems
    2. Toward a new global order, 1970–1991   In China, rapprochement
        a. National issues and international   with United States,
            realignment   1971; ascendancy of
                (1) Economic trends and crises   Deng Xiaoping, a
                (2) Domestic challenges and changes   pragmatic leader,
                     in the United States and in   1976–1989; "Massacre
                     the Soviet Union   of Tiananmen Square,"
        b. Problems with a global dimension   Peking, 1989;
                (1) Exploding populations   resurgence of
                (2) Growing environmental issues   hardliners, 1989–

C. The End of Modernism and the Birth of   In Japan, Prime Minister
    Post-Modernism   Yasukiro Nakasone, the
    1. Philosophical, political, and   "Japanese Reagan,"
        social thought   two terms in the
        a. Existentialism   1980s
        b. Structuralism   OPEC "oil crisis," 1974
        c. Feminism   In Japan, Socialist
        d. Black consciousness movement   party headed by a
    2. Science and technology   woman, Takako Doi,
        a. Communications and computers   1989–
        b. Medical discoveries   China explodes a hydrogen
    3. The literature of Late Modernism: bomb, 1967
        fiction, poetry, and drama   Pablo Neruda, Chilean
        a. Existentialist writings   poet, 1904–1973; winner
                (1) Sartre   Nobel prize, 1971
                (2) Camus   Taha Jussein, Egyptian
        b. Black literature   author, 1888–1973
                (1) Richard Wright   Yusunari Kawabata,
                (2) James Baldwin   1899–1972, Japanese
        c. The novel and other literary forms   novelist; *Snow
                (1) Norman Mailer   Country*, 1948; Nobel
                (2) Alexander Solzhenitsyn   Prize for literature,
                (3) Dylan Thomas   1968
                (4) Alan Ginsberg   V. S. Naipaul, 1932–,
                (5) Samuel Beckett   Trinidadian novelist
    4. The literature of Post-Modernism   Fugard, Kani, Ntshona
        a. Latin American writers   write plays on treatment
                (1) Borges   of blacks in South
                (2) Marquez   Africa, 1975
        b. Eastern European writers—Milan   Junji Kinoshita, 1914–,

5. Late Modernism and the arts
   a. Painting
      (1) Pollock
      (2) Rothko
      (3) Frankenthaler
      (4) Johns
      (5) Rauschenberg
      (6) Warhol
   b. Sculpture
      (1) Smith
      (2) Nevelson
      (3) Segal
   c. Architecture—Mies van der Rohe
6. Post-Modernism and the arts
   a. Painting
      (1) Pearlstein
      (2) Kiefer
      (3) Roberts
      (4) Stella
   b. Sculpture—De Andrea
   c. Architecture
      (1) Venturi
      (2) Rogers and Piano
      (3) Johnson
7. Late Modern and Post-Modern music
   a. Stravinsky
   b. Cage
   c. Glass
   d. Wilson
8. Mass culture
   a. More technology and
      communication
   b. Popular music

D. A Summing Up
   1. Political, racial, and economic trends
   2. Beyond Post-Modernism
   3. The future of the Western humanities

Japanese dramatist;
Twilight Crane, 1949
Yuichi Inoue: *Fish*, a
Japanese painting, 1959

Josaku Maeda: *Mystagogie
d'espace*, a Japanese
painting, 1965
Aquiles Badi, Argentinian
semi-abstract painter,
1893–1976
David Siqueiros, Mexican
muralist, 1897–1974
Tsugouharu Foujita, Japanese
painter, 1899–1968
Kenzo Tange, 1913–,
Japanese architect
and town planner;
Peace Center,
Hiroshima, 1955
Oscar Niemeyer, 1970–,
Brazilian architect;
designer of city of
Brasilia, 1956–1963
Minoru Takeyama,
Japanese architect;
Tokyo department
store
Carlos Chavez, Mexican
composer, 1899–1978
Zubin Mehta, Indian-born
conductor, chosen to
lead New York
Philharmonic, 1978
Tutuola, 1920–, Nigerian
storyteller, *Palm
Wine Drinkard*, 1952
Ravi Shankar, 1920–,
Indian sitar player

III. LEARNING OBJECTIVES

To learn:

1. The differences between Late Modernism and Post-Modernism

2. The causes and characteristics of the two postwar economic and political systems of the superpowers and their allies

3. The major economic and political trends among the nations of western Europe

4. Domestic developments within the Soviet Union from 1945 to 1970

5. Domestic developments within the United States from 1945 to 1970

6. The origins and course of the Cold War

7. The causes and results of the emergence of the Third World states

8. The causes of the changes in international relations since 1970

9. The course and results of Soviet-American relations from 1970 to 1991

10. The major global problems confronting the world in 1991

11. The major intellectual and cultural movements and their leaders since 1945

12. The discoveries and inventions in science and technology and their impact on Western culture from 1945 to 1991

13. The characteristics of Existentialism, its major voices, and representative literature

14. The development of the novel and poetry after World War II

15. The trends and changes in the theater after World War II

16. The Post-Modern novel and novelists

17. The characteristics, innovations, and themes of Late Modernist painting, examples of these changes, and the leading artists

18. The major developments, trends, and sculptors of Late Modernism

19. Late Modernist architecture and architects

20. The general characteristics of Post-Modernism and its most important features

21. The Post-Modernist painters, sculptors, and architects and representative works

22. The key developments, important innovations, and leading composers in Late Modernist and Post-Modern music

23. The rise and meaning of mass culture

24. The world in 1991, reflecting its heritage from earlier civilizations: making militant nationalism once again a force for disruptive change around the world, specifically in the Soviet Union and Yugoslavia; moving away from an international scene dominated by the superpowers to one governed by a multipolar arrangement; continuing Classical influences in the Post-Modernist arts and architecture; updating nineteenth-century Expressionism and Realism as trends in Post-Modernism; reviving and drastically refurbishing Hellenistic attitudes in Post-Modernist literature and philosophy and in the multiethnic, multiracial, multicultural states that seem to be emerging, particularly in the United States and Great Britain; returning to the roots of Western civilization in Mesopotamia and Egypt in the works of Anselm Kiefer, perhaps the most influential artist working today; and restoring harmonious sounds and simple techniques to the music of Post-Modernism

IV. SUGGESTIONS FOR FILMS

American Art in the Sixties. Blackwood Productions, 58 min., color.

American Sculpture of the Sixties. Visual Resources, 19 min., color.

Cold War. McGraw-Hill, 20 min., black and white.

Europe, the Mighty Continent [The concluding films in this thirteen-part series examine the decline of Europe and European unification.]. Time-Life, 52 min., color.

Music: Electronic Edge. Documents Associates, 22 min., color.

Today and Tomorrow. Films for the Humanities, 60 min., color.

A Woman's Place. Xerox Films, 52 min., color.

V. SUGGESTIONS FOR MUSIC

Cage, John. *The Seasons (ballet) (1947).* Davies, American Composers Orchestra, CRI S-410.

————. *Sonatas and Interludes for Prepared Piano (1946–1948).* Fremy. Etcetera ETC-2001; KTC-2001 [CD].

————. *Song Books I–II (1970); Empty Words III (1975).* For Speaker and Chorus. Cage, Schola Cantorum. Wergo 60074.

Glass, Philip. *Einstein on the Beach.* Glass Ensemble. CBS M4-38875; M4K-38875 (CD); MXT-38875 [cassette].

————. *Glassworks.* Glass Ensemble. CBS FM-37265; MK-37265 (CD); FMT-37265.

————. *The Photographer, for Violin, Chorus & Instruments (1982).* Kukovsky, Glass Ensemble. CBS FM-37849; MK-37849 [CD].

————. *Koyanisqaatsi.* Antilles/New Direction 90626-1; 906260-2 [CD]; 90626-4 [cassette].

Stravinsky, Igor. *Agon (ballet) (1957).* Irving, New York City Ballet Orchestra. Elektra/Nonesuch 79135-1; 79135-2 (CD) 79135-4 [cassette].

————. *Elegy for J.F.K. (1964).* Fischer-Dieskau, Gruber, Adler, Berger. Orfeo S-015821 A.

VI. SUGGESTIONS FOR FURTHER READING

Hoffmann, S. *Culture and Society in Contemporary Europe.* London: Allen & Unwin, 1981.

Hughes, R. *Shock of the New.* New York: Knopf, 1981.

Johnson, E. *American Artists on Art: From 1940 to 1980.* New York: Harper & Row, 1982.

Johnson, P. *Modern Times: The World from the Twenties to the Eighties.* New York: Harper & Row, 1983.

Keylor, W. *Twentieth Century World: An International History.* New York: Oxford University Press, 1984.

LaCapra, D., and Kaplan, S. *Modern European Intellectual History: Reappraisals and New Perspectives.* Ithaca: Cornell University Press, 1985.

Von Laue, T. *The World Revolution of Westernization.* Oxford: Oxford University Press, 1989.

Wegs, J. R. *Europe Since 1945: A Concise History.* New York: St. Martin's, 1984.

VII. IDENTIFICATIONS

Late Modernism	Pop Art
Post-Modernism	Neorealism
structuralism	Neoexpressionism
theater of the absurd	Neoclassicism
magic realism	high tech
Abstract Expressionism	synthesizer
assemblage art	

VIII. DISCUSSION/ESSAY QUESTIONS

1. Define the terms *Late Modernism* and *Post-Modernism* and explain the differences between the two terms.
2. What is meant by the term *Cold War?* Which nations were involved in this conflict, and what were the causes of this "war"?
3. Discuss the ways that both the defeated and victorious nations confronted the postwar years and describe their successes and failures.
4. Discuss the Soviet Union's domestic and foreign policies from 1945 to 1970.
5. What were the major internal problems confronting the United States from 1945 to 1970, and how successful was it in solving these problems?
6. What were the reasons for the end of European colonialism after 1945, and how did colonialism end in Asia and Africa?
7. Discuss the forces and issues that have led to a new global order since 1970.
8. Analyze the reasons for the end of the Cold War, and note how the internal policies of the United States and the Soviet Union influenced the course of events.
9. Briefly describe the major global problems confronting the world today.
10. Define structuralism and discuss some of its major supporters and their works.
11. Analyze the role of Simone de Beauvoir in the feminist movement, and trace the history of this movement into the 1980s.
12. Discuss black consciousness, its definition, and the reasons for its birth, using the writings and actions of its chief supporters as background for your discussion.
13. Show how Existentialism was expressed in the works of Sartre and Camus.
14. Describe the major developments in Late Modern literature, and give representative examples of writers working in this field.
15. Define the *theater of the absurd*, using the dramas of Beckett as the basis for your discussion.
16. Compare and contrast Post-Modernist with Late Modernist literature. Discuss at least two Late Modernist and Post-Modernist writers and their works in the essay.
17. Define Abstract Expressionism; how was it manifested in painting, and who were its most important painters?
18. What is meant by Pop Art? Which artists were associated with this movement?
19. Write a brief essay setting forth the differences between Late Modern and Post-Modern painting, focusing on at least two painters working in each style.
20. What distinguishes Late Modern from Post-Modern architecture, and who are the leading representatives of each style?
21. Discuss the contributions of Cage, Glass, and Wilson to music after 1945. How is Post-Modernism reflected in today's music?
22. What is meant by mass culture, and how is it a reflection of the influence of the United States in the expanding world culture?

IX. MULTIPLE-CHOICE QUESTIONS

1. The greatest threat in the immediate postwar years was:
    a. the fear of the Germans and the Japanese rearming
    *   b. the fear of nuclear war (p. 553)
    c. the fear of uprisings in the Third World
    d. the fear of an international economic depression

2. International tensions increased between 1945 and 1970 because of:
    a. differences between the Soviet Union and the United States
    b. developments in Third World countries
    c. rising nationalism in central and eastern Europe
    *   d. a and b but not c (pp. 553–554)

3. In framing the postwar recovery, the allies thought that this country held the key:
    a. Japan
    b. France
    *   c. Germany (p. 556)
    d. Italy

4. The postwar world was characterized by:
    a. democracies in the American bloc, collectivist regimes in the Soviet bloc
    b. piecemeal social welfare in the American bloc, comprehensive social welfare in the Soviet bloc
    c. booming economies in the American bloc, stagnating or slow-growth economies in the Soviet bloc
    *   d. all of the above (p. 555)

5. Prosperity and stability finally came to France under:
    *   a. de Gaulle (p. 556)
    b. Pétain
    c. Foch
    d. Leclear

6. Why did France and West Germany join in founding the Common Market?
    a. They wanted to ensure peace in Europe.
    b. They hoped to create economic stability.
    c. They recognized that the era of the small state was over.
    *   d. all of the above (p. 556)

7. All of these were Soviet policies between the death of Stalin in 1953 and the death of Brezhnev in 1982 EXCEPT:
    a. press censorship and repression of dissent
    b. increase in consumer goods and space exploration
    *   c. decentralized government and *laissez-faire* attitude toward satellite states in central and Eastern Europe (p. 557)
    d. nuclear weapons buildup and an effective military machine

8. In the 1950s the United States:
    *   a. emerged as the leader of the democracies around the world (p. 557)
    b. continued to struggle with its low standard of living
    c. was unable to return to a peacetime economy
    d. found itself torn by racial riots and social problems

9. What sparked the civil rights movement in the United States in the 1950s?
    a. the 1954 Supreme Court decision that declared "separate but equal" schools were unconstitutional
    b. the leadership of Martin Luther King
    c. the refusal of Rosa Parks to sit in the back of a bus in Alabama
    *   d. all of the above (p. 557)

10. A sign of the Cold War was:
    a. the race to stockpile weapons by the two superpowers
    b. the forming of NATO and the Warsaw Pact alliance
    c. the outbreak of the Korean War and the Cuban missile crisis
    *   d. all of the above (pp. 557–558)

11. A consequence of the U.S. failure in Vietnam was that:
    a. The U.S. emerged as a divided nation over the war and its goals.
    b. The U.S.'s leaders were now reluctant to exercise military power abroad except in the Western Hemisphere.
    c. The U.S. was perceived to be weakened as a superpower.
    *   d. all of the above (p. 560)

12. The first Third World country to win independent status after 1945 was:
    a. Algeria
    *   b. the Philippines (p. 560)
    c. India
    d. Union of South Africa

13. The shift in Soviet-American relations that eased international tensions starting about 1970 is known as:
    a. *laissez-faire*
    b. bilateral agreements
    *   c. *detente* (p. 560)
    d. *glasnost*

14. Under Richard Nixon, the United States:
    a. began to end the Vietnam war
    b. opened relations with China
    c. suffered through the Watergate scandal
    *   d. all of the above (p. 561)

15. The reforms of Gorbachev in the Soviet Union had this result:
    a. a raised standard of living
    *   b. progress in opening up political debates (p. 561)
    c. tighter control over the member states of the Soviet Union
    d. an era of prosperity in eastern Europe

16. Today the two most pressing international issues are:
    a. nuclear war and the arms race
    b. the Cold War and regional tensions
    *   c. population explosion and a deteriorating environment (p. 563)
    d. growing famine and population migration

17. A characteristic of Late Modernism was:
    a. a commitment to randomness
    b. a fierce optimism

c.   a sense of saving Western civilization from itself
*   d.   a and c but not b (pp. 564–565)

18.   Unlike Late Modernism, Post-Modernism supported:
      a.   mass culture
      b.   existential thinking
      c.   a global civilization
*   d.   a and c but not b (p. 565)

19.   Characteristics of Post-Modernism are that:
      a.   It looks backward to the roots of the Western tradition.
      b.   It welcomes the contributions of women, minority group members, and representatives of the
           Third World.
      c.   It stresses a playful approach to creativity.
*   d.   all of the above (p. 565)

20.   The intellectual movement identified with Post-Modernism is:
      a.   Existentialism
*   b.   Structuralism (p. 565)
      c.   Realism
      d.   Idealism

21.   Structuralists maintain that:
      a.   Human freedom is limited, not open to various choices.
      b.   Deep-seated modes of thought influence human thinking and behavior.
      c.   Human beings should forget the past and the future and live for today.
*   d.   a and b but not c (p. 565)

22.   How have Noam Chomsky and Claude Lévi-Strauss influenced Structuralism?
      a.   The theories of each imply that a common substructure exists in all human minds.
      b.   The theories of each hint that societies share some common subsurface characteristics.
      c.   The theories of each have led other researchers to focus on the subconscious mind.
*   d.   all of the above (pp. 565–566)

23.   The revival of the feminist movement after 1945 was first sparked by:
*   a.   Simone de Beauvoir (p. 566)
      b.   Betty Friedan
      c.   Alice Walker
      d.   Germaine Greer

24.   The earliest significant theorist of black identity was:
      a.   Martin Luther King, Jr.
*   b.   Franz Fanon (p. 567)
      c.   Malcolm X
      d.   Whitney Young

25.   Martin Luther King, Jr. was influenced by all of these EXCEPT:
      a.   the New Testament and the teachings of Jesus
*   b.   the philosophy of Nietzsche (p. 568)
      c.   the writings of Thoreau
      d.   the example of Gandhi

26. An important advance in technology after 1945 that changed habits and thinking around the world is:
    a. the birth control pill
    b. the communication satellite
    c. the computer
    * d. all of the above (p. 568)

27. The chief influences on Jean-Paul Sartre's literary works were:
    a. his Roman Catholic heritage
    * b. existentialism and Marxism (p. 568)
    c. Structuralism and Logical Positivism
    d. all of the above

28. In his novel, *The Fall*, Camus dealt with:
    a. the problem of the tragedy of death at an early age
    * b. the sense of guilt brought on by moral fraud (p. 568)
    c. the consequences of sin to a devout believer
    d. the never-ending quest for happiness

29. Black writers in the United States after 1945 discovered:
    a. that their works were often not well received at home by white critics and audiences
    b. that existentialism was one way for them to deal with their sense of isolation
    c. that exile in France was sometimes preferred to living with racial discrimination at home
    * d. all of the above (p. 569)

30. The assassination of Martin Luther King, Jr., affected James Baldwin in this way:
    a. It revived his faith in the American way of life.
    b. It persuaded him that an integrated society was the only solution to America's racism.
    * c. It convinced him that violence was the most effective way to change America's racial attitudes. (p. 569)
    d. It led him to dedicate his life to working among the urban poor.

31. Alexander Solzhenitsyn's novels express:
    a. his deep devotion to the religious beliefs of Roman Catholicism
    * b. his profound faith and trust in the Russian people (p. 569)
    c. his strong endorsement of Marxism
    d. his support for a centralized Soviet Union

32. The hero in Solzhenitsyn's *One Day in the Life of Ivan Denisovich*:
    a. is killed during a rebellion against the prison system
    * b. endures the hardships of the labor camp (p. 569)
    c. decides that life is not worth living and commits suicide
    d. renounces Marxism and is executed for his thought crime

33. Dylan Thomas's poetry:
    a. focused on themes accessible to most of his readers
    b. was filled with forceful and colorful language
    c. conveyed a simple moral lesson
    * d. a and b but not c (p. 569)

34. The poet who led the Beat Generation of the 1950s was:
* a. Allen Ginsberg (p. 570)
  b. Richard Wright
  c. James Baldwin
  d. Robert Frost

35. The theater of the absurd:
  a. shared existentialism's bleak vision
  b. focused on outrageous situations
  c. mixed tragedy with comedy
* d. all of the above (p. 570)

36. Beckett's play *Waiting for Godot:*
  a. contains little or no action
  b. borrows British music hall comedy routines
  c. expresses the idea of the futility of life
* d. all of the above (p. 570)

37. Post-Modern literature in Latin America is written in this style:
  a. social realism
* b. magic realism (p. 570)
  c. absurd naturalism
  d. Marxist naturalism

38. The novels of Gabriel Garcia Marquez reflect:
  a. the influence of American writers like William Faulkner
  b. the blending of the real and the incredible into the narrative
  c. the sense of place and a feeling for national traits
* d. all of the above (p. 571)

39. The Post-Modern novels of Milan Kundera stress:
* a. the identity of sexual freedom with political freedom (p. 571)
  b. the themes of fantasy and linguistic experimentation
  c. the principles of Christian fundamentalism and Slavophilism
  d. the ideals of revolutionary politics and social justice

40. The center of Western culture shifted after 1945 from Paris to:
  a. Tokyo
  b. London
* c. New York (p. 571)
  d. Rome

41. Abstract Expressionism can be described as a style of painting:
* a. that tries to liberate the painter from conventional painting methods (p. 572)
  b. that borrows themes from popular culture
  c. that is based on Classical values
  d. that is based on photographic clarity of detail

42. Which Abstract Expressionist is famous for "drip paintings"?
* a. Jackson Pollock (p. 572)
  b. Robert Rauschenberg
  c. Jasper Johns
  d. Mark Rothko

43. An "assemblage" is:
    a. an eclectic style that joins several styles of art into a single work
    * b. a put-together structure that mixes junk, odds and ends, and some paint (p. 575)
    c. a performance piece that blends art, music, dance, speech, and theater
    d. a collection of artists who work together simultaneously to create a work of art

44. These two Abstract Expressionists showed the way to Pop Art:
    a. Jackson Pollock and Willem deKooning
    * b. Jasper Johns and Robert Rauschenberg (p. 575)
    c. Mark Rothko and Helen Frankenthaler
    d. Kenneth Noland and Morris Louis

45. Pop Art focused on:
    * a. mass-produced products, like soup cans (p. 576)
    b. religious themes
    c. color, texture, and line
    d. a and b but not c

46. The most famous Pop Artist was:
    a. Picasso
    b. David Smith
    * c. Andy Warhol (p. 576)
    d. Jasper Johns

47. The Late Modernist architecture of Mies van der Rohe is characterized by:
    a. buildings treated as unified sculptures
    b. a reworking of the Classical orders
    * c. the "glass box" style (p. 580)
    d. all of the above

48. Which of the following art styles are identified with Post-Modernism?
    a. Neoimpressionism Neoabstractionism, and Neonaturalism
    * b. Neorealism, Neoexpressionism, and Neoclassicism (p. 582)
    c. Neocubism, Neoromanticism, and neogothicism
    d. Neorenaissance, Neobaroque, Neorococo

49. The Classical aspect of Post-Modernism is apparent in:
    a. Anselm Kiefer's *The High Priestess/The Land Between the Rivers*
    * b. Philip C. Johnson's AT&T Building, New York City (p. 585)
    c. Rogers and Piano's Pompidou Center, Paris
    d. all of the above

50. The Post-Modernist music of Philip Glass:
    a. continues the atonality of late Modern music
    * b. is emotionally appealing (p. 586)
    c. is composed using the Classical sonata form
    d. returns to the serial music style of Schoenberg

LISTENING GUIDES

The following pages contain a selection of listening guides developed by Jack Boyd for *Encore: A Guide to Enjoying Music* (Mayfield Publishing Company, 1991). These guides cover quite a variety of music, all of which is available on tape or cassette from Mayfield, without including so much detail that the music neophyte founders. The guides have been designed to keep the listener moving through the compositions, section by section, item by item. The nontechnical descriptions are coupled with notation to enhance the enjoyment of music readers. Permission is granted for photocopied reproduction of handouts given to students without charge.

LISTENING GUIDE

📼 & CD

CHARLES IVES · "AT THE RIVER" (1916)

Ives's version, approx. 1:20 min.

original ending of "Shall We Gather at the River"

Piano introduction

1. Shall we gather at the river,

2. Where bright angel feet have trod,

3. With its crystal tide forever

4. Growing by the throne of God

5. . . . gather at the river?

6. Yes, we'll gather at the river,

7. The beautiful, the beautiful river,

8. Yes, we'll gather at the river

9. That flows by the throne of God

Brief piano interlude

10. Shall we gather . . . shall we gather at the river?

Drifting, dreamlike harmonies.

The traditional hymn melody, until "by the throne of God," where the melody is altered.

The piano accompaniment is very independent.

The voice is meditative, remembering other times.

Traditional melody, with chiming sounds from the piano accompaniment.

Line 9 similar to line 4.

Meditative, similar to line 5, as the sounds drift away.

LISTENING GUIDE

📼 & CD

WOLFGANG AMADEUS MOZART · "LAUDATE DOMINUM," FROM *SOLEMN VESPERS OF THE CONFESSOR* (1780)

- The violins state the lyrical theme over a spare, elegant accompaniment.
- The solo soprano uses the same long, placid melody to present the Latin text of Psalm 113, *Laudate Dominum* (Praise the Lord).
- The chorus sings the same music, but now with the *Gloria Patri* (Glory to the Father) text.
- The soloist and chorus sing the concluding *Amen.*

ISTENING GUIDE & CD

ANTON WEBERN · *FIVE PIECES FOR ORCHESTRA, OP. 10, PIECE NO. 4* (1911–1913) (Flowing, extremely tender)

:00	Mandolin	6 notes, *dolce* (sweetly), *Zeit lassen* (strict time)
:01	Harp	3 notes at the same time, *pp*, slowing, then faster
:05	Viola	2 notes at the same time, *pp*
:06	Clarinet	a single note repeated 6 times, *ppp*
:07	Trumpet	4 disjointed notes, *dolce*
:11	Trombone	2 notes, *dolcissimo* (very sweetly), *sehr gebunden* (very controlled)
:14	Drum	3 strokes, *ppp*
:15	Harp	5 notes, gradually faster
	Clarinet	single note trilled
	Celeste	2 notes very close together, twice
	Harp	
	Mandolin	single note, 7 repetitions, *pp*
	Celeste/Harp	
:20	Violin	5 notes, *ppp*, "like a breath"
:25		silence

 ISTENING GUIDE & CD

IGOR STRAVINSKY · *THE FIREBIRD*, FINAL VARIATIONS (1910)

Theme (A)	First heard in the horns above a muttered string accompaniment, then repeated exactly.
Variation 1 (A')	Melody higher in violins, joined by flutes the second time through.
Variation 2 (A'')	Strings and woodwinds play the melody loudly, then other instruments join on the second playing.
Variation 3 (A''')	Introduced by sudden quiet muttering, followed by very loud, brassy, fast, shortened, and fragmented versions of the theme.
Variation 4 (A'''')	Melody slows as the full orchestra plays various sized pieces of the theme.
Conclusion	Very loud brassy chords, with a crescendo to the accented final note.

LISTENING GUIDE

■■ & CD

PETER TCHAIKOVSKY · "DANCE OF THE REED FLUTES," FROM *THE NUTCRACKER* (1892)

Although he had a full orchestra at his disposal, Tchaikovsky wisely limited himself to virtually a chamber music sound.

Introduction	plucked low strings
A	• Three flutes state the main melody, with the low strings accompanying.
	• The English horn (alto oboe) gives a smooth transitional melody.
	• Three flutes play the main melody again, with more instruments accompanying.

B	The trumpet, very low and in minor, presents a nervous, staccato melody, other brasses accompanying.
A'	Three flutes play the original melody again, with strings accompanying.

 ISTENING GUIDE   📼 & CD

LUDWIG VAN BEETHOVEN · "FÜR ELISE," BAGATELLE IN A MINOR (1808)

A   Slow, oscillating, trill-like opening figure, with simple upward accompanying notes in the left hand; the microform is **aababa**.

B   Soaring, songlike melody, ending with an echo of the opening slow oscillating notes.

A   As at the opening, except shorter, might now be thought of as **A'**; the microform is now **aba**.

C   *Ostinato* accompaniment (repeated notes) in the left hand, slow, interrupted melody in the right hand.

A   Same as the second **A** section (**A'**).

LISTENING GUIDE

& CD

TROUVÈRE SONG · "OR LA TRUIX" (14th century)

Or la truix trop— du - re———— te, voir, voir! A ceu k'elle est — sim - ple——— te.

"Or la truix" is in medieval Provençal French and compares wooing a girl with writing verse.

A   *Or la truix trop dure te, voir, voir!*
       (It is truly difficult to woo her, truly, truly!
       A ceu k'elle est simple te.
       Even if she looks simple.

b   *Trop por outrecuidiés me taius,*
       It may appear simple to the listeners,

b   *cant je cudoie estre certains*
       but in fact it is very difficult to put together,

a   *de ceu ke n'a ve-rai des mois,*
       oix, oix!
       Ah, me, Ah, me!

A   *Or la truix trop dure te, voir, voir!*
       It is truly difficult to woo her, truly, truly!
       A ceu k'elle est simple te.
       Even if she looks simple.)

LISTENING GUIDE

●● & CD

GUILLAUME DE MACHAUT • "KYRIE" FROM *NOTRE DAME MASS*

Machaut's mass, written c. 1350, is in six movements using a four-voice texture throughout.

Kyrie eleison
(Lord have mercy)

Upper two voices "busier" than lower voices. Top voice uses a syncopated rhythm four times.

Christe eleison
(Christ have mercy)

Syncopated, active top voice. Lower three voices almost like an accompaniment. Occasional long-held, chordlike notes.

Kyrie eleison
(Lord have mercy)

Exact repeat of the first *Kyrie.*

ISTENING GUIDE   ▭ & CD

THOMAS WEELKES · MADRIGAL, "AS VESTA WAS FROM LATMOS HILL DESCENDING," FROM *THE TRIUMPHS OF ORIANA* (1601)

As Vesta was from Latmos hill *descending*	Four high voices, then descending melodies.
She spied a maiden Queen the same *ascending*	Ascending melodies.
Attended on by *all* the shepherds swain,	All voices sing.
To whom Diana's darlings came *running down* amain.	Downward running notes.
First *two by two,*	Two voices echoed by two voices.
Then *three by three*	Three voices echoed by three voices.
Together,	All voices together.
Leaving their *Goddess*	Music in 3/4 time, the old Trinity concept.
All alone,	Single voice alone.
Hasted thither, and *mingling* with the shepherds of her train	Voices intertwining.
With *mirthful tunes* her presence entertain.	Pleasant tunes in all voices.
Then *sang* the shepherds and nymphs of Diana,	Stately, hymnlike introduction to this section
Long live fair Oriana!	Long notes in the bass voice, in the longest section of the work.

LISTENING GUIDE

⬛⬛ & CD

GIOVANNI GABRIELI · MOTET, *PLAUDITE, PSALLITE,* FROM *SACRAE SYMPHONIAE* (1597)

The organization is primarily in four sections, each section using a different brief psalm passage. Each section ends with an *Alleluia* setting. Although a single choir begins the individual sections and the *Alleluia* settings, all sections end with everyone singing (playing).

INTRODUCTION
Plaudite, psallite
(Clap hands, sing psalms

Three tenor voices in succession.

SECTION 1
Jubilate Deo omnis terra,
Give praise to God, all the earth

Choir 1 begins, then all voices enter at *omnis* (all).

Alleluia,
praise the Lord,

Choir 3 (low voices), then Choirs 1, 2, and 3 in succession.

SECTION 2
benedicant Dominum, omnes gentes,
bless the Lord, all peoples,

Again, Choir 1 begins and all voices enter at *omnes.*

collaudantes eum,
praising Him all together,

Alleluia,

Exactly as the first *Alleluia.*

SECTION 3
quia fecit nobiscum Dominus misericordiam suam,
because the mercy of the Lord has shown upon us

Choir 2 begins, Choirs 1 and 3 together, then all voices.

Alleluia,

Exactly as the first *Alleluia,*

SECTION 4
Et captivam duxit captivitatem, admirabilis et gloriosus in saecula.
He led captivity captive, this admirable and glorious one)

Choir 3 begins, then Choirs 2, 1, 2, and 3 with short phrases on *captivitatem. Gloriosus* sung in fanfarelike bursts.

Alleluia.

As at the first, but with a short extention to add finality.

 ISTENING GUIDE  & CD

ARCANGELO CORELLI · *CONCERTO GROSSO* IN G MINOR, OP. 6, NO. 8., MVT. 4, "PASTORALE" (pub. 1714)

This concerto grosso is in three sections, ABA', and uses two violins and a *basso continuo* for the *concertino*, with strings for the main body of the orchestra.

A

Concertino	Simple, lilting tune in 12/8 by the solo violins, accompanied by long notes in the string orchestra (imitating bagpipes?).
Ripieno	The orchestra concludes the opening section, then repeats the soloists' material.
Concertino	High but downward-pointing melodic sequence (series of similar phrases).
Ripieno	The orchestra finishes the *Concertino* section, then continues with its own statement of the music.
Concertino	High, slow, drooping violin notes, again with the phrase finished by the orchestra.
Ripieno	Orchestra continues in minor, ending the section with dramatic pauses.

B

Ripieno and *Concertino*	The full orchestra alternates loud and soft passages, interrupted by *concertino* passages.

A'

	A shortened version of the **A'** theme using only the first four divisions (**CRCR**).

HENRY PURCELL · "THY HAND, BELINDA" AND "WHEN I AM LAID IN EARTH" (DIDO'S LAMENT), FROM *DIDO AND AENEAS* (1689)

Thy hand, Be - lin - da! Dark - - - - - ness shades me,

RECITATIVE

Thy hand, Belinda! darkness shades me,
On thy bosom let me rest.
More I would, but death invades me.
Death is now a welcome guest!

Dido sings to her handmaid, with only a *basso continuo* accompaniment. Free rhythm, very emotional.

laid _____ in earth, may my wrongs_ cre - ate no trou - ble

When I am laid, am laid in earth, may my wrongs create no trouble in thy breast.

The ten-note ground (bass melody) is stated alone, then starts again as Dido sings. This vocal section repeats in most editions of this work.

Remember me, remember me, but ah! forget my fate.

This section is also repeated, then the aria concludes with a fully orchestrated playing of the ground.

The opera concludes with the polyphonic chorus of angels singing "With drooping wings, ye cupids come and scatter roses on her tomb."

LISTENING GUIDE

●● & CD

ANTONIO VIVALDI · "SPRING," FROM *IL QUATRO STAGIONE* (*THE FOUR SEASONS*), "ALLEGRO"

Tutti   Strongly rhythmic passage by the full orchestra with echoing loud and soft phrases.

Solo   Actually a violin trio picturing the songs of birds.

Tutti   A shortened version of the first *tutti*, leading directly into pictures of gentle zephyrs, another brief version of the first *tutti*, then a thunderstorm begins.

Solo   The solo violin enters with lightninglike flashes during the "thunderstorm."

Tutti   Very short modified version of the opening material, in minor.

Solo   The bird songs return.

Tutti   The "Zephyr" material of the second *tutti* returns.

Solo   Akin to the "Zephyr" music of the second *tutti*.

Tutti   Shortened version of the opening section, first loud, then soft.

LISTENING GUIDE

📼 & CD

J. S. BACH · CANTATA NO. 140, *WACHET AUF, RUFT UNS DIE STIMME* (WAKE UP, A VOICE CALLS US), MVT 1 (1731)

While listening to Movement 1, "Wachet auf," notice three musical components:

Wachet auf, ruft uns die Stimme
(Wake, awake, cries out the voice

der Wächter sehr hoch auf der Zinne,
the watchman high in the tower,

wach auf, du Stadt Jerusalem!
Wake up, you city of Jerusalem!

Mitternacht heisst diese Stunde;
This is the midnight hour;

sie rufen uns mit hellem Munde:
they cry to us with bright voices:

wo seid ihr klugen Jungfrauen? (etc.)
where are your wise virgins?)

LISTENING GUIDE

📼 & CD

J. S. BACH · FUGUE IN G MINOR ("LITTLE")

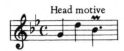

Three-note head motive (quarter notes)

Downward melody of eight notes (eighth notes)

Upward oscillating figure (sixteenth notes)

Complete fugue subject, voice 1

As voice 1 finishes with the subject, a few rapid notes lead into . . .

Following voice 2's presentation of the subject, there is an extended passage — the *codetta* — with free counterpoint. Soon voice 3 enters in the bass clef in the original key, voice 2 continues with the countersubject, and voice 1 presents new material.

In a passage exactly like the original entrance of voice 2, the deep, solid answer is presented in the pedal keyboard.

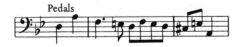

Listening Guides   277

LISTENING GUIDE

 & CD

W. A. MOZART · SYMPHONY NO. 40 IN G MINOR, K. 550, MVT. 4, *ALLEGRO ASSAI* (VERY FAST) (1788)

EXPOSITION

A   A fast, frantic upward melody (a typical "rocket theme") in G minor; no introduction.

Bridge   A long passage stringing out the A theme.

B   A gentler melody, in B-flat major, played softly first by the violins, next by the clarinet, then varied.

DEVELOPMENT

The first seven notes of the A theme are altered and revised in a jagged, almost frenetic passage, interrupted by fragments of the B theme. This reworking of the A theme continues throughout the Development.

RECAPITULATION

A   Returns much like the first statement.

Bridge   Again, stringing out material from the A theme.

B   Also returns, but in the original minor key.

CODETTA

Abrupt, loud, very fast passage for the full orchestra leading to the final chords.

LISTENING GUIDE

●● & CD

F. J. HAYDN · *SYMPHONY NO. 94 IN G MAJOR* ("SURPRISE"),
MVT. 2, *ANDANTE* (moving, going) (1791)

Theme	The little tune, consisting of two almost identical halves, has a certain folk song quality, a desirable trait in theme and variation because the listener has only one chance to learn the tune before being plunged into its variation.
Variation 1	The melody remains almost unchanged, but now violin I traces a filigree countermelody above the main melody.
Variation 2	The tonality changes from C major to C minor, and in the second half of the melody it temporarily jumps to the key of A-flat major.
Variation 3	The violins double the number of notes in the melody while the flute and oboe weave a new countermelody.
Variation 4	The woodwinds and brasses state the theme, then the violins play a more sharply rhythmic version.
Codetta	The basic melody returns in the oboe, the flute joins in, and the work concludes gently.

 ISTENING GUIDE  & CD

LUDWIG VAN BEETHOVEN · STRING QUARTET IN C MINOR, OP. 18, NO. 4, MVT. 4, "RONDO" (*ALLEGRO*) (fast) (1798)

A	Very rapid running notes, in C minor, reminiscent of a gypsy violinist.
B	A slower, songlike melody in A-flat major.
A	A virtual repeat of the opening **A** section.
C	Upward bursts of notes in (in order) cello, viola, violin II and I.
A	The gypsy song returns (**A**).
B	An almost identical repeat of the first **B** section.
A	The gypsy song returns, but much faster.
Codetta	A downward rush, some high repeated notes, then the upward bursts (borrowed from **C**) finish the movement.

ISTENING GUIDE & CD

LUDWIG VAN BEETHOVEN · *VIOLIN SONATA NO. 9 IN A MAJOR,*
OP. 47 ("KREUTZER"), MVT. 1
(1802–1803) [first 3:30]

Introduction	Solo violin, often using double stops, followed by a somber piano section, then both together.
A	Fast, short, agitated upward melodies by both instruments.
B	Slower, almost folklike theme, dominated at first by the violin.
(Continuation)	Both themes are taken apart and reworked during the development and recapitulation.

 **ISTENING GUIDE** & CD

ROBERT SCHUMANN · "DIE ROSE, DIE LILIE, DIE TAUBE, DIE SONNE" (1840)

Die Ro - se, die Li - lie, die Tau-be, die Son-ne, die liebt' ich einst al - le in Lie - bes-won-ne.

a *Die Rose, die Lilie, die Taube, die Sonne,*
(The rose, the lily, the dove, the sun,
Die liebt' ich einst alle in Liebeswonne.
I loved them all once with an ecstatic love.

a *Ich lieb' sie nicht mehr, ich liebe alleine*
I love them no more, I only love
Die Kleine, die Feine, die Reine, die Eine;
The Little One, the Dainty One, The Pure One, the One;

b *Sie selber, aller Liebe Wonne,*
She alone, of all love's delight,
Ist Rose und Lilie und Taube und Sonne.
Is rose and lily and dove and sun.
Ich liebe alleine Die Kleine, die Feine, die Reine, die Eine . . . die Eine.
I only love the Little One, the Dainty One, the Pure One, the One . . . the One.)

Headlong rush, starting before the piano.

Upward melody.

For emphasis, repeats some earlier text. Finishes completely out of breath, as the piano continues its accompanying figure, ending with two loud chords.

LISTENING GUIDE

📼 & CD

ROBERT SCHUMANN · "IM WUNDERSCHÖNEN MONAT MAI"
(1840)

Im wun - der-schö-ne Mo-nat Mai,   als al - le Knos - pen spring-en,   da

ist   in mei - nem Herz-en   die Lie - be auf - ge - gang-en.

A   Piano introduction.

B

a *Im wunderschönen Monat Mai,*   Simple, expressive.
       (In the beautiful month of May,
       Als alle Knospen sprangen,   Similar to first line.
       When all the leafbuds were
       opening,

b *Da ist in meinem Herzen*   Upward melody, building tension,
       Then in my heart   ending as if "breaking forth."
       Die Liebe aufgegangen.
       The Love broke forth.

A   Piano interlude same as the
                                              Introduction.

B

a *Im wunderschönen Monat Mai,*   Exactly the same melodic structure as
       In the beautiful month of May,   the first vocal section.
       Als alle Vögel sangen,
       As all the birds were singing,

b *Da hab' ich ihr gestanden*
       Then to her I confessed
       Mein Sehnen und Verlangen.
       My yearning and desire.)

A   Postlude same as the Introduction and
                                              Interlude, trailing off into nothing.

LISTENING GUIDE

📼 & CD

ROBERT SCHUMANN · "BLINDMAN'S BLUFF," FROM
KINDERSCENEN, OP. 15 (1838)

.15   Upward rushing melody, first section repeated. Then, downward melody in the same spirit. Much like a *moto perpetuo* (perpetual motion) or a fast round.

.26   Same melody again, but without the repeated first section.

.32   Shortened version of the melody.

 **ISTENING GUIDE**

📼 & CD

HECTOR BERLIOZ · "DIES IRAE," FROM *REQUIEM (GRANDE MESSE DES MORTS)* (1837, revised twice later)

poco f

[Di - es i - rae, di - es il - la,]

Introduction   Low strings, slow and soft, like a
                                     plainchant.

Di - es __ i - rae, di - es il - la.

Dies irae, dies illa,   Sopranos sing softly, gently accom-
(Day of wrath, day of judgment,   panied by orchestra. Basses, then ten-
solvet saeclum in favilla,   ors in two parts, followed by all three
when this age shall melt to ashes,   voices on the full text.
teste David cum Sibylla.
testified of David by the Sibyl.

Interlude   Full orchestra, animated.

Quantus tremor est futurus,   Tempo doubled, basses sing the *Dies
How great the trembling in the future,   Irae* melody, Sopranos on a single
quando Judex est venturus,   note, Tenors repeated accented state-
when that Judge shall come like the ments of *Dies irae, dies illa.*
wind,
cuncta stricte discussurus!
on whose sentence everyone depends!

Interlude   Full orchestra as before.

Quantus tremor est futurus, (etc.) Full chorus, very loud, with agitated
How great the trembling.)   sounds from the orchestra.

Interlude   Three measures similar to the first
                                     Interlude, then the four brass bands
                                     enter from four corners of the hall.

 ISTENING GUIDE &CD

FRANZ LISZT · HUNGARIAN RHAPSODY NO. 2 (1847)

Lassan

Introduction	Slow, deliberate, like a fanfare or roll on a drum.
Lassan	A leisurely, seductive, almost arrogant *molto espressivo* dance, with three interruptions for brilliant, free *glissandos* much like a gypsy instrumentalist. The accompaniment is marked *l'accompagnamento pesante* (peasantlike accompaniment). The *Lassan* melody comes back twice more before ending with material similar to the Introduction.

Friska

| *Friska* | Several sections, strongly rhythmic, beginning *pp* (very soft) and *vivace* (very fast), with a hopping, dotted rhythm. Several Liszt trademarks are used, including repeated trumpetlike notes, brilliant octaves, and fast chromatic passages. The work ends *prestissimo* (extremely fast) with the hands alternating octaves, followed by a pause, three slow, strong chords, then three fast, accented concluding chords. |

ISTENING GUIDE  & CD

MODEST MUSSORGSKY · "THE GREAT GATE AT KIEV,"
FROM *PICTURES AT AN EXHIBITION*
(1874; orchestral version, 1923)

Great Gate processional theme

A	A stately, dignified procession through the Great Gate, for full orchestra, loudly, with the brass stating the theme, which is then extended.
A	Repeat of the main theme, even louder.
B	Suddenly soft. Ancient Russian hymn played by the woodwinds imitating an organ.
A	Return of the procession played by the brass, while the strings play faster scale passages.
B	Slavonic chant, again played softly by the woodwinds.
Interlude	Bells (from the chapel of the Great Gate) sound, then the brasses play the melody of the Promenade (from earlier in the set) as the strings again play scales.
A	A triumphal ending for full orchestra using the orginal processional theme.

GIUSEPPE VERDI · "LIBIAMO," FROM *LA TRAVIATA* (1853)

Li - bia - mo, li-bia-mo ne' lie - ti ca - li-ci, che la _ bel -lez-za _ in - fio - ra;

Introduction

Orchestra, *allegretto* (moderately quick), with a bright waltz rhythm.

VIOLETTA

a   *Libiamo, libiamo ne' lieti calici,*
We find abandonment in this cup,
che la bellezza infiora;
which is the most beautiful flower;

The same melody as presented by the orchestra, ornamented and flowing.

a   *e la fuggevol, fuggevol ora*
it is a fleeting, fleeting hour
s'innebrii a voluttà.
it is an intoxicating delight.

b   *Libiam ne' dolci fremiti*
With sweet ecstasy of abandonment
che suscita l'amore,
let us drink to love,

b'   *poichè quell'occhio al core*
since such glances of the heart
onnipotente va.
overwhelm us.

a   *Libiamo, amor fra' calici*
Love and abandonment in the cup
più caldi baci avrà.
with many warm kisses.

SOLOISTS AND CHORUS

Ah! libiam, amor fra calici
Ah! love and abandonment in the cup
più caldi baci avrà.
with many warm kisses.

A rousing echo of Violetta's last phrase.

VIOLETTA

Violetta repeats her solo with more emphasis on friendship and happiness but with snide references to the fleeting quality of love.

SOLOISTS AND CHORUS

Everyone sings in unison, urging a night of revelry and wine.

VIOLETTA AND ALFREDO

The two lovers alternate phrases, then sing together of the joys of the evening. The chorus joins quietly, then all get gradually louder as they sing, "Let us enjoy every moment until the dawn."

ISTENING GUIDE

&CD

RICHARD WAGNER · "RIDE OF THE VALKYRIES,"
FROM *DIE WALKÜRE* (1870)

Ride of the Valkyries

Valkyries' war cry

Introduction		Agitated high string sounds, then low brass accents.
A	**a**	High brass present the Valkyries motive, which is then repeated to end in a new key. Fragments of the motive are developed into a fanfare.
	a'	Full brass on the motive, shorter section.
	b	Low brass, with downward rushes by the strings playing the Valkyries' war cry.
	a'	Brass repeat the Valkyries theme, ending with held sounds.
B		Sudden explosions, with trembling woodwinds, lightning flashes, and thunder.
A'	**a**	Return of the Valkyries theme in brass, with the sound of quavering woodwinds. Lightning flashes in the high instruments.
	a'	Final presentation of the Valkyries theme, very loud.

 ISTENING GUIDE    & CD

GABRIEL FAURÉ · "IN PARADISUM," FROM *MESSE DE REQUIEM*
(1887)

FIRST SECTION

In paradisum deducant angeli;
(In paradise may the angels receive you;
in tuo adventu suscipiant te martyres,
at your coming may the martyrs receive you,
te perducant te in civitatem sanctam Jerusalem.
And lead you into the Holy City of Jerusalem.

Serene, high oscillating piping and chiming accompaniment, as the sopranos sing the slow, seraphic, translucent melody. The rest of the voices enter on the word *Jerusalem.*

SECOND SECTION

Chorus angelorum te suscipiat,
There may the choir of angels receive you,
et cum Lazaro quondam paupere,
And with Lazarus, once a beggar,
aeternam habeas requiem.
may you have eternal rest.)

The silver chiming of angelic bells continues as the sopranos sing the melody. Again, the full chorus enters only on *requiem*, and then repeats the final phrase as the angelic chiming fades away.

LISTENING GUIDE

📼 & CD

CLAUDE DEBUSSY · "LA CATHÉDRALE ENGLOUTIE," NO. 10
FROM *PRÉLUDES*, BOOK 1 (1910)

(Repeated)

0:00 Gentle, almost random chiming, a wide range that narrows to four single notes, then expands. Two chords lead to . . .

0:50 Muttered low drone builds tension under harmonic chiming, building to . . .

1:29 Sounds similar to the opening, but fuller, louder, and more accented.

1:50 Chiming develops into a more melodic polyphonic section, first loud, then softer.

2:36 Single melody, developing to two-part, then fully harmonic.

3:47 Low rumbling drone section, with opening chimelike sounds, ending with a melody beginning in mid-range and moving upward. The misty chords gradually drift away.

**ISTENING GUIDE** & CD

ANTONÍN DVOŘÁK · *SLAVONIC DANCE NO.* 8, OP. 46 (1878)

A   Sections of strongly accented *hemiola* rhythms alternating with bouncy, peasantlike dance music, the first half of the melody in minor, the second half almost identical but in major.

B   Lyrical song by the oboe over muttering strings.

A   Sudden repeat of the opening material.

Coda A very short version of the **B** material, ending with a single explosion of the **A** motive.

ISTENING GUIDE

& CD

MAURICE RAVEL · *PAVANE FOR A DEAD PRINCESS*
(orchestral version) (1899)

A   Horn over *pizzicato* (plucked) strings. Two phrases divided by a harp glissando.

B   Two phrases, the first featuring the woodwinds, the second muted strings.

A   Similar to the first **A** section, with woodwinds playing the melody.

C   In minor, with various instruments on an upward-reaching melody.

A   Similar to the second **A** section, with added harp accents.

LISTENING GUIDE

 & CD

ARNOLD SCHOENBERG · "MONDESTRUNKEN" (MOONDRUNK),
FROM *PIERROT LUNAIRE,* OP. 21, for flute,
violin, cello, piano, and reciter (1912)

Den Wein, den man mit Augen trinkt (The wine that only eyes can drink *Giesst Nachts der Mond in Wogen nieder,* Pours nightly in waves from the moon,	Light, dancelike piano and flute, then other instruments, all in their upper register.
Und eine Springflut überschwemmt And a Springtide flood inundates *Den stillen Horizont.* The quiet horizon.	A sudden accent on "Springtide flood."
Gelüste schauerlich und süss, Desires, dreadful and sweet, *Durchschwimmen ohne Zahl die Fluten!* Swim through flutes without measure! *Den Wein, den man mit Augen trinkt,* The wine that only eyes can drink, *Giesst Nachts der Mond in Wogen nieder.* Pours nightly in waves from the moon.	Flute and violin introduce the second stanza. All instruments still in the upper register.
Der Dichter, den die Andacht triebt, The poet, under the impulse of piety, *Berauscht sich an dem heilgen Tranke,* Gets befuddled on the holy drink;	Suddenly louder and more agitated with the piano pounded.
Den Himmel wendet er verzückt He tilts backward toward heaven *Das Haupt und taumelnd saugt und schlüret er* His head, and sucks and sips *Den Wein, den man mit Augen trinkt.* The wine that only eyes can drink.)	Lighter on "heaven," ending with light, ethereal mistlike sounds.

LISTENING GUIDE

□□ & CD

GEORGE ANTHEIL · *BALLET MÉCHANIQUE* (1924, revised 1954)

0:00	Strict rhythm in tympani, followed immediately by the piano introducing the main "melodic" and rhythmic material.
0:25	Tympani and xylophone develop the main musical material.
0:55	Tympani roll into strong piano accents, xylophone dies away.
1:25	Piano alone, strong rhythms, nonmelodic.
2:35	Xylophone added to mostly piano material.
2:50	Xylophone, tympani dominate, then other instruments added.
3:35	Over a tympani roll, nonpredictable rhythms by other instruments.
4:05	The work continues with similar sounds.

LISTENING GUIDE

◫ & CD

VIRGIL THOMSON · "CATTLE," FROM THE ORCHESTRAL SUITE
THE PLOW THAT BROKE THE PLAINS (1936)

[I ride an old paint, I lead an old dan, I'm goin' to Mon-ta-na to throw a hoo-li-han.]

A   English horn (alto oboe) on "I Ride an Old Paint."

B   Clarinet, different key, "Laredo."

A   English horn, clarinet, English horn, with guitar.

B   Flute and guitar with faster notes. Then banjo, clarinet, oboe, flute, with *um-pa-pa* accompaniment, *crescendo*.

A   Full orchestra, loud-soft-loud.

B   Orchestra, strings predominate.

A   Trumpets loud, then soft, then strings and percussion.

B   English horn, flute, full orchestra, English horn that dies away.

LISTENING GUIDE

& CD

AARON COPLAND · "HOE-DOWN," MVT. 4 FROM *RODEO* (1942)

- The band tunes up, followed by a quieter section but still with strong rhythms.
- Sudden repetition of the opening music with a fiddle tune added.
- Trumpet, oboe, and fiddle alternate with the fiddle tune, then the full orchestra enters with the same tune.
- After a sudden stop, the percussion and other instruments play an accompanying figure as they gradually slow and stop.
- Sudden repetition of the opening music.

ISTENING GUIDE   📼 & CD

HENRY COWELL · *THE BANSHEE* (1925)

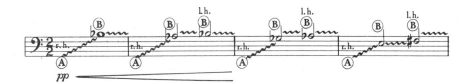

The Banshee is played on the open strings of the piano, the player standing at the crook. Another person must sit at the keyboard and operate the damper pedal throughout the composition. The whole work should be played an octave lower than written. R.H. stands for "right hand"; L.H. stands for "left hand." Different ways of playing the strings are indicated by a letter over each tone, as follows:

- Ⓐ indicates a sweep with the flesh of the finger from the lowest string up to the note given

- Ⓑ sweep lengthwise along the string of the note given with the flesh of finger

KRZYSZTOF PENDERECKI · *THRENODY FOR*
THE VICTIMS OF HIROSHIMA,
opening 3:10 (1960)

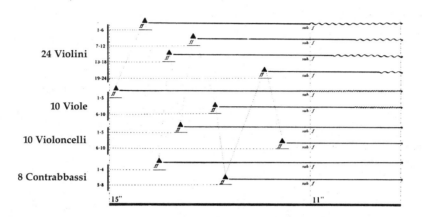

0:00 Extremely high screeches on the stringed instruments bowed right next to the fingers to form tone clusters. Diminishes.

0:47 *Pizzicato* (plucked) lower strings enter, high screaming pitches continue, solo instruments play brief two-, three-, and four-note "melodies." Gradually dies away.

1:45 Mid-range single tone forms, *pizzicato* notes gradually stop.

2:10 Low notes drift into a single tone, then drop a half-step.

2:20 Single tones blossom into discordant bursts of sound.

2:30 Repeated, very high.

3:00 High whine appears. The work continues.

LISTENING GUIDE

 & CD

LEONARD BERNSTEIN · *CHICHESTER PSALMS*, MVT. 1 (1965)

U - rah, ha - ne - vel!___   V'-chi - nor   u -   rah!___

Awake, harp and lyre! I will arouse the dawn!	Stately opening chorale-like passage using a text from Psalm 108:2.
Make a joyful noise to the Lord, all the earth. Serve the Lord with gladness; come before his presence with joyful songs. (etc.)	Loud, joyful, dancelike setting of Psalm 100 in highly accented 7/4 meter.
For the Lord is good, his mercy endures forever And his truth continues for all generations.	Bellike instrumental section introducing three vocal soloists.
Awake, harp and lyre! I will arouse the dawn!	The chorus enters briefly just before a loud, abrupt ending.

 ISTENING GUIDE & CD

HEITER VILLA-LOBOS · *BACHIANAS BRASILEIRAS, NO.* 5 for eight
cellos and soprano solo (1938–1945)

Introduction	Brief passage for *pizzicato* (plucked) cellos.
A	Soaring, wordless vocalise for soprano, with a solo cello paralleling the voice, but lower. Remaining cellos *pizzicato*.
A	Solo cello repeats the melody over *pizzicato* cellos.
B	Chantlike passage by soprano over rich harmonic cello foundation.
A	Repeat of the first A section.

LISTENING GUIDE

& CD

THE JAVANESE (SUNDANESE) GAMELAN · *BOPONG*

Bopong uses three musical components:
1. Continuous high, flute-like, highly ornamented chirpings.
2. Low to mid-range soft gongs, usually slow to medium speed.
3. High, brassy, chiming xylophones, generally fast and interrupting.

The gongs and flutes use a heterophonous texture with the gongs slower, the flutes faster and much more ornamented.

The brassy xylophones are mostly limited to swift, jangling, unpredictable interjections of very rapid notes, almost as if trying to interrupt the musical flow. They are actually marking the musical phrases. Under it all, the sauntering, majestic gongs keep up a placid, constantly evolving melody consisting of three slow notes followed by faster, higher tones.

Midway through, the gongs settle into a repeated 8 or 9 note melody. Twenty seconds before the end, all instruments change to a new, faster melody in unison.

LISTENING GUIDE

📼 & CD

BESSIE JONES · "BEGGIN' THE BLUES" (c. 1920)

Lord, I woke up this morn-in', I looked a-round in my room.

I woke up this mornin', I looked around in my room,
Well, I woke up this mornin' an' I looked around in my room,
I said, "Hello, blues, what you doin' in here so soon."

I knowed it was the blues, 'cause I heard him walkin' in my room,
I knowed it was the blues, 'cause I heard him walkin' in my room,
Lord, I wonder what's the matter, 'cause the blues won't leave me alone.

O the blues jumped a rabbit, run him a solid mile,
O the blues jumped a rabbit, run him a solid mile,
And the rabbit turned over and cried like a nachul chile.

He cried, "Blues, blues, you follow me everywhere,"
He cried, "Blues, blues, you follow me everywhere,
I don't know what's the matter, the blues jus' won't let me be."

LISTENING GUIDE

BOB NOLAN AND THE SONS OF THE PIONEERS ·
"CHANT OF THE WANDERER" (1946)

Introduction

Take a look at the sky where the whippoorwill trills;
At the mountain so high where the cataract spills.
Take a look at the falls and the rippling rills;
Hear the wanderer's call from the whispering hills,

Fast, slow, fast.
Bob Nolan solo.

Other voices enter.

CHORUS

The rippling rills,
The cataract spills,
The whippoorwill trills

Solo high tenor on a single yodel note,
as others sing twice.

Let me live on the range where the tumbleweeds grow;
Let the silver sands change where the prairie winds blow;
Let the wanderers sing where the wanderers go.
Let the melody ring, for it's happy I know.

CHORUS

The wanderers go,
The prairie winds blow,
The tumbleweeds go.

[Third stanza all instrumental, with flute on the high tenor note.]

[Fourth stanza similar to first two.]

LISTENING GUIDE

📼 & CD

LUDWIG VAN BEETHOVEN • *SYMPHONY NO. 5 IN C MINOR, OP. 67, MVT. 1, ALLEGRO CON BRIO (1807–1808)*

EXPOSITION

Theme A

A   Famous four-note motive, dot-dot-dot-dahhhh, then repeated and held.

Sequential treatment of the four-note motive, which is then expanded into a six-note version by the French horns (sometimes called a "Bridge Theme") to give a feeling of finality before the B theme.

Theme B

B   Short, lyrical, folklike theme, accompanied by versions of the four-note motive. This theme is given little attention before the return of the more important and dramatic A theme after a full stop by the orchestra.

DEVELOPMENT

A   As at the beginning, except a slow oboe cadenza replaces the third held note.

B   As before, except in a new key. The Recapitulation stays very close to the original version in the Exposition.

CODA

Directly into the coda without stopping from the Recapitulation, with an altered version of the Bridge Theme and a new march-like tune, ending with a strong, rhythmic, defiant, fist-shaking conclusion.

AARON COPLAND • *FANFARE FOR THE COMMON MAN* (1942–1943)

0:00   Strong, explosive accents by the tympani and cymbals, sounding almost improvised

0:25   Three trumpets present the theme, which features a bugle-like three-note head motive, ending with three loud tympani strokes

0:56   High brass in two parts, interrupted by two tympani strokes

1:29   Explosive percussion, again sounding improvised

1:40   Three-note head motive in low brass, followed by the high brass, with the tympani imitating the head motive

2:06   Full chords, punctuated by the tympani

2:22   The main theme for full brass, punctuated by tympani explosions

LISTENING GUIDE

FREDERIC CHOPIN • *SHERZO IN E MAJOR, OP. 54* (1843)

The word *scherzo* ("joke," or "game") is particularly apropos to this work. The entire eleven-minute composition has an impish, elflike flavor, with rapid changes of "altitude," as if a water sprite were flying from place to place on the piano. The melody and the connecting material is always very fast and unpredictable. Often it appears to be made up on the spot. There are five easily identified bits of musical material:

A	Opening four-note melody with a held chord
B	Altered, harmonized version of opening material
Chordal Arch	A fast, harmonized "arch" in the right hand
Slow Melodic Arch	Half melody, half harmonized
Fast Melodic Arch	Swirls of melody, usually in an arch form

The opening minute of the work uses the following outline:

0:00	**A**	melody (four notes with chord)
0:04	**B**	altered and harmonized melody
0:08		**Chordal arch**
0:12		**Slow melodic arch**
0:16	**A**	harmonized
0:20	**B**	as at the first
0:23		**Chordal arch**
0:27		**Slow melodic arch**
0:31		**Fast melodic arch**
0:34		A version of the **slow melodic arch**
0:38		**Fast melodic arch**
0:42		Another version of the **slow melodic arch**
0:47		**Fast melodic arch**, extended
0:52		Chordal punctuation
0:58		Fast melodic section, ending at . . .
1:02		Strong chord, after which the work continues

APPENDIX

BRIEF BIOGRAPHICAL DATA ON THE MAJOR CULTURAL FIGURES OF WESTERN CIVILIZATION

Showing Differences in Class, Sex, and Religious Beliefs. Keyed to Matthews & Platt's The Western Humanities.

THE ANCIENT WORLD TO 500 B.C.

Mesopotamia/Egypt [Chapter 1, *The Western Humanities*]

Few names of creative geniuses survive from Mesopotamia or Egypt; of those that do, such as Imhotep, the designer of Egypt's Step Pyramid, they appear to be members of the ruling elite.

Greece [Chapters 2–4, *The Western Humanities*]

In Greece, the ruling elite was at first defined narrowly: Greek males living in a particular polis. By 500 B.C. citizenship had become more democratic with the franchise opened up to new classes, so that all free Greek males, 18–21 years old or older, were given the vote—but only within a specific polis. After 334 B.C. another significant change occurred when the Greek world fell under Macedonia's sway; thereafter, in the Macedonian empire and the successor Hellenistic kingdoms, the self-governing polis came to an end but society grew more diverse as Greeks intermingled with Orientals, Persians, Jews, Egyptians, and Celts.

Aeschylus (about 525–about 456 B.C.), an Athenian aristocrat; one of the founders of the literary genre of tragedy.

Anaxagoras (about 500–428 B.C.), a citizen of the Greek polis of Clazomenae in Asia Minor; lived and taught philosophy in Athens until he was charged with impiety by city officials and forced into exile; an important philosopher who influenced Socrates.

Aristophanes (about 445–about 388 B.C.), probably a rich Athenian landowner; the founder of Old Comedy, the earliest type of stage comedy in the West.

Aristotle (384–322 B.C.), a Macedonian Greek, son of the court physician to the rough-living Macedonian court; tutor to Alexander who later became ruler of the Macedonian empire; studied philosophy in Athens under Plato and eventually set up his own school; the founder of Aristotelianism.

Carneades (about 214–129 B.C.), a Greek philosopher in the Hellenistic Age; born in Cyrene, North Africa, of a wealthy family; driven from Rome because his critical perspective was deemed subversive; a founder of Skepticism.

Democritus (about 460 B.C.–?), a wealthy citizen of Thrace; made important contributions to the atomic theory of the universe.

Diogenes (about 412–about 323 B.C.), a Greek; a social rebel who chose to live as a beggar; the first and most famous Cynic.

Empedocles (about 484–about 424 B.C.), a Greek born in Sicily; an important Pre-Socratic thinker who influenced Aristotle.

Epicurus (about 342–270 B.C.), a prosperous Athenian citizen who lived the first half (35 years) of his life outside Athens; the founder of the Epicurean philosophy.

Euripides (about 480–406 B.C.), a social rebel who was indicted on a charge of impiety by his fellow Athenians; probably of middle-class origins; a playwright; one of the founders of the literary genre of tragedy.

Heraclitus (about 545–about 485 B.C.), a prosperous citizen of the Greek polis of Ephesus in Asia Minor; one of the leading Pre–Socratic thinkers and the author of the first dialectical type of reasoning.

Herodotus (about 484–about 430 B.C.), a prosperous citizen of the Greek polis of Halicarnassus in Asia Minor; lived in exile in Athens after a failed revolt forced him from his home city; the founder of the West's tradition of secular history.

Homer (about 800 B.C.), by tradition, a blind Greek poet; the author of the first books of Western literature, the *Iliad* and *Odyssey*.

Menander (about 343–about 291 B.C.), a rich Greek of upper-class family; a dramatist; the supreme poet of New Comedy, the last phase of Greek stage comedy.

Parmenides (about 515 B.C.–?), a citizen of Elea, a Greek polis in southern Italy; one of the important Pre-Socratic thinkers.

Plato (about 427–347 B.C.), a member of a distinguished Athenian family; one of Greece's most important philosophers and the founder of Platonism.

Praxitiles (active in Athens from about 375 to 330 B.C.), a member of a family of Greek sculptors; the artist who sculpted *Hermes with the Infant Dionysus*.

Protagoras (about 481–411 B.C.), an Athenian thinker who won great fame and fortune as a teacher; forced into exile by the Athenian citizenry as a result of being convicted of impiety; the first Sophist.

Pythagoras (about 580–about 507 B.C.), a citizen of the Greek polis of Samos; settled in southern Italy, probably as a result of Samos's tyrannical government; an outstanding Pre-Socratic philosopher; the founder of Pythagoreanism.

Sappho (about 600 B.C.), a female member of an aristocratic family on the Greek island of Lesbos; a poet; considered by ancient authorities to be one of the greatest lyric poets of Greece.

Socrates (about 470–399 B.C.), a citizen of Athens; though well born, he fell into poverty in his later years; condemned by his fellow Athenians for impiety and corrupting the youth by his teachings; a thinker who reoriented philosophy from the study of the natural world to a consideration of human nature.

Sophocles (about 496–406 B.C.), son of a well-placed Athenian family; one of Greece's important playwrights; the author of *Oedipus Rex* and *Antigone.*

Thales (about 585 B.C.), by tradition, a wealthy citizen of the Greek polis of Miltetus in Asia Minor; the founder of European philosophy.

Theocritus (about 310–250 B.C.), a Greek from rural Sicily; flourished in Alexandria; founder of the literary genre known as the pastoral.

Thucydides (died about 401 B.C.), a member of a well-to-do Athenian family; a general during the Peloponnesian War; forced into a twenty-year exile when he failed to prevent a Spartan victory in battle; the founder of the tradition of scientific history.

Non-Christian Rome **[Chapters 5 and 6,** *The Western Humanities***]**

Non-Christian Rome, during its 1000-year history, was transformed from a tiny city-state, governed by a narrowly-defined elite, into a vast empire whose society was the most diverse of the ancient world. When Rome was founded, the patricians (nobles) constituted an exclusive ruling class; in 287 B.C., full citizenship was extended to the Roman plebeians, but still only those within the small city-state. In about 80 B.C., citizenship was conferred on all free Italians up and down the Italian peninsula; and, under the Roman empire, in A.D. 212, citizenship was given to virtually all free men throughout the vast Roman world.

Arrian (second century A.D.), a Greek noble, writer, and governor in the era of the Roman Empire; author of two manuals on Epictetus's teachings.

Catullus (about 84–about 57 B.C.), an aristocrat from northern Italy at a time when Italians enjoyed full Roman citizenship; his father was a friend of Julius Caesar; a poet.

Celsus (second century A.D.), probably a Greek aristocrat in the Roman empire; a philosopher.

Cicero (106–43 B.C.), an Italian, i.e., a non-Roman; born before Italians were given full Roman rights; Rome's most prolific writer and the creator of the Latin language's philosophic vocabulary.

Epictetus (about A.D. 55–115), an ex-slave and freedman; physically lame as a result of an injury; a Stoic philosopher who founded a school in Asia Minor.

Galen (about A.D. 130–about 201), a Greek physician; perhaps the most influential physician produced by Roman civilization.

Horace (65–8 B.C.), the son of an ex-slave; an Italian plebeian; one of the outstanding poets of the Golden Age of Roman letters.

Juvenal (about A.D. 60–about 140), a member of a well-to-do family; forced into exile in Egypt for unknown reasons; impoverished for much of his life; returned to Rome and lived on grudging handouts from the rich; author of satirical poems.

Lucretius (about 94–about 55 B.C.), probably a Roman noble; author of *On the Nature of Things,* a poem based on Epicurean ideas.

Marcus Aurelius (A.D. 121–180), a Roman emperor who followed Stoic ideals; author of the *Meditations.*

Origen (about 185–about 254), an Egyptian Christian who was persecuted by Roman authorities; an extreme ascetic, he emasculated himself; after his death, the church condemned his writings as heretical; his works influenced later Christian writers, including Augustine and Erasmus.

Ovid (43 B.C.–about A.D. 17), an aristocrat who was forced into exile from Rome to Tomis on the Black Sea, because his poems were judged obscene by the ruler, Augustus; the finest poet of love themes in Roman letters

Paul (about A.D. 5–about 65), an ex-Jew and a Christian during a period when both religions were persecuted in Rome; the first Christian theologian and the church's first outstanding missionary.

Plautus (about 254–184 B.C.), a plebeian and an Italian, i.e., a non-Roman; the founder of Roman Comedy.

Seneca (4 B.C.–A.D. 65), son of a teacher of rhetoric; descended from a wealthy family in Spain; the outstanding Roman intellectual of the mid–first century A.D.

Tacitus (A.D. 55?–117), a member of a family from Gaul, perhaps of Roman aristocratic background; a distinguished public career; the finest writer of history in the Latin language.

Terence (about 195–159 B.C.), a North African slave who was granted his freedom in Rome; one of Rome's two outstanding comic playwrights; his comic plays later influenced Shakespeare and Moliére.

Tertullian (about 160–about 230), a Christian convert at a time when Christians were persecuted in Rome, and a North African, reflecting the growing prominence of North Africa in the third-century Roman empire; a convert to the Christian heresy of Montanism made him anathema to orthodox Christians.

Judaism [Chapter 6, *The Western Humanities*]

Judaism originated outside of Greco-Roman civilization, although in the first century B.C. it passed under the hegemony of the Roman world. In early Judaism the key figures were simultaneously religious and political leaders, like Moses and David. After David and Solomon's unified Jewish state collapsed, the leading representatives of Judaism were prophets—charismatic figures whom later Jews regarded as divine emissaries. The prophets, by definition, were outsiders in Jewish society, since they condemned the wealthy and powerful and sided with the poor and downtrodden.

Christian Rome [Chapter 7, *The Western Humanities*]

In A.D. 311, after a decade-long attempt to stamp our Christianity had failed, then-emperor Constantine extended toleration to all Christians thus inaugurating a new era in Roman history. By A.D. 400 the Christian religion was adopted as the official faith of the empire and the old polytheistic religions were legislated out of existence.

Ambrose (about 340–397), a Christian from Gaul; his career as bishop of Milan reflects the ethnic diversity of the late Roman world.

Anthony (about 250–about 350), an Egyptian who was one of the first Christian monks.

Arius (about 250–about 336), a Greek priest in Alexandria; his teachings on the Trinity were condemned as heretical by the church in 325.

Athanasius (about 296–373), a Greek Christian who helped establish the church's doctrine of the Trinity.

Augustine (354–430), a North African; became a Christian in late pagan Rome; a church father.

Eusebius (about 260–about 340), a Greek Christian; lived through the Great Persecution; the founder of the literary genre of church history.

Jerome (about 340–420), a Christian writer from Dalmatia (modern Yugoslavia); his career reflects the ethnic diversity of late Rome; translator of the Greek Bible into Latin; a church father.

Pachomius (about 280–about 346), an Egyptian Christian; a founder of one of the first Christian monasteries.

Ulfilas (about 311–about 382), descended from Cappadocians who were captured by the Goths; converted to a heretical form of Christianity (Arianism); his translations of Christian scriptures into German (Gothic) were the first written works in the German language.

The Middle Ages [Chapters 8-10, *The Western Humanities*]

From the start of the Middle Ages until around 1400, European society was highly feudalized and was dominated by the feudal nobility and ecclesiatical leaders. Between 1400 and 1500 there were some changes, as feudal society began to decline and the earliest stage of commercial capitalism emerged. Untitled owners of large estates and prosperous merchants and businessmen in the larger cities now joined feudal lords and church leaders as members of the ruling elite. The status of skilled artisans and craftspeople, primarily in the arts, also improved but their position in society remained below that of the dominant groups.

Abelard (1079–1142), son of a Breton knight; castrated for having seduced his female pupil Heloise; embraced monasticism; solved the problem of universals, the intellectual controversy that dominated thought in the early twelfth century.

Alcuin of York (735–804), lived fifty years in Yorkshire, England, where he headed the York cathedral school for many years; at Charlemagne's invitation settled in Aachen (modern Germany) as head of the palace school; the foremost scholar of the Carolingian Renaissance.

Thomas Aquinas (1226–1274), son of a noble Italian family; a Dominican friar; some of his ideas were condemned after his death; the dominant intellectual of the thirteenth century.

Roger Bacon (about 1220–1292), member of a wealthy English family; a Franciscan friar and university professor; near the end of his life he was imprisoned briefly at the command of his fellow friars who questioned some of his teachings; an early exponent of the experimental method in science.

Bede (673–735), an Anglo-Saxon monk; entered a monastery at age seven; the author of the earliest history of the English church.

Benedict of Nursia (480–543), born of a good Italian family; a monk and head of his monastery; the founder of the monastic rule that became the model used in Western monasticism.

Bernard of Clairvaux (1090–1153), son of Burgundian aristocrats; a monk; a central figure in Cistercian monasticism; the "uncrowned pope" of the twelfth century.

Giovanni Boccaccio (1313–1375), offspring of a Tuscan merchant who disapproved of his son's literary efforts; occasional periods of poverty throughout his life; helped to establish the modern short story.

Boethius (about 480–524), a member of a distinguished Roman family; served the Ostrogothic king Theodoric, who ruled Italy; a philosopher whose writings dominated intellectual life for much of the Middle Ages.

Bonaventure (1221–1274), son of an Italian physician; a Franciscan monk and university professor; an important mystic.

Geoffrey Chaucer (about 1340–1400), son of a London wine merchant; courtier to English royalty; the first great writer in the English language.

Chrétien de Troyes (about 1148–about 1190), a frequenter of the court of Marie, countess of Champagne; the author of the first poetic verison of the legends of Arthur and the Knights of the Round Table.

Cimabue (about 1240–1302), the last great artist in the Italo-Byzantine style.

Dante Alighieri (1265–1321), a member of the Florentine aristocracy; a government official in Florence; died in exile, having been forced from nis native city-state by his political enemies; author of the outstanding literary work of the High Middle Ages.

Duns Scotus (about 1300–about 1349), a Franciscan friar; a Scottish thinker who lectured at Oxford, Paris, and Cologne universities; a major figure of the Late Middle Ages.

Meister Eckhart (about 1260–1328), a leader of the Dominican friars in Germany; some of his ideas were condemned as heretical by the pope in 1329; a great Christian mystic.

Einhard (about 770–840), of Frankish descent; a scholar and historian attached to Charlemagne's imperial court; author of the first medieval biography of a lay figure (Charlemagne).

Eleanor of Aquitaine (about 1122–1204), daughter of a distinguished family of Aquitainian nobility; queen first of France and then of England; a founder of the courtly love tradition.

Jan van Eyck (about 1370–about 1440), a Flemish painter; worked for various noble courts in northern Europe, notably that of the dukes of Burgundy; the outstanding painter in northern Europe in the early fifteenth century.

Francis of Assisi (1182–1226), son of a wealthy Italian cloth merchant; renounced his material goods and led a life of extreme poverty; the founder of the Franciscan order of friars.

Giotto (about 1276–1337), a student of the painter Cimabue; an Italian painter; introduced a new era in Western painting.

Gregory the Great (590–604), son of a distinguished Roman family; a brief career as a high-placed official; related by blood to earlier popes; one of the outstanding popes; standardized the use of music in worship services.

Gregory of Tours (about 538–593), a member of a distinguished Frankish family; a bishop and writer; the author of the only surviving contemporary history of the Merovingian kings.

Robert Grosseteste (about 1175–1253), a Franciscan friar and university professor; an English bishop; author of a scientific method that used mathematics and subjected hypotheses to repeated testings.

Guido of Arezzo (about 995–about 1050), an Italian monk; modernized music notation, an innovation that simplified the teaching of music.

Johann Gutenberg (about 1400–about 1468), son of a patrician of Mainz; exiled to Strasbourg because of an economic dispute; rendered destitute in later years as a result of litigation; blind in old age; a German printer and inventor; the inventor of moveable type.

Jan Hus (about 1369–1415), born of poor parents in southern Bohemia (modern Czechoslovakia); a Czech theologian; founder of a late medieval heresy that foreshadowed Luther's ideas.

Thomas à Kempis (1380–1471), a member of the Congregation of Windesheim, a German monastic order; a religious reformer; author of *The Imitation of Christ*, one of the outstanding devotional works of the Middle Ages.

William Langland (about 1332–1400), an English writer, perhaps a cleric in minor orders in London; used his writings to condemn the social and economic system of his time; author of the greatest example of alliterative poetry in Middle English.

The Limbourg Brothers, Pol, Herman, and Jean(about 1385–1416), the sons of a Flemish sculptor; employed by the Duke of Burgundy; painters of the most famous illuminated manuscript of the Late Middle Ages.

Thomas Malory (flourished around 1470), an English knight and writer; author of the first prose account in English of the rise and fall of King Arthur and his court.

William of Ockham (about 1300–about 1349), an English Fransican friar and theologian; excommunicated for his opposition to certain papal teachings; his style of reasoning dominated university theology from his day until 1600.

Francesco Petrarch (1304–1374), son of an Italian lay official at the papal court in Avignon; spent time at the papal court and various noble courts throughout Italy; a writer; helped revive the Classical forms of literature in the Late Middle Ages.

Giovanni Pisano (1245–1314), a member of a dynasty of Italian sculptors; his classically-inspired works foreshadowed later developments in Renaissance sculpture

Claus Sluter (about 1350–1406), a Netherlandish sculptor who was chief sculptor to the Duke of Burgundy; his works epitomized the Late Gothic style.

Suger (about 1081–1151), son of peasant parents; a monk and abbot; advisor to French kings; regent of France during the absence of King Louis VII on crusade; originator of Gothic-style architecture.

William of Champeaux (about 1070–1121), a French bishop and theologian; one of the leading intellectuals of the early twelfth century.

John Wycliffe (1320–1384), educated at Oxford; recipient of royal patronage and advisor to the English king; denounced by the clergy for his heretical views; founder of a religious heresy that anticipated many of Luther's ideas.

The Early Modern Period, 1400–1700 [Chapters 11–15, *The Western Humanities*]

The changes underway in late medieval society intensified during the early modern period, although the feudal and ecclesiastical elite still occupied the upper rungs of the social ladder. Untitled owners of large estates continued to gain social and political power, as did prosperous businessmen. Skilled painters, sculptors, and architects, if their manners were courtly, often became part of the cultural elite. Other influential social groups outside the feudal and ecclesiastical order also appeared upon the scene, such as religious reformers and secular writers and thinkers.

Leone Battista Alberti (1404–1472), an illegitimate son of a wealthy merchant-banker family in Florence; born during his father's exile from the city; reared by his real father and became his heir; entered holy orders though this had little impact on his career and life; an architect; the leading theoretician of Early Renaissance art.

Fra Angelico (about 1400–1455), a Dominican friar in Italy; an artist; helped to establish the Early Renaissance style of painting.

Johann Sebastian Bach (1685–1750), a member of a family of German musicians; parents died when he was ten years old; trained as a choirboy; court organist at Weimar and musician to the city of Leipzig; famous for his Baroque church music.

Francis Bacon (1561–1626), son of a powerful English court official who was a self-made man; educated at Cambridge; a high government official and scientist; impeached for abuse of office; instrumental in popularizing the new science.

Pierre Bayle (1647–1706), son of a Calvinist minister in the Netherlands; briefly a Roman Catholic; a professor at a Protestant academy; compiler and author of a famous dictionary that helped to inspire similar works during the Enlightenment.

Gianlorenzo Bernini (1598–1680), son of a Florentine sculptor; recipient of aristocratic and papal patronage; an architect; established the Florid Baroque style of architecture.

Bishop Bossuet (1627–1704), born into a family of French magistrates; educated by Jesuits; associated with the church from the age of ten onwards; a high church official; author of a work that defended the divine right of kings.

Sandro Botticelli (1445–1510), an Italian painter; associated with the Medici court; famous for his chaste nudes.

Robert Boyle (1627–1691), born into an English family of wealth and influence; a physicist; his research laid the groundwork for modern chemistry.

Tycho Brahe (1546–1601), son of a Danish government official; abducted by a wealthy and childless uncle who reared him in his own castle and financed his university studies; trained as a lawyer; an astronomer; made copious observations of planetary movement that were used by Kepler in his research.

Donato Bramante (1444–1514), son of well-to-do peasants; received patronage from Milan's Sforza family and Rome's popes.

Pieter Bruegel the Elder (about 1525–1569), a Flemish painter and founder of a painting dynasty; noted for his Mannerist style and his scenes of peasant life.

Filippo Brunelleschi (1377–1446), son of a Florentine notary; trained as a goldsmith and sculptor; an architect; a founder of the Early Renaissance style.

Leonardo Bruni (1374–1444), a Florentine political leader and scholar; an exemplar of civic humanism.

John Calvin (1509–1564), son of middle-class parents, the father a lay administrator for the local bishop in Noyon, France; a religious reformer; established his Calvinist ideals in Geneva, Switzerland, his spiritual home and secular refuge.

Caravaggio (Michelangelo Merisis) (1573–1610), son of a steward and architect; orphaned at eleven years of age; apprenticed to a painter; a social rebel; an outstanding artist in the Florid Baroque style.

Baldassare Castiglione (1478–1529), son of an illustrious family; a humanist and a bishop; an embodiment of the ideal courtier; author of a popular book on court etiquette.

Nicolas Copernicus (1473–1543), son of a well-to-do Polish merchant; university educated; an astronomer; revived the heliocentric theory of the university in modern times.

Pierre Corneille (1606–1684), born into a well-to-do, middle-class Norman family; educated in a Jesuit school; a legal official from 1628–1650; a playwright; author of *Le Cid*, one of the greatest dramas in the French language.

René Descartes (1596–1650), son of a wealthy French landowner; reared by a maternal grandmother when his mother died; a soldier and thinker; the founder of modern philosophy.

Donatello(1386–1466), son of a Florentine wool carder; trained as a sculptor; employed by the Medici and other nobles.

John Dunstable (1380–1453), served in the court of the Duke of Bedford who was regent of France from 1422 to 1435; an English composer; a key figure in the rise of Renaissance music.

Albrecht Dürer (1471–1528), son of a German goldsmith; apprenticed as a goldsmith to his father; famed for his engravings.

Desiderius Erasmus (about 1466–1536), illegitimate son of a Dutch priest; became a monk and a priest; active in English court and aristocratic circles; the outstanding Northern Humanist of the sixteenth century.

Marsilio Ficino (1433–1499), an Italian humanist and philosopher; protégé and tutor to the Medici family; directed the Florentine Academy.

Fontenelle (1657–1757), son of an impoverished nobleman; educated by Jesuits; composed libretti for operas; secretary of France's Academy of Science; a popularizer of the Scientific Revolution.

Galileo Galilei (1564–1642), son of an Italian musician; studied medicine at university; an astronomer; censured by the papacy for his scientific views; a key figure in the birth of modern science.

Lorenzo Ghiberti (about 1381–1455), unclear parentage, since his mother, while married to Cione Ghiberti, lived as the common-law wife of a goldsmith (Bartolo di Michele) whom she later married, after the death of Cione; trained as a goldsmith; the creator of "the Gates of Paradise," Michelangelo's term for the east doors of the Florentine Baptistery.

El Greco (Domenikos Theotokopoulos) (1541–1614), a Greek who spent most of his adult life in Italy and Spain; served various ecclesiastical and aristocratic patrons in Toledo, Spain, from 1577 to 1614; his art epitomized the Spanish Mannerist style.

Hugo Grotius (1583–1645), son of a civic and university official in the Netherlands; a child prodigy; university trained; the founder of the study of international law.

Matthias Grünewald (about 1460–1528), court painter and leading art official to the Archbishop of Mainz; numerous ecclesiastical commissions; famous for his *Isenheim Altarpiece.*

George Frederick Handel (1685–1759), son of a successful German surgeon and the daughter of a Lutheran clergyman; a composer; renowned for his Italian-style operas and the oratorio, *Messiah.*

Jules Hardouin-Mansart (1646–1708), a member of a family of distinguished French architects; official architect to King Louis XIV of France; one of the two architects who redesigned Versailles Palace.

William Harvey (1578–1657), son of a prosperous English businessman; university trained; a university professor at Padua, Italy; a scientist; proved that the blood circulated.

Henry VIII (1509–1547), king of England; founder of the Church of England.

Thomas Hobbes (1588–1679), son of an English priest who abandoned his family after a brawl outside his own church door; after the father's disappearance, the family was taken in by a well-to-do maker of gloves; educated at Oxford; a philosopher; author of *The Leviathan.*

Josquin des Prez (about 1440–1521), trained as a choirboy from an early age; a Burgundian; Europe's dominant composer in about 1500.

Johannes Kepler (1571–1630), son of a scruffy mercenary German soldier and the daughter of an innkeeper; a sickly child; university educated because of the generosity of the local dukes; served the Austrian Emperor; an astronomer; originator of three laws of planetary motion; a key figure in the Scientific Revolution.

Thomas Kyd (about 1557–1595), son of a London notary; arrested for treasonable activity; a playwright; author of an early version of *Hamlet.*

Andre Le Nôtre (1613–1700), son of the master gardener to France's King Louis XIII at the Tuileries; succeeded to his father's career; designed the park at Versailles Palace.

Louis Le Vau (1612–1670), son of a stonemason; chief architect to Louis XIV of France; one of the two architects who redesigned Versailles Palace.

Leonardo da Vinci (1452–1519), illegitimate son of a Florentine notary and a peasant woman who lived on his father's estate; apprenticed to the sculptor Verrochio; the outstanding example of a Renaissance man.

John Locke (1632–1704), son of an English lawyer of modest means; university educated; received the patronage of aristocrats; a scholar; the founder of modern liberalism; author of *Essay Concerning the Human Understanding.*

Ignatius Loyola (about 1493–1556), youngest son of a noble and wealthy Spanish family; a religious reformer; founder of the Jesuit order.

Jean-Baptiste Lully (1632–1687), an Italian, brought to France at a young age; trained as a musician; a naturalized French citizen; court composer to Louis XIV; founded French opera.

Martin Luther (1483–1546), son of a wealthy miner; a monk and a priest; educated at university; a religious reformer; condemned as a heretic and saved by German nobles; founded Lutheranism, the first Protestant Christian religion.

Niccoló Machiavelli (1469–1527), son of a prominent though poor Florentine family; important government official, 1498–1513; forced into exile by his political enemies; the founder of modern political theory.

Carlo Maderno (1556–1629), a member of a family of well-known architects; chief architect of St. Peter's; changed St. Peter's from a Greek crossshape to a Latin cross shape.

Christopher Marlowe (1564–1593), son of a middle-class tradesman, a shoemaker; violent and disreputable behavior often got him into trouble; a reputation for atheism; a playwright; the author of several important dramas, including *Dr. Faustus,* the first English stage version of the Faust legend.

Masaccio (1401–1428), son of an Italian notary and a daughter of an Italian innkeeper; trained as a painter; the first painter to master linear perspective in the Early Renaissance.

Michelangelo Buonarroti (1475–1564), son of a minor government official who had come down in the world; apprenticed briefly to the painter Ghirlandaio; taken under the wing of the Medici ruler of Florence; a painter, sculptor, and architect; one of the towering figures of Western art.

John Milton (1608–1674), son of an English Protestant notary and moneylender; educated at Cambridge university; supported the Puritan cause in the English civil war; blind at forty-three years of age; a poet; author of *Paradise Lost*

Moliére (Jean Baptiste Poquelin) (1622–1673), son of a furnisher of the royal household of the French king; confined to debtor's prison; toured for years with a traveling theater troupe as author, actor, and manager; official entertainer to Louis XIV; certain of his plays were banned by the church; the founder of modern stage comedy in France.

Michel de Montaigne (1533–1592), son of a French noble; a governmental official and thinker; the originator of modern skepticism.

Claudio Monteverdi (1567–1643), son of a barber-surgeon and chemist; trained as a musician; received aristocratic patronage; one of the founders of opera.

Thomas More (1478–1535), son of an English lawyer and judge; a political leader and humanist; beheaded by the English king, Henry VIII, for his political views; author of *Utopia.*

Isaac Newton (1642–1727), son of an English farmer of modest means; a sickly child; father died before Isaac was born and his mother later remarried, leaving the baby to be reared by a grandmother; tension between son and stepfather; educated at Cambridge; a scholar; one of the originator of calculus; completed the revolution in astronomy begun by Copernicus.

Giovanni Pierluigi da Palestrina (about 1525–1594), trained from an early age as a choirboy; wrote music for the papal court; the chief composer of the Counter-Reformation.

Palladio (Andrea di Pietro) (1508–1580), son of a miller; trained as a sculptor and architect; his works and writings launched Palladianism, a highly influential architectural tradition.

Parmigianino (1503–1540), trained as a painter by his uncles; served various noble and ecclesiastical patrons; a painter; helped to establish the Mannerist style.

Blaise Pascal (1623–1662), son of a French judge and mathematician; a child prodigy; a mathematician and philosopher; a forerunner of modern Christian existentialism.

Pico della Mirandola (1463–1494), son of an Italian prince of a minor principality; a humanist; a leading exponent of Renaissance Neo-Platonism.

Piero della Francesca (about 1420–1492), son of a tanner and shoemaker; trained as a painter; a member of the town council in Sansepolcro; associated with the noble court of Montefeltro; an important painter in the Early Renaissance style.

Pius II (1458–1464), son of a noble Italian family of reduced circumstances; a papal official and later a pope; a leading humanist of the Early Renaissance.

Nicolas Poussin (1594–1665), son of poor peasants; awakened to artistic abilities late, at age eighteen; a painter-philosopher in later life; the outstanding painter in the French Baroque style.

Andrea Pozzo (1642–1709), a Jesuit lay brother; trained as a painter and architect; noted for his illusionistic ceiling paintings in the Florid Baroque style.

Francois Rabelais (about 1494–1553), son of a rich landowner and a prominent lawyer; a Franciscan friar; studied medicine; his works were condemned as indecent and obscene by the Council of Trent; author of satirical books; a leading Northern Humanist.

Jean Racine (1639–1699), son of a French family of modest means, excise or legal officials; orphaned and penniless at age three; educated at a convent where his grandmother had settled; a playwright; after success as a playwright, he withdrew and became a court official; the outstanding author of tragedy in the French language.

Raphael Santi (1483–1520), son of a minor Italian painter; served various aristocrats and several popes; famous for his images of sweet madonnas; one of the geniuses of the High Renaissance.

Rembrandt van Rijn (1609–1669), son of a prosperous Dutch miller and a baker's daughter; trained as a painter; one of the greatest artists in the Western tradition.

Peter Paul Rubens (1577–1640), son of a Protestant courtier and lawyer; well-educated; trained as a painter; lucrative commissions from aristocrats in Italy, Spain, and France; one of the outstanding painters in the Florid Baroque style.

William Shakespeare (1564–1616), son of an English tradesman and alderman of Stratford-upon-Avon; a playwright and poet; revived stage comedy and tragedy for English-speaking audiences; the outstanding playwright in the English language.

Tintoretto (1518–1594), son of an Italian silk dyer; trained as a painter; a leading Venetian Mannerist.

Titian (about 1488–1576), son of a modest Italian official; trained as a painter; the supreme European painter around the middle of the sixteenth century.

Lorenzo Valla (1406–1457), son of a lawyer employed at the papal court in Rome; held heretical views but survived because of the protection of political and religious leaders, including the pope; proved that the Donation of Constantine was a forgery.

Anthony Van Dyck (1599–1641), son of a well-to-do Flemish silk merchant; trained as a painter; court painter in Italy and England; noted for his portraits of the English court.

Diego Velázquez (1599–1660), trained as a painter; official painter to the Spanish court; one of the masters of the Florid Baroque style.

Jan Vermeer (1632–1675), son of a tavern owner in Delft, where he lived for his entire life; a painter and art dealer; noted for his interior scenes, painted in the Protestant Baroque style.

Vesalius (1514–1564), a member of a family of physicians and pharmacists in Italy; a university professor; an important figure in establishing modern medicine.

Vittorini da Feltre (1378–1446), an Italian schoolmaster and humanist; one of the most significant educational reformers of the Early Renaissance.

Adrian Willaert (about 1490–1562), trained first as a lawyer, then as a musician; a Netherlandish composer who is considered the founder of the Venetian school of music.

Christopher Wren (1632–1723), son of a priest, later dean of Windsor; educated at Oxford; a university professor; an architect; rebuilt London's churches after the Great Fire of 1666; his masterpiece is St. Paul's Cathedral.

The Modern World, 1700–1914 [Chapters 16-19, *The Western Humanities*]

In 1700 the nobility and church leaders still constituted a ruling elite, although the middle class was rapidly gaining ground. During the course of this period, between 1700 and 1914, the middle class overtook and passed its old rivals, to become the ruling class, thus completing a rise to political and social power that had begin in the High Middle Ages.

Robert Adam (1728–1792), son of a Scottish architect; trained as an architect; built houses for English nobles and wealthy businessmen; a founder of Neoclassical-style architecture.

Jane Austen (1775–1817), daughter of an English priest; a novelist; author of gently satirical novels that portray the middle-class world from which she sprang.

Honoré de Balzac (1799–1850), middle-class background; son of a French governmental official; his mother was the daughter of prosperous cloth merchants; a writer; author of *The Human Comedy,* a series of nearly one hundred novels that depict French society in the early nineteenth century.

Charles Barry (1795–1860), son of an English stationer; trained as an architect; codesigned with Pugin the British Houses of Parliament.

Aubrey Beardsley (1872–1898), son of an English worker of odd jobs; an illustrator; associated with the late-nineteenth-century Decadent movement.

Pierre Beaumarchais (1732–1799), son of a French clockmaker; an accomplished harpist; a playwright; author of the satirical play that inspired Mozart's opera *The Marriage of Figaro.*

Ludwig van Beethoven (1770–1827), son and grandson of German court musicians; the family name shows a distant Dutch background; trained as a musician; supported himself through concerts, lessons, and the sales of his music; deaf in his later years; a composer; one of the West's greatest musicians.

Jeremy Bentham (1748–1832), a member of a prosperous English family of landowners; a child prodigy; the founder of Utilitarianism.

Hector Berlioz (1803–1869), son of a French physician; studied medicine and then music; a composer; a master of the Romantic style.

Umberto Boccioni (1882–1916), son of an Italian governmental employee; a sculptor; one of the Futurists.

Niels Bohr (1885–1962), son of an eminent Danish physiologist; a physicist; made major contributions to quantum theory.

Germain Boffrand (1667–1754), son of a minor French sculptor and architect; trained as an architect; designed the interior rooms of the Hotel de Soubise in Paris; worked in the Rococo style.

François Boucher (1703–1770), son of a French designer who kept an art shop near the Louvre; learned painting from his father; official painter to Louis XV; a master of the Rococo style.

Matthew Brady (about 1823–1896), of impoverished background; perhaps illiterate; blind in the prime of life; established a photographic studio in New York City when he was about twenty; died penniless; famed for his photographs of the American Civil War.

Johannes Brahms (1833–1897), son of a German musician; trained as a musician; a composer; the involuntary leader of the conservative anti-Wagner school in the late nineteenth century.

Georges Braque (1882–1963), son of a French painter and owner of a decorating business; a painter; with Picasso, a developer of Cubism.

Charlotte Brontë (1816–1855), daughter of an English clergyman; a member of a distinguished literary family; a novelist; author of *Wuthering Heights,* a masterpiece of Romantic fiction.

Emily Brontë (1818–1848), daughter of an English clergyman; a member of a distinguished literary family; a novelist; author of *Jane Eyre,* a masterpiece of Romantic fiction.

George Gordon, Lord Byron (1788–1824), a member of an impoverished noble family in England; physically handicapped; lived in the ruins of a castle inherited from his great uncle; a poet; in virtual exile from England because of his scandalous personal life; his behavior inspired Byronism, a nineteenth-century fashion that encouraged bohemian living; a master of Romanticism.

Mary Cassatt (1845–1967), daughter of an American banker; studied and lived in Paris; a painter; a leading Impressionist.

Paul Cezanne (1839–1906), son of a wealthy French banker and tradesman; a painter; a leading Post-Impressionist.

Anton Chekhov (1860–1904), son of a Russian former serf who became a struggling grocer; a playwright and short story writer; a major figure in Naturalism.

Samuel Taylor Coleridge (1772–1834), son of an English priest and schoolmaster; a poet; coauthor with Wordsworth of *Lyrical Ballads,* the first work of Romantic literature in England.

John Constable (1776–1837), son of a wealthy English miller; a painter; a master of the Romantic style.

François Couperin (1668–1733), born into a French family of musicians; trained as a musician; a leading musician in the Rococo style.

Gustave Courbet (1819–1877), son of a prosperous French farmer; trained as a painter; a painter; helped to establish the Realist style.

Marie Sklodowska Curie (1867–1934), daughter of a Polish teacher; a governess and then a scientist; first person to win two Nobel Prizes in science.

Pierre Curie (1859–1906), son of a French doctor; working with his wife, Marie, he identified two new radioactive elements, radium and polonium.

Louis-Jacques-Mandé Daguerre (1787–1851), an unstable background; son of a French minor government official and designer of stage sets; trained as a stage designer; one of the inventors of the photographic technique.

John Dalton (1766–1844), son of an English weaver; a Quaker in Anglican England; a teacher; contributed to modern atomic theory.

Charles Darwin (1809–1882), son of a well-to-do English physician; his mother was a member of the wealthy Wedgwood family who manufactured china; a scholar; author of on the *Origin of Species* and *Descent of Man*.

Honoré Daumier (1808–1879), born into a French family of glaziers, a lower-middle-class occupation; a caricaturist and painter; an early Realist.

Jacques-Louis David (1748–1825), son of a small but prosperous French textile-dealer; reared by uncles after the early death of the father; trained as a painter; the founder of Neoclassical painting.

Claude Debussy (1862–1918), born to an impoverished French family; a musician and composer; rescued by a wealthy Russian heiress who hired him to play duets with her and her children; helped to establish Impressionism.

Edgar Degas (1834–1917), son of a wealthy French family who had banking and other business connections; trained as an artist; a painter; a leading painter associated with both Impressionism and Post-Impressionism.

Eugene Delacroix (1798–1863), middle-class background, his father a government official and his mother a member of a family of furniture-makers for the royal court; trained as a painter; a painter; a master of the Romantic style.

Charles Dickens (1812–1870), son of an English governmental clerk whose impecunious habits landed him in debtors' prison; a journalist and novelist; the most popular novelist of the nineteenth century; a Realist.

Denis Diderot (1713–1784), son of a French cutler who specialized in surgical instruments; a writer; editor of the *Encyclopédie*, the monumental project that stands as a summation of the Enlightenment.

Feodor Dostoevsky (1821–1881), son of a Russian army doctor and landowner who was later murdered by his serfs; educated at an army engineering college; forced into exile in Siberia because of his liberal values; a writer; author of *Crime and Punishment*, one of the outstanding novels of Western literature.

Albert Einstein (1879–1955), born into a family of German Jews; father owned a small electrical plant and engineering works; a physicist; one of the founders of modern physics.

George Eliot (Mary Ann Evans) (1819–1880), daughter of an English estates-agent for a wealthy landowner; an outstanding Realist novelist.

Friedrich Engels (1820–1895), son of a family of German Jews; his father was a wealthy manufacturer; coauthor with Marx of *The Communist Manifesto*.

Johann Gottlieb Fichte (1762–1814), son of a German ribbon weaver; university educated; a philosopher and university professor; made important contributions to German Idealism.

Henry Fielding (1707–1754), an upper-middle-class background; his father was a colonel in the army and his mother was the daughter of a judge; a novelist; author of *Tom Jones*.

Gustave Flaubert (1821–1880), a member of a French family of physicians; his father was a surgeon and his mother the daughter of a doctor; a novelist; an outstanding Realist.

Charles Fourier (1772–1837), inherited his mother's estate; a leading Utopian Socialist.

Jean-Honoré Fragonard (1732–1806), son of a French haberdasher's assistant; apprenticed to a lawyer; trained as a painter; a master of the Rococo style.

Benjamin Franklin (1706–1790), son of a soap and candle maker in the North American British colonies; formal education ended at age twelve; apprenticed to his brother, a printer; a diplomat and hero of the American Revolutionary War.

Sigmund Freud (1856–1939), son of an Austrian Jewish wool merchant; a psychologist; the founder of psychoanalysis.

Caspar David Friedrich (1774–1840), son of a German candlemaker; trained as a painter; the outstanding German Romantic painter.

Elizabeth Gaskell (1810–1865), daughter of an English Unitarian minister; reared by a maternal aunt; a novelist; an outstanding Realist.

Paul Gauguin (1848–1903), son of a French father and a half-French, half Peruvian Creole mother; father was a journalist; spent most of his childhood in Peru; a sailor for six years; a bank clerk and a painter who exhibited with the Impressionists; abandoned Europe for the French colony of Tahiti in the South Pacific; a leading Post-Impressionist.

Theodore Gericault (1791–1824), son of French well-to-do parents; trained as a painter; a master of the Romantic style.

Edward Gibbon (1737–1794), a member of a prosperous, upper-middle-class English family; a man of independent means; a scholar; author of *History of the Decline and Fall of the Roman Empire*.

Johann Wolfgang von Goethe (1749–1832), of middle-class German stock, the father was a lawyer and the mother a daughter of a civic official; a writer and thinker; the greatest figure in German literature.

Francisco Goya (1746–1828), son of poor Spainish parents; trained as a painter; official painter to the Spanish court; the most significant painter in Spanish art.

Franz Joseph Haydn (1732–1809), son of a German wagon maker and house painter; trained as a musician; musical director for aristocrats; a composer; a master of Classical music.

Georg Wilhelm Friedrich Hegel (1770–1831), son of a German revenue official; university trained; a university professor and thinker; a contributor to German idealism and one of the most important Western thinkers.

William Hogarth (1697–1764), son of an English school teacher and minor writer; trained as a silversmith; a painter; the first major artist to produce multiple copies (engravings) from his works.

Victor Hugo (1802–1885), son of a French general in Napoleon's army; a writer; author of *Les Misérables*, one of the leading Romantic novels.

David Hume (1711–1766), a member of a Scottish middle-class family; the father was lord of a small estate and the mother was the daughter of a judge; an important philosopher in the Enlightenment.

Joris-Karl Huysmans (1848–1907), son of a French father and a Dutch mother; a civil servant; a founder of the Decadent movement.

Henrik Ibsen (1828–1906), son of a Norwegian businessman who went bankrupt; spent much of his life abroad in Italy; a playwright in the Naturalist style; the outstanding playwright of the nineteenth century.

Jean-Auguste-Dominique Ingres (1780–1867), son of a minor French artist; trained as a painter; a master of Neoclassicism.

Scott Joplin (1868–1917), born into a musical family of African Americans; his parents were former slaves; a musician and composer; popularized ragtime music

Carl Jung (1875–1961), son of a Swiss philologist and Protestant minister; a psychologist; the founder of Jungian therapy; famous for his theory of archetypes.

Franz Kafka (1883–1924), son of a Jewish merchant in Austria; overshadowed by a domineering father; a writer; author of *The Trial*, one of the classic works of Modernism.

Wassily Kandinsky (1866–1844), born into a well-to-do Russian family in Siberia; he was descended from Mongolian aristocrats; voluntary exile from his native Russia; a painter; founder of *Der Blaue Reiter (The Blue Rider)* school in Munich, Germany.

Immanuel Kant (1724–1804), son of a German saddler; university educated; a university professor and thinker; one of the most significant thinkers in the West.

Charles Lyell (1797–1875), descended from a Scottish family of aristocrats; his father was a naturalist; a geologist; his research on fossils proved that the earth was much older than Christians claimed.

Thomas Malthus (1766–1834), son of a prosperous English family; a clergyman; author of the groundbreaking essay *On Population*.

Edouard Manet (1832–1883), son of a high-placed French governmental official; a painter; his "art for art's sake" theory laid the groundwork for Modern art.

Karl Marx (1818–1883), a member of a German-Jewish family who had converted to Christianity; his father was a successful lawyer; exiled from Germany because of his political views; coauthor with Engels of *The Communist Manifesto*.

Henri Matisse (1869–1954), son of a French grain merchant; became an artist at age twenty; a painter and sculptor; a founder of Fauvism.

Dmitri Mendeleev (1834–1907), son of a Russian schoolmaster; his mother operated a glass factory that she leased; a scientist; worked out the periodic table of elements based on atomic weights.

John Stuart Mill (1806–1873), son of a well-known Scottish intellectual; a child prodigy; a leading Utilitarian.

Jean-François Millet (1814–1875), son of French peasants; trained as a painter; a member of the Barbizon school.

Claude Monet (1840–1926), son of a successful French businessman in ship-chandlering and groceries; trained as an artist; a painter; a founder of Impressionism.

Baron de Montesquieu (1689–1755), a member of a French aristocratic family; a major figure of the Enlightenment; author of *Spirit of the Laws*, one of the works that represented the beginning of the social sciences.

Berthe Morisot (1841–1895), a member of a wealthy French family of artists; her grandfather was Fragonard and she married Manet's brother; trained as a painter; a leading Impressionist.

Wolfgang Amadeus Mozart (1756–1791), son of a successful musician; a child prodigy; trained as a musician; served various aristocratic courts; a master of Classical music and one of the West's greatest musical geniuses.

Edvard Munch (1863–1944), a member of a distinguished and wealthy Norwegian family; a painter; experienced a nervous collapse in 1908–1909; a major Expressionist.

Balthasar Neumann (1687–1753), son of a poor German weaver; trained as a cannon and bell founder; studied architecture; designed the Residenz, the palace of the prince-bishop of Wurzburg

Friedrich Nietzsche (1844–1900), son and grandson of Lutheran ministers; after age five and the death of his father, reared in a household of women; university educated; abandoned a university career and lived abroad; suffered a nervous collapse in about 1890 from which he never recovered; a chief prophet of Modernism.

Robert Owen (1771–1858), son of an English saddler and ironmonger; trained as a clothier; a self-made man, he became a wealthy industrialist; a leading Utopian socialist.

Louis Pasteur (1822–1895), born into a family of French tanners; a scientist; established the germ theory of disease; a national hero in nineteenth-century France.

Pablo Picasso (1881–1973), son of a Spanish art teacher; trained as an artist; dominated Western painting from about 1906 until his death.

Camille Pissaro (1830–1903), born in the West Indies, the son of a Portuguese-Jewish father and a Creole mother; a prosperous family; lived in Paris after the age of twelve; a painter; a major Impressionist.

Max Planck (1858–1947), son of a distinguished German professor of law; university educated; a physicist; established quantum theory.

Alexander Pope (1688–1744), son of an English linen merchant; a Roman Catholic in Protestant England; severely physically handicapped; a poet; author of *Essay on Man*.

Marcel Proust (1871–1922), son of a wealthy French physician and a French Jewish mother; moved in the upper reaches of middle-class society; retreated to a cork-lined study to write; a novelist; a major figure in the Decadent movement.

A. W. N. Pugin (1812–1852), son of an English architect; trained as an architect; codesigned with Barry the British Houses of Parliament.

Jean-Philippe Rameau (1683–1764), son of a French church organist; trained as a musician; a master of the Rococo style.

Auguste Renoir (1841–1919), son of a French tailor; worked in a china factory at age thirteen, painting porcelain plates; a painter; a major figure in Impressionism.

David Ricardo (1772–1823), a member of an English Protestant family of converted Jews; his father made a fortune on the London stock exchange; a thinker; author of "the iron law of wages," a key concept in classical economics.

Samuel Richardson (1689–1761), son of an English tradesman; a novelist; author of *Pamela,* one of the first novels.

Auguste Rodin (1840–1917), born into a poor French family; trained as a mason; a sculptor; the leading Western sculptor in the early twentieth century.

Wilhelm Conrad Roentigen (1845–1923), son of a prosperous German textile merchant; expelled from secondary school; university educated; a scientist; discovered X rays.

Jean-Jacques Rousseau (1712–1778), son of a Swiss master watchmaker and sometime dancing master; changed religion several times; an unstable personality; a writer and thinker; one of the outstanding figures of the Enlightenment.

Comte de Saint-Simon (1760–1825), a member of a family of impoverished French aristocrats; an officer in the army, served with the Americans in their war for independence; a leading Utopian Socialist.

Friedrich Wilhelm Joseph von Schelling (1775–1854), son of a German Lutheran minister and professor of Oriental languages; a child prodigy; a thinker; a major figure in German idealism.

Arnold Schoenberg (1874–1951), son of an Austrian owner of a small business; a composer; the originator of serial music.

Franz Schubert (1797–1828), son of an Austrian schoolmaster; trained as a musician; a composer; perfected the German art song.

Georges Seurat (1859–1891), son of a French landowner of moderate means; a painter; a major Post-Impressionist.

Adam Smith (1723–1790), son of a Scottish governmental official; studied at Oxford; a thinker; the founder of laissez-faire economic theory.

Jacques Germain Soufflot (1713–1780), son of a French lawyer; an architect; designed the Panthéon in Paris; a master of Neoclassicism.

Igor Stravinsky (1882–1971), son of a distinguished Russian opera singer; trained as a musician; a composer; the head of the Neoclassical school of music after 1919.

August Strindberg (1849–1912), son of a Swedish aristocrat who had come down in the world, becoming a steamship agent; his mother was a former waitress; unstable childhood; a playwright; a leading figure of Expressionism.

Louis Sullivan (1856–1924), son of American immigrants, an Irish father and a Swiss mother; father was a dance instructor; university educated; an architect, the leader of the Chicago school.

William Henry Fox Talbot (1800–1877), born into an English middle-class family; university educated; one of the originators of the photographic process.

Giovanni Battista Tiepolo (1696–1770), son of a prosperous Venetian merchant; a painter; famous for his illusionistic ceiling paintings.

Leo Tolstoy (1828–1910), son of a Russian landowner; a military officer; a novelist; converted to fundamentalist Christianity; author of *War and Peace*; an outstanding Realist.

Joseph Mallord William Turner (1775–1851), son of an English barber; reared by an uncle after the age of ten; trained as a painter; a master of Romantic painting.

Vincent Van Gogh (1853–1890), son of a poor Dutch pastor; a failed career as a minister to the poor; a painter; emotionally unstable, he committed suicide; a major figure of Post-Impressionism.

Giuseppe Verdi (1813–1901), son of a poor Italian merchant and tavern owner; a composer; the greatest Italian composer of opera.

Louise-Elizabeth Vigée-Lebrun (1755–1842), daughter of a French painter; a portrait painter; court painter to Queen Marie Antoinette; a master of the Rococo style.

Voltaire (François-Marie Arouet) (1694–1778), son of a well-to-do French lawyer; educated by Jesuits; interned in the Bastille twice and exiled to England once; spent most of his career outside of Paris because of his unorthodox views; a writer and thinker; a major figure of the Enlightenment.

Richard Wagner (1813–1883), son of a German police chief; after the father's death, his mother wed an actor; university trained; a composer; composed *The Ring of the Nibelung,* the most famous cycle of operas in the repertory; the dominant musical figure at the end of the nineteenth century.

Jean-Antoine Watteau (1684–1721), son of a Flemish tiler; trained as a painter; a painter and decorator; founded the Rococo style.

John Wesley (1703–1791), a member of an English family of gentry and clergy; there were religious nonconformists in the family background; founded the Methodist religion.

Oscar Wilde (1854–1900), son of a wealthy Irish surgeon; university educated; imprisoned for homosexuality; author of *The Portrait of Dorian Gray;* a major figure in the Decadent movement.

William Wordsworth (1770–1850), son of an English businessman and the daughter of a linen merchant; a poet; coauthor with Samuel Taylor Coleridge of *Lyrical Ballads;* founded English Romantic poetry.

Frank Lloyd Wright (1869–1959), born into a middle-class family that had a precarious existence; the father was an itinerant minister and the mother a schoolteacher; an architect; the designer of the prototype of the "ranch house," the type of domestic architecture that dominated American suburbia in the mid–twentieth century.

Emile Zola (1840–1902), son of an Italian father and a French mother; a writer; a major figure in Naturalism.